Leadership of Organizations
The Executive's Complete Handbook

Leadership of Organizations
The Executive's Complete Handbook

Part I.   The Social

by   JOHN M. BRION

 JAI PRESS INC.

Greenwich, Connecticut   *London, England*

Library of Congress Cataloging-in-Publication Data

Brion, John M.
    Leadership of organizations : the executive's complete handbook /
by John M. Brion.
      p. cm.
    Includes bibliographical references and index.
    Contents: pt. 1. The social -- pt. 2. The technical -- pt.
3. Integration.
    ISBN 1-55938-934-3   (set : alk. paper). -- ISBN 1-55938-935-4
(part 1 : alk. paper)
    1. Leadership.   2. Executive ability.   3. Organizational behavior.
I. Title.
HD57.7.B745   1996
658.4'092—dc20

                95-16384
                CIP

Copyright © 1996 JAI PRESS INC.
55 Old Post Road No. 2
Greenwich, Connecticut 06836

JAI PRESS LTD.
The Courtyard
28 High Street
Hampton Hill
Middlesex TW12 1PD
England

ISBN: 1-55938-935-4 (Part I)
ISBN: 1-55938-936-2 (Part II)
ISBN: 1-55938-937-0 (Part III)
ISBN: 1-55938-934-3 (Set)

Library of Congress Catalog Card Number: 95-16384

Manufactured in the United States of America

About the Author

John M. Brion, a graduate of Yale University (B.S. in Industrial Administration) with a recent MBA from Pace University, is well qualified to write on organizational leadership, having had some 30 years in organizational leadership positions himself, positions that gave him a comprehensive knowledge of the management technology essentials for organizational excellence plus a wealth of people experience: District Sales Manager to V.P. of operations in one of the nation's largest metals distributors ($100 million sales), General Sales Manager of a metals rolling mill, Manger of Sales and General Administration in the Engineered Products Group of Crane Company, V.P. of a prominent New York consulting firm, and in-house management consultant at Johns-Manville Corporation (now Manville Corp.). The American Management Association published his *Decisions, Organizational Planning and the Marketing Concept* and John Wiley his *Corporate Marketing Planning*, both translated into Spanish. He has also been published by the American Marketing Association on Wholesaling and by the Marketing Communication Research Center on how 40 leading firms develop and introduce new products (in-depth analyses of each).

After Manville he spent the next 12 years researching the causes of the poor performances he had found in so many of the companies he had worked with. His book *Organizational Leadership of Human Resources* published by JAI Press in 1989 presented the good and bad of the human side of the subject; this one covers the total of organizational leadership, advancing the art-science of it to the new paradigm sketched in the third paragraph of the Foreword.

CONTENTS

PART II.   THE TECHNICAL

PART III.   INTEGRATION

Foreword

There's a new corporate world out there very different from but a few years ago and changing for the better at a rapidly expanding pace—Leadership, followership, strategies, structures, operating techniques, everything. Leaders and those hoping to be leaders who don't keep up will be dropped by the wayside.

The reader will find here the "how," all aspects of the subject with the latest developments needed by an executive to personally excel and lead an organization to competitive superiority. It is essentially the logical follow-on of the author's 1989 book on human resources leadership recommended by Harvard's organization behavior pioneer, Chris Argyris, this handbook containing the most advanced findings of research, technology and operating experience.

Leading an organization of course entails decisions and actions that account for all the variables of both the internal and external environment; thus, included is all the important knowledge required down through middle management on how to undertake successfully leadership development, upgrade as needed an organization's culture and climate, minimize bureaucracy, plan strategy, structure, operating systems, corporate policies, process teams and team development (at three levels), to reengineer with the latest information technology, computer networks and groupware, and to flatten the organization optimally for best performance. Supplementing this are many illustrative examples, including the changes and progress in such majors as GE, Motorola, Xerox, Texas Instruments, AT&T, IBM and GM.

And because some 50 percent of organizational leadership is leading and motivating its people, one therefore must first understand humans and their behavior, so all of the beginning, all of Part I, is dedicated to helping on at least the basic requisites.

It is primarily an executive's handbook but no less a college text, directed at not only executives, managers and staff but also students, any of all who are interested in finding out how to maximize organizational performance in corporations or non-profit institutions, with the assumptions that he or she has had some organizational experience or management courses.

The titles of the three Parts manifest the simple truth about what the executive has to do: gain an in-depth understanding of the *Social* factors of the organization, especially what makes the individual tick—personality, values, behavior, motivations, and so forth; about the *Technical* (management technology, principles, systems, skills, control, planning), with how to mold and operate the organization keeping employee needs and aspirations in mind as well as organizational goals; and finally the *Integration* of the social and technical for best performance and industry leadership.

There is of course the problem of just how much can be gained solely by reading, and to judge, it might be helpful to review briefly a comparison of the strengths and weaknesses of learning by reading with those of the other well-known educational alternatives believed worthwhile. Then, whichever is chosen, or before choosing, one can decide how best to proceed, and, how to fill the gaps left by any of them, virtually all having gaps, some very large.

There are essentially four choices extant, not including the school-of-hard-knocks, the sink-or-swim on your own still the policy of many traditional organizations, the results obvious enough to need no more comment. The four: (1) graduate business schools, (2) vendor leadership programs, (3) corporate in-house programs, and (4) the reading.

(1) A comprehensive critique of today's graduate business schools is covered at the end of Chapter 17 to which one should refer, particularly before deciding which school to select if you want to go to one. The large majority are not worth the investment for leadership development, but the good ones are now fairly effective, especially for building awareness of the demands of organizational leadership and the teaching and integration of the functional skills. Three major problems: the limited number of leadership skills that are teachable, the difficulty of changing unacceptable behaviors by classroom instruction, and the problem of transferring what is learned back to the workplace. See the elaboration in Chapter 17.

(2) A recent book *Learning to Lead*, by J.A. Conger,[a] gives an excellent description of the various types of professional vendor programs on the market and ticks off what he called an "ideal" against which one can evaluate each (and also apply to the schools and in-house programs). The ideal program will:

a. begin with a conceptual overview of organizational leadership, including the required skills and behaviors;
b. provide feedback on where participants stand with regard to each skill and behavior;
c. work on building the skills that are teachable;
d. for the very difficult skills to teach and the unteachable ones, focus on awareness building with the idea of participant self-development of what is needed over the long run back on the job as opportunities present.

Conger explained that there are broadly four categories of leadership training that vendors apply (he seems to deliberately avoid the word "development," perhaps because it takes considerably longer than the 5-10 days of vendor programs to achieve): training through personal growth, through conceptual understanding, through feedback, and through skills building.

The "personal growth" ones are based on the assumption that most managers ignore an inner calling to realize their potential to become leaders, and programs in this category aim to awaken the drive by outdoor adventure activities (e.g., mountain climbing, group camping) intended to arouse reflection on one's values, behaviors, motivations, interpersonal skills, and desire or not to lead others. They've helped some on self-awareness but clearly fail on all four of a to d.

"Conceptual understanding" programs are essentially off-site or on-site classroom courses covering all the basics like Theory Y, teamwork, participation, contingency models, etc., doing it via lectures, cases, discussion and review of what successful leaders have done. Skills building in these courses is also in lecture form with role playing for feedback but no real-world skills application. They are generally 4 to 5 day seminars or "workshops" that at least encourage thinking about leadership and what's involved.

Programs that are predominantly on "feedback" are also based on an assumption: that most of us already possess leadership skills in varying degrees, so the idea is to learn more about one's own, strengthen those that are weak, and develop what's missing. In one comprehensive program extensive feedback instruments are filled out before attending by the participants, by their job peers, subordinates, and bosses, then five days of skill exercises are given in class with class feedback, and on the sixth day each individual goes through a session of feedback back in the company from staff and class peers in discussions on what was learned and what more to work on, using all the pre-session feedback instruments to aid evaluation and the planning of a back-home program. A while later the peers, subordinates and boss may be asked to fill out new progress instruments, a program counselor contacts the participant, the two review them and replan the back-home program.

The designers of "skills building" programs generally recognize that it's difficult if not impossible to teach psychological and "vision" skills in the 5-day time they normally have for their programs, that in fact leadership skills that are teachable are largely limited to management technology skills (systems, planning, problem-solving, effectiveness techniques, etc.), plus a number of supporting social and interpersonal skills that are commonly taught by a combination of lectures, discussion, videotape of realistic examples, practice, class feedback, and planning utilization of the skills on the job. One program has structured 19 skill areas in 5 clusters, each cluster a function of the attending participants, for example, clusters on developing team performance, managing innovation and change, total quality management, and interpersonal skills. And since many skills even among these are too complex to teach, there's more stress on awareness building than training with the hope that the participants will be inspired to work on them over time back on the job.

As one can see, all types, except the "personal growth" ones, apply some of each of the four categories, one category being dominant, but there are some vendor programs that are quite comprehensive. An example: one has basically five parts: (a) each participant is assigned a "process advisor" who becomes a coach, friend, advocate, and support; about a month before the program the advisor sends the participant a pre-course packet to be filled in on the individual's life purposes, self-evaluation, and organizational situation and experiences; shortly after (still before the course) the advisor contacts the person, offers help on the packet and starts a friendship. (b) One of two full-time weeks of classroom sessions are attended, the advisor spot-checking to help as deemed needed, and 3-person teams of participants under the advisor are formed at the end for feedback, reinforcement, and planning. (c) Back to work for three months, during which the participant keeps a journal on leadership experiences, and is called occasionally by the advisor on progress and for discussion. (d) The journal is sent to the advisor just before the second session of 3-5 days and is used by the advisors with two other participants for evaluation, feedback and reinforcement. (e) Back on the job "change partners" are set up among participants who are encouraged to provide each other critiquing, support and truth for as long as they feel the urge.

(3) Increasingly large firms are undertaking corporate in-house management and leadership development programs for a variety of reasons: close control of program content and quality, designing to fit the needs of the firm, the program length governed by company objectives (not

principally to be made cost-attractive to prospects as on vendor ones); though the cost is too high for smaller firms, it's less expensive than other options when applied to full management teams in the thousands; and career-length development cohesion is possible so that the individual can build competence through the years to cover increases in job "scale" and "complexity" as the person rises in the hierarchy, the way GE does it (described in Chapter 17); GE's assumption as well as goal: "good material entering at the bottom will emerge exceptional material at the top.".. and they make it happen.

The good firms manifest the recognition that education must be a lifetime pursuit for all of us, and both national and global competition has made on-going human resources development and use of the talents of all employees mandatory for corporate survival let alone corporate leadership. It's a lucky person who works for such a progressive one.

(4) Finally, the reading. Tragically, the vast majority of managers feel (a) they're too busy to read books (one survey found that no one up through middle management in its large sample even knew the title of a current business book, only a handful of progressive senior executives did); (b) their managerial success in getting as far as they have implied to them they already knew enough. But of course, as said, it's a very different and much more complex ballgame than but a few years ago, and reading up-to-date books like this one can not only show what new should be learned but what successful competitors are doing and why they're succeeding.

Granted, the total of the three parts in this one adds up to an enormous amount of reading, but you're in fact not ready for leadership if you don't realize how huge and complex it is. If you are ready, consider that completing one chapter every two weeks will cover it in a year's time, after which it can be a very useful handbook on the office shelf or desk to refer to.

This is not to deny that reading is frequently seriously distorted by the reader's subjective vanity and misconceptions, that it cannot teach skills or *self-awareness* and that it lacks reality testing; but a good comprehensive book (or set of them) can go a long way toward the *skills* awareness-building mentioned and give important guidance as well on how to gain the needed self-knowledge along with all the other subjects herein.

A treatise of such magnitude certainly should be introduced by describing the framework of the basic approach, the key factors being the *technical* and *social* described, two words that concisely package what only a few business schools have successfully integrated, which probably explain along with the omissions why they've commonly developed only able number-crunchers rather than good leaders of people.

A major issue covered within the approach will be a fundamental flaw in many organizations produced by authoritarian or "directive" styles and ignorance, one that would be appropriately called *The Individual-Organization Gap*, labelling the appreciable difference between the attitude and feelings of employees about their work and those of the organization represented by superiors with such styles, and an inevitable consequence is that performance suffers, sometimes terminally.

Expertise in the technical is quite common now, and thanks to the behavioral sciences we know a great deal about the social and have many excellent books on how to manage it for better results, some in fact promising that competent management of the social is the key to maximum performance.

Experienced educators, however, readily agree that there's much more to it, and their teaching techniques are generally designed to embrace fully the technical and social together in a sociotechnical system as in the standard problem-solving procedure taught in many business schools. The procedure has in fact been made a pervasive feature of the text as it advances on both the social and technical through its stages, clarifying the steps and aiding a sense of continuity. Also, to help one relate the discourse and cases to one's own situation, it will be assumed that its performance could be a lot better (so the initial problem manifestation=unsatisfactory performance), that it has decided to undertake a project to define the problems (e.g., for one, what is the gap problem underlying its manifestations?) and what can be done about them; then it assigned the project to one of its best and most thorough executives.

Such a person would probably think immediately of the standard problem-solving procedure as an efficient way to go about it, so presuming all this has happened, it will be used:

Standard Problem-Solving Procedure

Step 1. *An informal investigation.*[b]
    a. An analysis of the manifestation(s)
    b. Preliminary information search
    c. Problem identification
    d. Problem definition

Step 2. *Conceptual preparation:*
    a. A statement of the assumptions
    b. A model of the problem's system (structures, process, human resources) and its functioning
    c. Hypotheses of the probable solution

Step 3. *Formal investigation*: the information search

Step 4. *Analysis*: study of all the most probably causes uncovered in the investigation; appraisal of their individual and collective contribution as causes of the problem; verification, or correction, of the systems model as consistent with the formal investigation findings.

Step 5. *Design*: development of the most probably alternative solutions other than the hypotheses that were suggested by the analysis.

Step 6. *Choice*: test of the alternatives and the hypotheses in the final system model and selection of the one that yields the best results.

The ultimate goal of the project, one can see, will be the Step 6 *Choice* for the solutions and decisions showing the management team how to implement each, including how to account for the multiplicity of organizational complexities and to deal with the realities of power, authority, and organizational politics.

One comment about the 6-step procedure might be helpful. Analysis is naturally a continuous process during an investigation, so that the write-up of the three Parts will include the analytic reasoning relevant to the details of each as the investigation progresses. The *Analysis* of Step 4, however, is essentially the final summary stage of it that leads to Steps 5 and 6, all of which will be undertaken in the last chapter.

NOTES

a. Conger, J.A., *Learning to Lead* (San Francisco: Jossey-Bass, 1992).
b. 1a through 1d are the steps for problem search if that is first necessary, after which the whole procedure is applied.

John M. Brion
Author

Part I

THE SOCIAL

Introduction

A brief sketch of the history of the conflict between the "individual" and "organization" will help one understand why it still exists and the reasoning behind the proposed solutions for which Part I on The Social lays the foundation.

When we look as far back as some 5000 years ago we find an organizational conflict pattern that existed then similar to the one in even technically well-run organizations today. Indeed, someone familiar with ancient history would point out that employee discontent has been with us since the building of the pyramids when the first known employee strike occurred and might add that it appears to be part of the organizational condition. Furthermore, since such conflict seems always to be present, and since virtually all organizations still have it, why be concerned, if you are, about its presence in your own?

Obviously, down through the ages it's been a matter of tolerance level, of what both sides would put up with, particularly the employees, and the dissatisfaction employees will tolerate is considerably less than what it was only twenty-five years ago let alone far back in history; moreover the unhappy now have the flexibility to move to other organizations or out of the market altogether, escaping their former necessity to resign themselves to a lifetime job of semi-, if not full, slavery.

Until the 20th century, we know, the employer had always been king, the worker a menial serf, employee opinion or feelings a minor employer consideration, and motivation was primarily by fear plus an always-inadequate reward. But during the three decades after 1900 management attitudes and methods apparently improved significantly, such that they were accepted by employees and the public alike because managements made the conditions endurable tradeoffs for supplying some individual needs and the immense requirements of the nation. Right up through the 1950s, surveys showed that the large majority had confidence in corporate purpose and leadership.

The 1929 Depression however proved to be far more than just an economic disaster; it was a traumatic and cataclysmic event that brought the whole

1

capitalistic free enterprise system into question: its inequities, social injustices, concentrations of power, human indifference, etc.; indeed it opened to question the lasting power of the whole system. Even such notable economists as John Maynard Keynes became convinced that certain basic characteristics of capitalism dictated eventual stagnation. (He did not take into account the dynamics of technological innovation or foresee that improving management and executive values might make a difference.)

The human misery of it all made it evident that unlimited free enterprise also had failed as a social system, and society must step in. Dealing only with the worst abuses in the beginning and treading with care to save what was good about it, the government set up only a few rules and controls, but it was like the camel's nose under the tent edge: it was only the beginning, and controls have increased through the years (almost always invited by mistreatment, malpractice, greed, fraud, etc.), so that the government currently manages directly about 10 percent of the nation's output, regulates in one way or another every major industry, finances much of the R&D, pays for at least some of every individual's costs from cradle to grave, and even has a policy and goal of "full employment" (even with the Republican 1995 "revolution").

Fifty years of more and more of this has naturally been a main reason for our phenomenal standard of living, high level of education, more equitable distribution of income (though not recently) and opportunity, and so on. Now with all this progress, one would hardly expect that any important degree of societal or employee discontent would be left, yet public opinion surveys and employee surveys portray an ominous negative picture.

It seems that few were aware at the start of the changes that the full social *Psychological* consequences of so much intervention would be: the changed and still changing personal values, attitudes and aspirations, an ever-increasing awareness of the poor qualitative state of society, and the constantly rising expectations of what should be. And certainly of dominant importance to management was the changed perception of the purpose of organizations, both private and public.

While the overall goals of society in the past were held to be primarily material, business and organizations were accepted as amoral means of fulfilling basic quantitative material and service needs. But no longer; not only have the goals been modified to include the qualitative, but these enterprises have become too large and important a part of our daily lives to be considered as only amoral product, service, and profit generators. We must consciously recognize the full measure of what they are: social systems—with all their moral implications—as well as economic systems, even though their basic purpose must be economic.

This calls on managers to try to better understand all the consequences that their decisions and behavior can have on subordinates' motivation and performance. Many are already aware, but it's the rare ones who are aware enough. In fact, for the vast majority it's a whole new world of demands that seem to be running increasingly counter to their goals and plans. Ahead is a lot of trouble for most and many are already in trouble without realizing it.

It had seemed propitious that the behavioral sciences, as mentioned in the Forward, have made such strides in learning how to help managers lead. The timing appeared ideal. But several decades of trying to apply the new principles have had negligible payoff, only bits and pieces are being adopted, and the quality of organizational life has not improved at the pace of employees' changing expectations, needs, or desires.

Clearly this is but more of what is at the bottom of the described *individual-organization gap* that surveys have shown and continue to show is causing widespread job dissatisfaction except in the progressive firms as will be described. The gap, moreover, has resulted in declining appeal of organizational careers to those who count most, the more intelligent college prospects and members of management alike. *Average* employees are willing to sublimate their intrinsic needs and accept their jobs as extrinsic means toward off-the-job satisfaction, and most students will continue to set their goals similarly since at their point in life they see their needs principally as material. But as the gap and its oppressiveness have become more widely known, a growing percentage of the best young brains are opting for professions and self-employment principally because of it, a not inconsiderable loss to future top managements and competitive competence in free enterprise.

It should be completely apparent too that employees who believe that all the intrinsic satisfactions of life are only available off the job invariably give only the minimum performance required.

Behaviorists have certainly been well aware of it all for some time, and though they seem to have largely avoided tackling systematically the fundamental cause, human values, they have at least correctly labeled two chief serious consequences of wrong values: (1) aversive authoritarianism and (2) the evils and havoc of misplaced interpersonal competition.

Authority and competition are indisputably indispensable; the problems arise out of how they are both practiced. The abuse of power and authority, we know, has been the bane of civilization since its beginning, and only now are we learning how to eliminate it while maintaining, indeed increasing, essential authority, a concurrence that will be explained in chapters ahead.

Competitions on, the other hand, has such appeal because of its benefits to our free enterprise system many people are convinced that any restraint is bad for the system, and they have a strong argument to buck. After all, the sophisticated harmonious-appearing behavior of management teams today does seem to indicate that present self-restraint is sufficient.

Figure A.1, however, translates that "harmony" into the subrosa condition and events that commonly occur, particularly in the medium and large scale firms. One can't help but ask, is such barbarity really necessary to the system? And what is the human and organizational price being paid for it?

Certainly, these negative aspects of the climate—the aversive authority, the misplaced competition, and the general job dissatisfaction—are also manifestations of the problem along with the internal unsatisfactory performance, and the analyzing executive would probably have them in the back of his mind as he started the informal investigation to clarify first the social part of the poor-performance problem, the task of Chapter 1.

Figure A.1.

Chapter 1

Paradox

A lucid picture was recently given us in the *Harvard Business Review* or the true conditions managers still all too often have to submit to in organizations, an article that tended to make evident that the heart of much poor organizational performance is most apt to be primarily the "social" aspects of leadership and managing more than management technology. It summarized the responses given in intensive interviews of over 100 managers in one very large firm, "speaking freely and sometimes humorously.[1,a]

We know that there are fundamentally two personal controls on managers in their pursuit of success in the organizations they work for: (1) the personal values they're committed to (whether consciously aware of them or not), and (2) the organization's own "rules of success," that is, what has to be done to advance. Those who gave the responses revealed directly or indirectly what was expected of them as well as its effects:

First, the rules here, as in most large organizations (and often in those of any size), were based on the fact that the hierarchical structure had evolved over time into a huge fealty system from the top to the lower reaches as a result of past and present practices and policies. The key components of the system: the leadership "style," the kind of behavior desired therefore rewarded, the method of selection for promotion, the management development technique, interpersonal competition, the way credit and blame were meted out, and the attitudes of all managers in general.

And it all started, as one would expect, at the top. New CEOs on taking over cleaned house of old fealties (as if they were immutable) and installed all new loyalties to themselves—a perfectly logical process if disloyalty is identified, but it was done without identifying it and regardless of competence or value to the organization.

The result was changes by bosses all the way down the chain as in political institutions following the example set by the CEO, and an awareness of its ever-present threat: that it will most probably happen not only at each periodic reorganization (under the same or any CEO), merger and divestiture but also whenever one's own boss is moved up or out, the boss's boss selecting the replacement principally in terms of believed loyalty, friendship and the desired behavior.

In a fairly short time any observant employee easily discerns that success depends not on competence and good performance but, as commented by the article's author, on a combination of the capriciousness of superiors and unpredictable events. Therefore the only solution for those who stick it out is to accept the inevitable on the events and work socially on the immediate superior and all other superiors up the line who might influence "promotability" (all quotes ahead are of either the article's author or interviewees).

Thus the focus for every aspiring manager was switched from performance to social factors, starting with conveying the right image:

- *Physical appearance*: Look the part of an executive: attractive and well-groomed.
- *Self-control*: hide all emotions and intentions.
- *The impression of a team player*: for example, long hours at the office and dedication to the rituals.
- *Personality style*: appearing knowledgeable (even in ignorance), sophisticated, witty, graceful, engaging, friendly.

The path to success became "playing the game." "It's the ability to play this system that determines whether you will rise... and part of the adeptness is determined by how much it bothers you" (a quote of one executive). The game: knowing the right people, developing a patron, saying the right things and only the right things (especially the boss's and CEO's incantations), wearing the right mask (the four points above), and making decisions "wisely."

The rules for making decisions "wisely" are a perfect illustration of how performance is destroyed by the requirements for advancement:

1. Avoid making any important decisions if at all feasible.
2. If one has to be made, involve as many people as you can to diffuse responsibility.
3. Choose short-term safety over long-term gain (managers are judged on short-term performance regardless of protestations to the contrary).
4. Plan and manipulate your career movement so you can outrun your mistakes.

And the underlying reason for them is the necessity to avoid blame, because "even correct decisions can shorten promising careers." The three leading techniques for those decisions that *have* to be made are numbers 2, 3, and 4. Both numbers 2 and 3 are obviously sensible defenses in the setup, number 2 to spread the blame if things go wrong and number 3 because "if you don't survive the short run the long run hardly matters."

And on number 4, the idea is to get promoted or transferred before superiors find out the consequences of bad (not infrequently deliberate) important decisions—like deferring maintenance expenditures for better current profits that profit pressure and fear of unjust blame induce)—so the replacement gets the blame. "The ideal situation, of course, is to be in a position (as the new superior) to fire one's successor for one's own previous mistakes!"

What you therefore have, the author observed, is "a vast system of organized irresponsibility" in a moral maze in which *the rules of success* are the components of "play the game" and make "wise" decisions (the four sub-rules). Apparently just enough good *unimportant* decisions are made to keep the organization going, and usually such companies are not seriously threatened competitively because their large powerful competitors are in the same condition.

Naturally, the climate is one of fear, distrust, suspicion, interpersonal dishonesty, and the relationship pictured in Figure A.1 on page 4. The good values managers are raised on by family and education, influence #1 on page 6, get buried by their psychological needs for recognition, promotion via these rules, the material promises higher up, and their heavy responsibilities at home. The truly superior managers with high market value leave as soon as they can. It reminds one of a statement by historian Arnold Toynbee: "From the standpoint of the employee, it is coming to make less and less practical difference to him what his country's ideology is and whether he happens to be employed by a government or commercial corporation."[2]

Plainly this description does not picture the managements and behavior in all large corporations, but it was the first research to get wide distribution giving the disturbing details of so many of them, and in doing so it helped counter to some degree the pleasing image portrayed by so much literature on the good example-setters like G.E., Xerox, Saturn and others.[b]

An excellent book published in 1988, *The Leadership Factor* by J.P. Kotter,[3] presented a number of additional examples manifesting inadequate to poor performance, all of the causes found to be largely traceable to inadequate to poor leadership, all tending to have cultural patterns much like the "Moral Mazes" one:

- *Short-sighted bosses*: unwilling to hire competence except for entry-level jobs (competitive fear), unwilling to transfer good subordinates across the organization for development, crony promoting, no coaching or development of subordinates, no thinking about the long-range leadership needs of the organization.

- *Hiring*: no criteria for hiring leadership potential, no college recruiting, hiring only, as implied, for entry-level competence into unchallenging entry-level jobs (when sudden high-level vacancies occur requiring outside recruiting of competence, the competent that were hired soon leave).
- *Promotion*: because of these hiring practices and lack of horizontal transfers for development, the career path is vertical and narrow so those promoted are unprepared for broader responsibility, and, those promoted are the ones who got short-term results, were politically astute, and were good at parochial infighting.
- *Organization structure*: centralized, functional, highly bureaucratic.

Of course one wonders, doubts, whether organizations that degenerate as far as the "Moral Maze" case can be turned around into honorable, positively-motivated high-performance places to work. The answer has proven to be yes though difficult and only over several years, so any less far-gone can be also. The chapters ahead will provide the detail of what to do and how, and the answers must naturally be in terms of both parties, the leaders (which imply the organizations they represent) and the subordinate managers, the best place to start being to ask what each expects of the other, how they accordingly behave, and what the consequences have been.

WHAT DO SUBORDINATE MANAGERS INDIVIDUALLY WANT AND EXPECT?

For the answers to this, one first has to examine a dynamic characteristic of all humans: their changing interests and goals as they advance in personal development and achievement, what they want out of jobs and what they expect from superiors and management in general.

As is well known by now, the nature of the changes and the sequencing are direct derivatives of basic needs, and the needs were identified and explained in 1943 by sociologist Abraham Maslow.[4] Logically, all people first aim to fill their basic physiological needs—food, shelter, and clothing—and after reaching about 85 percent satisfaction, their primary interest turns to safety. When safety is about 70 percent satisfied, they get yearnings for the social aspects of life; at around 50 percent of gratification, an urge to fulfill ego needs emerges; and finally, when the ego is some 40 percent indulged, the main drive becomes a desire for self-actualization, "to become everything one is capable of becoming."

The Maslow Hierarchy of Needs

5. Self-actualization
4. Ego: self-esteem, status, appreciation
3. Social: love, wife, children, membership
2. Safety: job security, insurance, savings
1. Basic physiological: food, shelter, clothing

Significantly, the self-actualization need is insatiable; when reached, it is never appeased and only under special circumstances, usually pathological, has it disappeared. The others though just become less and less motivating with higher levels of satiation and more so down the hierarchy.

The percentages, Maslow conceded, are unvalidated clinical estimates, and though the sequence is basic, circumstances can understandably push one back downward. Further, there are many determinants of behavior that can switch them around during the course of a person's life, such as societal value changes or momentous events.

The hierarchy is a reliable general guide that has proven invaluable to understanding behavior and motivation, and it is plainly also applicable to whole societies. Particularly important to an affluent one: as lower needs are satisfied, the drive for self-actualization becomes a primary pressure on its institutions.

So when one asks what do managers in advanced societies expect from jobs and management, knowing they are apt to be in the upper reaches of the Maslow needs hierarchy already, the foundation of the answers has been provided. The answers themselves, then, might be obtained by asking them in a survey either directly what they want or indirectly what their business- and society-related values are (because of the needs-values relationship that will be explained and illustrated in Chapter 5).

Unfortunately, neither type of survey has been undertaken that can confidently be said to be representative, but a comprehensive set of each type was administered in 1967, 1969, and 1973, the surveys designed to determine the values and expectations of college-age youth within the context of the changes and trends brought about by the events of the 1960s.[5] Since those tested are now members of our business and government organizations and their managements, the surveys not only suggest the relevant values of current managers but also the direction they are taking.

Interestingly, the 1967 and 1969 surveys showed that the radical views of the 1960s had no more than a minor values influence, and the 1973 one confirmed the solid traditional base revealed by the others and more recent

1973 Personal and Social Values of Youth†

	Non-College		College	
Beliefs in Traditional American Values				
● Doing any job well is important	89%		84%	
● Business is entitled to make a profit	85		85	
Commitment to a meaningful career is very important	79		81	
Duty comes before pleasure	66		54	
Man is basically good, but society corrupts	50		46	
Competition encourages excellence	66	(81)‡	62	(72)
● Hard work will always pay off	56	(79)	44	(57)
Activities Thought to be Morally Wrong				
Destroying private property	88		78	
Taking things without paying for them	88		84	
Collecting welfare when you could work	83		77	
Using violence to achieve worthwhile results	72		68	
Cheating big companies	66		50	
Restraints Willingly and Easily Accepted				
Power and authority of the police	60	(79)	48	(48)
● Power and authority of the boss at work	57	(71)	41	(49)
Conformity in dress and grooming	42		33	
Outward conformity for job/career advancement	37		20	
Abiding by laws you do not agree with	24		12	
Business and Society				
● Business is too concerned with profits, not with public responsibility	92		94	
● Society is democratic in name only; special interests run things	58		63	
● People's privacy is being destroyed	86		84	
We are losing our right to dissent	73		67	
We are a sick society	35		35	
There are flaws but we're flexible enough to solve them	67		56	
Institutions Needing Reform				
Political parties	64	(44)	61	(57)
● Big business	45	(24)	54	(37)
Trade unions	24	(28)	38	(43)
Mass media	37	(26)	27	(35)
Universities and colleges	21	(28)	31	(32)

● Findings of particular interest referred to ahead.
† From *The New Morality* by D. Yankelovich.
‡ Selected 1969 survey data in parenthesis.

Figure 1.1

studies. But the 1973 one also revealed significant changes compared with the then conventional thinking of both society and management and gave some important information about the dissatisfactions then and currently with institutions and corporate organizations.

Note in Figure 1.1 of the 1973 findings[c] with 1969 data in parentheses especially those opinions and values with an asterisk. Of particular interest to management too were the following results in 1973 on motivation and participation, opinions that will substantiate recommendations on them in chapters ahead:

	Non-College	College
I am more concerned with self-fulfillment than with economic security.	43	57
Participation in decisions that affect one's own work is a social right.	51	59

The linkage now of many of these values to needs can be traced through the definitions of success in an American Management Association (AMA) survey.[6] The AMA staff classified and ranked the 1,548 definitions received as follows:

1.	Achievement of goals	535
2.	Self-actualization	192
3.	Harmony among personal, professional, family, and social objectives	181
4.	Making a contribution to a greater good	121
5.	Happiness or peace of mind	115
6.	Greater job satisfaction	98
7.	Self-respect and the respect of others	49
8.	Enjoyment in doing or in being	39
9.	Job and financial security	38
10.	Honesty and personal integrity	37
11.	Spiritual growth	19
12.	Family	11
13.	Authority over others	5
14.	Other	97

If numbers 1 to 13 are grouped according to Maslow's levels, all but four (3, 5, 9, and 13) come out at levels 4 and 5 for a total of 78 percent of the responses. The unspecified "goals" of number 1 were described by the survey analysts as in part the goals of the position and in part those of their personal lives, the emphasis in both being on the idea of achievement, befitting our achievement-oriented culture and concurring with the asterisk in Figure 1.1.

Is management, as subordinates or superiors, being unreasonable to expect any satisfaction from the organization on the level of the ego and self-actualization desires the surveys show? The Maslow hierarchy suggests they are not. Their rising aspirations are no less than basic products of nature's workings; the massive rise of our citizenry up the material and education ladder makes the expectations unavoidable.

Additionally on the needs hierarchy information, any society can use it for self-analysis. Those at the lower part that are developing nations can look forward to higher aspirations among their people, and the evidence seems to indicate that those aspirations at or near the top will not backslide when reasonable economic stability has set in as in the United States, Europe, and Japan. Thus, there is a floor, a development period with milestones, and a very challenging top.

The problems for advanced societies now appear to be one of organizational lag; their institutions may be making good progress technically, but the evidence strongly indicates they are falling further and further behind the sophisticated psychological and emotional requirements of their individual members.

These characteristics of course underlie both (a) what managers look for in their work today and (b) what subordinates expect of their superiors, asking: are the superiors worth following as leaders?

(a) The "solid traditional base" portrayed in the AMA analysis on page 11 has been confirmed as still valid by a number of studies since then,[d] and the 1989 book *Leadership is an Art,*[7] nicely summarized it in the form of what all educated managers want from their jobs; briefly: meaningful work in a process that utilizes one's talents and potential, an opportunity to grow, reasonable control over one's destiny, and relationships that meet personal needs for belonging and contributing.

(b) We all have, at least unconsciously, certain decision criteria that tell us whether or not to follow the leadership of another. A 1978 internal survey at AT&T came up with some 20 characteristics that over 1,000 managers said they admired in superiors, which naturally translate into such criteria. The top five were: honesty (almost everyone listed as #1), competence, intelligence, forward looking, and inspiring - findings that seem to have been confirmed by a 1985 survey ,of some 1,500 managers by Posner, Kouzes and Schmit.[8] Pozner and Kouzes further expanded helpfully on the five in their book *The Leadership Challenge,*[9] noting that together these desires comprise "credibility."

Above all else, they concluded, we must be able to believe our leaders, believe they can be trusted, that they will do what they say they will do, that they have the competence and intelligence to do it, and that they have a positive, clear idea of where they want the organization to go in the years ahead, which implies the ability to communicate it and give subordinates the confidence that "it's good for me" as well as the organization. All this in fact telescopes many basics that will be elaborated ahead on how leaders can succeed, particularly with regard to the Integration in Part III.

WHAT DO ORGANIZATIONS AND SUPERIORS EXPECT OF SUBORDINATES?

The organization's need for goal achievement and performance naturally goes without saying. But what are superiors' demands on subordinates that can importantly influence their opinions and attitudes about the organizations they belong to, demands such as those imposed by decisions, orders, structures, processes, policies, methods?

We accept the hierarchical setup as necessary even to manage democracy, and submission to the structures of organizational anatomy, roles, policies and rules is a part of life. Certainly too, we are capable of not only tolerating but also enjoying organizational processes and methods as means of achieving our own as well as organizational goals whether they deal with control, communication, decision-making, manufacturing, marketing, etc.

It would furthermore seem reasonable for organizational goals per se to be an acceptable concept since their intent (assuming legitimate purposes) is to benefit society with products and services and corresponding compensation to the employees.

Yet the best of whole societies themselves and their cultures[e] rise and fall, though they give the appearance of being effective human organizations toward the common purpose of their members to survive and progress. One must either ascribe mystical destructive powers to organization per se (entropy) or look to humans and the way they manage their own kind in the application of structures and processes toward organizational goals.

Momentarily suspending the former idea, one can start an examination of the latter with the observation that, in managing their own kind, managers do seem to have created a curious paradox; they, the discontented, have produced the conditions that cause the discontent.

Two of the most well-known of the behaviorists, Chris Argyris and Douglas McGregor, have given the best explanations of how managers have done it, each from a different perspective.

"The human personality is a developing organism," Argyris pointed out: the individuals tend to develop as they progress from infant to and through adult:[10]

1. from a state of passivity (as infant) to a state of increasing activity (as adult);
2. from a state of dependence to relative independence;
3. from being capable of behaving in only a few ways to behaving in many different ways;
4. from having erratic, casual, shallow, quickly-dropped interests to having deeper interests;
5. from having a short time perspective (mainly the present) to much longer time perspectives (past, present and future);
6. from being in subordinate positions in the family to aspiring to occupying equal and/or superordinate ones relative to their peers;
7. from lack of awareness of self to awareness of and control over self.

However, he went on to describe the internal environment of the typical organization at the time (1957), conditions that are still common: if the principles of formal organization are used as defined (by management), employees will tend to work in an environment where (1) they are provided minimal control over their workaday world, (2) they are expected to be passive, dependent and subordinate, (3) they are expected to have a short time perspective, (4) they are induced to perfect and value the frequent use of a few skin-shallow abilities and, (5) they are expected to produce under conditions leading to psychological failure.

In effect, the management methods of organizations demand behavior that's less than mature from mature adults, and the adaptive response of adults is by any or a combination of leaving the organization, climbing the ladder, using defense mechanisms, or becoming apathetic and disinterested. Every job holder has observed at least several of the typical defense mechanisms.[11]

Aggression	Repression	Discriminatory decision
Guilt	Suppression	Over-compensation
Hostility	Inhibition	Vacillation
Denial	Identification	Ambivalence

Then management, on observing a variety of these or of apathy, blames the employees, sees them as lazy, disloyal, money hungry, wasteful and error prone, and "compounds the felony" by applying more authoritative leadership and tighter controls. If these do not work, the "let's-be-human" approach is invoked with sugar-coated programs that tackle and reflect management's worries instead of employee psychological needs.

While this description and treatment appears more typical of the rank-and-file and lower management than middle and upper, it is in fact characteristic of all levels, because (a) it is in the nature of authoritarian management, the "style" of most corporations and governmental bureaucracies, and (b) because those who rise from the lower levels are accordingly well versed and conditioned in the application of this style, they believe they are expected to administer a like dose to their own subordinates if they want to advance, so they naturally do.

One qualification: Chris Argyris himself pointed out in a recent discussion with the author that the situation he described is, though the predominant condition, admittedly only the number 4 in the matrix he designed shown below; number 1 is plainly the ideal, but there are plenty who prefer or accept the seemingly palatable match of number 4, people who either lack the energy to put in a full day's work or have psychological problems such as bureaupathics (Part II, page 452), and there are usually a substantial number of like-minded people in large organizations among the lower and middle management workhorses.

The Individual Character	*What Organizations Want*	
	Mature Autonomous	Immature Dependent
Mature Autonomous	1	2
Immature Dependent	3	4

Douglas McGregor agreed with Argyris, that the problem is principally in the methods of managing. And in probing deeper, he concluded that the character of the methods used is determined by the nature of the philosophical attitude managers have toward their subordinates. He called it Theory X, and proposed a Theory Y alternative, the two outlined in Figure 1.2.[12]

Drawing on his impressive experience in psychology, group dynamics and corporate consulting, he deduced that humans are not the apathetic, slothful dolts who have to be pushed that the Theory X view holds them to be. On the contrary, physical and mental effort is as natural as play and rest; they will, as Theory Y states, exercise self-direction and self-control toward objectives to which they are committed; they seek responsibility; and the job dissatisfaction and alienation are caused by the fact that the average employee is regarded by his or her superiors according to Theory X, a set of views that leads them to impose aversive authoritarian treatment and gravely underutilize their potential.

It is especially important to note the link McGregor expressed between self-direction, objectives, and commitment (Theory Y's #2). Recall the AMA analysis on page 11 that the achievement of goals (#1) counted most to managers by a wide margin. As the text progresses it will become increasingly evident that Theory X attitudes are in fact a major reason for subordinates not achieving job goals, because they create conflicts between the job goals assigned and the personal goals referred to. Thus the conflict prevents commitment and self-management toward goal achievement, and performance inevitably suffers.[f] McGregor's integration solution in his 1960 book (footnote #12) will be shown to be one of the most important contributions of the century to organizational leadership.

Still, on the subject of discontent, one of course doesn't want to ignore organizational realities. Anyone who has been exposed to an assembly line or worked in or near an acre of clerical and typists' desks knows all too well about the dissatisfaction caused mainly by the mind-deadening routine inherent in such mass production operations. Nevertheless, society now insists on the fruits of mass production (product availability and lower

Theory X and Y
by Douglas McGregor

Theory X:

1. The average human being has an inherent dislike of work and will avoid it if he can.
2. Because of this human characteristic of dislike of work, most people must be coerced, controlled, directed, threatened with punishment to get them to put forth adequate effort toward the achievement of organizational objectives.
3. The average human being prefers to be directed, wishes to avoid responsibility, has relatively little ambition, wants security above all.

Theory Y:

1. The expenditure of physical and mental effort in work is as natural as play or rest
2. External control and the threat of punishment are not the only means for bringing about effort toward organizational objectives. Man will exercise self-direction and self-control in the service of objectives to which he is committed.
3. Commitment to objectives is a function of the rewards associated with their achievement.
4. The average human being learns, under proper conditions, not only to accept but to seek responsibility.
5. The capacity to exercise a relatively high degree of imagination, ingenuity and creativity in the solution of organizational problems is widely, not narrowly, distributed in the population.
6. Under the conditions of modern industrial life, the intellectual potentialities of the average human being are only partially utilized.

Source: *The Human Side of Enterprise* (New York: McGraw-Hill, 1960), pp. 33 to 48.

Figure 1.2

prices); at successive steps up the ladder, the treatment tends to be less arbitrary, greater freedom is granted, the work is more interesting and there is more involvement; and the seemingly better climate up the ladder itself seems nevertheless to motivate a person to want to move up in the organization; it appears that one just has to have stick-to-itiveness.

(Sometimes the application of directive position authority is incorrectly judged always to be Theory X behavior. There are obviously circumstances when blunt direct orders by a Theory Y manager are essential to getting the work done; additionally, in some types of organizations Theory Y doesn't fit. All such situations will be covered ahead.)

According to the AMA and other surveys, though, it's often not working out that way, and one cogent way of looking at the subject is to examine the results of management's conduct with respect to the Theory X and Y factors and the consequent subordinate attitudes as Robert Presthus did, producing categories that can be very useful in judging others in one's own organization: upward mobiles (about 10% of the employees in conventional firms), indifferent (about 80%),[g] and ambivalents (the other 10%).[13]

The upward-mobiles are characterized by their ability to identify with their organization's goals and values, an ability that gives them a meaningful basis for participation, and a capacity for initiative and action. They generally plan their careers and are willing to conform and give all the necessary signs of loyalty to gain advancement. We're all familiar with the type and some of us may ourselves be among them, but many don't realize that presently in most firms, upward-mobility is bought at a personal cost, sometimes a great cost as in the "moral mazes" example.

The indifferent reject "the organizational bargain which promises authority, status, prestige and income in exchange for loyalty, hard work and identity with its values." They do only the amount of work they feel is necessary for self-respect, holding the job, and the pay necessary to buy fulfillment off-the-job; and the organization itself is seen as but "a calculated system of frustration."

Although Presthus' interest was mainly bureaucracy and not management per se, his description of the indifferent attitude and its causes are applicable to a large percentage of middle management. These people generally come to their organizations with high hopes, usually reasonable, only to find that the organization's values (as described by Argyris) are incompatible with their motivational needs, and its goals have no relationship to their own. The first reaction is alienation, then on deciding to remain in the organization this reaction is converted, as an accommodation, to indifference.

Presthus stated that it is the "reduced opportunity for real participation, as distinguished from mock participation, along with the lack of control over their own work, that underlies the indifferent reaction." It is by withdrawing that they recapture some of their identity; they withhold part of themselves.

A superior can, however, totally misinterpret it. Rejecting status and prestige values can result in appearing to be the most satisfied of organizational personnel. With no status anxiety, striving for promotion, or high self-discipline for achievement, they attain a kind of happy, tranquil emancipation; they even enhance their social appeal by being competitively non-threatening. And the organization gets at best mediocre effort and results.

Presthus' ambivalents are primarily a type of staff specialist or professional. They tend to be intellectual idealists with high aspirations who cannot resist organizational rewards, but who have great difficulty putting up with the tyrannies, injustices, and role requirements necessary to attain them.

In his description, the ambivalent is a person of limited flexibility, which may be due to personality, values, conditioning, or experience, one who lacks the adaptability necessary to play the contradictory roles demanded in a bureaucracy. "He rejects the compromises required to play the status game...has a temperamental inability to identify with group values...the majoritarian ethic of organizations repels him...and the most critical item is his fear of authority." But they play a critical organizational role, that of:

> providing the insight, motivation and the dialectic that inspires change. The upward-mobile honors the status quo, and the indifferent accepts it, but the ambivalent is always sensitive to the need for change...

which is after all essential for progress and performance improvement.

The three types are of course not always found in pure form, and some employees go through a continuum from upward mobile to ambivalent to indifferent, though not for Presthus' definition of ambivalent. There are many ambivalent line managers and staff managers who are well adjusted to the organizational norms and demands, can and do play the necessary roles, and are in fact of upward-mobile temperament, but they moved to the ambivalent stage or beyond because of the frustrations over the lack of growth opportunities, insufficient advancement by the management systems, archaic policies, stultifying climate, competitive aggression or disinterest of superiors, and so on.

The next step is alienation. But, in contrast to non-management personnel, managers are generally more action-oriented as well as growth-bent, and many move out to better opportunities elsewhere rather than move from the upward mobile to the ambivalent or indifferent accommodation.

In sum, one can logically conclude that the principal manager frustrations and dissatisfactions are largely due to superiors' behavior toward subordinates with regard to at least the first four needs listed in the AMA analysis on page 11: goal achievement, self-actualization, business personal life harmony, and making a contribution. Some examples of typical behavior of superiors in medium size and large organizations that observant subordinates or staff will readily certify:[h]

- Personal goals of subordinates ignored in job design, motivational techniques, and annual job planning (#1 on page 11);
- Unfair and/or unreasonable important performance goals set unilaterally by superiors (#1);
- Wholesale development programs that ignore managers' personal goals, or no development at all (#1);
- Promotion by friendship or nepotism instead of competence, ignoring the achievements of the competent (#1);
- Competitive superiors who bury competent persons out of sight in their departments so their own superiors will not notice them (#2);
- Upper executives, especially presidents and general managers, promoting mediocrity into their direct subordinate openings in order to look better themselves, thus blocking more competent people (#2);
- Refusal to promote subordinate managers because they do their jobs too well to lose (#2);
- Letting new or promoted managers sink or swim without training, development, or guidance for the new positions (#2);
- Setting subordinate managers competitively against each other for higher productivity (#3);
- Withholding a pay increase or an upgrading of a subordinate with competition potential in order to encourage the person to leave the company (#3);
- Lying to subordinates about corporate goals, actions or intentions to "protect" them from the truth "until they're ready for it" (#3);
- Hiring for a short time a person who recently departed from a competitor to milk competitive information (#4);
- Firing or easing out a subordinate whose offered contributions are too consistently superior to one's own (#4);
- Norms of fear, policies of secrecy and interpersonal competitiveness that block information sharing, problem solving and idea exploration (#4).

CONCLUSION

In sum, this first Chapter's informal investigation has verified that our society does in fact have the serious problem suggested in the Foreword: an individual-organization gap, a discrepancy between the respective needs and goals of individuals as subordinates and those of their organization through their superiors, in which:

1. there is the curious paradox that the individuals as managers are themselves causing the conditions that frustrate them as subordinates and makes them dissatisfied with their jobs;
2. the apparent basic reason for the dissatisfaction is the philosophy of managing, a compound of human values described by Argyris and by McGregor's Theory X;
3. the best management prospects of youth outside the organization are aware of it and tend to avoid entering;
4. a disturbingly large percentage of middle and upper managers inside, the backbone of organizations, are constantly thinking about or planning to leave (footnote b again);
5. the faster pace of rising social values and aspirations due to social progress compared to the slow-to-change organizational goals and methods ensure with current managerial behavior a steady increase in the gap.

And if one relates the described findings of Argyris, McGregor and Presthus to the survey data, it is difficult not to conclude that the manifested "unsatisfactory performance" was in large measure the consequence of the gap.

Item #5 above, the steady increase in the gap, is particularly ominous, because, due to organizational ability to pass on in price the resultant inefficiency costs, few in industry or government are fully aware of it, and there is in most organizations still little interest in taking corrective action.

On the other hand, some behaviorists have suggested that this is not the whole story about the trend, that it is as much due to a basic tendency of all organizations to disintegrate by a process of "entropy" because of an incompatibility between the individual members and a given characteristic of organizations per se. Another explanation: some philosophers have proposed that our egocentricity is fundamentally antisocial.

There will be more on entropy in Part III that will provide ample reason to doubt its validity, and our truly social nature is substantiated in Chapter 3. In this regard for the moment and until then, a cogent comment by psychologist B.F. Skinner:[14]

Without a social environment, a person remains essentially feral. A man who has been alone since birth will have no verbal behavior, will not be aware of himself as a person, will possess no techniques of self-management ... To be for oneself is almost to be nothing.

Additionally, many studies of isolation from society have shown that it becomes intolerable for most people, leading to hallucinations similar to those of hermits.

Yet we have this gap and paradox (Item 1) that can only be blamed on something about human beings. Could it be that even a well-meaning, careful, good manager, whether it be your superior, a peer, or yourself, steeped in such concepts as humanism, participation, MBO, and job enrichment, can foul up conscious efforts to do right without being aware of it?

With such subtleties and complexities, the need for a scientific problem-solving procedure like the one in Chapter 2 becomes all the more apparent.

NOTES

a.   All quotes ahead are of either the article's author or interviewees.

b.   In fact, a 1983 survey found that 42 percent of middle managers expected to leave their current jobs within five years. Reported in "Eyeball to Eyeball: Managers more Discontented than Execs Think," *Industry Week*, 3/19/84.

c.   3,522 respondents from 16 to 25 years of age, 1,006 of whom were college students, the responses from interviews of 1 or 2 hours long.

d.   On a more general level, a study at the American Enterprise Institute of surveys made from the 70s to 90s found that American attitudes about family, sex, and drugs have remained very stable and "traditional."

e.   "Culture" is not uncommonly used interchangeably with "society" by writers; however, a society refers to an autonomous population that maintains an interdependent association, whereas the culture of an organization (or group) is the pattern that develops over time of basic assumptions, mostly subconscious, brought about by leadership behavior and the values, beliefs and experiences of other members as they learn collectively to cope with external adaptation and internal integration. See pages 265-271 for more on the subject.

f.   In his latest book (1967), assembled by his wife after his death, McGregor was said to hold that X and Y are not to be used as opposite ends of a continuum, but different "cosmologies," beliefs of managers that help them impose order on reality. Since the continuum idea is now the universal conception, however, it will be maintained herein as done by others.

g.   Not to be directly related to the 80 percent approximation assigned earlier to the "mediocre."

h.   For some 40 more examples see *The Oppressed Middle* by Earle Shorris (New York: Anchor Press/Doubleday, 1981).

REFERENCES

1. Jackall, R., "Moral mazes: bureaucracy and managerial work," *Harvard Business Review*, September-October, 1983.

2. Toynbee, A., "Will business be civil servants?" *Harvard Business Reviews*, September-October 1958.

3. Kotter, J.P., *The Leadership Factor* (New York: Free Press, 1988).

4. Maslow, A.H., "A theory of human motivation," *Psychological Review*, Vol. 50, 1943.

5. Yankelovich, D., *The New Morality* (New York: McGraw-Hill, 1974).

6. Tarnowieski, D., *The Changing Success Ethic: An AMA Report* (New York: Amacom, 1973).

7. DePree, M., *Leadership is an Art* (New York: Doubleday, 1989).

8. Posner, B.Z., J.M. Kouzes, and W.H. Schmidt, "Shared values make a difference," *Human Resources Management*, 1985, 24.

9. Kouzes, J.M. and B.Z. Posner, *The Leadership Challenge* (San Francisco. Jossey-Bass, 1987), p. 16.

10. Argyris, C., *Personality and Organization* (New York: Harper & Row, 1957).

11. Ibid. Definitions on his pages 41-45.

12. McGregor, D., *The Human Side of Enterprise* (New York: McGraw-Hill, 1960), pp. 33 and 47.

13. Prosthus, R., "Toward a Theory of Organizational Behavior" *Administrative Science Quarterly*, Vol. 3, #1, 1958.

14. Skinner, B.F., *Beyond Freedom and Dignity* (New York: Knopf, 1971), p. 123.

Chapter 2

Conceptual Preparation
for Finding Solutions

As implied in the Forward, the "Standard Problem-solving Procedure" on page xxii is a universal one for organizational analysis, applicable to each of the social, technical and integration (thus each part of the work), and Steps 1a to 1d have been completed in Chapter 1 for the social.

So the fictional executive assigned to find the problems' solutions now moved on to Step 2, the conceptual preparation for the procedure.[a]

The principal element of this preparation is the theory he develops, that is, his hypothesis, about what the most probable solution would be, an opinion the informal investigation now allows him to develop with some degree of confidence. Needless to say, without the hypothesis he would have no idea of what to look for in the next step, the formal investigation, or where to look for it.

One can see that the hypothesis development is an entirely intellectual process of thinking through in a literally creative way all the information on the problem that's available in order to forecast in advance what one then attempts to validate. Two devices are crucial aids to the process: a statement of the assumptions that will be made and a blueprint, a model, of the locus of the problem showing the key constraints and variables and how they interact.

Assumptions (Step 2a)

One of the first things researchers and planners learn about their procedures is the importance of making a clear statement in the beginning of what will be assumed about those factors of uncertainty and ignorance that are either beyond the pale of research itself, too nebulous for desirable specificity or too expensive to determine accurately, factors that nevertheless can have a significant influence on the research, analyses, or conclusions or on the interpretations of users.

On such an enormous subject as organizational performance and the job dissatisfaction found in Chapter 1, one can imagine that many assumptions have to be made; the purpose of the statement, however, is to highlight only those that can have this significant influence, especially if there's a tendency to make wrong assumptions about them. There are two in particular in this category, to which the procedural assumptions of the research should be added.

The first is on the fundamental character of the individual, labeled by philosophers down through time as "the nature of man" (before they could be corrected by woman's lib). It will be shown ahead that whatever the assumption made, it not only will heavily affect the research analysis and conclusions, but it also has a heavy influence on much of the decision making and behavior of managers in their relations with subordinates, which correspondingly directly affects the gap.

. The second regards, the possibility of an incompatibility of the individual and the organization due to their respective natures. If it is true, then the search for solutions to the defined problem must take an entirely different direction than if it is not, so a stand has to be taken on it based on the knowledge possessed at this point, and the research to come may reinforce it or recommend change. Stating the two for a managerial context and adding the third on procedure:

The "nature of man": though Douglas McGregor's Theory Y cannot be positively proven, the preponderance of both direct and indirect evidence of behavioral research overwhelmingly recommends its acceptance, therefore acceptance of the assumption that people are basically neither evil nor neutral, but tend toward being good.

The individuals vs. the organization: while managements' efforts to fulfill organizational goals commonly conflict with individuals' goals, two points tend to negate the obvious conclusion of the incompatibility of the individual and organization: 1) the organization and its management are the product of people themselves, so we cannot ascribe mystical qualities to technology, structures or processes to explain the conflict; 2) changes of management philosophy, leadership style, climate and techniques that accommodate human psychological needs have demonstrated that organizations can not only fulfill the lower needs in the Maslow hierarchy but provide opportunities to fulfill the upper ones; thus their goals are not inherently incompatible, and the individual and organization can in fact be a synergistic combination.

The procedural assumptions: (1) Organizational resources in the technical-social-resource trilogy of managing will be assumed to be adequate and not a problem cause; (2) the technical competence of managing will also be assumed to be adequate. The management technology,[b] however, will be fully covered for two reasons: it comprises a large portion of the knowledge needed for integration skills; the assumption of technical competence can be checked for correction if it has been wrong, and if wrong can be developed along the way.

System Model (Step 2b)

The second of the conceptual preparation steps should sound practical. It is no more than a systems analysis technique of ensuring that the analysts or planners have an understanding of the total configural picture of the problem arena, a perceptual and intellectual framework for problem diagnosis that accounts for all relevant major constants and variables, their interrelationships, the functioning, and the feedback.

The analyzing executive undoubtedly knew that it had to be constructed of the two components, the technical and the social, and that they have to be integrated (though integration was only a vague intellectual idea to him), so the formula would be:

A technical model + a social model + integration = a sociotechnical model

A serious complication in developing the first, the technical model, is the infinite number of variables and of technical differences from one organization to another, such that it has to be custom tailored to each one as is done on the computerized simulation many large corporations have of their entire operations. All that is needed here, however, is the universal bare essentials of management technology as shown below.

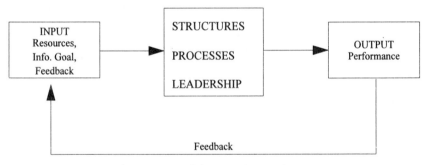

(money, materials, experience, change,
activities, interactions, sentiments)

Figure 2.1

By a "social" model is meant a behavioral one of how individuals function in the organizational environment, something that to practical managers may sound obvious and unnecessary to mention, but, as accurate as their intuitive knowledge may be, it has to be spelled out in terms of the major factors the way it does for the technical one, first, to fully understand what goes on, and second, to undertake the integration.

Those who have studied psychology will remember that Pavlov supplied the earliest formula for behavior, derived from his dog saliva experiments: Stimulus → Response, or S → R. Though crude, it still qualifies as a model.[1]

Subsequent behaviorists, however, soon recognized that it not only left out the important variables in the individual but also other crucial ones in the organizational environment. Kurt Lewin filled in most of the missing elements in a general way with his "Field Theory."[2] Applying Einstein's concept of fields of force to psychology, he theorized that any person (P) and his or her environment (E) form a "life space" (P,E), and behavior (B) is a function of it (the E in this instance referring to both the internal and external; usually it's only the external:

$$B = \int (P,E)$$

At the same time, the life space, he said, and the physical world outside this immediate environment of the person are capable of mutually influencing each other, an interaction the model doesn't show. Note that the model is a dynamic process: a change in E (e.g., an improvement in trust and openness) will change B, and a change in B will change P.

Lewin later reasoned that another factor had to be added to fully characterize the nature of the space—*climate*: "The atmosphere ... as important in psychology as, for instance, the field of gravity for the explanation of events in classical physics."[3]

Indeed, in subsequent studies he concluded that climate is not only the intervening variable and the essential link between the P and E, but is more powerful than previously acquired behavioral tendencies or traits.

The components of the three model factors can be generally specified as below, Environment referring to the most immediate community of which one's organization and oneself is a part:

The Person (the individual)
Physiological forces: The physical body and its processes
Constitutional tendencies (p. 46)
Psychological forces: Consciousness
Learning
The "self"
The personality components (p. 39)
The Environment
Physical: Inanimate and lower animate nature
Physical stimuli (energy, matter, light, heat, sound, etc.)
People and their movement

Psychological:	Culture
	Society and its institutions
	Organizations and groups[c]
	Other individuals and their behavior
	Climate and norms
	Events
Behavior	
Overt	
Covert	

And for "climate," something so important will be shown to also warrant an accurate definition and explanation. One of the better ones with an addendum by its authors—[4]

> The concept of climate describes a set or cluster of expectancies and incentives and represents a property of the environment that is perceived directly or indirectly by the individual in the environment ... (it is) considerably different from concepts of environmental influence, specifically refers to the subjectively perceived or experienced qualities of the total configural environment (that is, both internal and external to the organization).

Lewin never updated his original model to account for it, which would call for no more than an insertion of it in an intervening position as in Figure 2.2. We're also now more aware of the feedback effects shown that one's behavior has not only on the climate and general environment but also on one's own subsequent perceptions and behavior (in the P).

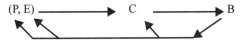

Figure 2.2

When applying this model to organizations of any size, however, there is one powerful factor buried in the E that, in light of our new appreciation of what is involved and what has to be done about it, should no longer be left hidden. It is the force of major importance within the E we call the *social system* of the organization made up of the key elements employees consider in drawing their conclusions and deciding their behavior and actions. It is composed of the **organization culture** (basic assumptions), the **social structure** (relationships, interdependencies, status and role systems), and the organization's **group dynamics** (the term used for the group behavior effects of the grouping, of specific structures and processes, and of leadership decisions and behavior), the three evolving the organization's climate, norms and, ultimately, employee performance (see chart for the discourse on "culture" on pages 265-271). Each of these, we now realize, has to be competently dealt with individually and also as a group for the organization to perform as desired. The chapters ahead will cover the key elements and what to do about them.

Before moving on to the final construction of the model for Step 2b, the technical and social models should of course be integrated, but one needs the more detailed information on the P (the individual) given in Chapters 3 to 6 to do it, so it will be postponed to Chapter 7. Nevertheless, enough is now available to think through what the hypothesis should be.

The Hypothesis (Step 2c)

Because the purpose of the adopted theory on the most likely solution is to direct the formal investigation concerning what to investigate and where to look for information, it is plainly the core of the whole problem-solving project. The analysis, therefore, that combines the information developed to this point with one's own learning and experience to produce the hypothesis must be comprehensive and done with the greatest care; indeed, for the project to produce a better solution than those being currently attempted—in this case, for example, to have a better chance of success than the current OD solution—the analysis must be creative if the end result of the project is to add to present knowledge or, as is often needed, to move the state of the subject's art a notch ahead.

In beginning this step, the executive analyst now felt more confident that the cause of the problem as defined may be any or a combination of:

The technical: It could be poor design or use of the structures, processes, or management technology, which can on their own motivate or amplify dysfunctional behavior producing the manifestations (unsatisfactory performance and the discovered disaffections).

The social: It could be an aversive philosophy, incorrect beliefs, or wrong assumptions on the part of managers as superiors, or it could be unsatisfied needs or frustrated aspirations on the part of subordinates (normalcy is assumed).

The integration: A failure to make the technical and social congruent (i.e., the organization and the individual) could occur out of ignorance of how to do it or failure on either the technical or social as stated above.

And because formulating the hypothetical solution is best started by looking at present conceptions of what the solution is—all of which are still alternatives to choose from—he first spelled out the views of conventional managers. These fall into three categories (the letters m to q are for summary use in the last chapter):

m. Theory X has not been effectively implemented; (a) give better training on the application of authority, controls and reward/punishment systems, and/or (b) remove and replace those who do not accept enthusiastically the dictates of the organization (superiors) with those who will.

n. Wherever possible, change the attitudes and behavior of those subordinates who are dysfunctional or do not concur with organizational goals and methods; that is, manipulate them to suit the needs of the organization by training, persuasion, rewards, penalties, and/or the implied threat of penalty.

o. Change the organization's goals and methods enough toward individual needs and expectations to placate employees on the differences—the theory of be nice, and the organization will be paid back in better performance.

Traditionalists holding the first view (m), having little comprehension of the social side of managing, almost naturally fall into the conviction that any problem of performance (to them satisfaction is not very relevant) is due to either not enough firmness on the part of superiors or the contrariness or incompetence of subordinates; their method is the to-be-expected sequel, unilateral directive authority. The description is called *the authority model.*

The second solution (n), known as *the leadership theorists' model,* emerged during the 1930s, the portrayal itself conveying the resentment, cynicism, and indifference it created. And the third (o), *the human relations* school approach, was the behaviorists' disaster of the 1950s in which they forgot to account for the need for *commitment* to organizational goals before any improvement in performance will occur.

Through the 1960s and 1970s, however, many progressive managers educated themselves about the individual-organization gap and somewhat modified their approach to one of *benevolent authoritarianism.* Their solution to the problem:

p. Maximize competence in management technology and implement it with "reasonable" consideration for the individuals' need for self-respect, personal growth, and return on their investment of effort.

But pragmatic behaviorists, now aware of the need for technical-social integration, realized that it would only occur if employees agree to the structures and processes with which they must comply. So they developed a range of behavior change techniques and assembled them into what is now known as the discipline of organization development as their solution:

q. Maximize the results of the planning and operation of the organization's management technology by bringing into the development of the parts those employees that are affected by them in participative decision-making, doing it in such a way that collaborative management of the organization and its culture occurs and is built into the management system as a continuous process.

Organization development, however, can hardly be called a success even when managements have enthusiastically embraced it and tried very hard to make it work. Some of the results have been impressive, but they have always soon faded, old behaviors and habits quickly returning. Either the behaviorists did not know how to teach effective implementation or they were leaving out essential elements.

But because those few good results showed it to have the best promise, the executive analyst decided to look more closely at the whole OD discipline, and his initial observation was that the OD procedures deal only with groups and whole organizations to which, according to the description above, the discipline is not necessarily limited, whereas the causes of the gap are obviously at least as much due to conflicts in the one-to-one superior subordinate relationships.

But he felt sure there must be more than this easy answer to current OD's inability to solve lastingly the defined problem, and that it would be necessary to go deeper, to in fact probe conflicts per se, since they seemed to be the fundamental origin of the problem, asking: in how many ways does the organization and how it's run (the technical) negatively affect an employee (the social) resulting in conflicts? Elemental logic of course provided the answers; there are two, each with sub-parts:

I. In a purely technical way:
   A. The planning or implementation of systems, procedures and controls, or compliance with their requirements, as described in a manual or impersonally instructed: differences of opinion are not emotionally significant, are due to differences of knowledge, so technical-social integration is not an issue;
   B. Technical job differentiation:[d] the technical differences of two or more specialized jobs; the-specializing causes biased opinions within each area as to how to do their own and other jobs and how to coordinate any interdependence that may exist toward a common goal. Personal needs and goals are not involved here either (the way they are in II below), but bona fide biased cognitive and emotional opinions are.
II. In a personal way, having an important impact as perceived by an individual on his or her personal needs, desires, motivation, goals, values, or beliefs:
   A. Emotionally, when attempting to change the person's behavior without applying the necessary techniques;
   B. *Directly* with respect to the individual's job goals,[e] job characteristics, career, and development—a consequence of the superior-subordinate interface and relationship concerning the subject person;

C. *Indirectly* through organizational structures, processes, policies, systems, methods, and norms, some of which factors are imposed by management above the direct superior.

From this it's possible to recognize that three kinds of conflict are involved:[f]

Technical conflict, the IA and IB: a difference of opinion on essentially technical job issues only; some behaviorists call it "substantive conflict" because it deals with the substance of the work.[g]

Social conflict, IIA: a difference of opinion that involves any of the personal values, assumptions, needs (including motivations, sense of worth, self-image, or identity), aspirations (including self-ideal), behavior, or expectations of one of the parties (individual or group). It has also been called "affective conflict" because it deals with the affective aspects of relationships, but it is more, much due to the social complexity in today's organizations, especially the interdependence and social diversity.

Technical-social conflict, IIB and IIC: a combination of technical conflict and part of the social, in that a difference of opinion of the technical occurs that has an impact either directly on the personal needs or aspirations of one of the parties in regard to the person's job or future, or indirectly through organization structures or processes.

And since all job-related conflicts between superiors and subordinates involve the technical to some degree, those conflicts fall in the first and third types. At the same time, when superiors do create technical-social conflict, it is because of social-category philosophy, values, and assumptions they apply in planning and/or administering the technical.

So two basically different types of solution are necessary to resolve the technical-social: a values change technique for the superiors' social misconceptions first, and after, an integration one for the technical-social. Then, because dysfunctional technical conflicts differ considerably from the two, a third is necessary for them (logic and maturity being the answer for the constructive ones); in fact, there has to be four to resolve all the dysfunctional: each of the two technical subtypes (IA and IB) and of the two social-technical (IIB and IIC) requires a specific one of its own.

A purely technical solution is all that is needed for IA, but a variation on it, called "the integration of job differentiation," is necessary for IB:

(a) *Technical integration* is the coordination of the technical elements of the industry, the organization, and its jobs from the options available in such a way as to maximize performance (there are no complications or managers' functional bias or impingement on subordinates' needs or aspirations); it is a vertical integration of the three elements with the implied internal horizontal integration of all functions and jobs (the term industry-organization-job match is used ahead to stress the components).

(b) *The integration of job differentiation* is the reconciliation of the bona fide specialization biases of the doers of two or more jobs sufficient to induce the needed cooperation and coordination between them to achieve their shared goals; personal needs, goals, and aspirations are not involved, only the biases and technical differences of opinion (that are essential to creative thinking and decisions)[h]

And naturally the term applied to resolving the technical-social conflict is *technical-social integration,* which is defined as achieving in a technical-social conflict situation a congruence of opinion between the individual(s) and the organization (represented by the superior) concerning their respective needs, goals, and methods.

Then because the direct and indirect conflicts in IIB and IIC are so different, two different techniques are necessary here also for a full achievement of technical-social integration. The two that have been developed:

(c) *Direct integration* is working through with each subordinate the characteristics and goals, the three kinds of goals (their personal jobs, career planning, and development planning), such that each sees the goals and needs of the organization as congruent with their personal goals and needs.

(d) *Indirect integration* is making a unit's or organization's goals, structures (e.g., regulations and policies), and processes (e.g., systems and procedures) congruent with the needs and aspirations of the individual(s) or group(s) concerned.[i]

Recalling that the words "direct" and "indirect" were also used to define climate on page 27, it comes to mind that its definition and these two are accordingly related: the objectives of the two techniques are to bring about a congruence between the organization's and employees' goals and needs directly and indirectly, such that the employees perceive the organization's structures, processes and leadership components of the climate as fostering their own interests and therefore warranting commitment.

Finally on the technical and technical-social, it will be shown in succeeding chapters that the ultimate goal after success on these four types of integration should be a fifth that interrelates the internal with the external.

(e) *Total integration* of the technical and social means the technical elements of the industry, the organization, and the jobs are effectively coordinated and integrated per (a) and (b) with the technical and social within the organization (commonly called the sociotechnical system).

One can see that success in any of (a) to (d) would contribute to reducing the Individual-Organization (I-O) gap, (a) and (b) included because of the potential of technical conflict to lead to technical-social ones; and we already know a lot about effecting each of them individually, though we have great difficulty combining them for the total integration of (e).

In brief, we know that management technology competence and interpersonal skills together can handle the (a) and (b) without difficulty, and the behaviorists have given us major advances for (c) and (d), starting with McGregor's contribution on the direct (c) in "The Human Side of Management," as mentioned in Chapter 1 (it is described in Chapter 20).

If one then relates the observation that current OD presently deals principally with groups to the description of the indirect technical-social conflict, it's apparent that OD attention has been on the indirect integration (d).

Unfortunately, it has been solely so. Unfortunately because, as elementary managing logic will tell one (and the text will confirm), neither the direct nor the indirect is sufficient on its own; both must be applied and in an interrelated manner; and no one is educating and training students or managers on the direct, which OD specialists are by far the most qualified to do.

There is an additional very important hang-up. Given success by the organization to the extent that the direct and indirect can be achieved, the entire effort will greatly reduce the gap, but it cannot do it to the extent desired or possible, that is, to the extent that the gap will be closed adequately.

This is because many of the most troublesome (to leadership) misconceptions are deep-seated values learned from and supported by society and its culture. A universally high level of technical education can help managers eliminate the technical conflicts and provide the technical base for technical-social integration; getting a sound education on the social does often lead to the upgrading of some values; and the organization itself can carry it considerably further by a systematic sustained application of OD (with the changes recommended in Part III); but a significant part of the values change can only be done by society.

Picking up now with the problem-solving procedure on page xxii having at this point completed steps 1 through 2b with the Chapter I information, the assumption and the model, the executive analyst, with this in front of him plus the complaints about the five current solution choices and the described need for at least the four types of integration of (a) through (d), he felt he was ready to formulate a respectable hypothesis (step 2c) of a solution to close the gap that will work. Keeping in mind that the organization's purpose as he saw it was maximum ethical organizational performance, he produced the following.

The hypothesis to guide the research for the best solution to the individual-organization gap problem must give due attention to both the technical and social components of organizational managing and leading and to do so necessitates three parts:

(i) Managements should plan and integrate technically their organizations' structures, processes, goals, strategies, programs, and methods for maximum effectiveness of the management technology toward the organization's purpose;

(ii) Then it is necessary to optimize the technical planning and its operation in terms of the social, that is, to manage the technical with due regard to the needs and aspirations of the organization's members, such that leadership planning, action and behavior will achieve the technical-social integration both directly and indirectly.

(iii) To achieve both (i) and (ii), organizations and society must each engage in the information education on the technical and social, the values change programs, and the skills training needed to remove the conflicts causing the gap.

Thus the thrust of the research and analyses to follow is spelled out quite clearly, the "social" as the presently least familiar, to be covered first:

- First, collect the latest relevant information about human behavior (personality, learning, motivation, and group dynamics) and values;
- Second, learn how to maximize competence ethically in all aspects of the management technology toward the organization's purpose, strategies and goals including their planning;
- Third, find out in detail the parts that behavior and values play in each major function of management technology (control, communication, decisions, planning, etc.);
- Fourth, determine from this knowledge what and how to teach on both the social and technical, to motivate managers and to undertake the technical-social integration wherever it's applicable.
- Finally, determine what society and its institutions must do beyond the power of organizations themselves to complete the changes in values, beliefs and assumptions needed to make possible the *total integration* of the industry, organization and jobs described in the (e) on page 32.

Addendum

Two additional matters qualify as important to one's "conceptual preparation": a clear understanding of (a) the difference between leadership and managing and (b) why the individual is placed first in the analysis of the problem.

(a) *Leadership* of people in organizations is (i) initiating, directing or guiding, controlling and/or influencing the activities, behavior, performance, attitudes and/or opinions of those people with their consent, and (ii) incorporating those qualities of personality and training that make the effort successful. *Managing* on the other hand is essentially supplying the supporting administration for getting there; planning the management technology, organizing, budgeting, and controlling, the emphasis being on formal structure, processes, systems and discipline. Naturally, both are necessary for successful organizational performance, so a key goal of leadership development is to develop both capabilities, optimally balanced, in those expected to lead.

Note the difference when the adjective "strong" is applied to each, that *strong* management is essentially close supervision with little participation and freedom, promoting bureaucracy. Strong leadership aims at and results in high levels of self-management, open communication and trust, thus a "freed-up" or "organic" organization (pages 447-448).

(b) The Individual is placed first in the analysis of the problem because, as is generally agreed, the individual is the *basic unit of analysis*, not the organization, its structures, or ' processes. If one wants to influence performance and output, a lot of time can be saved by starting, before attempting any technical changes, with an examination of and understanding of people in general, then those specifically involved, as will be done here, since they are the ones who shaped and operate the organization the way it currently is.

Thus, we first have to ask all the crucial questions about personality; along with its nature, learning, values, and motives, ask what are people's needs, aspirations, "predispositions," potentialities, and limits; how do they think, process information, feel, form opinions, and *become* motivated as desired; and what are the variables and the givens we're stuck with, realizing that some of the givens are more variable than commonly believed?

The chapters ahead will answer all of these.

A point to keep in mind: the reader will encounter in the text a number of reference dates that may seem to make the references obsolete, but judge whether or not the reference is a timeless fundamental, one that has been and always will be true.

NOTES

a.   One gender used for the executive to simplify the writing; apologies to the other.

b.   Technology and its subsumed types, like management technology, are defined in the beginning of the Part II "Introduction." The word "technical" has the broad meaning of technology; otherwise, in this work it will mean management technology. Note that management technology is a combination of hardware and software, whereas structures and processes therein generally refer only to software; however, for simplification, references to structures and processes together will be assumed to cover fully the management technology and vice versa.

c.　See Chapter 12 for definitions of groups.

d.　This has commonly been called "task differentiation," but tasks are the item components of a job. The concern here is with conflicts that occur between different specialized jobs and job groups or departments.

e.　The reference is to the three types of job goals: the defined purpose of the job, the long-range operating goals, and the annual operating goals.

f.　Discourses on "conflict" in organizational literature are always about interpersonal conflict only, exclusive of intrapersonal.

g.　Note that plain diversity of opinion as to knowledge contributes to the conflict and that such conflict is essential to creativity and superior decisions, which occur when the parties resolve it by objective collaborative reasoning. The technical and social terms are preferred here over the behaviorists' terms, being more suited to the vernacular of managers and more logical for the technical-social problems of the context.

h.　Explained under "Contingency factors" in Chapter 16.

i.　The point to be stressed is that while an individual's job, plans, and goals are structures and processes also, the issue is the difference between the direct personal impact of those in (c) vs. the less personal of these.

REFERENCES

1.　Pavlov, I.P., *Conditioned Reflexes*, trans., by G.V. Anrep, 1927. First publication in Russian in 1897.

2.　Lewin, K., *Principles of Topological Psychology* (New York: McGraw-Hill, 1936).

3.　Lewin, K., *Field Theory in Social Science* (New York: Harper, 1951).

4.　Litwin, G.H., and R.A. Stringer, Jr., *Motivation and Organizational Climate* (Boston: Harvard University, 1968), p. 29. Addendum from pp. 40-43. Italics added.

Chapter 3

The Human Factor

Obviously this subject is at the heart of performance and behavior. Understand the personality of your subordinates, co-workers and superiors, and with good values, you'll have a major part of all your managing problems solved. (Napoleon: "understanding man and his nature is the essence of generalship.").

Needless to say, personality can be very confusing. For example, the hypothetical problem-solving executive noted, like any aware manager, the significant ranges in the personality characteristics among employees in his own organization, e.g., from vigorous to passive, consistently social to truculent, achievement-oriented to political, well self-controlled at all times to not so under heavy stress, etc. So he naturally wondered whether or not personality is truly important to leadership.

He did discern however that the preponderance of the managers were inclined to be authoritarian. Why? Is it an inherent or a necessary leadership characteristic? Indeed, what kind of leader personality, what combination of characteristics, is ideal; that is, can an ideal leadership personality model be constructed? The knowledge of The Individual given in this and the next six chapters should go a long way toward supplying the answer.

This much he did know at this point from his own general knowledge: embedded in personality are the clues to what gives people the desire and drive to work with commitment, and it seems almost certain that a mismatch between a personality and an organization will result in an absence of that desire and drive.

It would therefore appear to be highly worthwhile for all managers to be well educated about personality in order to correctly understand and judge everyone in the organization, especially themselves and their subordinates.

Perhaps it should be mentioned, incidentally, that there are still some who hold to the idea that making judgments about subordinates' personality is equivalent to "playing God."[a] But as experienced managers know, it goes with the territory. In fact, failing on it is the sin, whether by avoiding it, neglecting it, or guessing at it with generalities or stereotypes, a sin through the injustices to the subordinates as well as the default on the major duty.

Learning to understand personality is clearly fundamental to leadership, and doing so naturally starts with a definition. For one about as simple yet complete as it can be made:

> *Personality* is an individual's unique pattern of characteristics with respect to intellect, motivations, traits, consistencies of behavior, dispositions, and acquired competencies.

Usually, it has been the general perception of the "whole person," and the word "pattern" carries the idea forward. The psychology pioneer, Gordon Allport, incorporated it this way: "Personality is the dynamic organization within the individual of the psychophysical systems that determine his unique adjustment to his environment,"[2] a definition that adds some idea of the causes and some broad clues to needed specificity.

Certainly it goes without saying that an understanding of the causes—how personality develops—and the specifics will also contribute to a knowledge of how to develop the desired caliber and an ability to discern if and how changes can be made.

Personality Development

There are five major determinants of personality, A to E below. From birth on, the individual combines them as encountered to develop in two ways—intellectually (the cognitive) and emotionally (the affective)—evolving a conception of the "self" and the surrounding environment's objects and people plus an astounding galaxy of personality ingredients.

The principal elements of the galaxy resulting from the five are the ten on the right of the chart, and the evolving concept of the "self" functions as an intervening force influencing how each of the ten develop, including factors subordinate to, synonymous with, or combinations of items of the ten like assumptions, perceptions, attitudes, and capabilities.[b]

Everyone knows of course that the process is one of continuous change through life, rapidly up to adulthood and slowing down from then on. A Swiss psychologist, Jean Piaget, identified three principal stages that provide a structure for the early part of the process:[3]

> *Stage I, sensory motor operations*: During the first 18 months, a child develops conceptions and memory of objects in the environment and of its own body.

> *Stage II, concrete thinking operations*: At about 18 to 24 months the child begins to solve simple problems above elementary motor manipulation, develops language and use of symbols, and at 7 to 8 years, to understand concepts.

> *Stage III, formal thinking operations*: At 11 to 12 years logical complex problem solving capability emerge.

Adverse circumstances in any of the A to E determinants can slow and reduce the amount of development within a given stage, which would be most serious, because the degree of development of each (not always complete) affects not only the cognitive development described but also the emotional development and social attitudes, even political attitudes. The third stage, understandably, eventually spells out the degree of the person's normality, maturity, and self-control.

The major determinants of and basic components of personality

Determinants	Intervening Influence	Basic Components
A. Consciousness		1. Knowledge (degree of)
B. Heredity		2. Intelligence
C. Environment^c	The "Self"	3. Opinions
D. Learning	Concept	4. Interests
E. Experience		5. Values
		6. Traits
		7. Motivations
		8. Valences
		9. Expectancies
		10. Emotions (control of)

There are some points about the five determinants and the "self" concept that are important to a sufficient comprehension of this development process.

Consciousness. Consciousness is a state of attention and awareness, the upper level of mental life as contrasted with its unconscious processes. It is one's sensory reaction to the environment that includes the arousing of the mind to being attentive, thinking, being aware of what is happening, and being aware that one is aware.

That awareness, however, is exceedingly limited in even the most alert person whether by vision, sound, feel, smell, or taste, so that it covers only a small fraction of *reality* (all the objective existence that is there). For example, the eyes, the major mechanism of awareness for people with vision, see but a sliver of the total range of light waves, themselves only a small portion of the total electromagnetic spectrum. (It's helpful for semantic clarity incidentally, to remind oneself that the subject of "perception," often confused with "consciousness," is only how one interprets the part of reality one is aware of, the perception generally a distortion.)

The eyes and other senses in the sensory system pick up no more information than is relevant to survival, safety, and the attainment of a

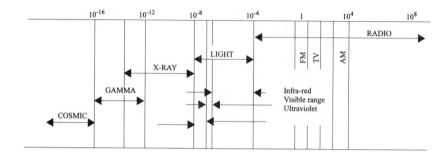

Electromagnetic Spectrum

limited set of goals the species considers as progress, leaving out all the rest, ignoring what appears to be "safe," except to the limited extent that a society has for one reason or another cultivated a greater sensitivity.

Interestingly, not only is the intake capacity limited, but the human psychophysiology puts a major limit on what is passed on to consciousness after it is admitted. A stimulus *change* in the environment, we know, is the event that attracts attention, but if the stimulus is repeated in a nonthreatening, uniform manner it soon drops out of consciousness whether it is internal (heart beat, swallowing, digestion, eye movement) or external (tick of a clock) in a process called "habituation" (or automatization), a primitive form of learning.

The initial attention causes at least three measurable things to happen: the heart beat increases, skin resistance drops, and the brain stops emitting alpha waves; after each stimulus repetition the attention declines, they all soon return to normal, and awareness of the stimulus is lost. We therefore note the scientific explanation of why the first step in advertising and selling must be to cause a change—to gain attention—and why annual auto design changes are a good way to increase their sales; the mind blocks out sameness.

We might therefore do better to visualize the consciousness-activating systems as a mechanism of awareness prevention as well as incitement; and, on top of that, both (a) our subconscious minds and (b) our culture, each in different ways, constrain even further the degree of consciousness we are capable of having.

Conspicuously, one must have consciousness first to exhibit any personality, and it makes sense that the caliber of the personality will be proportional to the degree of consciousness, which can range from that of a genius like Shakespeare down through the successively lower points of highly educated awareness, normalcy, drowsiness (partial sleep), and sleep to unconsciousness.

The way the subconscious mind, (a) above, limits consciousness falls into three categories in addition to habituation, and being consciously aware of what tends to happen at those times can help one counter them in oneself and better judge the thinking, decisions and behavior of others:

Operating constraints of the mind: (a) It can handle only one thought at a time with clarity; we're truly one-track minded; but (b) when having to deal with several messages at once, we can select one for clear attention while remembering the others; and (c) the mind does have the capacity to listen, think, and talk *almost simultaneously*, as demonstrated by a translator or by a steno typing a letter and talking to another steno about her boyfriend at the same time; but it is still a quick-switching process like that of a time-sharing computer (see "Limitations and distortions" in Chapter 14 for research on remembering).

Perceptual organization:[d] The mind creates both "consciousness constraints" of two types and "illusions": (1) the consciousness constraints may be either Gestalt constructs caused by a mental resistance to fractionism and an urge to see the whole for meaningfulness, as in filling in the lines of stenciling, or context constructs, simplifications to aid memory or handle information overloads, or as in any oversimplification where there was too much to remember or of something complex we do not understand. (2) "Illusions" are misjudgments of things, facts, or ideas (a delusion being about something that does not exist), many of which are subconscious, as the fact that busy patterns make a human figure look larger than solid colors.

Perceptual selection: The mind applies selective attention to certain factors in the setting traceable to our defense reactions, doing so at the expense of attention to other factors and the whole—
  Size: an unusually large man or object is noticed quickly with the exclusion of others, whether alone or in a group.
  Contrast: a normal size man in a group of small men will stand out and seem large.
  Intensity: intense noise, light, color, or smell stands out from weak ones, the first three universally applied in advertising.
  Motion: the upstaging actor, the moving display in the store window.
  Repetition: when the timing is not uniform and/or when the stimulus is complex, such as an ad, one is made more alert to it by one or more repetitions; further, a person is more apt to notice something if it was missed in the beginning. (This short-term repetition is to be contrasted with the long-term habituation.)
  Novelty: new objects or tasks in a familiar setting and familiar objects or tasks in a new setting, as applied to window displays or boring jobs.

The main way a culture, (b) above, limits consciousness is with respect to overemphasis of one of our two basic modes of thinking. There have been enough articles and books in the subject that now almost all educated people are familiar with the division of the intellect by the two lobes of the brain, the left one controlling the right side of the body, the right controlling the left side:

The *left side* of the brain is predominantly involved with linear thinking, sequential analysis, linear information processing, logic, math, and language.

The *right side* is predominantly involved with holistic thinking, intuitive evaluation, relational information processing, the artistic and creative, the "patterned whole," feelings, possibly all emotions.

Thus one is "linear" in nature, the other "holistic," and hemispherectomy has demonstrated that one side is sufficient to sustain a personality and an operational mind, but with some handicaps. For instance, disconnect the two sides, and English can be written with the right hand (controlled by the linear left lobe), but any former ability to draw (spatial) is seriously curtailed; even a square can't be copied. (This is based on right-handedness; left-handers may be the reverse, mixed, or similar to right-handers.)

A related aspect of the mind is a subconscious process that has been called "bimodal consciousness."[4] We know that the mind never stops functioning during life, and two states of functioning have been described for the awake person: an "active mode" that is a striving, goal-oriented, manipulating condition, and a "receptive mode" involving intake of the environment rather than manipulation of it.

During the active mode there is muscle tension, focal attention, and boundary perception (sense of self-object difference), and during the receptive there's relaxation (action is not contemplated), a decline in anxiety, a decrease in self-object differentiation, a sense of unity (becoming one with the environment instead of "I-it" manipulating), and an inclination toward a non-linear grasp of "wholeness." The parallels with the descriptions of the left and right lobe are obvious.

A major factor in our ability to survive and cope is the presence of these two modes and our ability to switch back and forth as needed, a process termed "congruity testing:" the mind constantly compares and tests its knowledge and past experience against the immediate present environment to determine what is safe versus what is threatening or dangerous. When it's safe, the receptive mode dominates and the active is quiescent, except for possible mild arousal by psychological motives; when it is not safe, the full forces of defense and offense stir up the active mode, and the receptive is turned off. And of course, motivation also arouses the active.

One can appreciate that fully developing both lobes and this bimodal faculty can make a significant difference in one's intellectual abilities, yet whole cultures have stunted one or the other as a result of regional, population, or religious pressures—for example, India's centuries of stressing the holistic resulted until recently in massive neglect of the linear essential to problem-solving, material advance, and control of the environment.

In contrast, the Western world's struggle for survival against the elements and for limited resources greatly stimulated the active mode and linear problem-solving, the latter leading to the "scientific approach" that denigrates the holistic as paranormal and mystical because it can't be explained by "scientific" methods and criteria. Naturally, the holistic potential of the right lobe has by and large remained underdeveloped.

There are two other reasons, along with gaining a general understanding of personality, why all of this information/research on consciousness and thinking is of value to managers. The first is to supply the foundation on which to comprehend the two fundamental types of problem-solver, the intuitive and the analytic, as important to fathoming the self as well as other managers; they will be explained in the problem-solving section of Chapter 13. The second is that the holistic thought of the right lobe is a major contributor to the faculty we call managerial judgment, the development of which is also presented in Chapter 14; it will be seen that knowing what is involved will contribute significantly to one's appreciation of how to develop judgment.

Finally, the knowledge of how our consciousness is limited inevitably leads a thinking person to wonder if the limitations can be reduced, if consciousness can be expanded in order to increase our cognitive capabilities. The answer is certainly yes, but not in the ways of the experimenting youth of the 1960s or their confused mentors (e.g., Charles Reich and his Consciousness III combination of ignorance, Utopia and self-destruction).

Consciousness expansion of course means increasing awareness of the stimuli impinging on one, such that either one's linear competence or holistic ability will be improved. What the youth of the 1960s didn't know was that an "altered state of consciousness" (ASC) is not expansion but a qualitative alteration of normal functioning; the psychedelic experience is no more than a hallucination, meaning brain malfunction, comparable to the sparks of a short-circuit. To interpret it as an expansion is comparable to finding truth in a firework's display.

There are *four ways to achieve expansion*, but not everyone is up to each: more intensive education, meditation, biofeedback and extrasensory perception (ESP).

The first, **education**, may seem too transparent to mention; we all know that all learning increases awareness (consciousness) and therefore the ability to think, and certainly, the passage from immaturity to maturity is a major educational advance. It also must be clear that with more knowledge and practice one becomes aware of more facets of problems (the prerequisite of solving them) and further, that the greatest drawback to problem-solving is being aware of too few alternatives. The value of an advanced management education, especially at the top of organizations, speaks for itself.

But more intensive education is also intended to refer to the combination of education, in-depth study and sweat that yields the special heights of creativity attained by all true leaders, whether in management, science or art. Even a non-artist, for example, with dedicated observing one hour a day once a week for six months in good museums, can develop an ability to pick up aesthetic messages—an exceptionally subtle form of learning— that would not otherwise be received. Over time, a sustained application of informed intellect to management problems can likewise comparably expand awareness toward superior solutions.

The second way, a passive type of achieving expansion, is **meditation** that we've now learned to use for tension and anxiety reduction, is still misunderstood by many in that it is not in that form a process of productive thought as is often believed but one of nonthought. Physiologically, it is a technique of slowing the mind's awake active Beta rate (14-21 cycles/sec.) to the quiescent relaxed Alpha rate (7-14), but short of the Theta (4-7) and Delta (1/2-4) degrees of sleep.

It has no more impressive a purpose than to turn off the linear by repeated cycling of a routine (gazing at an object, repeating a "mantra" or prayer, etc.) so the holistic state of Alpha can have a better chance of dominating. The "active mode" of Beta is turned down to allow the "receptive mode" to take over, producing the effects described on page 42.

As the writer of one book on consciousness well worth reading said, it is not quite so exotic as those who deliberately seek the esoteric might wish, nor is it an exercise in reason or problem-solving.[5] The consciousness expansion that the state can produce is only to the extent that relaxation of the linear can allow the holistic right lobe to integrate possessed knowledge into "intuitive" insights—which may come to the conscious surface on return to Beta but seldom do. Research on the subject has concluded that this process occurs because the neurons of the left and right lobes are able to interact freely at the alpha level and will do so subconsciously when one slows the pace to that level, a competence that may have been at the conscious level in primitive times and was suppressed by the overpowering survival need for the linear. A way of helping the insights rise to consciousness is presented in the "Thinking" subsection of Chapter 14 where creativity and intuition are described. Interestingly, dreaming during sleep, which occurs about every 1 1/2 hours for a short period takes place at Alpha's 7-14 cycles.

The last two ways of increasing consciousness, **biofeedback** and **ESP**, are as yet of doubtful value to managers and are only included for completeness. Briefly, the first, as most know, is an electroencephalogram (EEG) machine technique of increasing sensitivity to the body's alpha waves for control of internal functions of the body.

The second is an inherited sensitivity to wave lengths that are beyond the reach of "normal" sensory capabilities, and it comes in four forms: (1) mental telepathy (thought transference), (2) clairvoyance (perceptions without the use of sensory organs or nerves), (3) precognition of future events, and (4) psychokinesis (control of external events or objects through thought).

Freud thought that ESP was a left-over of an ability developed prior to language, a mode that has in fact been identified in lower mammals. If so, we might some day learn how to revive it, but even if we could, today's "gifted" have yet to demonstrate with any of the four variations an accuracy that could be of use to management.

Heredity and environment. When trying to comprehend human character and behavior it's necessary to consider the interaction of heredity and environment. The two are inseparable; one alone can never explain a trait, tendency, competence or action of an adult. A brief dissecting of each can provide what is needed to understand adequately the part each plays.

Our genetic instructions for growth and development can be said to be divided into two sets that operate at three levels. The first set is the automatically *programmed changes* that activate certain physical, cognitive and affective transfigurations, each at an "age-appropriate" time, from conception through adolescence; the second set is the *constitutional tendencies.*

The three levels are (1) the genetic instructions that make us one species, (2) those that make us members of a group such as a race and a family, and (3) those at the individual level that make a unique individual.

The automatically programmed physical changes of a child in the womb and after through adolescence are well known; Piaget's after-birth stages are still considered valid for the cognitive; and certain affective changes have also been found to be automatic at age-appropriate times (e.g., signs of affection for selected adults at the 10th to 11th month). All of them contribute to each level, either triggering an event or starting a capability.

The constitutional tendencies, interestingly, provide us with much the same list of characteristics for each level, the level differences being specificity, with the greatest specificity of course at the individual level. It is the instructions given for this last that is of greatest interest to managers, because they are the origin of all performance and behavior. One can easily visualize personality differences in the descriptions on the right below of the 10 basic constitutional tendencies on the left.

Constitutional Tendencies	*Capabilities*
Attention:	attention span, distractibility, intensity of response
Activity:	vigorous to quiet passiveness
Learning:	discovering, acquiring new information, habits, or abilities, and any modification of behavior due to contact with the environment
Thinking:	using acquired information
Striving and Coping:	trying to fill needs and desires, problem-solving, coming to terms rationally with the environment
Defending:	avoiding or escaping problems, repelling danger, protecting
Repairing:	recuperating from illness, mental upset, or injury
Feeling:	abilities of fear, anger, love, hate, joy, sorrow, humor, etc.
Disposition:	joyful, friendly, sullen, lethargic, querulous, etc.
Sensitivity:	degree of reaction to light, noise, feel, or other stimulation.

Certainly, no one would try to trace a performance or behavior back to this point, but as the "raw materials" that are combined with environment to produce personality characteristics, they're important building blocks of understanding.

For example, at a very early point an infant starts to relate its heritage and the environment in *a coping style,* a process of integrating its resources and energy to respond consistently for its own benefit to different events and people.

It is the beginning of personality during which some tendencies in the list influence consciousness and learning (A and D on page 39) amplifying their effect, and, if conditions are conducive, a number of complicated faculties develop: age-appropriate progressive neural changes in the brain (that deprivation can deter) necessary to achieve the full potential for intellectual, social, and emotional advance, the congruity testing mentioned, a related process called "reality testing" by which the coping style is built, and others.

The reality testing tells a lot about personality differences. It is the exploring and experimenting with the environment to discover the nature of things, people and events, one's own abilities and limitations, and the difference between the actual world and fantasy, a process that goes on through life that is especially critical in childhood.

Sociologists have been able to relate much of the end-result to socioeconomic class. To illustrate with one painful extant social disparity, social deprivation of infants in ghettos (insufficient mother care and love) from 6 weeks to 6 months typically results in thwarting the neural changes;

then the total absence of intellectual stimulation up through adolescence obstructs it even further, so that both learning ability and the capacity to form emotional attachments are stunted. One shouldn't be surprised by the consequent anti-social and hostile behavior.[e]

In contrast, most middle-class American parents, educated and motivated by the "agencies of socialization"—family, schools, peers, religious institutions, governmental and social work organizations—and the incentive systems they themselves developed, nurture their young to the fullest. They even take greater advantage of progressive programs designed to aid the poor (the principal conditions that cause faulty vs. healthy development are on pages 62-63).

One overriding factor: individuals do not inherit equally capable constitutional tendencies. Research is now beginning to verify conclusively that some people have more efficient neural systems than others, making them more capable on all of the first six. Upbringing may contribute, but heredity seems to be the major cause.

Looking again and more closely at the development of the coping style, one sees not just one but two dominant consequences. What has been described is the development of a set of strategies for dealing with events, people and problems as the person perceives certain behaviors in given settings will best fill needs and desires. But also, the unique "self" emerges at the same time.

The self. The babe at birth, it seems, doesn't know where its own body leaves off and the environment begins. Only gradually does it discover the boundary lines and learn to distinguish between the "me" and "not-me." At that time, blurry concepts start to clear up about nose, foot, mommy, daddy and on to its own name, others, toys.[6]

The parents begin to place demands on the child for self-control as to what's good behavior vs. bad, starting with toilet training, which leads to self-awareness and self-evaluation; the "me" becomes I, I am, I can, my feelings, my actions, and the *self-identity* begins to take form.

But for lack of any other basis of judging, the child must of course place total dependence on the opinions of those around to build his or her opinions of the self. What happens is familiar to us all. Being praised and seeing itself treated with warmth, consideration, and a desire to comfort and fill needs, the child builds a normal *self-esteem*.

With the reverse, the self-evaluation outcome is naturally negative. In either case, the treatment is generally recurrent and consistent, confirming the developing self-regard and setting the stage for all future hopes, fears, feelings, attitudes, and future interpretations of the environment.

A third self factor then begins to take shape. As the growing child first begins to want to be like the parent, finds additional models, and develops values, the self-identity and self-esteem combine with those influences and the efforts of all the agencies of socialization to produce a *self-ideal*, which, like identity and esteem, can be in accordance with reality or distorted by parental mishandling (e.g., by excessive praise causing over-confidence or excessive criticism destroying confidence).

Thus the **self-concept** has three interrelated parts, each of which must be of intimate concern for both parents during the early years in order for the child to make the most of its early development potential:

- *Self-identity*: the perception of what one is really like
- *Self-esteem*: the perception of worth through self-evaluation
- *Self-ideal*: the aspirations for growth and accomplishment.

And the treatment produces a "climate" that has exactly the same effect as the climate superiors produce in organizations: an aversive climate yields undesirable performance, behavior and growth; an encouraging one of supportiveness, trust, communication and development effort fosters the traits, motivation, growth and capabilities that produces the best results possible.

Learning and experience. Item D, Learning, in the personality chart on page 39 is so important to managing that all of the next chapter will be devoted to it, but it seems appropriate here, within the context of personality, to note a crucial connection between Learning, Experience (item E), and the holistic part of Consciousness (Item A).

When management development for those on the "key-position-ladder" (those believed to have top management potential—see Subject Index for ladder pages) is well planned and carried out, the result is a particular development of the right lobe of the brain that produces, as has been mentioned, the *managerial judgment* that is so important to leadership competence.

It is the success with which the three factors, A, D and E are combined that produces this personality attribute (combinations of the components on the right of the chart), and to combine them effectively plainly requires a knowledge of the inputs, the process, and the desired outputs.

Up to this point, the chapter has detailed what is known about the most important parts of the input except for the Learning (Experience meaning prior learning here and being important enough to input to stand alone), but it must be transparent that much is still unknown, which is what "theory" fills in. So at least a quick overview of the significant theories is needed, and conveniently they combine both input and process.

Personality theories

Few of the theories that are labeled personality started out as such; the title has in fact only been recently given to the lot of them by authorities in the field while attempting to organize them into a total picture. The theorists themselves originally called them psychological, social learning, motivation, or other category theories as they dealt with those specific aspects of personality—often attempting, however, to explain all of personality with only his or her specialty.

Managers don't need the fine points on them, but a general idea of the principal ones will not only help fill in the useful blanks, but also will explain much about present methods of teaching appraising, motivating and developing. They can be outlined in the following categories:

1. **Psychodynamic theories of personality**
   (a) The psychodynamic theory of Freud
   (b) The social psychology theories of Adler, Horney, Fromm and Sullivan
2. **Learning theory approaches to personality**
   (a) The psychodynamic behavior theory of Hull and of Dollard and Miller
   (b) The radical behavior theory of B. F. Skinner
   (c) Social behavior theory
3. **Type and trait theories**
   Jung, Sheldon, Allport, Cattell
4. **Self, holistic and phenomenology theories**
   Adler, Allport, Rogers, others.

Modern theories of personality deal mainly with what causes variations in personality, whereas the pioneers had to start in the beginning on the basic character of the species; this is what the first three categories (1a, 1b, and 2a) targeted. Parts or all of some are now obsolete, but each contributed thinking of great value to our present concepts.

Sigmund Freud's *psychodynamic theory* has been summed up as a personality called *Psychodynamic Man*[f] a relatively closed (from the environment) system in which three factors, id, ego, and superego, interact. One may recall that the ego, the human conscious reality-seeking intellect and reason, was described as continually striving to keep in check the id, the unconscious primitive instinctual drive of the libido toward sex, food, comfort, and aggression. The mostly unconscious superego, or *conscience*, aids in this struggle against the id by injecting the norms and values developed in it by the family and culture. The assistance is successful to the degree of the development, but when the ego's reasoning, as it sees reality, disagrees with the superego, a conflict occurs there also.

Although this theory and associated ones of Freud were brilliant insights, there were outstanding flaws: for example, the influence of the world external to the mind was ignored, no consideration was given to learning, sex (id) was considered the prime motivator for everyone (the superego only a modifier), and the idea of the human having instincts could only be judged as deterministic (the fallacy of the human "instinct" idea is described on page 153).

In all, his theories painted a very pessimistic picture of a creature with little self-control, inclined toward self-destruction (another instinct, his Thanatos theory he later withdrew), and not likely to find much satisfaction in life. Then there are his "methodology" flaws (to be kind) found now in his own writings: doctored evidence, apparent lies within his own accounts of individual cases, and his statement "The principle is that I should guess the secret (solution) and tell it to the patient straight out," like a detective who solves a crime before interviewing the first witness, e.g., the **Case of Dora**, his most famously botched analysis. Indeed he never proved a cause-effect relationship for any of his premises about repression, dreams, free association and others.[7] But his intuition was his genius; we've learned from him, for example that:

- The self and ego are the core of personality around which it develops.
- A superego is a valid construct, building and providing our conscience of standards and morality.
- Drives, motives, and emotions are basic causes of behavior.
- Many drives, motives and emotions are subconscious.
- Some motives and needs are more important than others though there's much disagreement and ignorance about the way we rank them
- When drives, motives or emotions are in conflict with needs or reason, anxiety results.
- When drives, motives, emotions or needs are frustrated, defense mechanisms develop and operate.

The second category, *the social psychology theories* (1b), was in fact a product of a group of his immediate followers who grew to disagree with some of his views as new information developed in the fields of anthropology and the newly emerging sociology. Among them were Adler, the most broadranging, Sullivan the innovator, and Horney and Fromm the neo-Freudian revisionists, the group adding the influences of social and environmental variables and downplaying the role of sex.[8] Some of the contributions of Adler and Fromm were especially noteworthy and will be described in chapters ahead.

But the key talent, learning, the process by which personality is built, had still been left out, even though Ivan Pavlov's dog saliva experiments on the subject were becoming widely known. It wasn't until 1929 that a scientist named Clark Hull injected it when he tried to explain Freud by what is known as his "Drive Theory." And for this act he has been called the first of the behaviorists; *Behavioristic Man* and **psychodynamic behavior theory** were born.

Again, however, deterministic instinct was retained, but in explaining the believed "instinctual" response a new feature was added. If the response, that has the purpose of reducing the drive pressure, is successful, it increases the probability, he said, that the response will be repeated in similar situations in the future. This was a major milestone because it in fact portrayed a *learning* event.

But the next milestone by two behavior researchers at Yale, Dollard and Miller, was equally if not more momentous (Category 2a). Applying their lab findings to Hull's Drive Theory, they concluded that all behavior is learned and went on to explain the consequence of repetition in similar situations of successful responses as a *reinforcement* principle.[h]

Unfortunately, they retained the idea that all the drives were instinctive and failed to see and account for the extent to which the environment does much of the teaching in the development of character, an issue another researcher, B. F. Skinner, was promoting at the time of their publication.

Skinner and his associates broke away completely from psychodynamics, rejecting all the earlier cherished explanations of personality—the reason why it was called the **radical behavior theory** (Category 2b). Instincts, drives, motives and traits were considered no more than inferences to be used as labels for the effects of deprivation and satiation.[9]

Personality should be viewed in terms of behavior, he contended, and the only way to understand behavior is to examine the events and circumstances that occur before and during it and identify those influences that tend to strengthen the future likelihood of the same behavior or to discourage it. When that is known, the knowledge has predictive value and can be used to control behavior by managing the influences.

Sometimes it is called the "pull" theory. One supposedly reacts only to rewards, punishments and pressures. Biological and psychological maintenance forces, motivations, perceptions, attitudes, cognition, emotions—the principal factors that account for the different reactions of different people to the same situation—all are totally repudiated, and self-actualization is considered but a fantasy we attribute to that idealistic construction out of ignorance we call "autonomous man."

Some of Skinner's conclusions have indeed been valuable contributions. But not this explanation of "the nature of man," which the text ahead will demonstrate is far too simplistic. Unsupportable assumptions are made, lab research on animals has been generalized to the complex human with insufficient scientific justification, and operant conditioning has proven unworkable except in tightly controlled clinical situations.

Those who pushed the next category of theory, **social behavior theory** (2c), nevertheless went even a step further in their simplification. They not only rejected traits but doubted the principle of reinforcement. While the radical view of traits was that such "consistencies of disposition across situations" occur only when the same behavior has been aroused by reinforcement in similar situations, the social behaviorists held that even that was improbable; our complexity has made us so discriminating that most of our behavior is too situation-specific to draw such conclusions.

For example, a man who is "independent-minded" with friends is commonly dependent with the boss and often with his wife, and it may vary with who is present. Instead of observing the person, we were told, look at what he or she does (thus their on-the-spot cognition and cognitive learning). It ignores the indispensible heredity, past experience, and motivation as well as traits, but their emphasis on observation and cognitive learning highlighted the factors' importance to analysis.

The third category, **type and trait theories**, covers the two more obvious possible explanations of personality that some scientists were trying to develop at the same time the Learning approach was getting under way.

The simple labeling of people as types goes back to Hippocrates in 400 B.C., but all of those proposed have quickly faded away, if not for limited applicability, then because of inflexibility; and today we realize too that they left out the same important variables other obsolete theories did—motives, traits, learning, the situation and the dynamics of personality change itself. In fact, the only type theories noted by the textbooks are those of Carl Jung and W. H. Sheldon,[10] and they are included just to illustrate their logic and present them as a passing phase.

Trait theories dropped by the wayside also not for lack of validity of traits but because their proponents tried to supply all the answers to personality and behavior with their theories about the one factor. Naturally, traits themselves remain an essential factor in the evaluation of leadership effectiveness. Indeed, the definitions of strong and weak personality generally accepted by behaviorists are in terms of traits:

Strong personality: Highly confident, outgoing, sociable, dominant, self-accepting.
Weak personality: Low in self-confidence, showing dependency needs, and tending to be socially weak and introverted.

For instance, the two best known trait theorists, Gordon Allport[11] and R. B. Cattell,[12] asserted that personality is a complex structure of traits, traits are stable subunits of basic motives, and behavior is driven by traits. Allport even believed at the time of his book on it that traits are actual neurophysical structures in the brain.

The value of traits in their own right, however, is not lessened by these opinions, and the work of scientists on the subject induced more thought on their usefulness to managers in appraising personality. Some interesting general information the research produced was:

- Most of the common traits follow a normal distribution pattern in the population; e.g., the traits of intelligence, creativity, sociability, extroversion, physical characteristics (height, weight, etc.).
- Variations in people are noted mainly by the:
  (a) nature of the trait (physical, emotional, intellectual),
  (b) amount of degree of the trait (that is, the amount inherited or developed),
  (c) degree of internal integration of traits (conflict resolution, maturity)
  (d) patterns of traits (combining to make up important aspects of personality).
- A trait's importance usually depends on the situation; for example:
  (a) general traits, like intelligence and self-control, are important in a wide range of situations, but not all;
  (b) specific traits, like claustrophobia, are important in only a few
  (c) if a trait of a person is much above or below the average of his or her group, it can play a more important role in the person's success or failure, e.g., self-confidence, querulousness.
- And the importance assigned to a trait by an observer may be tied to a total pattern of an individual's traits (e.g., assuming a pretty shapely female is dumb).

The last category on page 49, **Self, holistic, and phenomenology theories**, was a development process in itself that started with the early insights on the self by Alfred Adler back in 1914.[13] It evolved into present-day phenomenology, it seems, by adopting selected thinking of the emerging behavioral sciences along the way, especially from Allport, Maslow, and Rogers, in order to best fill the growing individual and organizational needs for its services.

The self-theorists have been labeled as such mainly because of their emphasis on the centrality of the self-concept that has been described (pages 47-48). They held that the self is at the root of both the uniqueness of and stable consistencies in personality, and the idea apparently led automatically to the "holistic" view—that, as per the definitions of personality (page 38), one should judge the whole person, who is always much more than the sum of the parts—and finally to the addition of phenomenology.

The word phenomenology means the search for essences, beyond assumptions and what is observable, which is also the definition of ontology. But phenomenology is a special branch of it that does in fact make two assumptions of its own for the search: contemporaneity and the holistic view.

Allport recommended among other points the contemporaneity, the word used earlier by Kurt Lewin, op. cit., 1936), a theory that *current* experience plays the most important part in a person's behavior compared to the past; the past does have an influence (versus the contentions of the social behaviorists), but it declines increasingly with time the way memory does. The human emphasis is on the immediate experience rather than a bundle of motives and traits "in a tangle with the person's past."[i]

Today's "phenomenology" is a label that encompasses not only these elements of the self, the "whole person" idea, and contemporaneity, but also *Humanistic Man*, a theory of "the nature of man" that will be described in Chapter 5 because of its relation to the information there.

Carl Rogers was the principal phenomenology integrator, combining the ideas of several others of the time, especially Allport and Maslow, with his own clinical practice conclusions, giving his interpretation a distinctive personal stamp. One statement of his in particular conveyed his thrust: "Behavior," he said, "is basically a goal-directed attempt of the organism to satisfy its needs as experienced in the field as perceived."[14]

The phenomenology contentions in sum: accept the influence of motives (especially the needs for autonomy, self-enhancement, and self-actualization), traits, and learning on personality but not as the only forces; don't waste time trying to fathom the unconscious like the Freudians; and don't rely heavily on environmental conditioning the way the radical behaviorists do. Instead, probe an individual's current behavior in the most recent situations in terms of the self. In any attempt to help or understand an individual *now* it is enough to determine just the characteristics of personality and the behavior that are relevant to the person's current environment.

It will be shown (in Chapter 18) that this thinking concurs with "social change theory" that crystallized at about the same time (Rogers undoubtedly influencing its formation), the theory leading to techniques of individual and organizational change ideally suited to organizational needs: the techniques have proven to be adequately effective with *normal* people, because they deal with current problems, and they are far less expensive than the main alternative, the psychoanalysis of psychodynamic theory.

Parenthetically, existentialism is a major **philosophic** expression of phenomenology, epitomized in Sartre's "existence precedes essence."[j] One first arrives, after which one defines oneself and makes oneself what one is. As with the social behaviorists, drives, motives, and traits are rejected, but so is the influence of the past, forcing the focus to be entirely on the present. Additionally, the existentialists waxed romantic by making the individual fully responsible—will power is supposedly the whole answer; even the forces of the situation are ignored.

Basic issues

In addition to what has been said about personality for understanding it, a most fundamental competence in judging it is of course to be able to discern the degree of normality, which in fact entails three other factors also; the four: *normality, maturity, self-control,* and *perception.* A grasp of all four, however, can be substantially aided by first getting straight a fundamental in "the nature of man:" whether or not we are social creatures or tend to be egocentric individualistic loners.

The social human. The exhortation of great Americans of the past to revere individualism,[k] our legal stress on individual rights, and the idealistic teaching of academe against conformity have in general created the impression that our natural inclination is to be totally independent, self sufficient, and alone, that our willingness to engage in group activities is in reality but an accommodation for practical reasons of defense, production, and/or self-gain.

However, anthropology, brain research and behavior research have now peremptorily dispelled the notion and shown that we unequivocally developed into social creatures aeons ago.

First, the most advanced paleoanthropological stand today is that the social nature of the hominid was a if not the prime reason why it emerged from apedome. Three fairly simultaneous events occurred between two and four million years ago while the brain was still ape-size: bipedalism, home bases, and the continuous availability of sex in monogamous pair bonding.

Small tools did not develop until about 2-3 million years ago, large ones around 1 million B.C. Thus bi-pedalism that preceded them, rather than to facilitate tool making (an old theory), seems to have occurred so that males and unencumbered females could carry food back to home base for child caring females, the injured, and the aging. And to encourage male cooperation, evolution changed the female so that she was available for sex at any time (vs. chimps, where the male is interested only when the female is in heat, which never occurs during babe-rearing, only before and after it's over, the rearing taking several years without male help).

Cooperation therefore, rather than aggression, competition or aloneness, evolved as a dominant characteristic at both the group and pair level. The females strengthened it further in their selection of cooperative males in lieu of socially disruptive ones and in their development of receptiveness to sex and their other attractions (an excellent description of the research is in the reference #16 article).

Second, neurologists have identified in the brains of all mammals not only a region dedicated to self-preservation but also another to the preservation of the species, which is consistent with the herding character of all mammals. No animals below them have it, and the one with the most highly developed is the human.

Third, combining the studies of anthropology, neurology, and behavior with how the brain developed from our primitive beginnings, scientists have concluded that a succession of neural changes occurred that added our capacities for feeling and empathy (undoubtedly from the pairing) and then, later, values and ideals for coping with the increasingly complex demands of social activity (described ahead beginning on page 146).[16]

Additionally, Douglas McGregor some years ago mentioned another point, one particularly relevant to management:[17]

> The available evidence strongly indicates that, throughout the long course of his evolution, man has been a group living form. Moreover it is very likely that the human group, throughout the history of the species, has been *a powerful problem solving tool, coping with all sorts of harsh and taxing environmental contingencies* (McGregor's italics). It has been an adaptive mechanism par excellence.
>
> (Furthermore,) individuals seek and find gratifying those situations that have been highly advantageous in survival of the species. That is, tasks that must be done (for species survival) tend to be quite pleasurable; they are easy to learn and hard to extinguish. Their blockage or deprivation leads to tension, anger, substitute activity and (if prolonged) depression.

Surely, most of us have suspected these traits; even a superficial reflection on the things that please normal people suggest our social nature—our emotional satisfaction in belonging, the enjoyment of affiliation, and the pleasure of group dance that goes back to prehistoric times.

At the same time too, we know that the benefits of membership have a price, one reason for our doubts: the requirement to conform to group norms in order to remain a member, which is often in direct conflict with our drive for self-determination. The idealists have unfortunately made an either/or dilemma of extremes out of it—egocentric individualism or demeaning submission—when the only solution is a compromise. Two behavioral scientists wrote one of the best responses some two decades ago:[18]

Nearly everyone is convinced that individuals should not be blind conformers to group norms, (but) perhaps we should also think of the consequences of the removal of individuals from group membership or the plight of the person who really does not belong to any group with clear-cut norms and values. It seems as if people who have no effective participation in such groups either crack up (as in alcoholism or suicide) or they seek out groups which will demand conformity. In discussing this process, Talcott Parsons writes: "In such a situation it is not surprising that large numbers of people should be attracted to a movement which can offer them membership in a group with a vigorous esprit de corps with submission to some strong authority and rigid system of belief; the individual thus finding a measure of escape from painful perplexities or from a situation of anomie."[19]

We seem, then, to face a dilemma: the individual needs social support for his values and social beliefs; he needs to be accepted as a valued member of some group which *he* values; failure to maintain such group membership produces anxiety and personal disorganization. But, on the other hand, group membership and group participation tend to cost the individual his individuality.

Is there an avenue of escape from this dilemma? Certainly, this issue is not as simple as we have described it. The need for social support for some values does not require conformity with respect to all values, beliefs and behavior. Any individual is a member of several groups, and he may be a successful deviate in one while conforming to another ... We must assert that we do *not* believe the basic dilemma can be escaped. To avoid complete personal disorganization man must conform to at least a minimal set of values required for participation in the groups to which he belongs.

How should one think of the relation between individuals and groups? Although research does not begin to provide all answers, we have found evidence which tends to support the following general statements:

- Strong groups do exert strong influences on members toward conformity. These conformity pressures, however, may be directed toward uniformity of thinking and behavior, or they may foster heterogeneity.
- Acceptance of these conformity pressures, toward uniformity or heterogeneity, may satisfy the emotional needs of some members and frustrate others. Similarly, it may support the potential creativity of some members and inhibit that of others.
- From their experiences of multiple membership and their personal synthesis of these experiences, individuals do have opportunities to achieve significant bases of individuality.
- Because each group is made up of members who are loyal members of other groups and who have unique individual interests, each group must continuously cope with deviancy tendencies of the members. These tendencies may represent a source of creative improvement in the life of the group or a source of destructive disruption.
- The resolution of these conflicting interests does not seem to be the strengthening of individuals and the weakening of groups, or the strengthening of groups and the weakening of individuals, but rather a strengthening of both by qualitative improvements in the nature of interdependence between integrated individuals and cohesive groups.

Normality. Human intricacy of course makes it impossible to put together a precise definition of either normality or maturity, yet the importance to managing people of knowing basic criteria for judging each and the difference between them is obvious. And the fact that one can be normal without being mature additionally complicates it.

One manifestation of that complexity is that mental normality has to be judged from five angles to embrace the full scope of its meaning: from the standpoint of **statistical averages, mental health, causality,** the **life-cycle process,** and **values,** the last being in this instance those of the relevant society.

On the first, it has been convenient for sociologists and anthropologists to describe both personality types and societies in terms of the statistical normal distributions of selected factors common to people in general, the middle of the curve being normal, the extremes abnormal.

Such "averages" can plainly be useful in describing large groups, but they can lead to undesirable, unintended implications when applied to the unique individual. For example, one might at first feel that, since the average person is socially acceptable, acceptance or rejection is a good, even quantifiable, measure of normality. Is it not then also a measure of conformity and subordination of personal convictions? Or if the factor to be averaged is intelligence, talent, enthusiasm, industry, etc., wouldn't normal (the middle of the curve) also mean mediocre, suggesting better is not desirable?

Yet there clearly is a place for averages in the definition. The unique Person is obviously too varied for fixed criteria, but on the other hand, averages that have adequate latitudinal ranges can often accommodate desirable differences.

The fields of psychoanalytic psychology and medicine have in the past defined normal as a state of "mental health." They held normality to be a negative issue: the absence of psychopathology and a reasonable freedom from undue discomfort, pain or disability. Now they've come to view it more positively, to mean the following conditions:

Criteria of Normalcy

1. A sound self-concept.
2. A reasonable degree of internal harmony in the coordination of thinking, feeling, and acting in the processes of problem-solving and coping.
3. A capacity for giving and accepting affiliation and maintaining constructive relationships
4. Absence of mental disorders (obsessions, disorientations, insanity) or extreme emotional distress (severe anxieties, fantasies, depression).

˙These are currently the criteria most commonly used, but they are, for understandable reasons, applied with considerable flexibility. We all tolerate as normal a level of functioning for any or all of the four that is considerably less than appealing, even behavior that includes types we don't want to associate with. There are some individuals who appear vulnerable in one respect but have inner offsetting strengths. Others who are taken for towers of strength have at times hidden critical weaknesses. And we all have breaking points (disorientation), which for most people have not been tested. But we and the others are no less normal personalities because of these variances.

"Causality" refers to the situational demands, and little comment should be necessary that what a situation requires of a person can span the behavioral spectrum, sometimes calling for extraordinary performance that doesn't seem to fit within the criteria. In a given case, normal behavior may be a matter of what others do or have done, of prudence beyond applicable norms, or whatever produces success within moral bounds. Or, in fact, standards may be wholly irrelevant. Causality thus becomes an added criterion to account for any unusual behavior that may have occurred.

The behavioral sciences, in contrast with psychoanalytic psychology and medicine, define normality dynamically, recommending that it be viewed as a biopsychosocial "life-cycle process" of development. Because life is a series of developmental stages, they say, it has to be judged by what should occur during each stage. Freud's four psychosexual stages (oral, anal, phallic, and genital), Piaget's three cognitive stages (page 38), and Erikson's eight psychosocial ones[1] are all valid bases in this regard.

Until recently, however, these and other descriptions concentrated on pre-adult development, so that we could only guess about changes throughout adulthood, the ones that are most important to organizations. Fortunately, a number of behaviorists noticed the vacuum and have now filled it. A write-up in *Time* magazine, Figure 3.1,[20] summarized a few of the contributions.

One can see that an opinion on normality that combines the five-dimensions (the fifth, values, covered in Chapters 5 and 6) is a matter of judgment. A manager's intellectual computer would have no difficulty doing it satisfactorily, given, say, a few months' experience with the person judged.

Maturity. The key word in the biopsychosocial process of maturation is "integration" (one more application of the word): the combining of thinking, sensing and emotions with one's energy, internal resources and available external resources in a harmonious, effective manner to cope with the range of environmental conditions ordinarily encountered.

Our usual reference to human maturity of course assumes completion of physical maturation and pertains to only the intellectual and psychological.

New Light on Adult Life Cycles

Freud, Spock and Piaget have charted almost every inch of childhood. Psychoanalyst Erik Erikson put the final touches on a convincing map of adolescence. Yet until very recently, most of the charting stopped near the age of 21—as if adults escape any sequence of further development. Now a growing number of researchers are surveying the adult life cycle.

The research so far has been narrow, concentrating largely on white, middle-class American males. But in separate studies, three of the most important life-cycle scholars—Psychiatrist Roger Gould of U.C.L.A., Yale Psychologist Daniel Levinson and Harvard Psychiatrist George Vaillant—have reached some remarkably similar conclusions that add new dimensions to the topography of postadolescent life. The main features:

16-22 LEAVING THE FAMILY. In this period, youthful fantasies about adulthood slowly give way. Young people begin to find their peers useful allies in an effort to break the hold of the family. Peer groups, in turn, tend to impose group beliefs. Emotions are kept under wraps, and friendships are brittle; any disagreement by a friend tends to be viewed as betrayal.

23-28: REACHING OUT. Following Erik Erikson, who found the dominant feature of the 20s to be a search for personal identity and an ability to develop intimacy, Gould, Levinson and Vaillant see this period as an age of reaching toward others. The growing adult is expansive, devoted to mastering the world; he avoids emotional extremes, rarely bothers to analyze commitments. To Levinson, this is a time for "togetherness" in marriage. It is also a time when a man is likely to acquire a mentor—a patron and supporter some eight to 15 years older.

TIME, APRIL 28, 1975

29-34: QUESTIONS, QUESTIONS. All the researchers agree that a crisis generally develops around age 30. Assurance wavers, life begins to look more difficult and painful, and self-reflection churns up new questions: "What is life all about? Why can't I be accepted for what I am, not what others (boss, society, spouse) expect me to be?" An active social life tends to decline during this period. So does marital satisfaction, and the spouse is often viewed as an obstacle instead of an asset. Marriage becomes particularly vulnerable to infidelity and divorce. Vaillant sees a crassness, callousness and materialism at this stage. Levinson detects a wrenching struggle among incompatible drives: for order and stability, for freedom from all restraints, for upward mobility at work. Says he: "If a man doesn't start to settle down by age 34, his chances of forming a reasonably satisfying life structure are quite small."

35-43: MID-LIFE EXPLOSION. Somewhere in this period comes the first emotional awareness that death will come and time is running out. The researchers see this stage as an unstable, explosive time resembling a second adolescence. All values are open to question, and the mid-lifer wonders, is there time to change? The mentor acquired in the mid-20s is cast aside, and the emphasis is on what Levinson calls BOOM-becoming one's own man. parents are blamed for unresolved personality problems. There is "one last chance to make it big" in one's career. Does all this add up to disaster? Not necessarily. "Mid-life crisis does not appear to portend decay," say Vaillant. "If often heralds a new stage of man." The way out of this turbulent stage, say the researchers, is through what Erickson calls "generativity"-nurturing, teaching and serving others. The successful mid-lifer emerges ready to be a mentor to a younger man.

Figure 3.1

44-50: SETTLING DOWN. A stable time: the die is cast, decisions must be lived with, and life settles down. There is increasing attention to a few old values and a few friends. Money is less important. Gould sees married people turning to their spouses for sympathy as they once did to their parents. Levinson notes that men tend to have fantasies of young, erotic girls as well as of older, nurturing women—all part of a final attempt to solve childhood problems and cut free from the mother.

AFTER 50: THE MELLOWING. These years are marked by a softening of feelings and relationships, a tendency to avoid emotion-laden issues, a preoccupation with everyday joys, triumphs, irritations. Parents are no longer blamed for personal problems. There is little concern for either past or future.

Like Freud and Erikson, the life-cycle researchers argue that personality disorders arise when, for one reason or another, the orderly march of life stages is disrupted. Vaillant's studies suggest, for instance, that men who fail to achieve an identity in adolescence sometimes sail through life with a happy-go-lucky air, but never achieve intimacy. BOOM or generativity. "They live out their lives like latency boys," he says, not mentally ill, but developmentally retarded at the childhood level.

The researchers' findings are tentative. So far, few minority group members of working class men have been studied, and the data on women is limited. Vaillant believes, however, that the female life pattern is much the same as the male, except that the drive for generativity that appears in men in their late 30s or early 40s may show up a decade earlier in women.

In any event, a thoroughly detailed portrait of adult life is still "many years away," as Gould concedes, and there is much skepticism in the academic world that one will ever appear. Yet the lifecycle researchers are confident that the threatening 30s and the mellowing 50s will some day become as universally accepted as, say, the terrible twos and the noisy nines of childhood.

DRAWING BY STEVENSON; ©1974 THE NEW YORKER MAGAZINE, INC.

"It seems like only yesterday I was on the verge of getting it all together."

Figure 3.1 (continued)

part of the integration, including meeting the demands of conventional social situations in relatively sound, realistic and non-defensive ways.

The word "relatively" permits an acknowledged range of anxiety, "normal" defensiveness and acceptable personality eccentricity; and anxiety can be "trait anxiety" or "state anxiety." The latter is the type we all get when aroused by a fearful situation. The former refers to a more stable overall level; some people are just more jumpy than others while fully capable of normalcy and maturity.

For both normalcy and maturity, therefore, one is talking about a perpetual change process through life of internal organization and reorganization of thinking, feeling, and sensing that moves toward an equilibrium appropriate to the state and situations of the being. Normalcy and maturity are reflected in the way one carries out roles and tasks during each period in Figure 3.1. The normal one succeeds in staying above a minimum stability level needed to cope, but may be short on self-control, have a number of self-damaging habits, and may be any or a mix of:

diffident, laconic, or truculent; obsequious, supercilious, or pusillanimous; torpid, tumid, or turgid; fatuous, captious, or vacuous; obtuse, irascible, or vindictive.

One may signal an abnormal condition, but a normal person may possess any of them as traits; a mature person is less likely to.

A psychologist's listing of causes of faulty development and of healthy development can provide a helpful base for further thought on the meaning of maturity:[21]

Causes of faulty development
1. Arrested development-immaturities and fixations that impair the individual's adjustive and integrative capabilities.
2. Distorted development—at either the physiological or psychological level, or the former leading to the latter, with such consequences as chronic delinquency, ruthlessness, extreme assumptions or attitudes (extreme racists, indifferent murderers, confidence men, many prostitutes).
3. Genetic and acquired defects—mutant genes, prenatal and birth difficulties.
4. Maternal deprivation.
5. Childhood trauma—for example, from serious parental complications.
6. Pathogenic family patterns (total family or family-child patterns)—rejection, overprotection, indulgence, excessive demands, faulty communication, sibling rivalry, undesirable parental models, disturbed family, antisocial family, disrupted family.
7. Social pathology—a disordered society or cultural deprivation.
8. Faulty self-structure, steering growth and development into distorted patterns.

Conditions fostering healthy development
1. Appropriate infant and childhood physical care.

2. Love and acceptance.
3. A stimulating, responsive, supportive, encouraging environment.
4. Structure and guidance:
   (a) Clearly defined standards and limits.
   (b) Adequately defined roles for older and younger members of the family.
   (c) Established methods of motivating and controlling the desired norms of behavior.
5. Success and recognition—the success-failure balance in favor of success with constructive use of the failures.
6. Early detection and considerate of defects.

And when the healthy development reaches the mid-twenties, at least the fundamentals of psychological maturity should have been the consequence over and above those of normalcy.

One can now combine this information with that on normalcy, our social character, and other knowledge we have of the human, such as our self-actualizing nature, to produce an elementary set of criteria of maturity:[23,m-]

Criteria of maturity

1. A secure *self-concept*—identity, worth, ideal.
2. A sound comprehension of *reality*
3. A *value system* worthy of respect (Chapter 5).
4. Reasonable *self-control* (ahead).
5. *Caring* and *warmth*
6. *Responsibility* toward one's small social groups, especially the family, and toward the larger important ones, the work organization and community.
7. The enjoyment of *work* and *productivity* in terms of one's capabilities (e.g., self-actualization).
8. *Resilience* under stress and after setbacks.

When this is achieved by a person, there are, along with the obvious advantages, an inner cohesion and ego strength that are open to rational thought on alternatives involving values or emotions that seem to be missing in the immature.[n]

Self-control. It is surprising that the psychologist author (Cox) of the article referred to on maturity in preparing her own list of criteria omitted self-control (that was added by the present author) because it cannot be assumed within any of the other seven and at the same time can significantly influence each as well as stand alone. There is little question that it is an indispensible personality factor, and certain self-control traits are especially important requisites of managing others that warrant singling out. Here are five of the most critical ones:

1. **Low impulsiveness.** An impulsive person is one who reacts immediately to stimuli without deliberation. The extreme high condition would be unbridled conduct due to either no disciplinary breeding or an abnormality and includes the acutely neurotic who haven't solved their personal problems maturely, take offense easily, are overcontrolled and inclined to explode, or are excessively defensive. A low extreme condition would be phlegmatic insensitivity that can result in inertia or appear to be indifference or stupidity.

Clearly, the mature reasonably self-controlled person will be in between, and he or she will show low impulsiveness most of all by his or her ability to communicate honestly without threatening either the other person or the self.

2. **High hostility tolerance.** Highly affiliative managers, who seek to make everyone happy, tend to be low on hostility tolerance, (tolerance of others' hostility), and it has proven to be the Achilles heel of many sales managers who as salesmen were superior in pleasing all customers, but as managers were unable to accept the need at times to displease subordinates and to make unpopular decisions.

3. **High frustration tolerance.** It entails a combination of motivation (valence and expectancy on pages 230-231) and an ability to delay gratification that gives a person two faculties that are very important to management: (a) the tolerance to take one's own frustration of being behind schedule or of not achieving goals due to one's own failures or to those of subordinates, and (b) the related ability to keep trying (or urge others to) for as long a period as necessary to achieve them. Implied is the complicated mix of drive, the capacity to see the potential payoff, self-confidence in one's competence, or confidence in relevant others', and a belief that the chances of success are reasonably good.

Research on the subject of high frustration tolerance has produced some valuable information for judging the trait. For one point, certain other traits tend to correlate with its presence: the person generally has a higher achievement drive, higher aspirations, less uncontrolled impulsiveness, higher levels of competence, higher intelligence, greater capacity for sustaining attention to a subject, and more mature cognitive development than do persons with low frustration tolerance.

Further, the trait is found least often in low socioeconomic classes and most often in the middle and upper ones, which gives important support to a research conclusion that it is principally learned from the models of the environment (especially the family and peers) and its mores.

To illustrate, the lower class negroes in Trinidad have had a reputation for wanting immediate pleasure and being unable to delay gratification for greater reward later; the East Indians in the same town were reputedly the reverse. But research studies of the children of the two groups showed that both had low-control and high-control youngsters, and in each case the low self-control correlated with fatherless households. A number of complexities were involved, but the salient problems for both groups were the absence of self-control (on this trait) models, disrupted family cultures, broken promises, or hopelessness about future rewards, that promoted getting what you can now. Unexpectedly however, it was found that many of the same children needing immediate gratification in both groups did elaborate planning ahead for religious celebrations and carnivals well in the future, rewarding events they knew would take place.[24]

4. **Strong social inhibitions.** This endowment in a manager has a major influence on how the person exercises authority, and naturally it affects off-the job behavior as well. An example is given in Chapter 8 (pages 272-274) by two researchers on the subject of the "power" motive that graphically illustrates it, calling those with the inhibitions "socialized" managers.

Those who are socialized feel a sense of responsibility for their group, tend to be more considerate of individuals and are willing to sacrifice some of their own self-interests for the welfare of the group. Those who aren't commonly seek as much personal power as possible, exercise power impulsively, are more rude to people, exploit others, and put undue value on the symbols of personal prestige like large offices and fancy cars. There is even an inclination to drink too much.

5. **Attitudes.** Most people need a definition without realizing it. Attitudes are learned predispositions to react consistently in a given way—positively, negatively, or neutrally—toward certain things, people, ideas, or situations. Whereas a value is a single belief that transcends these subjects, an attitude refers to an organization of several beliefs all focused on a given thing, person, idea, or situation. Attitudes depend on preexisting values: they are functions of them.[25]

Therefore, an attitude qualifies as a value system, but one with only the general consequence described, whereas a philosophy, ideology, or religion is a value system that produces specific concepts. Nevertheless, as with them, attitudes do help us cope and make decisions on the subjects, though we may not have consciously clarified the attitudes in our minds.

Needless to say, a person's attitudes about responsibilities, duties, authority (and those who have it), ethics, and work have a paramount influence on maturation, compatibility, self-control, commitment, and performance.

Perceptions. Perception is defined as the subjective interpretation of incoming stimuli, which would be how several or all of the 1 to 10 in the chart on page 39 combine to produce an opinion of the stimuli.

The dynamics of the process are spectacular. In perceiving, what is already inside a person's mind is constantly applying changes to the stimuli input while the input is constantly changing what's inside, so that both ends of the giving-receiving event are changing in rapid-fire progression Consequently, not only is the interpretive output of different people on the same subject at least a little, and sometimes a good deal different, but also an individual may easily see the same thing somewhat to very differently at different times.

To rephrase it, what comes out, our interpretation of the world, is not the same as what goes in, the world as it is, and frequently it's markedly different. The confusing result: although true facts ought to be the basis of judging performance and behavior, people do their judging, acting, and reacting according to their perceptions of the world.

Fortunately a large volume of "facts" we take in are only mildly distorted mainly because we're emotionally indifferent to them. We and others can reason through a relatively close agreement on a description or definition of them, but everything does receive some twist. Naturally, agreement also occurs on the emotional, and aware people try to appreciate how much distortion has been folded into the agreements.

As a result of all this modifying, the perceived world turns out to be the important world whenever performance or behavior is involved. Any attempt therefore to improve, influence, or change someone's job performance modus operandi is apt to be futile without at least a fair understanding of his or her perceptions of the factors involved, and to gain the understanding requires consideration of several to many of these (lists not horizontally related):

Perceptual Forces and Inclinations	*Major Interpretive Processes*
Needs, aspirations, expectations	Cues
Climate and context	Sequence
Learning	Perceptual organization
Philosophy	Construct distortion
Motivation and interests	Social distortion
Personality	Illusion distortion
Emotion, stress, fears, anxieties	Perception selection, including:
Interpersonal factors (others)	Perceptual readiness
Group and organizational factors	Perceptual defense
Reinforcement	Feedback
	Verbal
	Nonverbal
	Kinesthetic

The interaction of the perceptual forces and the influences of the processes involved produces the perceptions. Additionally, under the processes one has to consider not only cues, sequencing, feedback and the tricks of the mind described on page 41, but how badly any of them may have been distorted as a result of the perceptual forces and inclinations—plus the person's perceptual readiness and defenses (described below) that are also inclinations. The minds of well-educated, mature managers who've worked a lot with people go through much of it with exceptional speed.

Perceptual readiness is the tendency to interpret in terms of one's motivational needs, desires, goals, expectations, and psychological and emotional need to be consistent. On desires, for example, because of our desire for recognition and appreciation, we exaggerate the importance of our own names. On goals and interests, managers tend to suboptimize the larger organization's goals and interests to those of their own department. And the need to be consistent can be explained by the Theory of Cognitive Dissonance: inconsistencies among related beliefs or perceptions generate cognitive dissonance and motivate the individual to do whatever is easiest to reduce the dissonance and establish consistency.[26]

Perceptual defense is the perception relative of the defenses referred to on page 14: falsely seeing or not seeing what one is afraid to see, or it might be hearing or feeling. Illustrations: a father not seeing the bad traits in the son, seeing a person standing in a back-ally doorway as a mugger, or believing that slowly approaching footsteps heard in a large, otherwise empty house are threatening. Another aspect of it:[27]

- People ignore what is mildly disturbing:
- They react to disturbances that persist or increase to the point of threat (naturally reacting also to what is threatening in the first place).

Note that these refer to initial stimuli and not to habituation from repeated intake.

On the point of threat of danger in the second, once more an appreciation of personal difference is vital. As Leavitt points out, the person whose world has been relatively helpful tends to see the environment as helpful; if it's been frustrating and insecure, it tends to appear more dangerous and threatening, especially new things or changes, as we see in timid employees.

Fundamentally, we are all just trying to protect ourselves and at the same time enhance our own impact on others, to make people think we are what we want to be—our self-ideal. Moreover, this effort is generally toward projecting a role: I want you to see me as an intelligent, perceptive, effective, decisive, considerate but strong executive, while you're trying to convince me of your own self-ideal for the related role you're playing. But you will accept my act only if the gap between act and "fact" as you perceive it is small, and I will do likewise with you. If the gap is big all sorts of roadblocks to communication pop up, especially distrust, followed by serious damage to the relationship. Considering all the distorting going on, along with all the acting, one would be justifiably surprised that any understanding or bona fide communicating ever occurs.

Of course, most of the time we do understand and communicate, and jobs do generally get done (aside from how well). Understanding these complications though in both the perceiver and the perceived can naturally greatly improve the interpretations of behavior, attitudes, intention, and communications, leading to better decisions, relationships, and performance. Perhaps the following summary can help.

The Perceiver (you):

1. Will do a better job of understanding, managing, and communicating to others when understanding his or her own perceptual mechanisms, inclination, and alterations.

2. Will see only part of the picture because of perceptual selection, and though it may be more than the perceived sees, it will not be the same.

3. Will classify what is seen into categories and constructs (perceptual organization) and mold them to fit personal needs, goals, fears, emotions, personality, and the urge to be consistent and to confirm beliefs.

4. Will have a readiness to see some things and not others that one is physiologically capable of seeing, depending on a multiplicity of interrelated subjective forces, climate context, etc.

5. Will tend to weight excessively the first impression of the perceived and will then attach personality traits to visually perceived characteristics.

6. Will be heavily dependent on feedback from the perceived in judging his or her interpersonal competence and leadership with any degree of accuracy.

The Perceived:

1. Will be strongly influenced by the context and situational factors, especially the character of the group, his or her role and status, the status of the perceiver, the climate, the locus of the contact, etc.

2. Will be judging the perceiver at the same time, putting the other in a category or construct, and in the process may influence the perceiver's feelings and attitude in subtle ways.

3. Will unfortunately affect the perception of the perceiver, and sometimes a great deal, by his or her own appearance, physical traits, and verbal agility or lack of it.

4. Will reflect any fears, competitiveness, or insecurity instilled by the perceiver in his or her own general behavior in ways that will skew the perception disadvantageously.
5. Will have constantly changing perceptions as the environment changes, including treatment received as a subordinate or employee (fixed opinions of anyone over time are invariably untrue and unfair).
6. Will depend heavily on feedback from the perceiver in judging with any degree of accuracy his or her own performance and the relationship with the perceiver.

Certainly, much of this is already intuitively picked up by many experienced managers. But even they gain in understanding by raising the intuitions to conscious awareness, increasing the odds that at least the elementary questions are asked, like: What effect is the context having? Have there been prior commitments motivating a defense? Is a functional specialization suboptimizing judgments? Do character constructs tend to be black and white?

A few business examples of important distortions we tend to overlook might be worth adding to the ones already given:

- A top executive's perception of investment risks and dangers, quantified by analysts as the "Utility Factor," is a major determinant of the firm's long-range profitability. Plainly, the more conservative the executive is (the mediocre and the misfit being the most conservative), the less will the investment choices maximize the utilization of resources.
- Anyone forecasting the results of one's own planning tends to exaggerate the probabilities of both success and return that in any way affects oneself, a perceptual readiness for a variety of reasons that can significantly influence choices of alternatives even within the plan.
- The tendency of people to judge a complex context or character by one factor or trait (the Halo Effect) is particularly relevant to climate and morale. Two researchers studying the perceptions of members of a company in receivership found they reviled the company for that fact even though they had relatively high wages, good working conditions, and good supervision; one bad element in this climate made them overlook all the good.[28]
- Since all marketing functions are dependent on the perceptions of prospects, the design of new products (or redesign of old ones), ads, promotion, sales training, price, and services should be based on effective marketing research for that particular product. Yet in the vast majority of cases it's still done by the seat-of-the-pants even though the cost would be a negligible fraction of the total to get it to market.

- A supervisor's failure to obtain compliance with instructions is often a lucid example of insufficient perception of the subordinate's view and of substituting an easy assumption; for example, a salesman's failure to make new-account cold calls as instructed is not necessarily laziness or incompetence; it's more apt to be a defense against the often encountered unpleasant reception or high probability of failure to get an order. The usual recourse of a superior to nag, ignore, or fire might be expanded if he or she first examined a greater number of workable options, such as:

  a. Joint-calls to observe and help the person overcome the defense.
  b. Special training with cold-call role playing to do the same.
  c. An added monetary incentive or penalty.
  d. A combination of the above.
  e. A strong warning that will not be ignored to override the defense (the second generality on page 67).
  f. Transfer of the cold-call prospects to another salesperson.
  g. Set up a new-account specialist to cover all territories (sometimes the best answer).

Values and maturity. Interestingly, although there are many differences in the character of societies, they all try to advance their members toward maturity through similar continua:[29]

Dependence to self-direction
Pleasure to reality
Ignorance to knowledge
Incompetence to competence
Diffuse sexuality to heterosexuality
Amorality to morality
Self-centered to self-other-centered.

And the end-result is to a large extent pervasively determined by the way the society combines its values into systems of philosophy and ideology. We need but consider the simplest contrast of authoritarian governments vs. democracies.

It is in fact the value systems of philosophy adopted by a society (or community) that, more than any other general influence and more than individual values themselves, help or hinder movement of the society's members up the ladder of maturation, because values in a system mutually reinforce their own individual and collective validity, making them more or less inflexible to new learning. Thus combinations (systems) that frustrate development almost inevitably close off alternative thinking. One can only conclude that a relationship exists between value systems and maturity whenever one or the other is a factor; thus by deduction, value systems can range from immature to mature.

Douglas McGregor's Theory X is a prime example. The consequence to a whole society of adopting it zealously for the management of its organizations (aside from politics) can be illustrated by the effect of only two of its by-product tenets: excessive demand for conformity and its suppression of all conflict. Progress would be doomed and survival very much in doubt.

At the personal level, one can see that individual values have an impact on each of the eight criteria of maturity on page 63, but it is also not difficult to appreciate that, although the "value system" is presented as but one of the eight, a person's adopted system has a telling influence on all the other seven. It shows particularly on the "caring and warmth" criterion (number 5) which reflects one's attitude about "the nature of man." It's common knowledge that immature managers have a negative view and prefer immature docile subordinates. So do Theory X managers. In contrast, mature and Theory Y ones have positive attitudes, want mature subordinates and strive to give them mature environments.

Furthermore, behavior research has consistently found that confirmed Theory X managers generally fail to understand others and have very little genuine interest in them (non-caring), and they tenaciously resist even the consideration of Theory Y (examples in Chapter 19). Yet those who adhere to Theory X behavior because of a combination of ignorance and the modeling of superiors—they do not have the deep-seated value misconceptions of the confirmed—can be flipped over by processes of education on the subject.°

Others in the organization, however, judge by observed behavior, not distinguishing between those who are Theory X managers out of conviction vs. those who are out of ignorance, and they make the linkage to degree of maturity if only intuitively. Perhaps if all who use the Theory X approach knew it gave such an unfavorable impression, they might take the trouble to learn more about alternatives.

A Brief Summary

Recall that the problem-solving executive had asked himself four questions at the beginning of his research on personality:

1. With such great differences of personality among managers, does personality in general really have much influence on their leadership success?

2. What about the authoritarian inclination of most of the organization's managers? Is it an inherent characteristic, is it good or needed, or is it bad? And should or can anything be done about it?
3. Is it possible to construct a personality model of the ideal leader, one who would minimize dysfunctional conflict and inspire subordinate commitment?
4. Can education and/or the organization do anything toward developing such leaders?

And on reviewing his findings he found that, although none could as yet be answered adequately, he had gained not only a good general idea of the human issues involved but important leads on where to look further toward answering them.

For example, it's quite apparent that personality per se evolves from a combination of heredity and environment (family—including genes—community and society), and he sensed from what he had collected so far that learning probably plays the most important role in its development in that it either develops or heavily contributes to not only all the components in the page 39 chart but also the consciousness and experience determinants and the formation of the self.

This much can be said for the four questions: the answer to #1 seems to be yes, but to verify it one first needs to know the requisites of leadership, thus the rest of the book. For #2, one has to be able to distinguish between habitual authoritarianism and justifiable applications of authority vs. the alternatives, and to determine the wisdom, possibilities, and probabilities of trying to change habitual authoritarian behavior and/or the extent to which it can be done in given cases. The answers turned out to be too complex for this "Personality" chapter alone; Chapters 5 and 11 will add what is needed to get at them.

For the model in #3, the information given in the chapters ahead on the values and motivation components of personality (numbers 5 and 6 on page 39) is particularly necessary, so it will be assembled right after them (in Chapter 9). And on #4, the subject of *learning* again comes to the fore, a subject the problem-solving executive had to admit he also needed much more on for the answers, starting with the fundamentals ... which appeared to be the best area of in-depth inquiry to pursue next.

First, however, note a fairly recent development: the conclusion by research that a combination of the described personality traits they've labeled "emotional intelligence," though difficult to measure precisely, can be a valuable gauge for selecting leaders of people (an evaluation competent superiors commonly apply intuitively). Although IQ is still crucial on functions like financial analysis, the most valuable and productive employees who must manage people, especially teams, have been empirically found to be those who are superior on rapport, empathy, cooperation, pursuasion, the abilities to build consensus, control their own impulses, and maintain resolve and hope in the face of setbacks, all of which adds up to emotional intelligence.

Over the past decade the trait in American teenagers at all economic strata has declined, probably contributing importantly to teenage dropouts and crime; but it can be taught; in fact a few pioneering schools have been teaching the basics, with the added bonus of better achievement scores (courses by the Yale Child Study Center).

NOTES

a.   It's generally overlooked that this quote of a manager interviewed by Douglas McGregor back in the 1950s was the person's subjective description of the pain caused by his appraisal ignorance and inadequacy, pain that's no longer necessary. Furthermore, McGregor pointed out at the time that appraising is still an essential managerial responsibility.[1]

b.   Note, for example, that assumptions are a product of information (or lack of it), intelligence and values, and they could be classified under opinions or values. Managerial *competence* and *skills* would be a combination of knowledge, traits and intelligence, *work habits* a combination of knowledge, motivations and traits.

c.   It may be well to note here that "the situation" as referred to in management literature and ahead is intended to describe an event of narrower scope and shorter duration than "environment," such that it can and usually does influence behavior and leadership style but not the development of personality.

d.   "Character constructs," such a stereotyping and classifying by antonym extremes (e.g., good or bad, strong or weak) are also perceptual organization, but are (usually) developments of sloppy thinking rather than subconscious mental tendencies.

e.   For example, insufficient protein intake apparently reduces internal protein production, and the internal is important to problem-solving, a larger amount than normal being generated in the early period of coping with a problem; without enough of it, problem-solving ability is greatly reduced. One sees evidence of it in performance comparisons of protein-deficient children among ill-fed poor families and middle class children in the same classroom.

f.   The historians of psychology have classified the advance of theories about the "nature of man" in four stages: "Basic Conflict Man," the original-sin belief of religion in which good and evil battle for control of the mind, Freud's "Psychodynamic Man," which is also a conflict interpretation, "Behavioristic Man," which holds people to be basically neither good nor bad but neutral, and "Humanistic Man," affirming that we have an inclination to be good.

g.   Although Carl Jung was influenced by Freud during their 8-year friendship, he was not a member of the group, he had apparently started his own theory of psychoanalysis, known as "analytical psychology" before meeting him, continued to develop it during that time and finalized it after departing in mutual animosity.

h.   The first theoretical expression of reinforcement is attributed to E. L. Thorndike and his "Law and Effect" published in *Animal Intelligence* (New York: MacMillan and Company, 1911).

i.   Gordon Allport was a good example of how the leading pioneers of the new *behavioral sciences* not only contributed the components of the foundation, but developed and flexibly modified their thinking as the field rapidly progressed, usually keeping ahead of it and adding to the structure in the building process.

His stature was illustrated by a 1951 American Psychological Association survey that asked practicing clinical psychologists what personality theorist was of greatest value to them in their day-to-day clinical work. Freud was first (by a large majority) and Allport was second.

j. Philosophic phenomenology is defined as a technique of penetrating "presupposition-less" search for essences applicable to any branch of learning, the best known efforts being on "truths" about the social world.

k. For example, Emerson's ideal: "the grandly isolated man, nakedly alone, gladly bereft of friends, and heroically self-sufficient."[15]

l. Oral sensory (trust vs. distrust), muscular anal (autonomy vs. doubt), locomotor genital (initiative vs. guilt), latency (industry vs. inferiority), adolescence (identity vs. role diffusion), young adulthood (intimacy vs. isolation), adulthood (generativity vs. stagnation), maturity (ego integrity vs. despair).

m. While these are the psychological basics of adult maturity, Exhibit 3.1 describes modifying attitudinal characteristics.

n. "Task-relevant maturity" of subordinates is another way managers might view the subject. The two behaviorists who coined the phrase defined it as a combination of "job maturity" (technical competence) and "psychological maturity" (their description: self-confidence, self-respect, motivation).[22] It may not be adequate, however, for judging the maturity of subordinate managers whose attitudes about others, that are not included, can be crucial.

o. For example, Prentice on page 274.

REFERENCES

1. McGregor, D., "An Uneasy Look at Performance Appraisal," Harvard Business Review, May-June, 1957.

2. Allport, C. W., *Personality: A Psychological Interpretation*, (New York: Holt, 1937), p. 48.

3. Piaget, J. "The General Problems of the Psychobiological Development of the Child," *Discussions on Child Development*, edited by J. M. Tanner and B. Inhelder. (New York: International Universities Press, Inc., 1960).

4. Deikman, A. J. "Bimodal Consciousness," *Archives of Central Psychiatry*, (Dec, 1971), pp. 481-489, American Medical Association. Also published in The Nature of Human Consciousness, edited by R. E. Ornstein (San Francisco: W. H. Freeman and Company, 1973).

5. Ornstein, R. E., *The Psychology of Consciousness* (San Francisco, W. H. Freeman and Company, 1972).

6. Coleman, J. C., *Psychology and Effective Behavior* (Glenview, IL: Scott, Foresman, 1969), p. 62.

7. Esterson, A., *Seductive Mirage: An Exploration of the Works of Sigmund Freud* (Chicago: Open Court, 1993).

8. Dollard, J. and N. Miller, *Personality and Psychotherapy* (New York: McGraw-Hill, 1950).

9. Skinner, B. F., *Sciences and Human Behavior* (N.Y.: MacMillan, 1954).

10. Sheldon, W. H., *The Varieties of Temperament: A Psychology of Constitutional Differences* (New York: Harper, 1942).

11. Allport, G. W. op. cit. (1937).

12.   Cattell, R. B. *Personality: A Systematic and Factual Study* (New York: McGraw-Hill, 1950).

13.   Adler, A. *Practice and Theory of Individual Psychology* (London: Lund-Humphries, 1923, the first English publication).

14.   Rogers, C. R. *Client-centered therapy: its current practice, implications and theory* (Boston: Houghton-Mifflin, 1951).

15.   Emerson, R. W. "Politics," *Selections from Ralph Waldo Emerson*, edited by S. E. Whicher (Boston: Houghton Mifflin, 1957), pp. 249-250.

16.   Rensberger, B., "What Made Humans Human?" *New York Times Magazine*, April 8, 1984.

17.   McGregor, D. *The Professional Manager*, edited by C. McGregor and W. G. Bennis (New York: McGraw Hill Book Company, 1967), pp. 26-27.

18.   Cartwright, D., and R. Lippitt, "Group Dynamics and the Individual," *International Journal of Group Psychotherapy*, 7, January 1957. pp. 86-102. Reprinted in *Organizational Behavior and The Practice of Management*, edited by D. R. Hampton, D. E. Summer, and R. A. Webber (Glenview, Ill.: .Scott, Foresman and Company, 1968), p. 310.

19.   Parsons, T. *Essays in Sociological Theory* (Glencoe, Ill.: Free Press, 1954).

20.   *Time*, April 28, 1975, p, 69. Drawing by Stevenson;© 1974 The New Yorker Magazine Inc.

21.   Coleman, op. cit., pp. 108-138 (a condensation).

22.   Hersey, P., and K. H. Blanchard, *Management of Organizational Behavior* (Englewood Cliffs, N.J.: Prentice-Hall, 1977, 3rd edition).

23.   Adapted from Cox, R. D. "The Concept of Psychological Maturity," *American Handbook of Psychiatry"* edited by S. Arieti (New York: Basic Books, 1974) pp. 214-233, except for #4 on self-control, added by the author.

24.   Mischel, W., "Preference for delayed reinforcement and social responsibility," *Journal of Abnormal and Social Psychology, 62*, 161.

25.   Rokeach, M. *The Nature of Human Values.* (New York.: The Free Press,·1973), p. 18.

26.   Festinger, L. *A Theory of Cognitive Dissonance* (Stanford, Cal.: Stanford University Press, 1957).

27.   Leavitt, H. *Managerial Psychology.* (Chicago: University of Chicago Press, 1964).

28.   Grove, B. A., and W. A. Kerr, "Specific Evidence on Origin of Halo Effect in Measurement of Employee Morale," *Journal of Abnormal and Social Psychology*, July 1946, p. 258.

29.   Coleman, J. C., op. cit., pp. 73-77.

Chapter 4

Learning in Organizations

Although the general meaning of the word *learning* is simple enough to everyone, it's been found to be one of the most complicated of all human activities. For a quick overview of just the general miscellaneous knowledge that research has developed about it:

Everyone can learn, even the most ill-equipped person, and adults can learn and change well past 80, some past 100; observed declines with age where there is no obvious physiological impairment are due mostly to declines in motivation or to depression.

There are fast and slow learners, not good or poor learners, so teaching technique is most often the answer to effective learning; those who teach professionally should learn the Carroll-Bloom secondchance "Mastery Learning" technique that capitalizes on this fact.

Readiness of a person for learning depends on numerous factors, especially (a) the expected payback (one normally only goes as far as one thinks necessary), (b) physical capability, (c) emotional readiness, (d) intellectual curiosity in the subject, (3) relative maturity, (f) mastery of the prerequisites, and (g) immediacy of application.

Adult learners want the teaching to be problem-centered and will learn best if it's given a conceptual overlap with what they already know and accounts for the growth and life stage they're in at the time.

Preliminary orientation and organization can be very important to motivation, learning, and remembering; particularly important to motivation: being given the total picture, seeing the meaningfulness and payback, and participating in the program planning.

Motivation to learn is also importantly affected by the prospects of success: it's greatest when success appears possible but not too easy, least when it appears too difficult or too easy.

A psychological environment of openness, trust, and apparent good will is naturally most conducive to learning, gives a learner a feeling that he or she can optimize potential in the situation.

Instructions and rules on what learning behavior patterns produce the best results and which are detrimental can save the learner much time-wasting and trial-and-error; rules can also pre-relate for one an otherwise unrelated miscellany of information bits.

Excessive direction by the instructor generally produces boredom, indifferent conformity and/or absenteeism, rebellion, and maybe sabotage.

Lecturing is inferior to a group discussion approach (one research case: supervisors lectured on how to improve their job-rating skills did not improve; groups asked to analyze among themselves their methods and how to improve them did so significantly).

The learning advantage of one long learning period vs. numerous short ones depends on the nature of the task: a long one is best for complex material requiring much thinking: spaced short ones are best for rote memorizing and simple detail work.

Review for remembering should be done right after the original learning, when memory traces are still tenuous and fade most rapidly.

When learning from reading, more is learned by recalling what has been read along the way than by rereading; periodic reviews are usually necessary to retain it.

Something forgotten can be relearned more easily than first-time learning.

Whenever possible, learning should be on the job where it will be used, hopefully just before the work to which it is related, when the lesson will be more likely to stick.

An instructor should never lose sight of the importance of reinforcing good learning patterns and behavior and should do so as soon after as possible to raise the repeat probability.

Never criticize a learner directly for poor performance.

When the learning is principally one of changing behavior, values, or attitudes, the need to "unfreeze" what is to be changed comes into play; the method is described in Chapter 18.

Punishment, or threat of it, to bring about either learning or doing is a complex technique of limited use, and it takes considerable understanding of it to make it work, even when it may be applicable, without undesirable side effects (see pp. 105-111).

Feedback of results and progress is crucial, and the methods are many, including reinforcement, quizzes, self-checks, counselling, critiquing, role-playing, compliments, etc. Even repetition and practice need feedback of progress to keep effort from declining. More on it in a coming section of the chapter.

To teach either knowledge or skills, professional educators consider 6 basic factors, whether dealing with one-to-one instruction or a group, that influence learning effectiveness:

1. *The organization's (or unit's) culture and climate*—democratic or authoritative behavioral patterns (any obstructive ones to correct first?), norms, member interrelationships if a group, etc. (also see Figure 8.2, p. 278).
2. *Conduciveness of conditions*-physical conditions, tools, adequacy of resources, distractions, time pressures.
3. *The learner*-prior learning, interest, educability, readiness, motivation, energy, health, study skills (need for instruction on it), maturity.
4. *The task*-type of learning (motor skills, verbal skills, math skills, interpersonal skills, etc.), amount of new knowledge needed, complexity, familiarity with the subject, amount of ambiguity, time required.
5. *Incentives*-intrinsic, extrinsic, desirable rewards vs. punishment.

6. *Teaching methods*-preliminary instructions (orientation), techniques, program (including sequencing), schedule, reviews, testing, rules, standards.

Why take the trouble to be well informed about such details beyond the reasons given so far? Two particularly urgent ones, often overlooked by busy managers, that should be stressed: (1) that almost everything any organizational member does on the job involves learning whether the teaching is formal, informal, intentional, or accidental, and (2) managers, as the dominant force in their units, constantly teach subordinates by whatever they say or do to perform and behave one way or another, such that a lot of wrong and unintended learning goes on at considerable cost to the organization as well as the individual subordinates.

The importance of appropriate effective learning to leadership is certainly glaring. The greatest tragedy of course is the Peter Principle manager, the politically selected one, or "buddy," none of whom even know *what* to teach.

Therefore, to avoid the misguiding—as well as the failure to guide—it's imperative to know not only the *what* but also the *how*, which includes the foregoing information and:

- how individuals actually learn,
- the variety of teaching and learning theories and the techniques actually available to managers, and
- the consequences of each technique in each situation.

Some fundamentals

Three are particularly important to management: a definition of learning to specify, classify and circumscribe the word, the learning curve, and scheduling.

Definition. The way most behaviorists define it: learning is a process by which new knowledge, intelligence, opinions, attitudes, perceptions, and skills are acquired through contact with the environment (people, events, conditions, things), resulting in a relatively permanent change of thinking and/or behavior.[a] The modes of learning involved have been divided by them into three categories:

Direct instruction is the simple communication of information, but to bring about the "relatively permanent change," cognitive learning (page 90) has to be activated in the process, which may be in the form of latent learning;[b] also, direct instruction may occur during either simple or complex learning.

Simple learning is the category that embraces both classical conditioning and operant conditioning, each of which can include some direct instruction and may at times entail some complex learning.

Complex learning (that will be shown ahead to be synonymous with "cognitive learning") is a complex mix of mental processes, cognitive and psychological, and a switching around of and among the processes can occur during the event as needed; further, direct instruction and/or simple learning can take place during the event. There are three major sub-types that are particularly important to management, and externally programmed complex training could be considered a fourth; listed as discoursed:

> Social learning
> Feedback learning
> Complex training designs
> Punishment

The three are in fact too confusing, should be broken down into the clear, easy to understand components, that is, the seven ways people learn:

1. *Acquisition*—much of technical training, management development, classroom learning, self-instruction (reading, information-gathering), manuals, memos, etc. Because it is so elementary and well understood, no more need be said.
2. *Insight*—generally a by-product of thinking, producing a mental illumination-"Eureka!" or "Aha!" How to encourage it is described in Chapter 13 on pages 640 to 643.
3. *Conditioning*—the two types (in "simple learning" above) are techniques of bringing about desired behavior by targeting it among the alternatives with rewards for that behavior. More on it detailed ahead.
4. *Learned anxiety*—This is Edgar Schein's term for the first of Kurt Lewin's three-step process for changing individual or group behavior: the "unfreeze-change-refreeze" process. By showing the individual or group that their current way of acting or behavior in a given situation is unsatisfactory, their confidence is destabilized (unfrozen), and they're made ready for learning (change to) more effective behavior and attitudes, after the adoption of which the new behavior and attitudes are reinforced in one way or another, demonstrating that they are better (refreezing). It is a fundamental OD approach and is described in the two OD chapters 18 and 19.
5. *Social learning*—This of course refers to the learning we pick up from our society and its institutions, much by osmosis, on how to behave

and function in that society; thus it is essentially indirect conditioning vs. B.F. Skinner's direct. Its learning subdivisions are socialization, observation and social interaction, descriptions following the "conditioning" section.

6. *Feedback*—Feedback is not ordinarily listed as a learning technique, but so much is learned by individuals, groups and organizations through feedback of one sort or another, it qualifies as crucial in many instances and situations. It will be seen in the section following "social learning" that one need but ask what would happen (or not) without it?

7. *Punishment*—managers had better learn the full story to come about this sorely misunderstood technique that, intending to improve performance, most often causes the reverse.

The learning curve. This was discovered in England during World War II in connection with production planning, and from then on it has been an important factor in all aerospace and high tech contracts for estimating actual development and production costs for innovations. The concept is also applicable to every really-new product developed.

Only rarely do people learn according to line A in the chart below, a "curve of equal return" in which the same improvement occurs in each subsequent trial. Most learning in industry follows the decreasing B curve, in which a great deal is learned quickly with a little less in following trials; it is especially applicable when averaging the work of many engineers and is the one used by the Department of Defense on new weapons production contracts.

Occasionally when a job is totally new and mostly intellectual, as with certain staff, consulting, and R&D projects, the beginning will be a curve C, but it generally then evolves into a D (the S-curve), which is only a combination of B of C.

Curve E is an unsmoothed one that pictures the unevenness that normally occurs in continuous learning as in high school, a combination of A, B, and C plus periodic plateaus. Adolescents in particular have to be taught not to be discouraged with the plateaus, because both latent learning and holistic summarizing seems to be going on during them, learning that is necessary to advance further and start up toward the next higher plateau.

Scheduling. Scheduling is the administration of timing and frequency, and the consequences of different scheduling are usually predictable but are sometimes surprising. (What reinforcers to use and how much are also vital administrative matters, but entail factors of leadership and judgment beyond the scope of this section.)

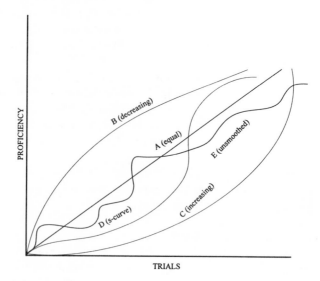

TRIALS

There are four main types, and they are easiest to understand when one assumes the same reward and amount, say, for each reward:

- *Fixed ratio* scheduling: the reward is given consistently after a certain number of responses.
- *Fixed interval* scheduling: it is given a fixed period of time measured from the last reinforced response.
- *Variable ratio* scheduling: it is given after a varying number of responses, with each having a chance of being reinforced.
- *Variable interval* scheduling: the period of *time* after the last reinforced response is varied.

Most elementary learning has to start with a fixed ratio of 1:1, a reward given for each response; with progress it can be increased to 5:1, 10:1, and often effectively up to 20:1; Skinner is said to have gotten rates with mice up to 182:1. The fixed ratio is the industrial piece-rate schedule that can obtain good, steady effort to the degree the worker is pressed for money at a given time.

The fixed interval—by the minute, hour, week, or month—has to be judged according to its two situations: (1) when the link between performance and reward has been kept clear to the recipient, an average improvement is obtained, but the improvement is cyclical: a drop-off of effort tends to occur right after the reward followed by a pick-up as the person gets closer to receiving the next one; (2) when the link is lost sight of and the reward is viewed as a base pay for minimum performance, the incentive value beyond that minimum is lost.

Both variable ratio and variable interval types have the effect of anticipation-plus-uncertainty that causes the worker to produce consistently at higher than average level. Knowing that each response (or unit) or each moment has an equal chance of being rewarded irrespective of the time of the last reward receipt, the person tends to maintain effort. And, for the same reason, both the variable ratio and variable interval have a high resistance to extinction from non-reinforcement.

Selection of one or the other of the two variable types naturally depends on the circumstances, but realistically the options are always limited with most present compensation systems. Almost all of them are on a fixed ratio or fixed interval basis, resulting in a low-level relationship between performance and reward. However, we know that all the intangible and social rewards—attention, recognition, appreciation, approval, etc.—are actually variably dispensed. A manager doesn't have to, and maybe shouldn't, give recognition and approval every time, but he or she needs to pay some attention to the interval.

There is also the important timing matter of immediacy. The effectiveness declines the longer a reward is delayed after performance, a reason why annual bonuses are seldom more than giveaways. Even piece-work compensation, already weakened by being paid on a fixed interval basis, is further debilitated by being paid 1 to 2 weeks later.

Conditioning

B. F. Skinner proposed, one recalls, that since each of us is constantly learning by conditioning, why not harness it and capitalize on it to the extent possible rather than leave it to chance. Unfortunately he grossly overrated what can be done by design, but the potential to significantly influence performance and behavior is there for managers who know what can and can't be done and when and how.[c]

Knowing the difference between the two types of "simple learning" in its definition on page 80 is important, and that famous first experiment of Pavlov best explains and illustrates the first, the classical conditioning.

Briefly for those not familiar with it, in a series of repetitions he rang a bell each time he gave food to a hungry dog that naturally salivated in each food giving instance, and eventually the dog would salivate for the bell tone without the food.

Three salient features of the event were: (a) the food stimulus was a primary physiological need that incited a natural response; (b) there was only one possible response, no alternative way the hungry dog could do so (as will be shown is present for operant conditioning); and (c) the consequence to the salivation response of the repeated feeding was reinforcement, which is defined as any action that strengthens a response to a performance or behavior and motivates repetition of that response in similar situations. The dog would salivate on hearing the bell even if less than hungry (probably not if stuffed).

Pavlov then paired the bell tone with a black square, such that in time the square alone made the dog salivate, and after, paired the square with a third item with success. But he could go no further with the dog.

The food, by filling a primary innate need, is called a primary reinforcer, the square and third item secondary and tertiary reinforcers, the actions first order, second-order and third-order conditioning. Note that the second- and third-order in the dog case remain classical like the first because b and c are still based on the primary need. Other related terms:

> *Unconditioned stimulus (US)—one that activates a primary human physiological need (see column 1, page 143).*
>
> *Unconditioned response (UR)—the consequence of a US.*
>
> *Conditioned stimulus (CS)-one that has resulted from pairing with another stimulus.*
>
> *Conditioned response (CR)—the response to a conditioned stimulus.*
>
> *Extinction*—caused by a failure to reinforce a CR often enough with a CS such that the CR weakens to eradication.
>
> *Generalization*—when a new but similar stimulus produces the same response as the original one, as when a child fears all dentists because the first one hurt (the mind engages in "pairing" on its own, helping one adapt to new situations by borrowing from past learning vs. going through new learning).
>
> *Discrimination*—a reaction to stimuli differences as compared to generalizing similarities, e.g., experience with other dentists showed that all do not hurt, so the child responded accordingly.

Psychologists believe that humans can and do go beyond to higher-order conditioning, which might help explain generalization and how a stimulus itself acquires reinforcement value. We call many things like money, attention, recognition, and approval secondary reinforcers because they are not primary and do not necessarily follow performance, yet they can become initial reinforcing stimuli just as many cues are reinforcing. They may in reality be third or of higher order; we don't know for sure.

In contrast to classical, operant conditioning[d] is what happens when, as mentioned above, there are two or more response alternatives, and a reward is given that encourages a repetition of only one, for example, complimenting one way among several of doing something. The table below compares the two types.

Classical Conditioning

	Stimulus Incentive	Response Alternatives	Responses
Step 1	US (food)	Dependable basic	$\longrightarrow$ UR $\longrightarrow$ r
Step 2	CS (tone)	reactions	$\longrightarrow$ CR $\longrightarrow$ r

Operant Conditioning

Stimulus (s)	Response Alternatives for the Subject	Reinforcement Applied	Future Response Probability
A situation,	R_1 $\longrightarrow$	None $\longrightarrow$	None
such as a	R_2 $\longrightarrow$	None $\longrightarrow$	None
task to be	R_3 $\longrightarrow$	r $\longrightarrow$	R_3
done	R_4 $\longrightarrow$	None $\longrightarrow$	None

r = reinforcement; for arrows, read "yields" or "is followed by."

Discernibly, the first occurrence of S in operant conditioning has to be reinforced at least once for the r to lead to R_3, at which time the situation is said to be contingent on an antecedent situation. Note that the stimulus is a situation vs. an incentive with classical.

Two other dimensions of conditioning are important: (1) positive and negative reinforcers and (2) extrinsic and intrinsic reinforcers. The positive and negative are a bit tricky in that both always do the same thing, always strengthen the association between the stimulus and the response. But they refer to different actions on the part of the administrator, actions that produce opposite effects. A positive reinforcer is something wanted that has been *applied* after an initial desired response; a negative reinforcer is something wanted that has been *withheld* or *terminated* after an undesirable response.

A manager who terminates a policy of employee participation in decisions affecting them is effecting a negative reinforcement, one that reduces their regard for the firm as well as for the manager. The relationship of the divestment, the manager, and R_3 in the table below have been closely associated.

Stimulus	Response Alternatives	Reinforcement Applied	Future Response Probability
Situation:	R_1 (High regard)	None	None
decision	R_2 (Indifference)	None	None
making	R_3 (Dislike)	Partic. Terminated	R_3

Then there is an overlap of the negative with *punishment*, for punishment is defined as either (a) the negative reinforcement of withholding or terminating something desired, or (b) the application of something disliked, called a noxious stimulus (e.g., an electric shock), or the threat of it, the threat called aversive conditioning. Because punishment is a leading means of management abuse, a special section is given to it ahead.

Extrinsic reinforcers are devices external to the individual that are applied by another party or by an organization—salary, incentives, praise, recognition, promotion, status, social acceptance, and security.

It's not as easy, however, to define the intrinsic reinforcers and pin them down to specific instruments. They are internal to the individual and refer to the effect that is inherent in an activity or behavior itself; it is the factor that produces an individual's satisfaction in a given task or position that comes from:

• The achievement of a goal
• A feeling of competence after doing a job well
• The acquisition of a new skill
• Successfully solving a problem
• A feeling of making a contribution
• A sense of personal growth
• Responsibility
• Autonomy, or a reasonable degree of it
• A feeling of some control over one's own destiny
• A feeling of self-respect
• Belief that one is optimizing one's potential.

The self-starter, the highly motivated, the person who needs little-to-no supervision, the one who has internalized goals of achievement—they have all received intrinsic reinforcement in some manner. And, unfortunately for the manipulative superior, the condition cannot be induced or controlled directly; it can be done only indirectly by leadership style, by climate, or by setting up the circumstances that foster it, such as job design, growth opportunity, supportiveness.

Management applications. One can easily appreciate that any of the two types of simple conditioning may be the result of either another's effort one's own effort, or experience. And certainly a lot of conditioning, whether in childhood or adulthood, is unplanned, unconscious, or subconscious. It is, in fact, not particularly important for managers to be able to distinguish operant from classical conditioning, since the difference is but the selection of the stimulus. Indeed, it's often quite difficult to distinguish whether the outcome is from one or the other. For example, a lot of our fears, likes, dislikes, and attitudes about others can either have linkage to innate needs or be due to operant conditioning.

We do know of course that whenever a repeat of good performance or behavior is desired one can generally motivate it with compliments, supportiveness and other rewards, and that extinction is apt to take place without them. The needs appear to be classical, but a line manager would tend to feel about the distinction "so what?" What counts is results.

The utility for organizations of *operant* conditioning on the other hand is very restricted, a statement that warrants explanation both to delimit the great promise erroneously accorded it over the past two decades and to specify where it *can* be of service.

Its principal constraints are the very complexity of all that is involved: the individual in general, the organization, society, and the person administering it. Concerning the individual, as a child's and adolescent's thinking ability develops, the complex learning (defined on page 80), a mostly subconscious process, increases to being the dominant mode. Learning more and more involves past learning, past experiences, psychology, and personal motivation, and individuals themselves become with growth more personally independent.

Naturally, the consequence is less and less susceptibility to administered operant conditioning, and when the myriad of organizational and societal variables is added, it becomes very difficult for the administrator to determine how the person will interpret or react to any given stimulus.

For example, with a little thought, one realizes that a given stimulus cannot be counted on always to elicit the same response automatically. The response is invariably the result of an integration of the stimulus with a number of others, and the result, further, can vary at different times with the same person and be the opposite for different people. For a sampling of influences:

- The intended meaning of the administrator
- How it is presented (labels, instructions, cue meanings, symbols, rules, timing)
- The administrator's organizational and/or social status
- The administrator's authority
- The subject's appraisal of the climate, context, situation, peer opinion, group pressures
- Alternative reinforcers and what others get
- Personal expectations, incentives, utility (risk tolerance), and ranking of all the stimuli encountered
- The person's state of satiation or deprivation

- The person's many personality traits
- Who is present

There are just too many strong variables like these in all organizational situations to be able deliberately to manage a person's motivation by the technique.ᵉ Additionally, because organizations are multivariate open systems with many cues and influences hitting each individual all the time, even the assumptions one has to make to undertake it can only be naive. For instance, one has to assume, as Chris Argyris pointed out, that the recipient will interpret the reinforcement precisely as intended, not add meanings, will not associate it with other and previous reinforcements producing an unintended new meaning, and will not discuss it overtly or covertly with anyone else *or* oneself.[2]

Other complications:

- The organizational person is a member of many groups, formal and informal, each group meting out rewards and penalties; and, there are at least five reinforcement systems impinging on a group member:
  The formal base pay compensation
  The formal departmental and individual incentive systems
  The department manager's informal personal techniques
  The informal pressures of others regarded highly
  Those of subgroups such as bowling teams, after-work socializing, etc.
- Very close supervision is necessary to make it work since the desired performance first has to be identified each time to be reinforced, and the identification is necessary for the operation of a schedule; no reinforcement or inadequate reinforcement of course leads to extinction in such a situation.
- Then not only would the close supervision be anathema to good management (and impossible on middle and upper managers), but also the dispenser might be justifiably accused of applying Taylorian "scientific management" under a different name.
- It's the rare manager in a medium size or large operation that has or can get the authority to vary either the amount or the timing of a subordinate manager's base pay or money incentives.

We have to concede therefore that operant conditioning is of little use to the leading of subordinates on the job, especially subordinate managers whose work is an inordinate complex of components, many of them qualitative that are difficult to identify and impossible to measure. For instance, what do you try to reinforce among which alternative responses to evoke a creative decision or the solution to a complicated problem?

When *can* it be used? In training and management development where reactions to selected stimuli and response alternatives are simple and clear. All good professional instructors count on it in such cases as an important tool to accelerate learning.

One final comment about conditioning. Some who have feared *its power to manipulate*, especially fearing operant conditioning without appreciating its limits, have raised questions about the ethics of applying conditioning to someone.

Plainly, **manipulation** goes on constantly in many if not most social situations, both consciously and unconsciously, as attempts to **persuade** or **influence**. It's normal and obviously not all immoral. So one has to distinguish between what is and isn't **moral**, which can be done by first correctly defining four terms (substituting the philosophic concept of "good" for "moral" in this situation):

To manipulate is to change another's performance, behavior, personality, or perceptions without the person's knowledge or voluntary consent.

To influence (ethically) is to affect or alter another's performance, behavior, personality, or perceptions by direct, indirect or intangible means, the person given freedom of choice (which may be not to choose) without penalty or threat of it and aware of the freedom.

To persuade (ethically) is to move to a belief or opinion by discussion or argument, again, the choice free without penalty or threat of it.

Good is whatever fosters others and society's welfare and the healthy development and one's own growth.

We know of course that the words "persuade" and "influence" are commonly applied to efforts without the free choice, in which instances they should have been called coercion or manipulation.

Consciously reinforcing in a normal adult desired beneficial performance or behavior, on the other hand, is influence when it can be assumed, as it usually can, that the recipient is awake enough to be aware that it is an attempt to influence and not coerce. If it is unconsciously done or the person is unaware, it might be either influence or "good" manipulating, in which case why not make the elementary distinction that all good manipulation be called influence, all unethical be called "manipulation."

This differentiation will also lead to the answers for any conditioning that may be involved. To judge its morality, its two uses must be considered: "behavior modification" for mental illness or child development (the modification feasible in a closely controlled environment) and application to normal adults. In the former the recipient is not competent to make a conscious choice, so it's morally acceptable to omit notification or an attempt to explain.

Such reasoning provides the answer for the latter: any time an employee is subjected to a beneficial direct conditioning effort, the person is invariably aware, at least intuitively, that it's an influence based on a mutually beneficial trade of performance or compliance for the incentive offered (more on its nature under "social exchange" ahead) and that there's free choice to reject it.

But negative conditioning of any type is another story, and the coming discourse on punishment will make evident that much of what is done in organizations is in fact unethical.

Social learning

Early in the chapter two reasons in particular why managers should learn about learning in detail were stressed: organizational members are always learning and superiors are always teaching whether they are conscious of it or not. And two things were quite clear to the problem solving executive (hypothesized for the text): each of the four sub-types of complex learning was a major way that learning and teaching take place, and a substantial amount of the social and feedback learning and all the punishment in all organizations turn out to be negative, all serious drags on performance. Were they significant problems in his own organization?

Reviewing first the definition of complex learning on page 80, that it is a complex mix of mental processes, cognitive and psychological, he felt that he understood well enough the psychological processes of this mix and that they included the emotional. But his understanding of the cognitive, or *cognition*, needed some clearing up.

A little digging elicited the fact that it is the cerebral process of being aware, knowing, and thinking that includes several to many of its subprocesses of directing attention, goal-seeking (therefore motivation), memory, perceiving, relating, reasoning, anticipating, imagining, choosing, conceiving, judging, and abstract thought--much of which transparently involves the psychological also.

It is in effect information processing and manipulation toward the solution of a perceived problem, however subtle or remote, and if it yields, even without a solution, at least new arrangements of facts, some learning called cognitive learning, occurs.

So cognitive and complex learning are in reality synonymous. Psychology researchers seem to prefer the cognitive label, behaviorists the complex. Whichever, it was clear to both disciplines that a study of how a person does it would explain a lot about the person's performance and behavior.

Both researchers and behaviorists know they still have a long way to go, but the study to date did provide knowledge crucial to management. For example, on social learning, the learning that occurs by accident or design on how to function in one's social group, organization or society, an understanding of this process was aided by subdividing it into its three principal modes (which, understandably, possess a great deal of overlap) and probing them individually; the three: socialization, observation, and social interaction. (They are so familiar to us that unfortunately some very obvious facts have to be stated to bring out those that can be of important use to managers.)

Socialization. This is the process of learning and integrating into one's personality the culture (e on page 21) of one's society, which includes those immediate influential groups known as agencies of socialization. The agencies as said before - family, schools, peers, religious institutions, social, governmental and work organizations. And the process can be divided for management purposes into the influencing forces external to the organization and those internal to it, the internal being the way organizational members make sense of their environment by learning the assumptions of the organization's culture and the character of the climate.

Conveniently, being social creatures with part of the brain devoted to survival of the species, we have, with normal development, a natural inclination to go along with the socialization efforts of one's own society. Still, to be sure of success, the society has to, and does, use every method in the book to achieve it, backing it up with reward/punishment systems and no end of incentives and reinforcements, formal and informal, to direct choices and discriminations or simply to motivate desired thought or action.

On the segment of greater concern to managers, the work-organization, it was found, is now becoming accepted as a complex *social learning system,* that is, the "social system" described on page 27 is one of continuous complex learning. Not long after being set up, a firm or unit quickly begins to develop its own set of intellectual, emotional, and behavioral patterns believed by management to be best for it to prevail in the environment. But the larger the organization grows, the more apt it is to have also a number of nationalities, ethnic types, and regional differences that enter the organization; even the differences among specialized professional groups and old-timers vs. young managers can have important impact. And then there is "the informal organization," a term sometimes incorrectly equated with organizational culture; it is a mix of informal relationships forming a "subcutaneous" pattern or set of patterns under the formal one (see below and pages 554-556).

Each significant internal group, like the external culture, attempts to motivate *identification* with itself and adherence to its norms and behavior patterns, and those that have some success inevitably have an influence on performance and behavior.

The basic norms of formal organizations or units that are successful can be assumed to have a net beneficial effect, and ordinarily different subordinate national and ethnic ones do too (when they don't produce conflictful behavior) because of the diversity of views they contribute. Some of the serious determental conflicts that occur are plainly due to general management, for example, along with those caused by value misconceptions (examples on page 118), when management's own behavior contradicts its policies, or it inadvertently creates systems conflicts (such as conflicting incentives in the reward system), or it fails to account for national cultural and value differences in overseas operations.[f] But those of particular importance to individual managers are most apt to be due to norms developed by emotional subgroups within their own units. When two or more subordinates (seldom over 6 to 8) associate emotionally in an informal relationship of mutual admiration, interdependence, or some common interest like defense against an aversive boss, it often functions as a mini-society whose effects are not always to the good of the unit.

The conglomeration of such groupings up, down and across the larger organization are, though unrelated, the aforementioned "informal organization," and they come in a variety of types that will be described under Communication in Chapter 12. But for the groupings within one's own unit, every manager, especially one new in a position, needs to be aware that such developments can occur very subtly and should try to determine:

- What groupings exist, and who is the leader or model of each?
- Are there desirable effects on performance or behavior toward organizational goals (e.g., mutual assistance of value)?
- Are there any undesirable ones (e.g., the propping up of non-producers, or norms encouraging secrecy, hostility, cheating, dependency, doubt, or indifference)?
- Who is the leader and by what means—expertise, charisma, wit, cunning, warmth, or seniority?

If the effects are positive, one need only keep an eye on the group. If negative, can diplomacy and leadership turn it around? Negative ones developed under a recent previous leader usually can be, and the effort is usually well worth it; a positive group can be a valuable asset. If negative, a change is imperative, perhaps a complete break-up of the group.

Observation. In this wholly self-evident method of social learning, one observational technique—learning through models—deserves comment if only as a reminder to capitalize on it wherever possible. There are two applications: emulation, that combines identification with imitation, and skills modeling, that engages imitation only.

As is well known, emulation is unquestionably the main way managers come by much, if not most, of the managerial knowledge, judgment, and behavior they develop on the job, occasionally carrying it to the extreme of hero worship when the superior has strong "personal power" (See **Types of Power**, Ch. 11).

On the assumption that managers generally retain their jobs because they perform as desired, most organizations have a standard rule that no manager gets promoted who hasn't developed a competent replacement, because they expect much of the development to occur through modeling even though an increasing number of organizations supplement it with formal development. General Motors relies heavily on the formal up through middle management, stops it there, and relies entirely on interface modeling above that level where they do not even have manuals. Success is expected to breed success.

The use of **skills** modeling is now becoming widespread. One technique: the filming or videotaping for imitation of good managing for a wide variety of specific problem situations (examples are given in a discourse on **Current Practices**, Ch. 17). Large progressive firms add a feature well worth consideration by those that have the staff to do it: evaluating their current managers on the positive-negative modeling they convey and providing education to those found negative on how to be positive. Of course it can work only on skills, not negative "styles," and all parties should not lose sight of the fact that imitation in both applications is an unthinking mechanical process that does not in itself encourage a better or more creative approach. Indeed, it lends to rote, conformity, and the passing on of prejudices.

Social interaction. The growing use of social interaction techniques in organizational teaching in itself warrants that it be singled out. Aside from its informal part in socialization and modeling, it is also the underlying force in virtually all of the formal teaching that isn't direct instruction, the most advanced being the techniques of OD, that capitalize on the described phenomenology described on pages 54-55.

A full chapter is devoted to OD in Part III, but one of its techniques may be learned and used independently of OD (an OD staff person can be helpful in the first application), one that's able to resolve a very common managerial problem. It's called "role prescription" and is used for situations where poor performance or conflicts between a superior and one or more subordinates is discerned as perhaps due to a misunderstanding of mutual expectations or assigned responsibilities.

In organizations, we know, one can have the role of a superior, subordinate or peer, a marketer, accountant or scientist, a programmer, typist or machine operator, a staff or line employee, and will usually have several at one time.

The role is the position's expectations as to the behavior needed to perform its tasks effectively, and every role in an organization has one or more "reciprocal" roles—the other party or parties in the act—a prime illustration being the way the role of a superior requires one or more to be willing to play the role of subordinate.

If the relative expectations, adaptations, and returns appear mutually advantageous to both parties, all should go smoothly, but we know they often don't. Expectations do not always appear to both to be mutually balanced, or they are not understood (role ambiguity), or there are incompatible expectations within one's own or with another's role (role conflict). Or one's role has too many expectations (role overload), or sometimes the role/role-reciprocal relationship develops unpleasant problems that can lead to rupture. And, then there are misunderstandings about responsibilities.

Role prescription engages the concerned parties in a seven-step participative resolution.[3]

1. The manager (or peer or subordinate), called the actor, writes down a list of statements that he or she believes characterize his or her functions and behavior toward the reciprocals (subordinates or others in the group) that need clarification.
2. The reciprocals, operating as a panel, write down how they would like to see the actor perform and behave (or there may be only one reciprocal).
3. All engage in a group discussion of the lists, remove the unrealistic, do some compromising and arrive at a tentative prescription for the actor to follow.
4. The actor role-plays the prescription with members of the panel, possibly replaying some past interpersonal problems.
5. All analyze jointly how well the prescription worked, and make changes as they appear needed.
6. The final agreed-on one is applied on-the-job for 2-3 weeks for a pilot test, after which—
7. Another meeting is held to critique both the prescription and the actor's performance and make needed modifications.

It goes without saying that no obdurate Theory X manager would submit to doing this with subordinates, or could apply it objectively *to* a subordinate without manipulating. But given a trusting climate and a reasonably open-minded, flexible manager, the technique's potential for making a unit an appealing place to work is impressive.[8]

One can see too that it can be a good way to clarify a new role that hasn't been defined or is difficult to define, but, additionally, that there are plenty of superior-subordinate conflicts in which it *isn't* applicable, like:

- Unconscious dysfunctional behavior of either party
- Personality misunderstandings
- Non-performance of an important role requirement (e.g., failure of a superior to develop subordinate managers)

- Task or interpersonal skill inadequacy (e.g., handling a performance review)
- A job misfit that has not become apparent
- Judgmental incompetence.

Special note should be given, incidentally, to the role-playing technique in Step 4; it should be kept in mind for the many situations in which it will pay off, e.g., dry-running with an associate a presentation to a top executive or board, playing out a big sale to a client, and any occasion when seeing the other's point of view with clarity is critical. What happens in these dialogues is even visible: the real-life immediate feedback of the impact of one's words and actions, which is no less than the third complex learning process, one that has complexities of its own of such importance to performance that it requires a closer look.

Feedback learning

On subdividing it one quickly realizes that each of its three levels is a critical learning function in itself:

> Individual feedback learning
> Group feedback learning
> Organizational fee back learning

Individual feedback learning. This of course refers to both directions in the superior-subordinate or any other one-to-one relationship. The *subordinate's* need for it from the superior will come out again and again in the chapters ahead on motivation and management processes, particularly with regard to its importance to the individual's motivation for achievement. All achievement-oriented problem-solvers are frustrated without feedback on both their quantitative and qualitative performance for reasons of personal cybernetic self-control, and, for the attention, recognition, and appreciation favorable feedback can manifest.[h] Thus, in those instances some of the experience is learning, some is reinforcement, and some is both.

For an example of a *superior's* need from a subordinate, one has only to recall any recent observation of a typical authoritarian boss, maybe your own, describing to a subordinate manager, naturally courteously, a project to be carried out, with the steps to be taken and the schedule to be followed. The subordinate nods at the right times, says OK, accepts the papers presented, if any, and leaves. The boss receives no indication that:

(a)   the plan could be improved;

(b)   some errors of judgment or calculation in the plan may have been made;

(c)   the timing may be wrong;
(d)   significant resources (money, materials, workers) may not be available, which becomes evident when the goal is only partly achieved;
(e)   there are better ways to measure the progress and end result.

Because of the unilateral presentation of the project the superior has blocked learning about all of these and guaranteed his or her own ignorance concerning the subordinate's opinions and attitudes about the whole matter.

If a sign of subordinate resistance or non-acceptance appears, the sequel is quite familiar: the traditional approach to *persuasion* of upping the pressure with a sales pitch, a special reward or even a direct order, each having an unspoken threat behind it, each a coercive one-way proposition, and all demeaning events that leave the subordinate with at least a subconscious feeling of frustration, resentment, and/or demotivation.

Moreover the authoritarian climate is one in which subordinates will not risk being candid, and the consequence, as Argyris has pointed out, is that valid information is not volunteered on important problems—because it can so often affect one or both parties personally—is volunteered only on the unimportant. Indeed, superiors in such situations frequently behave that way because, besides the know-it-all mind-set, they at least intuitively realize that they've already predetermined non-communication by the climate they've created and, as a result, will get no feedback. They've sorely handicapped the building of a lasting productive relationship of any sort.

One of the best tools the behavioral educator has to demonstrate what's wrong with much superior-subordinate interpersonal communication and the mutuality of the feedback involved has been the chart below known as the "Johari Window"[4] concerning the superior's side of the picture:

	Concerning My Motivation and Behavior ...	
	Known to Myself	Unknown to Myself
Known to other(s)	1. *We both know:* I know about myself. Other(s) know about me.	2. *I am kept blind:* I don't know about myself. other(s) know about me.
Unknown to other(s)	3. *Other(s) are kept blind:* I know about myself. Other(s) don't know about me.	4 *We both don't know:* I don't know about myself. Other(s) don't know about me.

Most authoritarians, we know, aim at box #3; being untrusting they reveal nothing about themselves, which itself discourages feedback. Boxes #2 and #4 are more pathetic varieties; the superior in both is handicapped also by his/her own psychological inclination to close the eyes to many truths about he self.

Plainly, the solution to the example on page 96 is genuine participation with its two-way transactional communication, which, repeated over time in such situations, produces the conditions in box 1. If, then, in the process a difference of opinion or resistance to a request is perceived, it's time for *ethical persuasion,* a subject so crucial to effective leadership that every manager should go well beyond the definition on page 89 to study at least he following.

First, be particularly impressed that it is fundamental not only to successful subordinate relations but also to wherever there's a dependence on peers or others to gain collaboration as well. The occasions in outline:

1. Where there's a power differential (e.g., superior-subordinate)
   (a) to debate a point
   (b) to obtain compliance
2. In lateral relations (no formal authority over the other)
   (a) to debate a point
   (b) to obtain collaboration

Kurt Lewin supplied the concept, a solution that works in all four situations and one that even most traditional managers would be willing to undertake. Elaborating on his "Field Theory" and behavior model on page 26, he explained that to influence another's behavior when there's resistance to an idea or request, all the reasons for the resistance should be considered by carefully examining the total picture as that person sees it—his or her life space," the (P,E), which is, in this instance the combination of the driving forces of the "persuader" (E) and the individual's restraining forces (P). Unilateral pressure or traditional persuasion plainly ignores the person's needs, values, ideas, feelings, personal problems, and the like that cause or are related to the resistance.[5] The persuader is in effect saying he doesn't give a damn about them, only about "winning" or using the other as a tool.

In the case of a superior who wants to inspire motivation and commitment as well as compliance, successful persuasion, he explained, can only occur when the superior explores in a considerate discussion what the relevant ideas, feelings, needs, etc. are that are obstructing agreement. On the first sign of opposition or hesitancy, switch to questioning the other's point of view, discern with your knowledge of normal humans what's causing it, and jointly develop an agreement that satisfies both parties.

The end-result: "life space" ethical persuasion, a feedback learning process for both that was in fact the precursor of the principle underlying the *direct integration* described by Douglas McGregor a decade later, a technique of genuine participation that integrates individual and organizational goals and interests (in Chapter 20).

Group feedback learning. This is naturally more complex in that, along with the individual's feedback needs mentioned above, it involves those of group dynamics and team management. Each of the other issues will be covered where it is believed to fit best, but a clear conception of the group feedback learning requisites will supply a valuable preface to each.

Chris Argyris gave these requisites to us with his "Model I" and "Model II" renditions that elaborate on the Lewin approach, showing the basic idea to be applicable to leadership in both the individual and group feedback processes.[6] Model 1, he said, pictures the interpersonal relations with subordinates of traditional managers, relations that are the consequence of a set of four goals the managers establish *for themselves* whether dealing with individuals or groups:

1. Achieve the purpose at hand as they themselves define it.
2. Win, don t lose.
3. Suppress negative feelings.
4. Emphasize rationality.

The managers, as a result, seek to control unilaterally all aspects of the relationships—the environment, the tasks, and the others—such that there's little public testing of ideas, little to no effort to get feedback on one's own actions or thinking, a tendency for all concerned to play it safe and not upset others, and no inquiry into the validity of the task objectives set or the values implicit in the situation.

The feedback learning that does occur, if any, is conspicuously one-way what Argyris called single-loop learning, and the environment virtually precludes effective problem-solving and decision-making. Instead, it's a situation of defensiveness (self-protection), closedness, mistrust, conformity uncertainty, avoidance, saving face, intragroup rivalry, miscommunications misperceptions, parochial interests. And as mentioned valid informational feedback occurs for only unimportant problems, none for the important ones.

Model II was presented as a solution, one that is not the opposite of Model 1. The goals:

1. An environment in which the others are encouraged to participate in the goal-setting and planning.

2. Joint control of the task by the members.
3. A win-win attitude among them.
4. Protection of the self made a joint enterprise oriented toward growth.

The individuals are able to be articulate and precise about their own purposes and are capable of the advocacy and control attempts that may be necessary to win, but they incorporate a sincere invitation to the others to confront their own views and are willing and ready to alter and improve them, such that the others can, as participants, become internally committed to the final product.

The consequences: an open free-choice climate, shared power, minimal defensiveness, valid information, a willingness to risk public testing of ideas, minimized one-upmanship, and a mutual effort to help each other contribute. Learning is "double-loop" and problem-solving and decision-making effectiveness maximized.

Note too that the goals of both Model I and II are the result of the superior's personal values, so that if anything is to be done about Model , the values that evoke the Model I goals have to be changed (solutions n Chapter 18).

Organizational feedback learning. This obviously enlarges the subject much further to include, and require, feedback from all levels—individual group, unit, the organization as a whole, the external environment—all of it necessary if the management is to "optimize the utilization of all available and potential resources toward the organization's long-term functioning."[7]

Every respectable management system does have, we know, a whole array of techniques and devices for getting, providing, digesting, and disseminating information (the new knowledge itself being learning). Note in the list of 29 control devices in the beginning of Chapter 11 (p. 460) that all of 17 through 29 except 18 and 21 qualify, the others being techniques of knowledge utilization (a number of the 29 serving both purposes).

In many industries, however, the whole process has become almost desperately chaotic. In stable environments the standard techniques and devices can be counted on to keep everyone abreast of the times, but how many are there today that can be called stable? The record shows very few; indeed, not only have many changed toward the unstable (along a continuum) but some have become so radically unstable that their organizations have had to make major structural changes to maintain the effectiveness of their organizational information, learning, and control systems.

To illustrate, in the past virtually all firms could plod along counting on the common-sense reactions of their managers to events (a poor form of feedback learning) to operate the organizations adequately, and in stable mechanistic environments it's still possible. But not only is the pace of change today greater for most, the pace itself is increasing. The table below generalizes these changes of technique and pace and the coping method that have ensued over the last three and a half decades.

In column 1, the *external* environment has now become so unpredictable that economic forecasting is suspect, and the *internal* environment, as described in Chapter 1, is one of at least quiet turmoil and reluctant acquiescence to the relatively inflexible processes and policies. Management's interpretations of what its main problems were in each decade in column 2 were tackled by the methods in column 3, all the important decisions being centralized at the top of each unit, whether the corporation, a division, or a department (column 4).

The two most telling variables are patently the *instability* and *unpredictability* shown in the first column. Up to the 1950s the pace of technological and social change was relatively moderate, so a competent person or group at the top could think through and test solutions in time. But for any industry that's moderately dynamic or more, the stepped-up pace of change amplifying the instability now requires a speeded up rate of appropriate responses, responses that can't wait for a slow trickle-up of key

Management's Response to Environmental Change

Period	(1) Environment, External and Internal	(2) Main Operational Concern	(3) Organizational Approach	(4) Who Handled Adaptation
Late 1940s	Stable and predictable	Growth techniques	Firefighting	Top management
The 1950s	Stable and predictable	R & D, creativity	Corporate planning and mergers	Top management and Staff
The 1960s	Becoming unpredictable	Organizational structure and processes	Corporate planning and systems anal.	Top management and staff
The 1970s and on	Unstable and unpredictable	External and internal environmental change	All the above plus emphasis on strategies and info. technology	Top management and staff

information to the top (and assume its reliability) or for the slow gyration of decisions down through large headquarters staff departments.

Further, the changes are increasingly becoming unprecedented in nature, barring extrapolation of past experience and adding to the unpredictability, such that more and more of the decisions to be made are unique and must be thought through from scratch.

Conventionally operated organizations in such environments therefore have an inherent set of circumstances built for trouble that require quick and significant change of operating policies, structures, and processes, starting with pushing decisions down as close as possible to where they are implemented in order to involve those most knowledgeable about the subjects and most affected, which is no less than the delegation and participation argument that currently barrages every student of management.

But now it's important for much more than reasons of motivation. First, relying on the same small elite group at the top to handle the growing volume will result in unacceptable delays, by-passed decisions, and failure to see all the needs for decisions. Second, in addition to the accelerating volume, the unpredictable uniqueness of changes obviously demands the full creative resources of more echelons, preferably the entire management team.

And finally, when social (especially the internal) and technological changes are repeatedly unique once responding decisions are made, fast feedback of decision outcome must certainly be built into the decision-making system so that each subsequent related decision can capitalize on those outcomes in a sequential learning process. The decision-makers must learn results at a pace that's at least as fast as the rate of change. The needed cybernetic systems will be described under "Control design" in Chapter 11.

But pushing decisions down and installing fast-feedback systems plainly constitutes only the management technology part. The other, and in fact first subject that has to be tackled, is the leadership style and all that it entails: the philosophy (including "team philosophy" pp. 584-599), values, skills and managerial competence, necessary to implement and operate it effectively. What organizations need on both scores in any environment would be the consequences of the recommendations of the balance of the book.

Complex training design

Listing this as a type of complex learning on page 80 is admittedly a bit contrived, but complex combinations of techniques are required for leader managers to learn many of the managerial skills and behaviors they need, and the result is complex learning though externally programmed, applying concepts that must underlie the training and development described in Chapters 17 and 20.

One has only to consider the types of learning involved in courses that include case studies, role-playing (and add videotaping with critiques), problem discussion and debate, simulation games, interpersonal skills, team building skills. Any will incorporate some to many types of learning through new information, conditioning, reinforcement, socialization observation, social interaction, feedback, identification, emulation, imitation and perhaps a little unintended punishment. And the trainer will do his or her best to develop a "Model II" group climate to foster this learning.

Designing courses is certainly the province of professional trainers, and to be good at it they have to first research the teaching process, studying such works as "Cognitive Style, Learning Style, and Transfer Skill Acquisition."[8] But here are some introductory thoughts for trainer trainees, a few ideas which all leaders should know for their own informal teaching and in order to understand subordinates' reactions to it.

The foundation is the list of "general miscellaneous knowledge" on pages 77-78, the six basic factors on 78, and the information from there to here. But particularly important is the additional fact that just as people think differently they also learn best in different ways. Therefore, the most basic design principle is to fit the teaching techniques to the individual's dominant learning mode or preferences, of course incorporating the above knowledge and factors. The word dominant is inserted because few people are purely in one category, might have characteristics in several, but one does tend to dominate.

As for the modes, there have been many theories going back to Carl Jung, but education research has recently made much progress, pinning them down to a reliable four, though different researchers use different emphases and labels. A particularly intelligible and helpful set was recently offered and explained by L.D. Ward in *Training* magazine: the idealistic, the pragmatic, the realistic, and the existentialist tabulated on page 103.[9]

Quoting from her article, the *idealistic* adult learner is the builder, thinker, and reasoner, who likes to discover deductively the skills needed for different tasks. Thus they like self-governed, self-paced learning as in group discussions, sharing, self-appraisal, case studies, interactive video and democratic planning.

The *pragmatic* says I'll buy it when I see it work on the job and believes his or her situation is unique (e.g., an example of the solution for Company Z is unacceptable), which is perhaps a defense because the type usually has difficulty transferring skills from one setting to another. So the preferences are on-the-job training, coaching, mentorship, and material specific to his or her job.

The *realistic* wants fast-paced nuts-and-bolts programs devoid of human relations and the concerns they require, is often low on interpersonal skills, intellectualizing, and team-building competence, saying "just tell me what needs to be done." The preferences: structured programs, how-to workshops, explicit goals, step-by-step procedures.

And the *existentialist* learner is a humanistic participative type that has a high regard for the diversity of strengths and abilities, their own and others', believing there are many ways to get effective results. Their preferences: training based on contingency theory (see "Contingency factors" in Chapter 16), requiring inductive reasoning and stressing human relations and respect for alternative solutions offered by others.

But how do you identify the dominant mode of each subordinate? Appraisal records developed by techniques in Chapter 9 and its accompanying comments by the professional appraisers may give important clues, and there are a few commercial instruments trainers can apply to participants in a training class. For one, some help can be gained from an evaluation of values by the "Study of Values" on pages 138-139 (Spranger categories).

Nevertheless, superiors, and most of the time trainers, ordinarily have to rely on self-trained judgment from personal relations and observations in sizing them up, being ever ready to change opinions and careful about stereotyping. The self-training might include an integration of different dimensions from one's own learning, such as the relevant Spranger values categories, dominant motivations (in Chapters 7, and 8), and the above. Definitions of each classification suggest the following loose relationships:

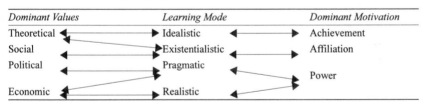

Dominant Values	Learning Mode	Dominant Motivation
Theoretical	Idealistic	Achievement
Social	Existentialistic	Affiliation
Political	Pragmatic	
		Power
Economic	Realistic	

Your identification of one of these aspects in a subordinate should lead to a mental association with those connected to it.

And rules-of-thumb are possible: promising managers on the key-position ladder to the top (see index) are most apt to be best served by boxes 1, 4, or a mix of both on page 104; the nature of lower and middle management work generally recommends boxes 2, 3, or a mix of both; in group instruction, trainers can apply technique variations to "idealistic" and "existentialistic" standouts in classes for boxes 2 or 3.

Two caveats: (1) One should try to judge whether or not value misconceptions (page 118) would override the mode/technique issue, obstructing learning, in which case refer to Chapter 18, including its

Sample Training Methodologies for Four Types of Learners

Box 1	*Box 2*	*Box 3*	*Box 4*
Sample training methodologies for the **idealistic learner:**	Sample training methodologies for the **pragmatic learner:**	Sample training methodologies for the **realistic learner:**	Sample training methodologies for the **existentialistic learner:**
• Discussion • Democratic Planning Groups • Case Study • Problem-solving • Goal Setting • Discovery • Inquiry Training • Interactive Video Instruction • Role Play • Lecture • Quality Circles • Critical Incident • Brainstorming • Debate • Reading Assignments • Parables	• Custom-designed, Job specific Training Materials • Simulation • Role Play • Value Clarification • Job-related Games • Individualized Instruction • On-the-job Demonstration and Practice	• Goals Identification • Programmed Instruction • Behavior Modeling • Job-description, Competency Identification • Simulation • Role Play • Video and Computer-Assisted Instruction • Off-the-shelf Training Materials • Example/Non-Examples • Question/Answer • Audiovisual (showing "how to" procedures) • In-class Demonstration and Practice • Reading Assignments (emphasizing "how to" procedures) • Testing/Feedback	• Team Building • Group Dynamics • Value Clarification • Person Goal Setting • Expectation Theory • Interpersonal Games • Inductive Reasoning • Contingency or Situational-based Competency Design • Transactional Analysis • Quality Circles • Individualized Instruction • Participant Presentations

different approaches for young managers open to quick change versus experienced ones who are not. (2) Never underestimate the mind's ability to grow intellectually from boxes 2 or 3 to boxes 1 or 4, sometimes rapidly, which often happens with promotion and new job experience. Superiors who feel responsible (as they should) for the development of their team members should find the skill of appraising their learning mode very helpful in coaching (pages 410-414) and particularly so in the joint career and development planning for them recommended on page 367.

Punishment

Punishment was defined earlier as learning by the effect of either (a) the negative reinforcement of withholding or terminating something desired, or (b) the application of something disliked, called a noxious stimulus (e.g., an electric shock) or the threat of it (the threat called aversive conditioning), both (a) and (b) intended to remove undesirable behavior, the interest here being only in organizational applications.

Almost everyone is unsure and somewhat confused about the subject, and some behaviorists espousing set ideas seem to be equally so. Enough is known, however, that a number of reliable guides can be put together; foremost among them is the guiding fact that punishment of adults is in general quite unreliable.

First, it can't be denied that punishment is necessary in rearing children, and for the same reason it's applicable to quite a few adults who don't grow up. Jean Piaget's stages of learning (page 38), the growth of the "self" (page 47), and the values development in the next chapter, all make it clear that reasoning ability is absent in the infant and grows slowly. For some time, therefore, the parent has to apply blunt imperatives, and only when hints of thinking begin to appear can reasoning "requests" be substituted little by little for the imperatives. The more abstract the subject, like "don't tell lies," the longer it takes. It's ordinarily not until the mid-teens that the reasons for this one, the full consequences of both lying and not lying, really sink in.

So in the beginning we have to lay down a number of do's and don't's with the threat of punishment, periodically applying it as the child tests the threats in order to maintain the strength of the threat (or it will "extinguish"); it's the only thing that works until greater maturity arrives. As one psychiatrist dramatically explained it in regard to the abstracts of morality:[10]

The mistake we still make is to hope that more and more citizens will have developed a mature morality, one they have critically tested against experience, without first having been subject as children to a stringent morality based on fear and trembling ...

While conscience develops on the basis of fear, learning depends on prior formation of conscience, which, in the process of learning, is more and more modified by reason.

It is true that too much fear interferes with learning, but for a long time learning does not proceed well unless motivated also by fear ... Later, in the process of gaining maturity, one can slowly free oneself of some of the fear and begin to question the absolute tenets.

Education must reach the child where he is in order to guide him where he is not, (and) the child must fear something if he is to apply himself to the arduous task of learning.

But while accepting the need of children, we also realize that:

• not all adults advance to maturity,
• many are mature and reasoning in some ways and not in others,
• we will always have those who disagree with society's norms and rules or just want to kick over the bucket at society's expense,
• there are those who are basically or incorrigibly abnormally unreasoning, illogical, destructive, anarchistic or hostile.

So we must concede that some punishment will probably always have to be applied to a segment of the adult population too.

Therefore, to understand when to use it and *how* and when not to use it and *why*, one might start with an outline of the types of punishment and the problems they present. There broadly are three, with overlaps due to application degree:[i]

Type	*Description*	*Examples*
I. Corporal punishment	Application of noxious stimulus or treatment	Confinement, hard labor, electric shock, hitting, beating, torture, killing.
II. Aversive punishment	(a) *Strong:* threat of corporal punishment	Clenched fist, shouting, strong commands, pay cut, demotion, firing.
	(b) *Mild:*	
	1. Threat of material punishment	Threats of demotion, transfer, pay
	2. Threat of psycho-logical punishment	cut; criticizing, disapproving frowns, gestures.[j]
	3. Applied programmed punishment	Task-cost techniques, Time-out techniques, A scheduling technique.
III. Negative reinforcement	(a) Withholding or terminating a reinforcer being received	(1) Ceasing attention, approval, praise, etc. (2) No bonus on sales or profit below quota.

(b) Withholding a desired reinforcer not yet received	No pay increase, promotion or perquisite that was wanted or expected.

Problems. Type I can of course be passed over as either illegal, socially unacceptable or irrelevant in civil organizations. Type II(a) is complicated in that along with the obvious, it includes a strange mix, such as the inflictor's loss of self-control in the form of exasperation or anger, the periodic application of threatened punishment to keep the threat from "extinguishing," and punishments like "firing" that terminate the control. The mild threats of II(b) point up the fact that threats are commonly just as potent as their application, providing they are occasionally carried out; they may be on an extended variable schedule and/or may be experienced only vicariously (seen applied to someone else).

The programmed punishment applications of type II(b)3 are admittedly exceptions to the definition but are new concepts; they are techniques recommended in preference to any other when negative reinforcement (III) is too weak or will take too long to have timely effect. A "task-cost" technique is one in which, to reduce an undesirable behavior, a task is required that could be perceived by the person as costing more to do than continuing the behavior, such as a chronic complainer being asked to fill out lengthy bureaucratic forms on each complaint.

The "time-out" technique is a temporary removal of a positive reinforcer already being received, like putting a rule-breaking hockey player in the penalty box for two minutes, keeping a child after school reducing play period, withholding a leniency on the production line. The "scheduling technique" is simply an application of the principle described on pages 81-83.

If the time element *does* permit negative reinforcement and punishment cannot be avoided, the Type III(a) and (b) are the methods most recommended by behaviorists, because they are the least aversive (therefore lowest on immorality), do not engage aggression, and have the lowest potential for undesirable results.

Type III(a) is usually the most humanitarian, but the message may not become apparent or may be too vague, and there's no denying it is capable of raising a person in a sensitive situation to considerable anxiety. Type III(a)2 is, we know, a well-accepted part of formal organizational incentive systems. The impact item III(b), on the other hand, is highly dependent on expectations; it can have a minimum aversive affect if they're low, but a strong effect if they're high; it may indeed be most painful since it frequently affects self-esteem as well as the pocketbook.

It shouldn't be necessary to argue that inflicting pain is basically immoral and that, even for the exceptions mentioned, we're obligated to keep it to a minimum. But there are also some very convincing *practical* reasons for avoiding it:

1. The punisher teachers two things, not just to stop certain behavior: aggression is also taught by modeling it, setting an example that may be interpreted by the punished as the way to handle the disciplining of their own subordinates, and they are also likely to interpret the bosses' aversiveness as necessary behavior to be considered an effective manager; in the home a child told not to aggress is confused to see the parent do it to himself or herself, and ends up copying because it gets results.

2. Punishment fails to tell the recipient the correct behavior to be substituted for the undesirable behavior, so the undesirable is generally suppressed only to reappear later when the punishment seems less likely to be repeated. "Quite literally a person may subsequently behave *in order to avoid punishment.* He or she can avoid it by not behaving in punishing ways, but there are other possible reactions, some disruptive and maladaptive or neurotic."[11]

3. Different people are affected in both different ways by the same punishment and differently themselves in different circumstances. It may have no effect on a defiant one, please a masochist, give status where a group dislikes a punisher, cause serious psychological damage to another, generate a guilt complex in a child, effect a sudden reflex attack on the punisher or an innocent bystander, or instill a lasting desire for revenge.

4. The punished one may develop such a dislike and disrespect for the punisher, the latter's opinions and disapproval may be held in contempt and held so permanently.

The first two are, with few exceptions, quite predictable, but the second two are not at all so; in fact #3 and #4 are the real dilemmas to the aware punisher—who generally knows that there are at least a dozen major variables that could directly upset the planned outcome, and that there are therefore at least 12 x 12 possible combinations:

1. The type of punishment
2. The frequency of application
3. The intensity
4. The schedule of delivery
5. Stimulus control

6. Personality and behavior of the administrator
7. Personality and behavior of the subject
8. Past and present relationship of the two
9. Influence and reaction of peers or friends
10. The locus of the event
11. Control of peripheral variables (environment)
12. Sensitivity of the recipient to pain

Even when mildly punishing a subordinate by chewing the person out, one should recognize that it's a moot question which affects behavior more and in what way, the criticizing or the cessation of it. One pertinent question is, if desired results do seem, to occur, will they last or will the undesirable conduct recur in one's absence; further just how much have future relations with the person been damaged irreparably.

So, aside from the question of morality, the practical reasons for keeping punishment to the minimum are overwhelming. But then when to use it and "how" in the unavoidable situations ...

Consideration. It goes without saying that no manager is ever expected to go by-the-book with all the advice and rules given on how better to lead. It is only hoped that knowledge of them will increase the probability that more and better alternatives will occur to each of them at the appropriate time.

In what appears to be a punishable event, one of the more simple rules is to make a quick analysis of whether the event is a:

misbehavior

or

performance failure.

Treating both alike is at the heart of the great majority of abuses against people of all ages and walks, which is especially true in the business world where poor performance is universally punished even though maximum effort was applied by the subordinate, inadequate training had been given, mitigating circumstances were involved, or there was a total absence of motivation from the superior.

Here also lies the reason why the bragged-about open door policy seldom succeeds. Being the locus of perceived or experienced unjustified punishment, the office is secondarily conditioned as a torture chamber to be avoided.

On the other hand, when misbehavior is the problem, the first recourse as recommended earlier would be a form of negative reinforcement, the second a mild programmed punishment, and on up the ladder of types on page 106, the cases in which the more stringent punishments are plainly unavoidable being:

- Aggression.
- Sabotage.
- Behavior that is clearly disruptive without time for gradual reduction of the behavior or gradual increase of punishment.
- Undesirable behavior that can lead to mass followership by a group or crowd.

Here are some rules of thumb either for maximizing results or as alternatives, rules that tend to make up for some of the weaknesses of punishment, though far from all of them:[12]

(a)   Deliver the punishment as soon after the misbehavior as possible.

(b)   Make the initial intensity really significant.

(c)   Deliver the punishment for each behavior occurrence, or do it as frequently as possible after each.

(d)   Provide an alternative behavior that will not be punished, preferably one that can give the subject at least as much satisfaction.

(e)   If an alternative is not available, provide an adequate release, face-saving and/or safety valve.

(f)   When the desired behavior is substituted by the subject, it should be duly reinforced positively.

(g)   Remove, if possible, any and all reinforcement being supplied the undesirable behavior.

(h)   There should be an indication that the undesired behavior is decreasing; if it is not, a reanalysis is in order for a change of treatment (type of punishment, cessation, dismissal, therapy, scheduling, etc.).

(i)   There are always some insensitive managers who need to be told not to criticize an employee in front of others, the punishing criticism compounded by the punishing loss of face, followed by a determination of revenge for the humiliation.

Admittedly, the conditions necessary for applying a number of these are not common. As one critic stated, "It is frequently impossible to punish problem responses immediately, severely, consistently, and without associating punishment with certain socially desirable consequences such as attention"[13]—not to mention the administration problems on page 108, and the usual lack of time to work your way up the page 106 ladder.

Again, it can only be concluded that the best policy is to avoid punishing others if at all possible. Here are some guides to aid in this too, some quite obvious:

1. Remove, or don't set up, temptations (such as not locking the car when you leave it), or change the nature of the situation so that punishable behavior will not be invited.
2. Remove the appeals of punishable behavior (e.g. don't give attention if that's being sought).
3. When misbehavior can be anticipated or forecasted, suggest alternatives or sublimation of the punishable behavior in advance.
4. Provide "rules" that can clear up doubts or ambiguous situations, but first find out how to design them (in **Rules**, Chapter 11 on control).
5. Understand the "non-compliance" situations that do and don't require the use of power and punishment so that you understand the other's problem and you know your alternatives (**Compliance** in Chapter 11) and you don't overreact.

Unfortunately, for traditional managers to apply much of these recommendations requires first giving up the traditional conception that misconduct and unsatisfactory performance should be punished, and that clearly entails behavior change, which can seldom occur with just reading about the subject. There is however one exception, the IIb3 "scheduling technique" on page 106, a total system of handling punishable behavior short of behavior change by OD or integration methods, one that's duly benevolent and considerate, an organizational discipline that should be taught in all management development programs.

Organizational discipline. A growing number of organizations have found that their managers can in fact be made very receptive to the application of the technique to subordinates for misbehavior because of its simple logic. The best known formula is the one known as the Huberman nonpunitive system, a mild programmed approach in which subordinates work themselves up the punishment ladder or not in three steps by their own decisions.[14] After the punishable event, instead of a demeaning chewing out:

> First, no comment. A private meeting is held as soon as possible to discuss what happened and what should have happened, and the superior gains an agreement on what will be done in the future, in effect a commitment to meet reasonable standards of performance and behavior. The meeting is documented, with copies to the employee and a "working" file but not put in the individual's personnel file.

Second, if the conduct is repeated, a written "reminder" is given restating the responsibility agreed to vs. the usual threatening warning. A meeting follows quickly to review the commitment, analyze the failure, agree on a solution once more, and prepare an "action plan." No threats. A memo is sent to the person summarizing the meeting, copies to the employee and to the personnel file this time.

Third, if it happens again, the person is given a paid one-day "decision-making leave," returns the next day for a meeting with the superior, and announces the decision to change and stay or to quit. If stay, a new "action plan" is prepared with the understanding that another failure means termination. A third memo with copies to the employee and personnel file.

The goal of superiors from the beginning: get subordinates' commitment to be responsible for their own change, which is the most mutually beneficial and likely method to accomplish it. Moreover by doing so, the focus of future infractions is placed on the employees' failure to abide by his or her own agreements. And, if an employee, in the first or any meeting, refuses to agree to reasonable performance and behavior standards, the organization has a sound basis for termination.

One can see that this system is applicable anywhere in the organization up through middle management and especially at the lower levels where problems of job performance and behavior are most frequent—the factory floor, supervisors (e.g., unacceptable supervising), white collar employees and technicians.

The gains for the organization as experienced by GE, Union Carbide, and others who have instituted it:

A substantial reduction in disciplinary incidents, discipline-related grievances, arbitration and suits; minimized wrongful terminations; elimination of rule or standard misunderstanding and difference of opinion as issues; reduced absenteeism and turnover; a noticeable increase in morale; a much more collaborative climate; and positive mature interpersonal relations.

The personal gains to supervisors:

Greater self-confidence in handling such events; greater self-regard due to the organization's philosophy and its trust that they can handle them equitably; the troubling task of fitting the punishment to the crime replaced by efforts to explore positive ways to build commitment and a sense of responsibility; responsibility for termination decisions for these infractions transferred to the subordinates.

The gains to subordinates:

The elimination of misunderstandings about rules or standards and of opinion differences as issues is to their gain also as is the elimination of irrelevant accusations and emotions; a hearing on their side of the occurrence; full participation in planning the alternatives and being the one who makes the choice (vs. the unilateral decision of the superior); maintenance of self-respect by the paid decision-making leave.

Warning: setup of a Huberman system cannot be a do-it-yourself project. Each organization must develop its own system around this structure to fit its own characteristics and activities. However, if your personnel department doesn't have the professionals experienced in the procedure and necessary training, outside assistance is essential. After their orientation of the upper executives, they recommend, organize, and guide a task force team of select managers in planning the system, educating the departments to be covered (if not the whole organization), and implementing the start-up. Particularly important:

> The general education of all the involved employees: explanation of the system, relevant philosophy, objectives, and ethics; the organizations' belief in fairness, open discussion of such problems, and respect for and trust of its members.

> The training program: the education of the managers on the nature of punishment (e.g., this chapter subsection) and the training in conducting the meetings, the interpersonal skills needed, how to instill commitment and a sense of responsibility, and how to do the action planning. It typically takes several months.

> System integration: with the appraisal procedures, the grievance system if any, and the due process system if any (**Due Process**, Ch. 21).

> System maintenance: periodic refresher training for all managers; assignment of monitoring responsibility to the personnel department requiring annual reports to top management executives of rates and trends of discipline-related grievances, absenteeism, turnover, employee survey findings, and morale; appropriate written material for new employees, and periodic bulletins.

The article on the technique in the July-August 1985 issue of *Harvard Business Review*[15] is recommended for an excellent example.

NOTES

    a.   Note that the mode of acquisition is not relevant to the definition, whether it is brought about by parents, schools, models, norms, experience, reinforcement, punishment, management development, role playing, assertiveness training, organization development, etc.

    b.   Latent learning is learning not manifested in performance but revealed in later unrelated performance (cognitive, affective, or physical).

    c.   A clear distinction between the words behavior and performance is important in discussions of managing the generally accepted definitions for an organizational context are (also see footnote m on page 340): Behavior is a motivational or emotional response to stimuli, which is what is happening in the Lewin formula on page 26. Performance is the consequence of technical execution (from good to bad) of a task or function toward a predetermined goal, the execution process however almost always possessing motivational or emotional (therefor behavioral) components.

    d.   Operant conditioning is also called instrumental conditioning and positiv reinforcement. "Operant" refers to what the individual does, not what someone does to th individual. The someone admittedly selects the stimulus that will elicit the desired respons but the individual then in response "operates" on or modifies the environment to achieve th goal.

    e.   The closest the researchers have come to the operant conditioning of a complex tas is a technique called "shaping": the task is subdivided into its simple component parts, th individual components taught, and their performance motivated separately. then the parts a reassembled. It has been found to be too cumbersome and impractical for anything outsid the lab.

    f.   For national differences and values, see G. Hofstede, "Motivation, Leadership, an Organization: Do American Theories Apply Abroad." (AMA: Organizational Dynamic Summer 1980).

    g.   The technique called "role analysis" has not been included here because interactio is not involved; each party writes down his or her perceived responsibilities and what is expecte of the other, a third-party intermediary analyzes and resolves the differences with the superio and the subordinate is unilaterally informed of the results.

    h.   It is interesting that an individual also needs an internal feedback system for matur behavior—introspection as to one's own thoughts and actions to control excesses, whether the be aggression, dependence, withdrawal, or others. Its inadequacy in the excessivel authoritarian, status conscious, or power-driven person is usually evident.

    i.   One should keep in mind the two basic sides of the punishment subject: the receip of one of the following types and the avoidance of it. The latter is or course a natural reactio for normal people in most situations, but it may have to be taught to the less-than-norma The technique is called "avoidance learning:" learning to avoid a punishment by making th required responses.

    j.   Note that otherwise neutral frowns, gestures, and the sight and sound of many thing can be punishing as a result of secondary conditioning.

REFERENCES

1.   Schein, E.H., "How Can Organizations Learn Faster?" *Sloan Management Review* Winter 1993.

2.   Argyris, C. "'Beyond Freedom and Dignity' by B.F. Skinner, A Review Essay," *Harvar Education Review*, Vol. 41, No. 4 (1971), p. 550.

3.   Margulies, N. and J. Wallace *Organizational Change* (Glenview, Ill.: Scott, Foresma and Company, 1973). (See their pp. 92-97 for more detail).

4.   Luft, J., "The Johari Window," *Human Relations Training News*, Vol. 5, pp. 6-: 1961.

5.   Lewin, K., op. cit., 1951.

6.   Argyris, C. *Increasing Leadership Effectiveness* (New York: John Wiley, 1976, pp. 1 23.

7.   Campbell, J.P., M.D. Dunnette, E.E. Lawler III, and K.E. Weick, Jr., *Managemen Behavior, Performance and Effectiveness* (New York: McGraw-Hill, 1970), p. 105.

8.   By the National Center for Research in Vocational Education, Ohio State University Columbus, Ohio, 1979.

9. *Training*, November. 1983, pp. 31-33.
10. Bettelheim, B., "Moral Education." *Moral Education*, op. cit., pages 87-91.
11. Skinner, B.F. op. cit., 1971, p. 62.
12. Some of these from "Punishment" by Azrin, N. H. and Holtz, W. C. in *Operant Behavior*, edited by W. K. Honig (New York: Appleton-Century-Croft, 1966).
13. Stuart, R. B., "Behavior modification techniques for the education technologist," *The School in the Community* (eds) R. C. Sarri & F. F. Maple (New York: National Association of Social Workers, 1972).
14. Huberman, J., "Discipline Without Punishment," *Harvard Business Review*, July-August 1964.
15. Campbell, D. N., R. L. Fleming and R. C. Grote. "Discipline without punishment—at last," *Harvard Business Review*, July-August 1985.

Chapter 5

The Behavioral Fundamental—Values

There are few managers today who are not aware of the important part values play in performance and behavior. Still, few of those who are have given them much thought if any with respect to either their own self management or the management of subordinates if not because of the pressures of work because of the vacuum in their education on the subject. Note: The values of primary concern in this book are those dealing with interpersonal relations and the management of people within an organization).

Yet we know that wrong values are at the bottom of most of the dissatisfaction and alienation described in Chapter 1, and research has conclusively identified many of the value culprits in management, prime examples being those in Figure 5.1 that were found to govern the decisions and judgments involving people in conventionally managed organizations.

Indeed values are the fundamental force directly controlling all behavior, the impact correspondingly carrying over to all associated performance, and, unfortunately for the function of leadership, they're inordinately complicated. Those in the Figure list are the most easy to recognize; they might be called the black-and-white, many of which people-conscious managers tend to disagree with intuitively. But even for a humanist, many values are far less obvious, and their application are commonly dilemmas. Moreover, decision-making on any can be sorely complicated by the situation.

For effective leadership one needs a thorough comprehension of their basic nature (to be able to identify them), how they develop, how our minds combine them in systems, and what can be done, if anything, about those that need to be improved or changed.

For the basic nature of a value, the general meaning is fairly well known: a value is a standard by which one judges as to goodness, performance, importance, appropriateness, or desirability. A precise definition:[1]

A value is a conception, explicit or implicit, distinctive of an individual or characteristic of a group, of the desirable (to the value holder) which influences the selection from available modes, means and ends of action.

117

Common Organizational Value Misconceptions

General

- The average human being has an inherent dislike of work and will avoid it if he can (Theory X, #1).
- The average human being prefers to be directed, wishes to avoid responsibility, has relatively little ambition, wants security above all (#3).
- Individualism is one's highest achievement; conformity is slavery.
- The intellectually inclined individual brings unrealistic ideas, turmoil, and discontent to an organization.
- Self-fulfillment is solely the individual's responsibility.
- The corporate world is (in corporation) the reason for being, its goals the measure of what is worthwhile in life.
- People must in the final analysis be subordinated to economic objectives.

Power, authority, and leadership:

- Power (and authority) is a constant; a decrease by one party (e.g., the superior) results in an increase by the other (the subordinate).
- Authority in an organization always flows down from the top.
- A "boss" is essential to every group.
- Strong leadership is unilateral and dominating.
- Be firm (directive) and fair, using the carrot and stick.
- Fear, money, and close control are the most effective means of inducing subordinates to work.
- Leadership guided by Theory X is strong, by Theory Y weak.

Competition:

- Winning is everything; losing is dishonor.
- The most important factor of success in any endeavor is superiority and/or dominance over the others involved.
- Competition always produces more effective results than collaboration.
- Interpersonal aggression (for men) is manly, admirable and essential to organizational vitality.
- Interpersonal competition always improves performance.

Participation:

- Participative management is permissive.
- Participation is inefficient on cost/effectiveness and wastes time.
- To share power is to reduce one's own and consequently one's ability to get the job done.
- Participation invites resentment backlash from subordinates when their proposals are rejected.
- Broad involvement is fine, but management by committee only leads to weaknesses and compromise decisions.
- A group does not make decisions; it annoints them.
- Group activity forces excessive conformity and obstructs individuality and creativity.
- Leaderless groups (without a boss) are socialistic or communistic.

Emotions:

- Feelings and work are mutually exclusive.
- Expressing feelings is effeminate.
- Effective employees keep emotions separated from their work.
- The soundest decisions evolve from purely rational thinking.

Figure 5.1

And there are two basic types:

- An asocial value: a standard that is set for a thing or abstract idea.
- A social value: a standard that guides human thought, decisions, or endeavor that affect humans directly or indirectly (many of course applicable also to all other living creatures).

Each then subdivides into two of their own, the asocial, as stated, into things and ideas (the ideas also called non-moral values), the social into moral and immoral or anti-social ideas, as shown in this elementary chart:

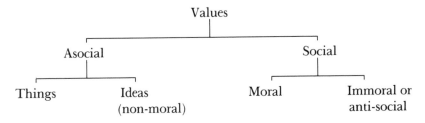

But from there on it's not so elementary. Even Plato got off on the wrong track when he assumed that all values are *absolute*, that each has an intrinsic or precise value of its own whether asocial or social when in fact they are all *relative*. The value given a thing is a relationship between the person and the thing; the value attributed to an idea (asocial or social) is a relationship between the person and the idea.[a]

Then under the social, we know that sometimes so many variables must be taken into account that being sure one's thought or decision is moral may be exceedingly difficult. However, one can be quite specific about what social values are. Elaborating on the foregoing description, they are the standards involved in voluntary ideas, judgments, intentions, decisions, or actions that concern or have a bearing on:

(a) other individuals,
(b) institutions of society, or
(c) the formation of one's own character.

And we can also generalize that moral conduct is doing good and avoiding evil with respect to (a), (b) and (c), while still recognizing that what good and evil are is at the heart of ethics philosophy controversy, particularly in the gray area.

For examples of the two basic types, the values concerning asocial things are obviously the ones that would be assigned to metals, gems, clothing, and the ones on asocial ideas would be applied to such issues as:

Productivity	Aesthetics	Work (the ethic)
Autonomy	Knowledge	Leisure
Money	Wisdom	Eating
Innovation	Science	Talking
Economics	Skills	Sleeping

But we know also that such applications of these values may or may not involve people, and when they do, complying with (a), (b), or (c) above, they become social. Illustrations: the achievement of productivity by forced labor or of autonomy for oneself by the enslavement of another.

An excellent detailing of moral values is presented in Exhibit I in the Appendix, but lest there be any doubt that values can be *immoral*, consider the one of white supremacy in South Africa or any type of ethnic prejudice. Indeed, with a little thought, one will come to realize that virtually all organization decisions and actions can have a bearing on (a), (b) or (c) and therefore become social with moral implications. When one moreover considers that at least half of all the decisions of managers are about either (a) or (b), their societal responsibility is clearly considerable. Take for instance the importance of *greed* and the effects of what happened in the 80s that thousands of employees, stockholders and all society has had to pay heavily for in the 90s. Managers in particular need to know how to define it. One of the best definitions was presented in *Business Week* magazine (p. 104, 7/6/87):

> In an economic system energized by the hope of gain there is a point where legitimate expectations of profit stop and greed begins. It is when the drive to acquire wealth overrides fundamental values—respect for the law, for other people, for one's own conscience. Avarice deforms the human spirit and alienates it from those things that truly matter.

Fortunately, the advanced cultures of the world have done a sufficiently good job of values conditioning on persons who have reached management in those societies that their general morality through the years to the 1950s, although below employee hopes and expectations, seems to have been tolerable.

But, as Chapter 1 has shown, no longer. The discrepancies between rising follower expectations and standards arrayed against insufficiently upgraded concepts of leading and managing have grown to a point of unacceptability. Something has to give. It will not be the expectations and standards. On the other hand, the fact that we constantly change values to suit our personal needs would suggest that we can also change those underlying the behavior in managing and leading.

Value development

The way values develop ought to, and will, give some clues on how to either reverse the process, change existing concepts, or develop new ones. There are two parts to it: the indigenous forces within individuals that induce or influence development, and the exogenous forces that both utilize the indigenous and mold or influence development in a conditioning process.

Indigenous forces. These can be divided into two subparts: first, the constitutional tendency of the person (page 46) to engage in valuing from infancy as a babe and how it is done; second the characteristics integral to the process that must be taken into account in any attempt to influence it.

The best explanation to date of the former has been provided by Carl Rogers and of the latter by Lawrence Kohlberg.

Roger's extensive research led him to conclude that infants have at a very early stage a clear organismic valuing process that is neither conscious nor symbolic.[2] A child's reaction to pain, sudden noises, insecurity and hunger are obvious, as is the positive response to their relief, but particularly impressive was the fact that, when a score or more of dishes of natural (unflavored) foods were spread in front of a sampling of infants over a period of time, they clearly tended in the long run to value the foods that enhanced their own survival, growth, and development. If for a while a child gorged itself on starches, it would soon balance the excess with a protein binge; if the diet was vitamin deficient for a period, it would be followed by vitamin rich selections. The infant's own senses, uninfluenced by parents, did the valuing.

As the infant grows out of the crib and moves into the living room, though, its internal valuing processes become altered by the disciplining necessary to control behavior. When a boy indulges in the enjoyable act of pulling little sister's hair, he is called "bad boy," his hand is slapped, and mother's affection is temporarily withdrawn. Accordingly, his values are externally manipulated by challenging his basic need for security and love. The next time he pulls her hair he may be heard to intone "bad boy," evaluating himself and his action not by his own natural system but by another's judgment, in effect distrusting his own as a guide to behavior.

The pattern is the influence in our growing up that has turned the majority of us into what David Riesman called "other-directed" personalities. The values so developed become set as in concrete because we're not allowed to test them, and an added result is that we're unable to resolve the many conflicts that occur among them.

This is a picture of most of us. However, some individuals who have had the good fortune of an environment that encouraged a fair degree of autonomy have developed their personality without suppressing the organismic contact. The valuing process that develops in them is fully capable of adopting taught or learned ideas and beliefs that are logically good, doing it in a way that's similar to the infant's, albeit with much more complexity, scope and sweep. The growth direction is toward self enhancement, the key feature being confidence in one's own worth and trust in one's own judgment, the growth proportional to openness to the experiencing going on within.

The logical extrapolation to the management of people: treat employees not like children the way most authoritarians do but as self-respecting adults entitled to freedom of thought and freedom from domination and fear of criticism if you want them to maximize performance and creativity.

Provocatively, Rogers also concluded from the universality he found of this organismic process that the consequent individual self-enhancement impetus carries over to community enhancement and species enhancement, which concurs with the physiological discovery about the same time in line with McGregor's comments on page 56, the brain has an area devoted to the advancement of the species.

On the second factor in values development referred to at the start of the section (page 121)—the characteristics of the development process that must be taken into account in order to influence it—the principal one is the fact found by Lawrence Kohlberg that values develop in stages according to the cognitive development of the individual.

In the extensive research study that led to the conclusion, Kohlberg and his associates, concentrating on moral values, interviewed large samples about "right" and "wrong" in The United States, Britain, Turkey, Taiwan, and The Yucatan, the ages ranging from 10 years up through adulthood. The six stages in Figure 5.2 were identified, Kohlberg illustrating them in his own words as follows:[3]

Here's a question we have asked: Before the Civil War we had laws that allowed slavery. According to the law if a slave escaped he had to be returned. Some people who didn't believe in slavery disobeyed the law and helped runaway slaves escape. Were they doing right or wrong?

A bright. middle-class boy, Johnny, answers the question this way when he is ten: "They were doing wrong because the slave ran away himself." Johnny's response is Stage 1 *punishment and obedience orientation.*

Three years later he is asked the same question. His answer is mainly Stage 2: *instrumental relativism.* "If a person is against slavery and maybe likes the slave or maybe dislikes the owner, it's OK for him to break the law if he likes, provided he doesn't

Levels and Stages in Moral Development

Levels	Basis of Moral Judgment	Stage of Development
I	Moral value resides in external, quasiphysical happenings, in bad acts, or in quasiphysical needs rather than in persons and standards.	*Stage 1: Obedience and punishment orientation.* Egocentric deference to superior power or prestige, or a trouble-avoiding set. Objective responsibility.
		Stage 2: Naively egoistic orientation. Right action is that instrumentally satisfying the self's needs and occasionally others'. Awareness of relativism of value to each actor's needs and perspective. Naive egalitarianism and orientation to exchange and reciprocity.
II	Moral value resides in performing good or right roles, in maintaining the conventional order, and the expectancies of others	*Stage 3: Good-boy orientation.* Orientation to approval and to pleasing and helping others. Conformity to stereotypical images of majority or natural role behavior, and judgment by intentions.
		Stage 4: Authority and social-order-maintaining orientation. Orientation to "doing duty" and to showing respect for authority and maintaining the given social order for its own sake. Regard for earned expectations of others.
III	Moral value resides in conformity by the self to shared or sharable standards, rights, or duties	*Stage 5: Contractual legalistic orientation.* Recognition of an arbitrary element or starting point in rules or expectations for the sake of agreement. Duty defined in terms of contract, general avoidance of violation of the will or rights of others, and majority will and welfare.
		Stage 6: Conscience or principle orientation. Orientation not only to actually ordained social rules but also to principles of choice involving appeal to logical universality and consistency. Orientation to conscience as a directing agent and to mutual respect and trust.

Figure 5.2

get caught" (Differences of titles with Figure 5.2 are apparently additional descriptions by Kohlberg of the stages.). In effect, his orientation to sympathy and love indicates Stage 3 also: *orientation to approval, affection, and helpfulness.*

At age nineteen, in college, Johnny is Stage 4: *orientation to maintaining a social order by rules and rights.* He says: "They were right in my point of view. I hate the actual aspect of slavery, the imprisonment of one man rule over another. They drive them too hard and they don't get anything in return. It's not right to disobey the law, no, but you might do it if you feel it's wrong. If 50,000 people break the law, can 50,000 people be wrong?"

Johnny here is oriented to the rightness and wrongness of slavery itself and of obedience to the law. He doesn't see the wrongness of slavery in terms of equal human rights but in terms of an unfair economic relation ... he is still not *just.* Not only does he fail to ground the rights of Negroes on *principles* but he fails to ground respect for the law on this base. Respect for the law is respect for the majority.

From this position, progress in development leads the individual to *social contract legalism,* Stage 5, in which justice is generally understood, but there is still a fairly naive commitment to the concept of the law, making respect for the law and the majority inflexible; it is equivalent to saying, if you don't like the law of the majority, you can move to another community or country.

In Stage 6, principle becomes guiding.[b] For example, one understands the majority's potential for tyranny, and when it happens, recognizing "all that is necessary for evil to triumph is for good men to do nothing," one disobeys the law in protest, willing at the same time to pay the penalty. Martin Luther King's letter from a Birmingham jail is a crowning example. He wrote:

One may well ask, "how can you advocate breaking some laws and obeying others?" The answer lies in the fact that there are two types of laws, just and unjust. One has not only a legal and moral responsibility to obey just laws, one has a moral responsibility to disobey unjust laws ... Any law that uplifts human personality is just, any law that degrades human personality is unjust...

I do not advocate evading or defying the law as would the rabid segregationists. That would lead to anarchy. One who breaks an unjust law must do so openly, lovingly, and with a willingness to accept the penalty ... (this) is in reality expressing the highest respect for the law.

Thus as King makes clear, morality is the highest type of law, in a sense is behavior as we at our best would have it, guided by principles of true justice; indeed, he's induced us to respond to America's racial problems in terms of justice.[4]

Particularly impressive was the fact that these six stages and the same quality of moral thinking were found in all the cultures studied. Moreover, specific universal associated factors important to values development were also found by two follow-up studies.

One discovered that both adolescents and adults rank as the "best" moral opinion on a subject that stage of reasoning they can comprehend; and they can often comprehend one stage, even two stages, higher than the one they abide by, though they usually cannot verbally express them. Furthermore, they tend to prefer the higher one, and through a standard teaching technique—"cognitive conflict" with a higher stage—they can be provided enough cognitive experience to move up.

A characteristic of major importance that emerged: no one skipped a stage in the upward movement; each had to be experienced in its proper sequence, which is an interesting parallel to the trip up Maslow's hierarchy of needs. The international Kohlberg study of Figure 5.2 produced the same finding: no short cuts.

In the second study, the moral interviews of the international study were given to 100 sixth graders, and it was found that the majority were at the first four moral levels, a minority actually at the sixth, the *principal* level. They were then subjected to experimental cheating tests in which 75 percent of the lower and 20 percent of the higher group cheated.

When the same procedure was applied to college students, 42 percent of the lower group and only 11 percent of the higher one cheated. The ratio of change between the sixth graders and college students showed an improvement of 75/20 percent and 42/11 percent. Although education and maturation can't guarantee the elimination of cheating (or immorality), they do seem to decrease significantly their probability.

One of course should not lose sight of the fact that all three of these studies were applied to school children and young people *within* the system, reared essentially according to universal moral codes from the start. Obviously, battered children, many slum children, and many badly reared children who have not been so blessed acquire very different moral values. Fortunately, those within the system are the large majority, giving our educational instructions a base of sorts on which to build, and it's encouraging to have found from national surveys that four out of five adults now favor moral education.

Exogenous Forces. To pick up social values development from the infant entry the living room (page 121), societies, we know, have applied four methods of development and control for over 5,000 years: (1) formal law; (2) religion, (3) formal civil institutions, especially the education one, (4) the informal techniques of family and social groups; and added to them, now more than ever, is the pervasive fifth that includes the four: (5) the collective changing forces of and in the environment—economic, social political, technical and intellectual.

The dynamics of the five are of course complex, but we do realize that too much is now expected of the law and religion, too little is done about values in formal education, and a consequence of the educational neglect is an appalling ignorance passed on to each succeeding generation.

Formal law (1) is, after all, formulated as a last resort when other institutions and family have failed. Its coverage must be minimal to keep the legal processes manageable, and it doesn't motivate moral conduct; like punishment, it motivates the avoidance of a penalty.

On religion (2), studies have shown that in advanced societies it has little impact on social morality (its power in primitive societies, and still today, being primarily fear) and virtually none in commerce. Indeed, executives rarely solicit the clergy's judgment on moral problems for very logical reasons: (a) the irrelevance of religion to economics, (b) the ignorance of the clergy about business and its interpersonal relations, (c) the clergy's commitment to the tenets of the faith, precluding their objectivity, and (d) the clergy's affiliative urge to fill the needs of individuals, resulting in insufficient concern for those of the larger group or organization.

Although higher education (3) is beginning to take an interest in at least the development of an awareness of values, the Board of Regent in every state except California have blocked values development for grammar and high schools in spite of the national survey just mentioned. For example, the New York State Board has for years refused, and still at this date has refused to pass on even a statement of *policy*, an action that's been attempted each year, after which approval has to be obtained on *what* to teach and *how*.

(And now we have that life-and-death necessity for sex education to fight the proliferating disease of AIDS, sex education being a subject that must involve values, such as the stand to take on premarital sex, homosexuality, abortion, anal sex, contraception-dispensing clinics in or near schools, etc.).

The problem has been a general failure of plain people (who make up the boards) to realize that "there is no morality-free school, no valueless teaching,"[5] that the personal biases, misconceptions, likes and dislikes of each limited teacher, bad and good, are passed on anyhow. As a consequence, the most an elementary school gives a youngster is a code of commandments on the back wall of the classroom, such as:[6]

Be a good citizen	Play nicely and fairly
Be generous by	Be neat and clean
helping your friends	Mind your own business
Be prepared	Work quietly
Raise your hand	No fighting
Be polite	

Thus the required learning is left to the unknown random values of the chain of teachers to whom the child is exposed.[c] Other institutions do attempt to impose their own "bag of virtues," for example, the boy scouts' "be honest, loyal, reverent, clean and brave" and the church's Ten Commandments. But as Kohlberg has pointed out, there are no such things in practice as virtues and vices per se: they are "labels by which people award praise and blame toward others. But the way people use praise and blame toward others is not the way they think when making decisions about themselves." This was found over 50 years ago in a study on cheating that concluded:[7]

- You can't divide the world into honest and dishonest people. Almost everyone cheats some of the time.
- If a person cheats in one situation, it doesn't mean he will in another.
- People's verbal moral values about honesty have little to do with how, they act.

This was before the idea of values education, but it does describe today also. Still, societies prevail or collapse to the extent that their individual members set firm standards of honesty and truth for themselves.

There is the negative challenge of the opponents who ask, "Who has the right to decide what values are right, which to teach?" But haven't the basic ones already been decided, the basic ones, in addition to honesty and truth, of liberty, equality, justice, fairness, responsibility, citizenship, kindness, tolerance (all examined ahead). Yet we don't even teach that liberty—vs. tyranny—involves value choices and responsibility.

So the uninformed children become adults, teachers, and parents (4) and pass on their ignorance, including such myths that support the opposition to values education as in "mother knows best," knows instinctively what to do. "Most women don't. In fact, if educators have had a single message for parents during the past decade, it has been that parents have done a generally good job of messing things up."[8] The consequences of the educational vacuum? Along with the I-O gap, self-indulgence, everyone-for-himself, materialism gone amuck, and the present scandals at all levels of our society. Fortunately, there does seem to be an awakening going on about the myth, a realization by an increasing number of communities that their schools must teach at least the agreed-on values.

Finally, there is (5) the powerful dynamic molding and conditioning influence of the total environment (which includes the above four), the continuously changing economic, social, political, technical, and intellectual forces that individually and in combination influence and change values constantly.

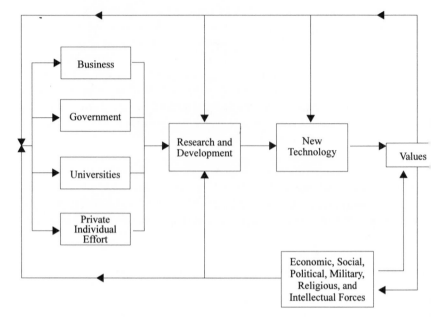

Figure 5.3

Figure 5.3 illustrates it.[9] The four factors on the left work individuall
or jointly, as a result of people and events (lower left-hand box) to produc
new ideas, opinions, norms, products, processes and structures that lead t
new technologies (definitions in the Introduction to Part II) and the value
to the right, the values also created or altered directly by elements in th
box. We need but look at the automobile for a perfect illustration o
technology's impact on values, its upgrading of those values concernin
pleasure, self-reliance, convenience, leisure, privacy, and human dignit
and at the same time the concomitant downgrading of those concernin
rationality, power, law, reverence for life, courtesy, family, and the qualit
of the environment.

Developed Values

The values end-result of all these forces, indigenous and exogenous, i
a multilevel-structure, the six major levels (for organizational personnel
being:

1. *Personal*: truth, honesty, integrity, fairness, consideration, success
   numerous qualitative goals.

2. *Interpersonal*: concern for others, their views, welfare, self-respect and dignity; and their rights to privacy, justice, a say in their destiny, and the pursuit of growth, self-actualization, and happiness. Also, values involved in control, power, authority, responsibility, interpersonal competition, and toward different groups.

3. *Internal-organizational*: obligations and responsibilities toward assigned tasks, authorities, employees, stockholders, organizational assets and goals, the organization as an entity, the quality of organizational life.

4. *External-organizational*: numbers 1 and 2 with customers, suppliers, creditors, unions, community, and nation.

5. *Professional/technical*: standards of product and technical performance, and of professional behavior and responsibilities.

6. *Legal*: the laws, product performance, and warranties.

Since a major problem at hand is the I-O gap, a major interest is of course the values of managers (particularly as superiors), and it's quickly discernible that those they hold in regard to the first three are the relevant ones here, the ones responsible for the gap.

These three are combined as patterns and systems to suit cognitive and affective needs. Managers tend to group selected ones in ways that help them carry out managerial functions producing consistent patterns, for example, for the five subjects in Figure 5.4. Additionally, they package them, often subconsciously, as specific systems that help them balance and integrate their personalities, social learning, and environment, the systems we call ideologies, orientations, and philosophies.

Managers' Values. What we've had on the subject up to fairly recently has been limited to the general wisdom of organization behaviorists and that only by inference from consulting and research on other topics (e.g., motivation). Figure 5.1 is a collection of the negative ones, euphemistically called misconceptions because in large measure they are, values that are seldom intentionally hostile (though they may give that impression), concepts that are mostly due to ignorance or picked up from models, hearsay wrong literature, some deep-seated, others less so.

But one project specifically referring to managers' values has gone a long way toward filling the void, and although the conclusions were also drawn by inference, the systematic methodology applied has given it an assuring degree of reliability.[10]

Some 200 concepts important to management were classified and reduced to the 66 in Figure 5.4, then rated by executives in a survey (1,072 responses from a random sample of 2,043 out of the 1965 Poor's Directory of

Concepts used to measure managers' values

Goals of Business Organizations	Personal Goals of Individuals	Groups of People
High Productivity	Leisure	Employees
Industry Leadership	Dignity	Customers
Employee Welfare	Achievement	My Co-workers
Organizational Stability	Autonomy	Craftsmen
Profit Maximization	Money	My Boss
Organizational Efficiency	Individuality	Managers
Social Welfare	Job Satisfaction	Owners
Organizational Growth	Influence	My Subordinates
	Security	Laborers
	Power	My Company
	Creativity	Blue Collar Workers
	Success	Government
	Prestige	Stockholders
		Technical Employees
		Labor Unions
		White Collar Employees

Ideas Associated with People	Ideas About General Topics
Ambition	Authority
Ability	Caution
Obedience	Change
Trust	Competition
Aggressiveness	Compromise
Loyally	Conflict
Prejudice	Conservatism
Compassion	Emotions
Skill	Equality
Cooperation	Force
Tolerance	Liberalism
Conformity	Property
Honor	Rationality
	Religion
	Risk

Figure 5.4

Corporations) on the degree of importance of each to their managing an⟨ in what way.

They simply checked the degree of importance in boxes like the one⟨ below using 1, 2, and 3 for ranking as to success (indicating pragmatic)⟨ rightness (morality), and pleasantness (emotional effect on self or others)⟨

Although the end result was not the specific values of managers, th⟨ rankings made it possible to infer them with respect to both broad valuativ⟨

```
                    Organizational Growth

    High      ┌──────┐ ┌──────┐ ┌──────┐   Low
    Importance└──────┘ └──────┘ └──────┘   Importance


_____ pleasant

_____ successful

_____ right
```

.ttitudes and the five categories in Figure 5.4. Importantly too, the validity
»f the findings, checked and verified 6 years later (1972),[11] confirmed a
tability of managers' values comparable to the stability of societal ones
ound by the Yankelovich studies in Chapter 1.

Most managers, the research concluded, are primarily pragmatic
verifying a characteristic we've always assumed) with ethics and affect in
econd and third positions of importance. Some, though pragmatic, are
trongly ethical, and a few are greatly concerned about the affective
onsequences of their decisions, possibly primarily so (refer to the affiliation
notive on pages 237-239.

The values themselves were interestingly subdivided in yet another way,
»ne that added insights into behavior: (1) *operative* values, those that are
he principal determinants of managers' decisions and behavior; (2)*intended*
alues that are normative socioculturally induced, are important to life but
ot found useful to organizational performance (surprisingly, rationality
vas one, as was trust, honor, and loyalty); and (3) *adopted* values that are
ituationally induced by observation of their success in managing but are
ot easily internalized (examples: equality, compromise, conflict).

Transparently, the most significant to managing are the operative, and
hey can be deduced from the concept ratings of both "high importance"
ind "successful" in the last columns of the Figure 5.5 charts.

In the first of the charts (5.5A) the three goals in the top subset (the subsets
»eing groupings of declining managerial weight that loosely follow the
l, 2, and 3 applied to the box above) are clearly of major weight to the
:ategory, well above all the others in deciding organizational goals. Those
n the second subset were found to be important, but were used to test
ilternative primary goals rather than serve as primary ones themselves. The
:ulturally induced bottom two were rated as having low relevance to
managing.

Behavior Analysis of Values (N = 1,072)

	% High Importance	% Successful 1st Ranked	% High Importance and Successful 1st Ranked
A. Goals of Business Organizations			
Organizational Efficiency	81	71	60
High Productivity	80	70	60
Profit Maximization	72	70	56
Organizational Growth	60	72	48
Industrial Leadership	58	64	43
Organization Stability	58	54	38
Employee Welfare	65	20	17
Social Welfare	41	8	4
B. Ideas Associated with People			
Ability	84	72	65
Ambition	75	73	57
Skill	70	75	55
Cooperation	78	46	40
Aggressiveness	42	76	33
Loyalty	80	19	18
Trust	91	18	18
Honor	86	12	12
Tolerance	39	18	12
Prejudice	11	36	10
Obedience	30	19	8
Compassion	29	10	8
Conformity	6	23	4
C. Personal Goals of Individuals			
Achievement	83	69	63
Success	70	64	53
Creativity	70	63	50
Job Satisfaction	88	41	41
Individuality	53	29	21
Money	28	46	20
Influence	18	47	15
Prestige	21	35	14
Autonomy	20	31	13
Dignity	56	20	13
Security	29	21	12
Power	10	52	9
Leisure	11	7	4

Figure 5.5

The second chart (5.5B) is particularly meaningful to interpersonal relations. The top three ratings are consistent enough with our expectations; managers judge others' managing as well as their own first by these criteria. But the conflicts in the rest of the chart are revealing. Outstanding is the fact that the culturally induced *cooperation* is held very high in importance in principle but not for achieving success, and the scoring on the situationally learned *aggression* is almost exactly the reverse. Then the culturally learned loyalty, trust, and honor take a nosedive on "success," which may explain a lot of organizational conduct.

In Figure 5.5C on personal goals, the analysts interpreted the top three as key motivational forces because of their high operative rating, but the second level given by managers to job satisfaction suggested that they held it to be a cultural value more applicable to others (mainly subordinates) than to themselves. The ranking of several in the third subset as having low relevance to managing may be as much due to uncertainty about them as to perceptions about utility.

The chart for "Groups of People" is not shown because its main revelation could be stated briefly: managers identify mainly with My Company, My Customers, and Managers (as an occupation). And the same was true of "General Topics": managers assigned low importance to emotions, quality, conflict, force, and religion.

The summary of the study was careful to qualify these findings as to their averaging nature, concealing the great variety and complexity of views possessed within this special segment (managers) of our society:

Some managers have a very small set of operative values while others have a large set and seem to be influenced by many strong values. The operant values of some managers include concepts which are almost solely related to organizational life while others include a wide range of personal and philosophical concepts. Some managers have what might be termed individualistic values as opposed to group-oriented ones. Some appear to be highly achievement-oriented as compared with others who seem to value status and position more highly. Finally, it is clear that some have a personal value system that might be characterized as "hard." Their operative values include concepts such as Ambition, Obedience, Aggressiveness, Achievement, Success, Competition, Risk and Force. Others have value systems that are often thought of as "soft" and include concepts such as Loyalty, Trust, Cooperation, Compassion, Tolerance, Employee Welfare, Social Welfare and Religion.

Yet while duly honoring differences and uniqueness, when one considers that managers' values influence all their:[12]

- perceptions of the situations and problems faced,
- decisions and solutions to the problems,

- the way they evaluate other individuals and groups,
- perceptions of individual and organizational success and achievemen
- concepts of ethical behavior and limits, and
- the extent to which they accept or resist organizational pressures an goals,

... it's obvious that values are a key factor in effective leadership, one that often overlooked, and not only from the standpoint of managers' attitude decisions and actions as herein described but also as to the quality of th organization collectively—manifested as the *organization* values, those th; develop from the pattern over time of the leadership, especially at the toɪ Consider, for example, these typical specific organization values, good an bad, that impinge on people, often becoming embedded in and part of th organization's culture: attitudes pro or con about caring for peoplɪ participation, justice, open communication, fairness, seniority, longevity o the job, firing (a last resort?), privacy, a supervisor's responsibility for his her subordinates' success; authoritarianism, status quos, politics, and don'ɪ rock-the-boat attitudes, and the values supporting the "moral mazes" i Chapter 1.

Idealogies. Just as values have different levels of manifestation so to do value systems. Those at the societal level are ideologies, value orientatioɪ (mostly at the subconscious level of the individual), and philosophiɪ (commonly at the conscious level). Indeed, in most instances only a carefu evaluation of one's stand brings each to full and clear consciousness.

What's to be gained by doing so? Certainly we form value systems as natural cognitive process of simplification, like stereotyping, as integratioɪ of the many bits of knowledge we have on the subject the system is abouɪ giving ourselves summary meaning for an orderly basis of thought an consistent action on it.

The system may be constructed of all good apples (values) or have onɪ to many bad ones, and naturally any that are bad will lessen the effectivenes of the system to serve its purpose. And importantly, as a system it has moɪ power thari any its parts to impel us toward not just individual acts bu into a comprehensive viewpoint and pattern of behavior. Needless to saɪ it's a good idea to know clearly what your inclinations are so that you caɪ better control your thoughts and actions to your best advantage ... and helɪ society as a whole to do the same if its collective concepts are found wantinɡ

The most fundamental of these systems, ideologies, singularly incorporat not only individual values but philosophies as well. So it's necessary tɪ define a philosophy first (values defined on page 117) in order to describ an ideology: a philosophy *is a body of principles* (fundamental laws and or assumptions) underlying a branch of learning, the prominent formal ones being on ontology, ethics, religion, aesthetics, logic, economics, politics and sociology. An ideology is *an intellectual pattern* of a culture, group or individual that combines values with philosophies held, consciously or not, on the last three—economics, politics and sociology.

In economics there are seven basic theories of distributive justice (theories of how to divide social material benefits and burdens where there's some measure of scarcity), one or more providing the foundation of the five major economic philosophies. The seven are:

1. To each an equal share: *egalitarianism*;
2. To each according to fundamental need, e.g., a safety net;
3. To each according to rights: the *libertarian* thesis of the right to social and economic liberty unimpeded by governmental regulation or taxing;
4. To each according to individual effort;
5. To each according to merit;
6. To each according to social contribution;
7. Any mix of the six that will maximize public and private benefit and minimize harm: *utilitarianism*.

And the five economic philosophies are:[d]

- **Classical liberalism**—the pure libertarian laissez-faire of Adam Smith stressing the law of supply and demand (market forces), the power of self-interest, and survival of the fittest.
- **Neoliberalism**—the same as classical with a few changes to fit today's circumstances: market forces will solve all, including inequities and responsibilities; government intervention is acceptable only to manage the money and see that the rules of competition are obeyed. Its leading advocates are Milton Friedman who objects to even to licenses for doctors (purportedly an AMA monopoly) and Robert Nozick who philosophically objects to *all* government action except to protect fundamental human rights.
- **Conservatism**—a form of neoliberalism in that it is based on its premises but at the same time accepts the social and statutory changes to date that have worked well for and not adversely to me; the key thrust: maintenance of the status quo or return to when it was better for me.
- **Reform liberalism**—neoliberalism modified by adding social responsibility, social justice, and human rights, with a reliance on law, fiscal policy, and unions to correct the inequities that would be caused by unrestrained market forces; the best known proponent is Keynes.

- **Marxism**—a pure egalitarian principle of distributive justice, a philosophy that the individual has an economic right to an equal share of production based on a concept of equal material need (not solely a fundamental need as per the table on page 143).

The political and social philosophies that are most relevant to ideologies are essentially econo-socio-political amalgams, the dominant ones being:[e]

Capitalism, an application of the libertarian classical laissez-faire not found today in its pure form, though the word is loosely applied to the neo- and reform types. It is a private enterprise economic system energized by expectations of profit and wealth, largely unfettered by economic and legal limitations (relate to the definition of "greed" on page 120).

Socialism, a leftist interpretation of reform liberalism that imposes state control over social functions but allows free enterprise for non-social ones.

Social democracy, the combination of socialism and reform liberalism that has free enterprise for most social functions as well and includes the safety net "justice of enough" to be described on page 161.

Communism (pure), socialism with no free enterprise, every function considered to be social requiring centrally controlled social-based goals and planning. The view of egalitarians—equality of both kind and degree.

And the mix of philosophies in any one ideology reveals its principal thrust, the subject and its view always considered by the society and its indoctrinated members to be crucial to their survival and progress. Ordinarily members unconsciously adopt their society's or group's views that themselves evolve unplanned from its experiences and developing mores. But of course individuals are quite capable of consciously thinking through their own and, when in conflict with the society's, capable of influencing the society's thinking, at least by means of minority groupings.

Again, with ideologies themselves we have levels—an institutional and a personal one. At the institutional level, two have been identified in corporate management:[13]

- *The classical ideology*, based on the classical liberalism philosophy, manifesting a strong hostility to government and a conviction that management's responsibility is to stockholders only.
- *The managerial ideology*, that lands between the neo-liberalism and reform liberalism with a sense of responsibility toward employees and society as well as the stockholders (who remain first) and an acceptance of and cooperation with the government.

And on the personal level the pertinent ones encountered are *individualism* and *communitarianism,* two that are so important they should be examined closely.

The ideology of John Locke some 300 years ago depicted the essence of the former: a combination of self-centered self-reliance, private property, free competition, and minimum government regardless of population density and societal complexity.

Communitarianism, in contrast, sees the individual as an inseparable part of a community:[14]

> Individual fulfillment and self respect are the result of one's place in an organic social process. A well designed group makes full use of our capacities ... government must set the community's goals and coordinate their implementation. The perception of reality requires an awareness of whole systems and of the interrelationships.

One can immediately imagine the threat the latter might be to someone committed to the former, that it appears to constitute no less than submission to conformity and Sartre's "nothingness."

It must be evident also that the choice or mix a manager makes between the two will have a major impact on the person's conceptions about leadership, especially power, authority, control, participation, interpersonal relations, and an organization's responsibilities toward employees and society. However, because, as said, people usually adopt their ideologies unconsciously from their society, what they do adopt is sometimes in conflict with other convictions they hold consciously—the "professed" vs. "in-use" dichotomy. A subtle management example of the individualism/communitarianism subject is the widespread belief in the rightness and value of decision participation but very little genuine application of it.

The business article just quoted pointed out two additional reasons why coming to a conscious personal decision on ideology is especially important right now: the significance of the ideology to the success of the society as a whole, and the transition from the individualism to communitarianism that's taking place now with little appreciation of its occurrence or importance:

> Ideology legitimizes a community's institutions—business, government, universities, or whatever—and thus it underlies the authority and the rights of those who manage the institutions. It is a particularly useful concept in the United States today, because (as many believe) we are in the midst of an ideological transition.

> Pretending to lack an ideology, we have ignored it (and) a society that ignores ideological change may promote the anarchy that inevitably leads to totalitarian temptations; history is replete with examples of active, planning states that imprison as well as plan. There may also arise problems of motivation in a society where the necessities are provided for all.

How far our own society should go toward communitarianism—the blend of the two best for its long-range welfare—will clearly depend on what its leaders develop as personal ideologies.

Interestingly, a potent movement on the subject is now underway and gaining momentum, "The Communitarian Network" in Washington D.C., with a widely distributed 10-point platform "The Responsive Communitarian Platform: Rights and Responsibilities" and a quarterly journal called "The Communitarian Reporter" (much credit for all to founding father Amitai Etzioni).

Two paragraphs in the platform combined explain its goals: "A communitarian perspective recognizes that the preservation of individual liberty depends on the active maintenance of the institutions of civil society where citizens learn respect for others as well as self-respect; where we acquire a living sense of our personal and civic responsibilities, along with an appreciation of our own rights and the rights of others. The basic communitarian quest for balances between individuals and groups, rights and responsibilities, and among the institutions of state, market, and civil society is a constant ongoing enterprise."

Note too the impact of personal ideology within organizations, that what is at stake is the relationship of the individual and organization in a holistic sense: "A corporate tradition that encourages freedom of inquiry, supports personal values, and reinforces a focused sense of direction can fulfill the need for individuality along with the prosperity and success of the group. Without such corporate support, the individual is lost, doesn't know how to act . It is management's challenge to be sensitive to individual needs and direct and focus them for the benefit of the group as a whole."[15]

Value orientations.   Suppose you as head of a unit or organization are trying to plan a growth strategy for the next 5 years, knowing you need the concurrence and commitment of your top team of executives for it to succeed, but you find you have irreconcilable people. What's wrong and what can be done about it?

A recent *Harvard Business Review* article gave an excellent illustration of how to answer both questions.[16] The value orientations of people can apparently be sufficiently different to account for such problems, and to resolve them one can find out what the orientations are and with the knowledge collaboratively develop a plan that, by accounting for the differences, is acceptable to all.

A well-known psychological test called the "Study of Values" by Allport, Vernon and Lindzey[17] proved to be ideally suited to the identification task. It's based on six classifications provided back in the 1920s by the German philosopher Edvard Spranger.[18]

- The *theoretical*: their primary interests are truth, systematic ordering, critical intellectual reasoning; both beauty and utility are secondary.
- The *economic*: G.W. England's "pragmatic," principally concerned with business, profits, economic resource utilization, accumulation of wealth.
- The *aesthetic*: their chief interests are in form, harmony, the artistic aspects of life.
- The *social*: love of people, altruism, kindness; the golden rule dominates; to them the three types above are cold.
- The *political*: power, not necessarily in politics, is the primary orientation in whatever area the individual functions, driving the person to gain greater influence, control, recognition.
- The *religious*: they seek to relate themselves to the universe in a meaningful way, have a mystical orientation and may feel strongly about imperatives.

The average normal adult with at least a high school education is a fairly balanced mix of the descriptions, ranging from 10 to 20 percent each of the total. No one is ever wholly one type, but most people do stress one over the other in their thinking, decisions, and actions.

The test can uncover which one is dominant in an individual and the proportional weight given each. The two Harvard Business School writers of the article gave it to about 1,000 executives attending the Advanced Management and other programs at Harvard over a period of 4 years[f] and supplemented it with additional questions to determine their impact on the respondents' managerial judgment and decision-making.

Figure 5.6a shows a sampling of the results the average profile produced, indicating the average was dominantly economic, and what four of the other dominant types in the sample looked like, the views of three of them graphically portrayed in 5.6b. One can see that the research mangers, the middle of the three, gave themselves a 49 on theoretical values while the executives rated them a very high 60; at the same time, the scientists saw the researchers as 48 and the researchers saw the scientists as 60 and so on.

The supplemental questions then revealed that the dominant orientation would indeed influence their judgments and decisions, biasing them toward the orientation. For examples of a top executive's views:

- On growth rate, a dominantly *social* profile would prefer the more intimate environment of slow growth to the more impersonal one of fast growth and large size.
- On basic product strategy, a dominantly *aesthetic* profile would want top quality with aesthetic appeal and would tend to oppose any competition on price.

Average Profile

Value	Score
Economic	45
Theoretical	44
Political	44
Religious	39
Aesthetic	35
Social	33
	240

Value Profiles for Four Top Executives

Mr. A		Mr. B		Mr. C		Mr. D	
Value	Score	Value	Score	Value	Score	Value	Score
Religious	57	Theoretical	65	Aesthetic	48	Economic	58
Political	41	Aesthetic	45	Social	44	Political	49
Theoretical	36	Religious	37	Economic	43	Theoretical	37
Economic	36	Political	33	Theoretical	36	Religious	37
Aesthetic	35	Economic	32	Political	35	Social	31
Social	35	Social	28	Religious	34	Aesthetic	28

Figure 5.6a

Self Ratings Versus Ratings From Others

	SCIENTISTS			RESEARCH MANAGERS			EXECUTIVES
THEORETICAL	51	60	48	49	60	41	44
ECONOMIC	41	41	51	44	46	55	45
AESTHETIC	38	42	32	37	39	34	35
SOCIAL	34	28	31	32	27	31	33
POLITICAL	41	38	50	42	37	51	44
RELIGIOUS	35	31	28	36	31	28	39

Figure 5.6b

- On marketing strategy, a dominantly *theoretical* would tend to insist on strict truth and integrity in advertising, regardless of the industry's universal degree of puffery.

The article authors demonstrated the influences with a case they'd experienced. A perceptive president of a medium size research and development firm had a pretty good idea of his own values, that they were almost equally balanced among economic, scientific and human relations concerns and that he liked working closely and productively with a tightly knit, involved group. He had drafted the following three alternative long-range growth strategies and presented them to his three-man top team, feeling that their agreement with and commitment to the final choice was crucial to implementation and the future of the firm:

1. Attempt to triple over the next three to five years the company volume of business by broadening its base of research "products," capturing a larger share of the then growing government expenditures for space exploration.
2. Aim for the same growth objective, but achieve it through the development of commercially exploitable hardware products generated in the research activity.
3. Aim for a slower rate of growth, continuing the business along the lines in which it had achieved its present position.

Three long arduous meetings were held and proved fruitless; each executive selected a different strategy without concession to the others. So the president felt his only recourse was to dig deeper into the reasons for their differences of opinion and find out on what points each might be willing to yield a little. His conclusions (mentally going through a procedure for each along the lines of the Allport test): Executive 1 was a businessman-scientist and favored the first because he wanted economic size but wanted the firm remain a research company. Executive 2 was a wholly economic man and favored the second. Executive 3 was so completely a scientist (theoretical), commercial products or bureaucratic size alarmed him and he wanted only the third strategy.

Though he himself favored the first alternative, the president modified the third to a doubling of size in 5 years within the same lines as the present ones, the consensus he sought was achieved, and the subsequent implementation success indicated to him that the decision was sound.

In sum, the HBR article attempted to make managers more aware of four points:

- The impact of one's dominant value category on attitudes and decisions.
- The potential gains, especially for leaders, of being sensitive to and knowledgeable about the dominant category of oneself and those one deals with.
- The dominant value is usually not a great deal more potent than the others, adding to the danger of using the categories as stereotypes.
- The fact that we can misjudge the opinions of others (Figure 5.6b), and how we can correct it.

Philosophy and moral values. Among the philosophies in the definitions on pages 135-136, the factor of direct concern to managers in their dealings with people is of course ethics, which, because of the subject, has to be a system of moral values. One's own system is generally assembled unconsciously over time from education, experience, models and observation is the best way to cope with interpersonal situations, treat people, and make decisions that involve or affect people. So as a first step toward better coping, judgments, and decisions, it would appear wise to bring to full consciousness the true nature of your own moral philosophy and values.

But there will still remain the question whether or not a connection exists between the *morality* of people-decisions and the decisions' effectiveness, especially in gaining compliance and commitment. If moral decisions can be shown to produce positive results and immoral ones negative results, we'd have the answer.

True, that still wouldn't prove that philosophy is the only route to finding out what is and isn't moral. In fact, most behavioral scientists are convinced they can get to it or have gotten to it, at least understand what's involved, via their research. So let's first look at what they've done.

The scientists. Knowing that the action necessary to induce a person to positive effort (let alone commitment) is motivation, psychologists and behaviorists even well before Freud (probably clued in by Aristotle) have also known that the core factor is human needs. But only in the last 30 years or so have they developed the clear picture of them portrayed in the chart below, including as shown the determination of what is and isn't learned, and we now appreciate too the linkage between motives, needs, and values.

Physiological and Psychological Needs

Unlearned		Learned
(1)	*(2)*	*(3)*
Physiological Maintenance Drives	Psychological Maintenance Motives	Psychological Maintenance and Self-actualiz. Motives
Breathing	Consciousness	Affiliation
Eating	Cognition	Competence
Drinking	Activity	Achievement
Sleeping	Exploration/	Power
Maintenance of	Curiosity	Status
temperature tolerance	Manipulation	Recognition
Avoidance of pain	Security/safety	Appreciation
Safety (short-range)	(long-range)	Prestige
Sex	Affection	Self-esteem
	Nurturance	Autonomy
		Creativity ⎫ Higher-
		Responsibility ⎬ order
		Self-actualization ⎭ needs

Figure 5.7

"Higher-order" here is in terms of the Maslow hierarchy. Some behaviorists have used it to mean a cluster of needs, e.g, oxygen + food + water = a higher-order survival need. Others have said they are the intrinsic needs, those that only the individual can satisfy.

The table itself defines "needs" for us, though it doesn't distinguish them from "wants," which the scientists have either overlooked or incorrectly assumed most people have thought through; take a quick glance ahead at pages 160-161 if you're not sure. A *motive* is an internal state based on personal needs that energizes and directs one toward a particular goal. And a value, as explained, is a normative standard that guides one's behavior with regard to both oneself and others. (Future references to values will be the social ones, moral or immoral, when "social" is not stated.) Naturally the needs, and consequent motives, play a major part in molding one's standards, therefore *values*, in the process of maintaining one's internal harmony among goals, behavior, and conscience.

As for the values-needs connection one has but to observe how each of the needs in column #3 above will be frustrated in one way or another by virtually any of the value misconceptions on page 118. And the annals of behavior research are packed with evidence on the needs-motives connection. However, there's also plenty of on-the-job evidence about which little is said, that negative results frequently occur when the right actions for satisfaction *are* administered; examples: when power granted to one is a violation of rights of others, the delegation of autonomy to one is an injustice to others, treating all in a group equally is demotivating to the more competent, or untruthful compliments result in mistrust to describe only obvious ones.

The fact is that psychology scientists in their concentration on *observable* behavior have not given us all the information we need to consistently and successfully motivate; they omitted the unobservable abstracts, in particular justice, equality, liberty, truth, and goodness—all related to psychological needs. The scientists left them out for lack of research susceptibility. Motivating subordinates is not just a matter of filling the needs they've described in the ways they've recommended; misjudging or mismanaging any of these abstracts in people-decisions can mess up the best of intentions.

However, a change in the discipline has been taking place. Prior to Lawrence Kohlberg's 1969 exposition of stages of social cognitive development and the research described on pages 122-124 the subject of morality was largely ignored, even frowned upon; it was considered a function of social learning and a consequence of conditioning. But since then interest has been growing, one encounters an increasing amount of research and books on the subject (for example, the research and references in the book in footnote 20), and a journal was even started in England in 1971.[g]

Kohlberg's work was a major milestone for several reasons, especially his determination of the presence of stages of social cognitive development, his solid empirical support of them through stage 4 (stages 5 and 6 relying more on theory), the incontrovertible movement from stage to stage, the universality of the process, and the apparent irreversibility.[19]

But he also injected for the first time the concept of *moral cognitive development* with a theory of moral development that he claimed the data showing the cognitive development process supported with equal validity, backing it up with the research on pages 122-124.

Two definitions are necessary to understand what's involved, one on cognitive development per se and one on the movement from stage to stage:[20]

Cognitive development means increasing ability to comprehend what is relevant to the social perspective-taking and reasoning process of relating to reality, and increasing the capacity to organize and reorganize conceptualization and construal to take account of this comprehension.

Stage transition involves the breaking down of the cognitive structure built by the development process within a stage, and the development of a new more complex and more differentiated structure that can accommodate the latest learning that overloaded the earlier structure.

The question at stake: is moral cognitive development incorporated in general cognitive development (which by definition must involve conclusions concerning morality), or is it produced by additional forces in the individual? Kohlberg theorized the latter and that there are principally four factors involved: normative order, utility, ideal self, and justice, with justice the core element and major additional force.

Others disagree. Psychologist Helen Weinreich-Haste (referred to in the footnote for the definitions above), for example, has stated, "The data do not support the view that there is a 'moral domain' with special characteristics." And the reliance of the whole process on growth through the combination of social perspective-taking, reasoning and reality seems to support her stand.[21]

Nonetheless, the reader now has from science two of the four parts needed for management decision-making on social issues:

- The Figure 5.7 knowledge supplied by orthodox psychologists from observable behavior—part of the *content* needed, that is, part of "what" has to be learned;
- The social cognitive development *process* of relating to reality providing valuable information on "how" to teach the "what."

Still missing is the unobservable abstract part of the *content* an convincing evidence that moral decisions are more effective than immora ones. A sound foundation on which to build the answers can be obtaine from the philosophers.

The Philosophers. It's difficult for many, especially the very religiou to accept the fact that there are no absolute values (page 119), a fact tha applies also to value systems, and then to accept too that not only are al values and philosophies relative but that they're constantly changing. If yo want to keep your own views current for best interpersonal results, you' have to allow yourself to be convinced of these points in order to be ope to changing what you've been taught or have learned. A brief look at th history of philosophy should convince one of this changeability, showin that it is integral to its cultural function.

From tribal days, humans have apparently had the intelligence to wonde "what is the meaning of life and its purpose," and in the beginning thei societies intuitively supplied rudimentary answers in terms of essentia activities, particularly the need to survive against the elements and prevai against enemies, e.g., to build shelters, hunt, raise a strong family (especiall sons), be brave in battle, fashion good weapons, be truthful, and be loya to the hierarchy.

The consequence was a close cause-effect relationship between all neede activities of the community and its general rules of behavior:[22]

> In its early stage, morality boiled down to 'doing the done thing' ... primitive ethics was *deontological*, a matter of rigid duties, taboos, customs and commandments imposed by those in authority for enforcing cooperation; there was no room for criticism.

> However, the methods used in primitive communities to harmonize the desires and actions of their members were very crude, although they may at first have done their job, something always happened to throw them in doubt.

Conflicts in the rules came to light, changes occurred in the community and contacts were made with other communities having different codes, al i of which raised questions about the inconsistencies and the rightness o some . I of the rules involved. The authorities would stand their groun for a while until additional change forced replacement of either the rule or the rulers, and the confrontation started a process by which many mora codes and behavioral decisions even today emerge from conflicts between people of interest or of decision dilemmas, that of *teleology*, the reasoning through of what it would take to produce the best results. The consequence was to complement the deontology such that in unambiguous case deontology's specific rules and duties remained mandatory, but in equivoca ones the teleology recommended the more general approach of using logic to come up with the best end-result for those involved or affected.

Each of these two concepts had over time two stages of development forming the basic structure or philosophy. Their essence in outline:

Deontology (moral duties, rules)
The classic, as described above and as promoted by religions (God's will).
The modern, especially Kant's "Categorical Imperative" as fundamental (1791). More on it ahead (pp. 172-173).
Note: both deal with specific personal behavior for interpersonal relations, for the welfare of others, and the interest is morality, not happiness.

Teleology (purpose, results)
The classic of Plato and Aristotle that one's objective should be a good life, one of happiness, obtainable only through good behavior, good a fundamental absolute. To Plato it would result from knowledge, to Aristotle by the development of reasoned-through virtues; they would answer the two key questions:

- What is the good life for a person?
- How should a person behave to achieve it?

In sum, how should one live, not asking about specific acts for specific situations, but requiring reflection on life as a whole. More on Aristotle ahead.
The modern, especially the utilitarian of Bentham and Mill (in the 1700s). Good is not viewed as absolute, and virtues are not addressed; the heart of it is reasoning toward good ends for collective welfare: in any moral decision maximize the happiness and/or benefits for the greatest number of people.
Note: both the classic and modern deal with general not specific requirements, and both are purposive, deemphasizing moral obligation and implying the self-interest importance of basic moral rules.

Of course, all philosophies regardless of category have, as they've advanced down through the ages, been the philosophers' answers to how individuals and societies can attain individually and collectively the goal of "a good life." But in the West they haven't kept up to date along the way. In the last thousand years our Western civilization advanced at such an accelerating rate—from blue paint on the face to knights in armor and on to the industrial revolution—that experiences and knowledge continuously outpaced current established beliefs, values and philosophies. A chasm developed between cause and effect and between the real world and professed ideals, so reinterpretations were required time after time to reduce it to tolerable proportions.

Providing the reinterpretations has been the main function and service of the philosophers, that is, giving us the intellectual follow-on to cultural change due to progress, and the task has been made exceedingly difficult by the necessity to reassess knowledge itself due to its evolving changes from *certainty* to *uncertainty* to *ignorance.*

For example, for centuries to the middle of the last one, certainty was attributed to all physical and moral laws, both types believed wholly independent of the constantly changing environment around them. Reality was believed known or knowable, the clarity of Darwin's explanation of evolution reinforced the belief as recently as 1859.

In the second half of the century, however, scientists began to question the absoluteness of many of their supposedly universal laws; uncertainty was setting in. The more perceptive philosophers took notice, began to wonder if moral laws also were susceptible to doubt.

Then at the start of the twentieth century, Einstein supplied the telling blow to the absolutists by making apparent the extent to which we are condemned beyond uncertainty, to ignorance. The intangibles of time, space and cosmology became essential considerations in any theory about humanity, and a large part of reality was recognized as unknowable. The realization spread that the scientific method and our limited senses can go just so far, and beyond that point it's like giving a fly a calculus problem to solve.

The reaction of some philosophers was "philosophical analysis," a kind of turning-within escape, but nonetheless a sorely needed return to the basics of defining what they really meant by right, wrong, good, bad, and key philosophy phrases, and of spelling out the assumptions behind statements and theories. It is now acknowledged to be a necessary professional tool of every philosophical endeavor.

Nevertheless, one parallel of ethics philosophy to science was well recognized if only intuitively, that just as science hypotheses on uncertainties and unknowns are necessary to forge ahead in science, so too philosophies on the uncertainties and unknowns of ethics serve the same purpose in human behavior. Constant societal change in its many forms, as said, necessitates repeated modifications of ethics philosophies to maintain their validity. Indeed, the forced continuous reassessment and updating should help answer why the philosophers have never conclusively explained the riddles of the universe. (There's a note of ironic logic in T.S. Eliot's statement that the purpose of life, the most perplexing of the riddles, is to find the purpose.) Surely they seem to have presented us with more questions than answers on all subjects and in so doing remind us that, as in all problem-solving, the right questions not only have to precede the right answer, but they add valuable insights into the problem.

Two important general characteristics of the great philosophers that will help understand them: first, they always took their own cultures as given and starting points for their thinking, accepting the majority of the values and behavior of the societies. New philosophies have never been truly new, only modifications, largely reflecting the changes they proposed in the values and behaviors they found unacceptable.

Second, most of the classical philosophers tended to claim their one concept to be the unconditional solution to all situations, which fits the belief of the earlier philosophers in absolutes, but it's a flaw of some of the moderns too. However, each who has survived in the literature contributed something significant to the solution of major ethical problems and is therefore important reading for a comprehensive picture of particular ethical topics.

As for the philosophies themselves, historians have loosely divided them into two categories, classical and modern, most known by the leading proponent, some as schools of thought. Those who have contributed concepts of particular importance to the management of people are:

Classical Philosophers		Modern Philosophers(ies)	
Plato	Spinoza	Bergson	Existentialism
Aristotle	Kant	James	"Good reason"
Epicurus	Bentham (J. S.)	Dewey	Fromm
Christ	Mill		

There is no precise dividing line between the two, but it's usually placed at the time of the mid-19th century philosophical rebellion in America against the European metaphysical theories, views that seemed to have lost touch with the social and intellectual changes that had taken place on both sides of the Atlantic.

Certainly for management applications, managers or students needn't swamp themselves with a detailed knowledge of all 14, each of which has been built to some extent on those that preceded it. In fact one can get the basics of what is required from only the few mentioned ahead within the discourse on the three specific moral philosophies most relevant to leadership, those on:

"The nature of man."
Why be moral?
Authority.

But first, one final point on all is worth noting: the impact over tim of the social sciences on all ethics philosophies. Psychology, sociology, an anthropology are, we know, also about human thought and behavior bu are *descriptive*; they treat the what, how, and why of the subjects, a compared to ethics' *normative* nature which deals with the "ought" o rightness, wrongness, goodness, and badness. The former influences th latter through the need of the latter to reflect reality. Logically, ethica principles, and therefore moral judgments based on them too, will be cleare and sounder the more they reflect the facts developed by the sciences correspondingly, as the philosophies incorporate the new knowledge, the naturally become more convincing, indeed more "certain" for that poin in time.

"The nature of man"[h] How many times have you yourself thought abou the unsatisfactory performance of a subordinate and fairly quickl concluded the person is either incompetent, indifferent, or lazy, being sur you don't have to look deeper? And perhaps your own boss has at time had the same thoughts about you.

Can a simple set of thoughts or ideas like that have anything to do wit philosophy? Surprisingly enough to even many progressive-thinkin people, it definitely does. Indeed, personal judgments, regardless of wha they are, are commonly based on our most elementary one of all, th judgment about the true nature of the human, about whether people ar fundamentally good or evil.

In fact most of us, as managers or not, would come to this same conclusio without appreciating that a force of philosophy that lodged in our mind long ago predetermines it, and moreover that the force has a lot to do wit our ability to relate to and motivate others because of the resultan assumptions we hold about everything they do.

So it would pay to become fully aware of what we actually believe, wher it leads, and how well it concurs with reality. Of course the ingeniousnes of the mind to rationalize our view, especially if it is the predominan philosophy of society, will make alteration difficult. But if the las subsection sufficiently conveyed the possibility of either your own or a whol society's philosophy being obsolete, and that, by extension, your own min might therefore be in need of change, a look at the history of this particula concept and how the sciences have updated it may suggest modification for greater personal effectiveness.

Footnote f on page 73 outlines this history, and finding out why i happened that way will help explain the consequences of locating philosophy at each spot on the good-evil continuum and therefore help t determine the best place to be for the kind of results you want.

As stated there, the historians have recorded a progression of four stages of thought on the subject of what we are like, entitling them Basic Conflict Man, Psychodynamic Man, Behavioristic Man, and Humanistic Man, the first two alleging an instinctive tendency to be evil.

The ancient philosophers, who were also the religious leaders of their time, originated the *Basic Conflict Man* concept as the answer to much of the inexplicable about the human. We also know that religions have passed it down in the doctrine of original sin in which there's a battle of good and evil drives within us to control the mind. It had the convenient advantage of providing control by fear, a fear of the supernatural, which is still a major force in many societies, especially in underdeveloped countries.

Furthermore, belief was continually reinforced by the simple observation of how people react to the laws and orders of their rulers, that fear was the only thing keeping them in line. So the classical philosophers continued the idea, the dominant Western legal system was based on it (Napoleonic law stating that one is guilty until proven innocent), and even economists adopted it to help solve their problems.

The ultimate *negative* philosophy on how leaders should deal with this evil nature was of course Machiavelli's self-serving treatises, *The Prince* and *The Discourses,* published in 1530,[i] and it wasn't for another century that constructive contributions of any persuasiveness emerged that intelligently countered his recommendations.

The first was Thomas Hobbes' *Leviathan* of 1651. Picking up Plato's social contract idea, he said that individuals covet power, prestige, and material goods and will get them at their discretion. As a result, they will produce chaos and mayhem if they don't enter into a social contract of governing laws to keep the peace.

Then there was a lapse of 75 years when an economics philosopher came to the fore. Adam Smith (who also wrote on ethics) in *Wealth of Nations* (1776) stated that although people are inclined to be evil, you can count on reason and self-interest. In a social environment, a law of economics takes hold—the allocation of resources by supply, demand, and price; so the best econo-political philosophy is "laissez-faire."

But there was no challenge by a philosopher of any stripe to the idea of inherent evil until the twentieth century, and of course organizational leaders and managers adopted it as the justification of their authoritarianism. Indeed, the high point of its acceptance in management was its formalization in the first decade by Max Weber in Europe followed by Frederick Taylor in the United States.

With this notion in mind, Weber concluded that workers have to be viewed as cogs in the organizational machine—he was the first to label them collectively as bureaucracies—who should be tightly controlled by means of an authoritarian hierarchy, written policies, rules, and impersonality (1904). In fact, "The more the bureaucracy is dehumanized," he said, "the more completely it succeeds in eliminating from official business love, hatred, and all purely personal, irrational and emotional elements which escape calculation." Furthermore, the more successful the dehumanizing the more it succeeds in securing the desired "stability, continuity and predictability of product."[23]

Historians have labeled this Weber's "bureaucratic model" of how to manage, and it's obviously the origin of some of our worst managing misconceptions. The Englishman Babbage is also entitled to some credit for suggesting some of these ideas as far back as 1850.

Most students of management know that Taylor promoted the concepts as "scientific management" (1909). The employee, he said, is a "constant" of fixed nature in the production equation. He or she is prone to inefficiency and waste unless properly programmed, is lazy and wholly self-interested, but is also fiercely competitive with peers. To gain a worker's full potential, therefore, tight controls and external motivation must be applied. Recent surveys have shown that the large majority of prominent business leaders of major corporations still hold these beliefs today in a general way with only minor modification if any.

At about the same time, the first science explanation was developed, that of Sigmund Freud. But he too held to the same basic conflict and evil nature concepts with his *Psychodynamic Man* (described on page 49), the closed system of id, ego, and superego that pessimistically portrayed the human as primarily emotional and often out of control of the self.

Shortly after, however, his theory's omissions (especially external forces and learning) and principal weaknesses (e.g., the use largely of intuition, insufficient samples, and observations from the abnormal only) were appreciated, and the behaviorists, led by John B. Watson and Clark Hull, began to be influential. Through observation of overt behavior, stimulus-response (S-R) analysis sprung up and *Behavioristic Man* became the general explanation.

This school of thought had two phases. The early behaviorists seemed mainly to *react* to Freud's introspection and turn wholly to external stimulation in interaction with our "instinctive" drives and emotions; concentration was on the "S" of the S-R equation.

Research progress[j] then led to the realization that things were a lot more complicated, producing the second phase, the "modern" behaviorists. They recognized that the highly complex person in the middle and the many variations that personality traits can cause had been ignored. Moreover, on closer analysis of the "R," they concluded that not only was the idea of instinct too simplistic but that there was another factor, one of primary importance, following the "R" that had been overlooked—the "reinforcement" that the response brought about, the phenomenon described on pages 83-86.

The key development in all this was a new understanding of learning and of an individual's ability to do it in a much more complex manner than animals. It became apparent that although instincts[k] may be developments in the small brains of animals necessary to their basic survival needs, our brains have been advanced to such competence that the characteristic disappeared long ago—just as one's body no longer needs the appendix. We transcended instincts probably somewhere between "lowbrow" homo erectus (c. 5 million B.C.) and homo sapiens (c. 200,000 B.C.), and probably because automatic responses are clearly restrictive and dangerous when inappropriate. The more obvious researched "proof" we now have indicates that not only is there often a lack of correlation between supposed instinct "dispositions" and behavior that should have occurred, but also the wide range of "disposition" strengths in different people cannot be fitted into an instinct concept.[1]

Modern behaviorists therefore hold that although we do have some unlearned drives of hunger, thirst, sex, sleep, and the like as implied in the Maslow theory and shown on page 143, the pieces of information that are available about them indicate they probably are largely unlearned motivations, unexplainable due to our present inability to really fathom the unconscious; all other drives are learned. Thus in their view we do not have any instincts to be evil *or* good; we start out neutral, as described in the often ignored philosophic proposal of John Locke back in the seventeenth century: one's mind at birth is like a blank page.

Plainly, these modern behaviorists had achieved a quantum leap forward in understanding "the nature of man" even though they still had quite a way to go. In addition to the above point, they showed us, first, that behavior is always preceded by the cause, that is, a stimulus in the environment; second, that behavior is an interaction of prior learning with the stimulus confronting us; and, third, that some "wattage" (reinforcement) may be generated along with the response, a fact that can be utilized to reproduce desired behavior or discourage undesirable behavior.

But their findings had no impact at all on applied leadership behavior until after the great depression of 1929. As the industrial revolution picked up steam from the middle of the nineteenth century on, leaders and workers mutually agreed that there was an evil intent of the other, Adam Smith's view and solution suited those in economic and political power to a T, and societies on both sides of the Atlantic took the painful lumps of laissez-faire's abuses without much complaint, as if they were a necessary part of the burden of life (which Samuel Beckett called a terminal illness, a misdeal!).

Coincidentally, the great Hawthorne experiment began just before it in 1927, and by the time of its completion in 1932 the study had prompted a considerable interest in organization behavior and the true nature of workers.

Though the interpretations of Hawthorne were uncertain at first, three points were quite clear within a short period: (1) the scientific management principles of Weber and Taylor (based on evil man) were seriously myopic; (2) the human side of the work organization is very complex and must be studied with behavioral research techniques; and (3) a key determinant of worker satisfaction and productivity is the *climate* created by supervision. The "Human Relations" school was born.

So when the crash occurred, the stage was set for a fairly ready acceptance to change particularly regarding the school's recommendations. Still, only the most progressive firms made a serious effort to test its principles, and at that, within a few years the whole effort ground to a halt. The behaviorists had sold them on the idea that a "be nice" approach to employees can improve performance, an idea concluded from the Hawthorne experience with insufficient double-checking on their assumptions. It didn't work. More will he given on it in Chapter 8.

But the organizational experience was well worth it. The new management attitude for the 1930s opened a few doors to the behavioral researchers compared to almost none open formerly, problems were solved in the real world instead of only in laboratories, new managing principles were developed, and even a few senior executives began to realize that workers are no more lazy, apathetic, or evil by nature than they are themselves.

While this small amount of cautious progress was going on within organizations, the momentous controversy among modern behaviorists described on pages 49-55 (under personality theories) was taking place. And particularly noteworthy with regard to "the nature of man" were the contentions of the radical behaviorists, that all our actions, decisions, and behavior are a consequence of environmental conditioning, and that our believed self-control and will power is no more than egocentric self-deception—all convincingly summarized by Skinner in his *Beyond Freedom and Dignity* in which he eloquently attempts to inter "Autonomous Man."

However, the radicals' generalizations from simple lab animals to complex humans were too much for a number of prominent psychologist behaviorists whose combined research and organization experience brought them to very different conclusions—that humans not only have purposiveness toward good but also a capacity for some independent will power.

In fact, they had but to ask, would not the absence of will be as dangerous, with its consequent inability to handle unique situations, as instincts? Their own proposal was *Humanistic Man.* Maslow, understandably was one of them as was Allport, and Rogers' deductions on pages 121-122 make evident that he was also. But the person who seemed to tie it all together best was Eric Fromm whose summary of it (in 1947) well suits the explanation of the alternatives for a philosophy of authority, so it will be described there (on pages 166-169).

From this point on the development of the science of organization behavior began to take off at an accelerating pace, led particularly by Kurt Lewin, Douglas McGregor, and Chris Argyris. That humans have a tendency toward good underlies all their contributions, and they eminently validated it through the consultative application of their research findings, raising the "good" trait from nebulous philosophical insight to a reliable principle of behavior.

This is not to say that all scientists now agree. Physiologists in general, for example, especially those studying aggression, are as yet quite pessimistic. Says one, "Man has innate neural and endocrine organizations which when activated result in hostile thoughts and behaviors ... whether man is born good or evil is a value judgment and depends on the frame of reference of the evaluator."[24] But the fact that such conclusions are drawn almost entirely from research on the drug control of pathological hostility or hyperemotional conditions would seem to disqualify them. The question is, what are the forces in relatively *normal* people?

And there are a fair number of blank-page behaviorists along with the radical behavior determinists. But Skinner himself made statements that appear to be contradictory. For instance, while humans are controlled by their environment, he stated, today it is an environment almost entirely of their own making. "Man as we know him, for better or worse, is what man has made of man... the product of the culture man has devised."[25]

If, as this suggests, and all scientists agree, that every culture strives to induce cooperative, harmonious behavior toward a better, happier way of life, must not the culture makers be basically good?

Let it be summarized here that the end result, the decision-making result, of one's own philosophy of "the nature of man" is inclined to be as follows. If we assume that people are basically evil, we naturally start with the idea that their poor performance or undesirable behavior is caused by something within themselves that neither they nor we can alter. So we decide that the only solution is to apply tight rules and control, limiting their freedom, and to administer penalties for violations.

If we believe they are basically good, we start with the possibility that poor performance or misbehavior may be a reaction to their environment or to management, and we review the whole range of external potential causes first.

Additionally, how you yourself approach human relations problems can help you locate on the good/evil continuum where your true belief about the nature of man lies. (You might ask a good staff behaviorist for an objective analysis.) Having done so, you'll be able to better understand much of your treatment of subordinates and your selection among the leadership style options to be described ahead. Note then also how it influences all your social business relations, your communications, the policies you formulate, and the reward/penalty structures you set up and apply.

Why be moral? We know that, although the long-run gains to society of being so is easy to understand and accept as a general proposition, the personal advantages for the short run are not at all wholly evident to a large percentage of us, Indeed, as long as it looks like—and we're not taught or conditioned to see otherwise—one can gain so much with a little cleverness by being immoral, it's going to continue to be very popular.

But whether for the short- or long-range, personal or organizational, there are many everyday people-decisions made in management based on moral values, some that are very subtle. For example, in time all managers find themselves wondering, if not bluntly asking themselves, about such questions as:

- Should an executive allow subordinate managers to be as "tough" as they want if it seems to get the desired results?
- Do employees actually have a right to participate in decisions affecting them (59% of college students thought so on page 11).
- Is there a moral obligation of superiors to help subordinates develop themselves?
- Isn't it democratically correct to treat all in a group equally?
- Can morality be a factor in an across-the-board pay change?
- What's wrong, if anything, about a manager having "career authority" over subordinates (control over promotions in "The selection system," Chapter 17)?
- Since a subordinate's desk is company property and the person is hired by the firm, isn't it permissible to search the person's desk if you suspect activities contrary to the interests of the firm?
- Why in a hierarchical organization should its management have an obligation to set up a due process for the adjudication of grievances that challenge a benevolent management's judgment?
- It was implied that many in the list of actions on page 19 are unjust. Are they, and why in each case?

Aside from the question of morality, it happens that the wrong decisions or actions in every instance are an unnecessary cost to the organization, and managers brought up with traditional values are most often wrong on them.

But before going into what the morally right decisions are and whether or not "right" will be most effective, if managers do learn what is right from the philosophers or anyone, will that persuade them to change the wrong ones to the right? For the answer, start with a quick review of some points that have already been made from the search for what's in their minds before learning: they either possess on the subjects (a) moral values, (b) immoral values learned in some way or other that they are to their advantage, or (c) no value convictions due to ignorance (lack of experience or learning).

Presenting the connection between (a) and effectiveness is the intent of the discourse; for the moment, consider it a hypothesis to be verified. When (b) is the situation, just getting the information on what is moral will not, we know, change the behavior and decisions; techniques that have to be applied will be described in Part III. But when immoral decisions or actions are due to no convictions or value misconceptions caused by ignorance (c), men and women of goodwill will normally correct them upon learning the missing information if not blocked by a deep-seated contradicting value.[m]

In fact, that is the first step of the most advanced values change techniques, and it alone usually works quite well on task-specific behaviors. But for all the moral decisions and actions that are not task-specific there's often no clear-cut proof of right and wrong, which is the case on most of the nine questions just asked. We have only the logic of motivation by the satisfaction of bone fide basic needs for deciding and doing what is effective, and even that logic often gives us either vague or no help.

The scientists have certainly been on the right track in determining the fundamental motivators in Figure 5.7, but their research tools and rules forced them to stop short of finding out all that is required for the full spectrum of decisions and actions of determining the universal values needed to channel the motives toward morality.

Granted, it had seemed safe to assume that mature adults are well aware (from personal experience, education, and intuition) of what appear to be relatively clear and uncomplicated values in regard to that channeling like honesty, respect, and responsibility, and that a lack of any will yield bad results in interpersonal relations. But aside from the fact that they shouldn't be assumed, should be stressed in training, and seldom are, *liberty, equality,* and *justice,* the three other principal ones in dealing with people (collectively referred to as the "constitutional values"), which may also seem clear, are complex well beyond general realization. Most of us think we know enough about them, may even ask if they have any relevance to management in a hierarchical organization, yet a closer look at the first three questions in the foregoing list (page 156) will make apparent (if not already noticed) that they are principally issues of liberty, the second three of equality, and the last three of justice and rights.

Ironically enough, philosophers demonstrated over 2,000 years ago how they are linked to human needs, which leads to how they're related to decision effectiveness. We know that all societies that have survived down through time have learned through experience and intuition that morality was essential to survival, morality for a long while consisting of only the obvious issues and up to about 500 B.C. imposed entirely by fear of punishment. Then came the Greeks trying to sell the idea through *reason*— Teleology—and every important moral philosopher from then on including deontologists appealed to the use of reason as a basis of principles; reason's function was found to be essential. Indeed, what the Greeks produced was so advanced we've done little better to date. So it's an ideal point from which to start one's thinking, even if one is not interested in morality, only maximum decision effectiveness.

(Parenthetically, all philosophers appreciate the regrettable limitation of all moral philosophy: that you can't sell morality to the amoralist, the irrational, or basically evil; only those already disposed to hear will be receptive, those open to moral discourse and reasoning. Fortunately, the inaccessible are a minority in the organizational world.)

It may be recalled that Plato in his *Republic* attempted to sell morality through Glaucon's discussion with Socrates of the then fashionable attitude that people are by nature evil and will always try to profit at the expense of others.[26]

Socrates had proposed that all evil is due to the lack of knowledge, that knowledge autonomically leads people to the discovery of what is *good*, that knowledge is the essence of the good life, and that with the knowledge people will try to act in ways that will achieve the good life... a view that appears to hold us to be neutral between good and evil.

Glaucon challenged Socrates with the story of Gyges who succeeded in becoming a successful happy king through a series of undetected bloody crimes, asking him to explain why Gyges was less happy than, say, a just, good person who had been accidentally punished for a crime not committed as so often has happened.

Plato clearly appreciated the enigma by posing the question (through Glaucon), but he then responded somewhat evasively (through Socrates) with his "philosophical idealism": *good* is an absolute, independent of the individual; the more people know about it the more "good" and happier they will be whether conscious of it or not and vice versa. Moreover, since this good is the essence of life, there is only one good life for everyone.

Those may be acceptable explanations for some, but it's obvious that having one ideal good life to aim at is a little restrictive; there's also the fact that people often act evilly even though they know what is good and right; and Plato gave little help as to what good really means; moreover, his "ethical egoism" as it came to be called was doomed because the underlying concept of self-interest was intellectually illogical: how can self-interest by sold as morality when morality by definition imposes obligations in the interest of others?

The modern teleological utilitarianism (p. 147), also called "consequentialism," did provide a credible solution to this in requiring consideration for others, but it was criticized for its important inadequacies: its failure to account for justice toward minorities, for conditions, for exceptions, and for the often impossible task of measuring consequences of alternatives needed to make comparisons and implement the concept.

As for deontology, common sense tells us we must hold some basic moral rules as ethical "absolutes" for the species to survive whether or not they can be proved as such, but the imperatives-of-authority idea is not very impressive; we know that those interpreting God's will disagree greatly with each other, and the conscience of even one "good" individual gives conflicting answers; then on codes of conduct, they vary unbelievably with the culture. One South Sea tribe feels it a duty to kill its elderly at a given age. More in the comments about Kant on page 172.

At the same time, teleology and deontology are major tools of philosophical thinking that are ethically applicable in a variety of sub-forms and specific situations, complications that are covered in specialized business ethics texts. Before going into any of them however, ethical problem-solving in general can be greatly aided and simplified by first building a solid foundation on which to stand, a feature that seems to have eluded many of the texts.

Aristotle, one of Plato's younger associates (by some 41 years) at his Academy in Athens, supplied the key ideas. He was not satisfied with the one-good-life idea or with the practice of all Greek philosophers of relying solely on reasoning to develop their answers and theories. In his mind, to get to the truth reality has to be examined, so he innovatively engaged in the first market research for the answers to the two primary philosophical questions posed on page 147, interrogating a large number of people over time and then used the responses to develop his conclusions.[n]

On "what is the good life?" the inevitable response outcome was "happiness," but in his uncanny brilliance (for his time) he traced the fundamental issue back to human desires and then subdivided the desires into needs and wants. Needs, he pointed out, are the universal requirements for survival of all humans—also called real goods—and wants are the subjective other desires, material and emotional—also called apparent goods. Correspondingly, real happiness is based on real goods, apparent happiness on apparent goods.

If one then believes in the sensible rule that everyone has a right to life everyone therefore has a right to the basic needs, the real goods necessary to stay alive, and a right to the pursuit of real happiness, therefore too a right not to be impeded by others in the pursuit.

He further reasoned that, given all the evidence that it is not sufficient for a human just to survive, people have a right to a little more, indeed to live as well as their faculties will allow, doing it through the acquisition both of more real goods than actually needed and of apparent good (therefore a right to both real and apparent happiness), with the constraint that it does not impede others in *their* pursuit of happiness.

Out of these ideas can be seen an evolution of thinking about rights and justice, topics that are so important to human resources management. The good life, Aristotle declared in answer to the first question on page 147, is a life of happiness as described. And to the second he said one should behave so as to achieve happiness with the due regard for others in their own pursuit of it, and to develop the habit of making the right decisions that will produce these results.

The constraint of not impeding others is of course derived from the realization (along with Plato) that we are interdependent social creatures who have to cooperate with each other. So the "due regard" is crucial, and to command appropriate respect for it, societies have for a long time intuitively made it an imperative called justice; the definition: due concern for the rights that include their welfare, individually and collectively as institutions of society. In all instances of injustice to a person it is a violation of rights, and the ultimate injury is the effect it has on his or her happiness.

Thus while real happiness in terms of real goods is the same for all, the happiness he described, refuting Plato's one good life, can vary considerably among people depending on their wants; there's room for much diversity. We see that the right to life leads to the right to the basic needs, to the right to happiness: the pursuit of goods, he said, in the right order (the *real* first) and measure, and in such a way that (a) one's own real goods are not sacrificed and (b) one does not impede others in their pursuit or injure others in any way

Then his major means toward the end of happiness was the concept of virtues that he defined as (paraphrased) ethically admirable dispositions of action, desire, and intent, the principal goals being excellence and self-actualization; examples: knowledge, love, happiness, health, being fair-minded, generous, considerate, courageous, none of them moral rules but each a general characteristic with ethical implications. Thus the interest was less in morality and more in reasoned-through traits that he believed are ssential to happiness, the reasoning a combination of knowledge and wisdom.

This amazing intellect, moreover, also went two important steps further. Recognizing the obvious fact that inordinate success in accumulating the satisfaction of needs and wants can be bad for both the individual and society, he attempted to give the solution with what he called the "Golden Mean," a formula for applying reason to the development of virtues and desired traits (he of course assumed reasonable, well-intentioned individuals). An explanation of it here would be to probe deeper than intended, but a general feel of it might be gained from footnote.°

Second, with regard to the issue of rights, given the assumption of the right to a little more than the needs required to survive, the inevitable question is how much more? What did he mean by "the right measure?" His answer was certainly vague, but it was an important start. "Self-sufficiency and action," he said, "do not involve excess ... even with moderate advantages one can act virtuously ... it is enough."

From then on philosophers have worked on the *enough*, such that today the discipline has given us, if not the quantities, at least the structure of its meaning in the form of a set of principles, a set that might be called 'the justice of enough" (philosophers would call it a philosophy of 'distributive justice"):ᴾ

1. To all equally according to their natural needs; that is, all must be equal on the "enough" base line, the real goods and basic rights.
2. To each in varying degrees according to the function performed or the contribution made.
3. Any may acquire more real goods than needed and as much apparent goods as desired provided doing so does not
   (a) obstruct one's acquisition of any of the natural needs,
   (b) obstruct others from pursuing their happiness, or
   (c) injure others.

#1 and #2 comprise essentially a condensation of our present concept of equality and #1, #2 and #3 together are requisites of liberty.

For *equality*, we know there are two types: personal equalities (by endowment, e.g., being human, and by attainment as through education) and circumstantial equalities (equality of opportunity and equality of conditions—economic, social and political); and for both there are the two dimensions of **kind** (e.g., everyone having a car) and **degree** (everyone having the same number of cars). Certainly both should be, it they aren't already, of great interest to managers and politicians alike, the managers to motivate performances, the politicians for the vote.

Note that pure communism demands equality of both kind and degree while democracy seeks equality of kind but not degree as reflected in #1 an #2. In the #1 one recognizes the idea of treating equals equally, in #2 o treating unequals unequally in which *equality of opportunity* is necessar to facilitate its operation, providing equally favorable circumstances fo unequal talents in order to be fair to personal attributes and self developmen (inequalities) after principle #1 has been satisfied.

Then the #1, #2 and #3 jointly are rights of *liberty*, liberty having 3 types inherent (e.g, free will), acquired (the freedoms gained from education an the habit of making good decisions) and, again, circumstantial (such as thos made possible by birth, luck, being in a free society, etc.). In all they sa that because one has the right to basic needs and the pursuit of happines one has the right to be free to do the pursuing within the limits stipulate in #3.

So this is what the philosophers have given concerning the thre fundamentals (liberty, equality and justice) for dealing with others, makin; it evident that *these three constitutional values are the foundation of mora thinking.* And common sense can tie them to effective decisions. The ke· is reality, the one bona fide absolute in philosophy,[q] and that one absolut· is the basis of our best concepts of ethics; in short-hand form:

The reality	—	The basic needs.
The basic needs	—	They prescribe rights, equality, liberty.
Rights	—	The right to life and to basic needs.
Equality	—	Equality on basic needs and equality of opportunity.
Liberty	—	The freedom to pursue happiness.
Justice	—	The restraints with regard to others' rights and liberty.

Parenthetically, note that justice does not obligate one to help other· obtain their needs or rights, only to refrain from impeding their pursui or receipts; that helping feeling is Fromm's *love*: knowledge + care + respec + responsibility.[29]

Thus we see that justice is not limited (there will never be too much) whereas equality and freedom are. Too much freedom for anyone woul· plainly be dangerous for others, and too much liberty (that is, without th· constraint of justice) results in inordinate power for the "haves" to multipl· their wealth, which is so often at the expense of the "have-nots."

Social democracies like the advanced Western nations and Japan hav· developed a liberal conscience about it all and built a set of guidelines base· on "the justice of enough," guidelines for institutionalizing their fel·

ıbligation to quantitatively aid the pursuit of happiness in terms of their ıational objectives and resources:

(a) Services beyond the individual's capacity to obtain at the quantitative and qualitative levels necessary for the society's welfare and progress: schools, hospitals, fire and police protection, etc.
(b) The "safety net" for events and misfortunes not the fault of the individual: unemployment insurance, social security, disaster assistance, food stamps, shelter for the homeless, etc.

And the sages summarized it very simply some time ago for the individual ın the three-point "natural moral law," concurrent with the, (a), (b), and ıc), and generalization on page 119:

- Seek good and avoid evil.
- Do good and avoid doing evil to others.
- Act for the common good.

Though sounding a bit sanctimonious, one need but look at the ;onsequences for the connection to effective decision-making. A ıubordinate who believes a decision violates his or her rights to basic ıhysiological or psychological needs (Figure 5.7) will understandably not ıe committed to it and may sabotage it, whereas the probabilities are good ‛hat the commitment will be inspired by decisions that are recognized as ıntended to help on those needs, e.g., answering some of the questions on ıage 156:

On liberty, the delegation of autonomy or of participation in decisions that is in the interest of both the individual and organization; helping the person to develop and have the freedom to pursue self-actualization.

On equality, compensating on the basis of contribution; allowing equal opportunity for promotion throughout the organization.

On justice, respect for the rights to privacy; instituting a fair system, or support of it, to insure just treatment of grievances; promotion by competence, not favoritism.

Clearly, people-decisions that follow these precepts would motivate effective performance and inverse decisions would be ineffective—two inevitable equations therefore:

- Good decisions are effective.
- Poor decisions are from ineffective to dysfunctional.

It consequently follows therefore that decisions that attend to human needs and aspirations are good ones, are moral ones, and vice versa. Moral decisions pay, if not obviously in the short run, in the long run; immoral ones cost.

We now have all four values requisites needed for the most effective management decisions on social issues (picking up from page 147):

- The part of the *content* supplied by orthodox psychology—the motivational essentials obtainable from observable behavior (the page 143 table);
- The *process* from cognitive development research;
- The balance of the *content* from philosophy—the unobservable abstract essentials obtained by the same procedure used in the development research: reasoning applied to reality;
- The relationship of moral decisions to *effectiveness*.

Admittedly, a complaint of oversimplification can be charged. The large number of variables involved in many moral decisions can stump the smartest well-intentioned person; and too, there are all those decisions to be made in the gray area (discoursed ahead). But a solid foundation on the basics like this should make it easy on the black and white issues and also provide a great deal of help on the gray.

Of course the absolute *proof* that one should be moral in dealing with others is still missing. But Aristotle himself was well aware of the difficulty of coming up with it, and he gave the clue to what one of the problems of proof on such subjects would always be: it takes a good individual, he said, to know what is good, a point that philosophers since then have appropriately extrapolated. Just as a being must be logical to recognize the force of logical argument (as given here), he or she has to be moral to be moved by moral reasoning.[30]

Nevertheless, we do have such evidence as the cognitive development research on pages 122-124 (Kohlberg) and 143-146 that there's a general correlation of morality with knowledge and maturity. But, the development of knowledge and maturity is obviously long-range, and having them doesn't help on-the-spot argumentation with an intractably evil person. The only immediate answer for coping with those insufficiently moral is structural safeguards and a strong reward-penalty system.

Still, there are those who are too skeptical (or indifferent or jaded?) to accept the idea of morality, are otherwise mature, and do not find this easoning sufficient. For them, one of the most cogent arguments was given ɔ us by, of all people, a determinist, B. F. Skinner (pages 51-52). One doesn't ᴧave to adopt the totality of his determinism while still accepting the xplanation. "In the scientific view," he began, "a person's behavior is ᴅetermined by a genetic endowment traceable to the evolutionary history ᴧf the species and the environmental circumstances."[31] Genes change ᴅecause of the environment, but the process is very slow. Fortunately, ᴧocieties intuitively discovered quite early the power of the operant ᴄonditioning process with suitable reinforcers to supplement the genetic ᴧystem to adjust to more current environmental changes.

For example, following the formulas described on page 85, when the ᴅressures of needs (e.g, food, sex, and status) and wants were found to be ᴧmenable to reinforcers, the society set values of *good* or *bad* on the ᴄeinforcers for both ends and means depending on whether they worked ᴅositively or negatively toward the species' survival and progress.

Skinner called survival-based reinforcers *personal reinforcers*; all others, ᴄonditional reinforcers. Food and the pleasure of sex are plainly survival ᴅased and status is not. The desire for status is induced by one's society to ᴧotivate commendable conduct, which in this case naturally means conduct ᴄoward others. His operant conditioning explanation:[32]

> How one feels about behaving for the good of others depends on the reinforcers (rewards and sanctions) used ... not because of a feeling of belongingness. We are likely to appeal to some inner virtue to explain why a person behaves well with respect to his fellow men, but he does so not because his fellow men have endowed him with a sense of responsibility, or obligation or with loyalty or respect for others but because they have arranged effective social contingencies.

The effectiveness of the arrangement over several thousand years has been to make the desirability of these traits quite firmly deep-seated.[33]

> Man has not evolved as an ethical or moral animal. He has evolved to the point at which he has constructed an ethical or moral culture. He differs from the other animals not in possessing a moral or ethical sense but in having been able to generate a moral or ethical social environment.

The ingeniousness of this creation called a culture is manifested particularly in the way it accomplishes two vital functions.

First, a complication of motivation-by-consequence is that the more remote in the future the consequence the less concerned is the individual, the less influenced by that consequence. In Skinner's example, a construction worker wears a hard hat because the rule says he'll be discharged if he doesn't; it has to be a strong rule because the possibility of injury or death from a falling object is too remote and infrequent for the construction company just to issue the hat and say use it.

By the same token, "Ethics and morals are particularly concerned with bringing the remoter consequences of behavior into play." Since injustice, dishonesty, and greed, for instance, can have attractive short-term payoffs, all cultures have had to convey their long-range threat to their survival starting with folk wisdoms, maxims, and proverbs, followed by religious and governmental laws, and formal education imparts the rules.

Second, because the genetic evolution process is so slow, the human species has been and still is vulnerable to even moderately paced significant changes in the physical environment, as many *extinct* species have taught us. Cultures have had the same problem with technological development, major sociological and psychological changes, and such processes as degeneration from the "complacency of success" that we've seen in many civilizations and often see in the behavior of corporate managements.

A major function of a culture therefore has been to accelerate the development and institution of norms and behaviors that provide adequate adjustment to these changes in time to avoid being destroyed by them. As Skinner put it, "Biological evolution has made the human species more *sensitive to* its environment and, more skillful in dealing with it. Cultural evolution ... has brought the human organism under a much more sweeping *control of* the environment,"[34] which includes adjustment to it.

So, in final answer to why be moral or why be concerned about the survival of my culture, which will last at least as long as I live, he commented:[35]

> We do not really need an explanation ... just as we do not need to explain the origin of the genetic mutation in order to account for its effect in natural selection. The only answer to that kind of question seems to be this: there is no reason why you should be concerned, but if your culture has not convinced you that there is (a need to be moral), so much the worse for your culture.

Still, it's plain that cultural evolution, while adequate in prior centuries, is itself no longer sufficient. The evidence is manifold, for example, the special interest politics destroying our method of government, the refusal of professions to discipline themselves, indifference to poverty, the violence, manifold social crimes, and for managers and subordinates all the causes of the I-O gap.

Authority. This third moral philosophy of major importance to leadership (page 149) is determined to a significant extent by the answers adopted for the first two ("the nature of man" and "why be moral?"). Thus to ascertain how to exercise authority for the *best* result involves, in addition to the relevant management technology, all of psychology, behavior, sociology, and ethics to which, it will be shown in later chapters, has to be added organization design and the art-science of organizational Leadership.

As for any complex endeavor involving many variables and intangibles, the first requisite is a theory of what will work best, in this case a philosophy of authority that combines psychology, sociology, and ethics, one with which the design and leadership will comply and foster.

The greatest contribution has come from a psychologist, Erich Fromm. As a behavioral scientist, practicing psychologist, and philosophical thinker as well, he was ideally suited intellectually to formulate this base, and he provided it within the answers he developed for the two original questions of philosophy: what is the good life and how should one behave to get it?

Fromm was the first to point out that the answers to the questions involved both psychology and ethics, that for this subject the two disciplines were inseparable, and that they were correspondingly the foundation for the best philosophy of authority. Ethics is no more than mature behavior (the values-maturity relationship described on pages 70-71), and maturity can only be achieved through psychological growth, for which the human has a basic drive.

Indeed, the modicum of free will humans have at birth (per humanist scientists' conclusions) is one of the best manifestations of their latent potentiality for psychological growth. Moreover, if society, circumstance, or the individual doesn't stifle the modicum, the advance of growth toward maturity will continuously increase the degree and scope of free will in a circular feedback process.

The requisite growth conditions, Fromm said, are (a) optimum freedom from internal and external authority, and (b) a meaningful context in which to grow and mature. One can see in (a) the need, because of free will, for some say over one's destiny (at least a partially satisfying measure of autonomy), the need ordaining specific characteristics to the authority, and in (b) the importance of climate (e.g, the nine dimensions defined on page 278).

Applying the standard approach to building a theory or philosophy—starting with an examination of the current alternative types of authority and their consequences (which will verify these points)—Fromm described the two major ones, which he called "rational" and "irrational." Rational authority is the kind that has its source in *competence*; the superior doesn't have to intimidate or rely on charisma or magic and views the subordinate as an equal, differing only with regard to knowledge and/or skills. Irrational authority is the application of *power*—physical, mental, realistic, or relative—power on the one side, fear on the other.[36]

To select which is best and right, one has to study the norms and consequences of each. Fromm described the simple logic of it: to be effective, norms must be accepted by those expected to abide by them. That means they must at least be ethical (per the conclusion on page 163), and valid ethical norms have to be the outcome of reason (vs. religion, relativism, subjective preference), reason based on knowledge of humans as to what is good and bad for them.

As for the meaning of "good," it's quite evident from the foregoing in this chapter that it has been established solidly down through the ages as being based on the nature of the human, that is, as implied above, whatever is fundamentally good for the individual and society. And in relation to that, from the sciences and philosophers together we have the psychological needs listed on pages 163-164 plus our examination of the abstracts: liberty, equality, justice, rights, responsibility, and respect. Fromm's phrasing: "Good in humanistic ethics is the affirmation of life, the unfolding of man's powers; it is whatever fosters the individual's or humanity's welfare and healthy development. Virtue is responsibility toward existence and development; evil constitutes the crippling of man's powers; vice is irresponsibility toward himself."[37,r]

Needless to say, the "rational" authority spells out the norms of humanistic ethics, in which the norms are based on the nature of the human and what's good for the human (so must be the consequence of human reasoning), not the dictates of a higher authority. The "irrational," in contrast, is the authoritarian approach, in which the authority is held to transcend the individual, is the decision-maker, and must not be questioned; moreover what is good is in the interest of the authority, not the individual. The differences in climate the two generate certainly need no comment.

These concepts can now be assembled as follows in two sets for quick reference. The *humanistic ethics* clearly assumes the human is fundamentally good and is "the measure of all things; there is nothing higher and nothing more dignified." As this philosopher-scientist so well explained, it holds that (relevant abstracts in parentheses):[s]

- "Good" is what is good for man, and "evil" is what is detrimental to man, the sole criterion of ethical value being man's welfare (thus the concern is rights and justice).
- Only man himself can determine the criteria for virtue (liberty and respect) and sin.
- Man himself is the norm giver as well as the subject of the norms (autonomy and liberty).
- "Virtue" is the pursuit of one's optimum potential and the acceptance of the responsibility to do so (adding responsibility).

● Authority has its source in competence and is based on equality of both authority and subject (equality).

On the other hand, *authoritarian ethics* is based on the assumption that we are inherently evil in nature and must be externally controlled by an authority:

● What is good or bad is primarily in terms of the interest of the authority, (the individual or the organization), not the interests of the subject; it is exploitive, though the subject may derive considerable benefit, both psychic and material, from it.
● Man (the average man) cannot know what is good or evil. Reason is not sufficient to determine it.
● An authority transcending the individual must state what is good for man and lay down the laws and norms of conduct.
● Obedience is the main virtue and disobedience the main sin; the unforgivable sin is rebellion.
● Authority is based on inequality, implying the differences in value— power on one side, fear on the other.

We see in these summations/sets no less than the key principles underlying Theories Y and X that followed 13 years later, providing us, it seems, with a persuasive explanation of why Theory Y should be adopted. Parenthetically, it is significant that for superiors to buy the authoritarian philosophy calls for the illogical assumption that they "transcend" their subordinates, are suprahuman!

Other Ethics Considerations

The telling impact of values and values systems on behavior and on social decisions seems evident, and this chapter has attempted to demonstrate that judgments can accordingly be improved, decisions be made more effective, and one's ability to motivate others be increased through knowledge about:

1. *Ideologies* (pages 134-138)—for analyzing one's own and others' gross conceptual approach to society as a whole.
2. *Value orientations* (pages 138-142)—for analyzing one's own and others' gross intellectual and emotional inclinations in general.
3. *Moral values and philosophies*—to understand and/or develop personality, behavior, maturity, and effective social decisions.

Also, we have the orthodox psychologists' guidance on motivation through satisfaction of basic needs having observable consequences, and the philosophers (including Fromm) provided the fundamental abstract values needed to channel the motives. However, comprehension of one more abstract value—truth—is transparently crucial to human relations. Additionally, one may wonder if any of the other philosophers mentioned on page 149 might have something to contribute or if further study is worth considering.

Truth. When you rely on a statement by a subordinate or anyone you believe to be telling the truth and later find it is not, was the person deceitfully lying? How should you go about judging it before reacting or responding?

Probably too, others have been confronted with statements of your own and asked themselves the same question. When you understand what truth is, you'll not only reduce the number of such incidents of doubt but anticipate and explain (to yourself) satisfactorily those that do occur. The aware manager has usually seen plenty of instances in which trust and relationships have been destroyed by wrong conclusions in each of these instances, instances that are then followed by wrong decisions.

An elementary comprehension of truth is all that is necessary to avoid such mishaps. To begin with, it's either subjective or objective, each with two subparts.[38]

1. *Subjective truths*[t]
    a. Statements of taste, for example, those on customs, beauty, and life style; differences are irreconcilable; there's no point in arguing.
    b. Subjective value judgments (judging good, bad, right, and wrong), judgments in which there's insufficient factual support available; one is claiming the veracity of one's own opinion; it's true to me (often because it satisfies a need or want).
2. *Objective truths*
    a. Strong truths—self-evident truths that do not require supporting evidence, reasoning, or argument; common sense is sufficient to judge them, e.g., "I am alive," "a circle has no corners."
    b. Weak truths—those that have been resolved by experts considered qualified to judge in a reasoning process of resolving differences of opinion; they're no longer in dispute until new information or a consensus of the experts changes them; they are truths "with a future." The truths pursued by all the sciences and humanities (thus philosophical "truths" too) are in this category, as would be any assertions of truth based on them."[u]

It's easy enough to identify statements that are matters of taste (1a) and accept them for what they are, and it's generally agreed that life can be enriched by hearing and accepting differences of opinion on them. But in the organizational world most of the problems arise on subjective judgments (1b) and the weak truths (2b), the two normally separable without difficulty because of the tendency of subjectivity to be apparent.

In either case, it's particularly important to appreciate that other than the self-evident, there are no absolute enduring truths, so that if, for example, a subjective statement by a subordinate on his/her own performance or behavior or a weak truth on any other subject is found later to be untrue, the logical approach is to try to evaluate what motivated it (assuming a normally sincere otherwise truthful individual).

You'll probably have to brace yourself and accept the fact that fear was at the bottom of it, and it was no less than a defense on real needs, telling you (the boss) what he/she believed you wanted to hear or not telling you what you don't. Would it then be fair or in your own interest to punish the person or be better to do something about the cause?

The idea here is only to try to avoid destroying any existing good relations you may have through the application of an intelligent understanding of the subjectivity contained in the 1b and 2b forms of lying. But equally important-especially for top management-is to size up the extent to which lying may be permeating all the upward communication of your unit or the whole organization because of leadership style. Look forward for a moment to the Argyris on page 222 and ask yourself whether or not you might be contributing to that.

Plainly too, to facilitate acceptance of your own statements by anyone, being aware of the category it's in and sensitizing yourself to the amount of subjectivity you've injected (of either type) will naturally incline you to improve both your mode of expression and any explanations that may be needed, helping to build and sustain trust. The author also found that for one's own underlying motivation to always tell the truth, a comment of a college professor to his class left an indelible imprint: "Ask yourself," he said, "If you can't always be an honorable person, who can?" Doing so periodically works. Of course "honorable" covers honesty in all regards.

It might be helpful to add the following about the occasional temptation to get one's way with a little "white" lie. One is either a liar or not in such circumstances, and the "white" is a lie to oneself. Moreover, almost always, with a little imagination you can get your way without lying - or, you can say nothing. The only time a violation (a lie) is acceptable: to avoid serious harm to someone.

Other Philosophies. Most top executives of major corporations have heard of the Aspen Institute in the Rockies that holds philosophy seminars for those at their level, an effort to make them more aware of moral issues. A goal of this chapter has been to do the same for everyone in management, preferably well before they do damage on the way up.

Some of the principal philosophers they cover were listed on page 149 along with the comment that learning about only a few will supply the necessary basics, but a reading of the others also and what their critics have said would surely be proportionately better. The most prominent concepts of all (shown below) suggest the variety of approaches possible to morality in general, and clues may be found in them for further study toward solutions of specific problems at hand:

Plato - If you learn about "good" you will lead a virtuous life, and it will be a good life.

Aristotle - Needs, wants, happiness, rights, justice, the "Golden Mean."

Epicurus - Live moderately but pleasurably.

Christ - Love God and obey his absolute laws.

Spinoza - The good life is achieved by a resigned attitude toward predetermined life.

Bentham and Mill - An action is right if it tends to produce the greatest happiness for the greatest number.

Kant - "The categorical imperative": act in a way that can become universal law;[v] treat human beings in every case as ends withal, never only as means (respect their dignity and individuality).

James and Dewey - If it works for the benefit of both the individual and society in the long run, it's good and right.

Existentialism - One is wholly responsible for one's own destiny, for becoming a "being" or "nothingness."

"Good Reason" - Moral decisions are made when universalizable reason is applied to the situation.

Fromm - The good life is through love and work toward Good under conditions of freedom and a meaningful context: the humanistic ethic versus the authoritarian ethic.

Skinner - "If your culture has not convinced you there is (reason to be moral), so much the worse for - your culture.

Two of these are so important that they warrant elaboration: Kant and "Good Reason." But first a few points on the semantic difference between ethics and morality that might help an analysis of an event (e.g., in the 4-step *ethics analysis* procedure ahead).

Moral behavior, as said, deal essentially with interpersonal behavior, and philosophers divide it into four types, distinguishing two of them as "ethics" and two as factors of "morality," two words commonly considered synonymous (as will be done ahead for simplification). Briefly, *ethics* for them refers to the discipline in general of dealing with what is good and bad, right or wrong, ethics itself having two levels: *ethical principles—*

standards that provide general behavioral assistance, such as respect for others' individuality; and *ethical guidelines*—behavioral standards oriented toward tasks of specific functions or professions; for example, protecting confidentiality in doctor-patient relations.

The two categories of *morality* are: (a) *Moral rules* that are generally accepted standards and norms, the standards being essentially "don't', aimed at minimizing harm and evil; basic ones: don't kill, cause pain or injury, lie, deceive, steal. And norms help indicate what circumstances can allow exceptions (while the "ethics analysis" technique on pages 178-179 provides a procedure for dealing with dilemmas). (b) *Moral ideals* are the positive side of the standards, for example, help others in distress, have empathy and compassion in relations.

For a further delineation of morality: these rules and ideals form a system of interrelated ideas having as its core the notion of a moral code with four characteristics: the code is paramount, universal (but not absolute), grounded in reason, and concerned principally with forbidding behaviors that tend to cause severe harm.[39]

Kant's Categorical Imperative, interestingly, is both a set of principles and moral rules; take your choice. In either case, the enigma certainly was how to sell it as a universal fundamental to skeptics. For those open to moral reasoning his own logic might be convincing.

The locus of moral values and law is in the human mind; they are not laws of God or abstracts of nature, but of human nature. Given that our natural attitude is one of self-love and self-interest, the species, to survive, has had to establish universal moral standards, and it's our reasoning that created them.

In short, reasoning by the species as a whole has produced the same results worldwide for what is basically good and bad for social harmony, and Kant concluded that, since the reasoning on these basics was universal, the moral laws produced are universal and as such qualify at least in theory for the label of "absolute,"[40] that is, absolutely essential to the human race, and especially for the two most fundamental rules in his Categorical Imperative—two that every superior has to try hard to honor to build commitment.

The precepts of the school of "Good Reason," a British group, are particularly useful to organizational leaders, because they added other basic ideas to the Categorical Imperative needed for decision-making. The group eclectically integrated the best of past key philosophers into an easy to remember procedure: each moral judgement or decision must be (1) capable of being a universalizeable standard (Kant), (2) congruent with the situation (James and Dewey), and (3) derived by the use of reason (Plato and all after him). One need only remember to tick off and apply them at the appropriate times.

Interestingly, on the second, the requisite of congruence with the situation not only emphasizes the importance of reality but is consistent with the simultaneously emerging appreciation by organization behaviorists (in the 1950s) of the significance of the situation to behavior and leadership style. It will be elaborated in Part III.

And the third requisite of reasoning leads a student of the subject to three observations about morality as a whole. First, the fact that both philosophy and psychology have independently arrived at the same conclusions on the relationship of motives, needs, and values provides indisputable evidence that:

1. Good ethical decisions produce the most desirable behavior on the part of the employees affected, making them both satisfied and motivated.
2. Bad decisions (violating the Good) cause virtually all the undesirable behavior in otherwise normal people, inducing them to rebel in many ways.

A product of "Good Reason" would therefore be the infallible rule of thumb for management decision-making—call it for reference *the behavioral pragmatism* of management—*that if it works behaviorally, it's right and good, and if it's right and good it will work behaviorally.* "It works' of course means it produces, or will, if not immediately then in the long run, optimum performance and satisfaction. It is assumed that the decision is good from the standpoint of management technology.

This of course presumes an honest interpretation of "it works," which leads to the second observation: "it works" also depends on the decision-maker's assumptions about the others involved, and surprisingly, the most common stumbling blocks for those benevolent enough to think of it is the golden rule because of the basic assumption integral to it: "Do unto others as you would have them do unto you" infers that others' needs and values are the same as your own... a useful uncomplicated imperative for the masses centuries ago but misleading for today.

Corrected for effective managing, it would become what has been called the *platinum rule:* "Do unto others as they would have you do unto them." In other words, attempt to discern the personal goals, value orientation, dominant motivation (explained in Chapter 8), values in general, and the important emotional needs of the individual (or group) affected before deciding. The simplest solution: ask them their opinions of the subject, discuss their interests, and have them participate in the decision.

The third observation is the extent to which it is now possible at this point in the text for managers to assemble general replacements for most

f the value misconceptions on page 118, that is, to generate basic broad-
auged criteria for moral decision-making. Perhaps Figure 5.8 can serve as
point of departure, or be used largely as is.

Doubtlessly, it looks too pious and goody to many for the crude realities
f survival in organizations, but all sages through the ages have advised or
warned that humanity must aim at such ideal goals to avoid degeneration
nd self-destruction. It will be shown herein repeatedly that virtually every
ecommendation of the most highly regarded authorities on organization
lesign and leadership is at least implicitly based on one or more of them.

The Gray Area, the Dilemmas. Finally these. The intent of all the
oregoing in the chapter has of course simply been to provide the knowledge
oundation that allows one to become aware of and handle all types of ethics
ituations, which is often enough in itself for "black and white" issues, those
on which right and wrong are quite evident to an educated person.

Reviewing it briefly, a reader starting to develop an ethical awareness from
cratch would now know how to determine whether or not a situation
nvolves ethics (from pages 119-120) and realizes that in organizational
eadership three elements have to be considered in any ethical situation:

- People factors in general—the impact on those involved of one's
  judgments, decisions, behavior, and actions;
- Organizational factors over which one may or may not have any say—
  the impact of plans, policies, structures, processes, culture/climate,
  training/development;
- Individual factors (one's own as well as those of others involved)—
  personality and history, individual perceptions of the subjects at hand,
  the responsibilities of each person as to roles, causes, and capacities.

And as complex as the situation may be an informed and reasonably
benevolent person who agrees with the generally accepted criteria on page
76 can, with a little objective thought, handle the black and white, the
chool of "Good Reason" rules helping to both formulate the best moral
udgment or decisions and evaluate the alternatives.

But a dilemma, we know, has no clear-cut right or wrong solution; a
choice has to be made among two or more options, none of which can satisfy
ll persons involved. Further, along with the complications of the factors
bove one has to consider in the least the side effects on everyone and the
organization, the urgency for a solution, the scope of the decision's impact,
nd the aftermath as to the effects on individual behaviors and the future
f the organization or unit.

Criteria For Moral Decisions

A. *Concerning others:*

1. *Personal welfare*: the right of others to life and the pursuit of health, emotiona security, economic security, and happiness.
2. *Respect*: the right to be treated "as an end, never as a means only," to be accorde self-respect and dignity.
3. *Personal liberty*: the right to have a major say in one's direct on-the-job welfa and destiny and to determine one's off-the-job activities that do not clearly affec the organization adversely.
4. *Justice*: the right to freedom of speech and conscience, to privacy, to freedom fron slander, and to due process.
5. *Growth and self-actualization*: the right to the pursuit of the optimum growt and development of one's intellect, emotions, character, and competence.

B. *Concerning obligations to society and its institutions:*

6. *Duty* is love in the form of advancing the full potential of the self, others, an the institutions of society, in which love is knowledge + care + respect responsibility, knowledge being of values, psychology, others' needs, priorities.
7. *Society's welfare*:   peace, justice, charity;
   freedom from hunger and deprivation;
   equality of opportunity;
   the quality of life and environment;
   intellectual and cultural achievement;
   material improvement.
8. Good citizenship: involvement, public service;
   I am my brother's keeper to a significant degree;
   abidance by the law at the level of principle (page 123)

C. *Concerning the development of oneself:*

9. *One's moral conduct in action:*
   performance of A and B with honesty, fairness, trustworthiness, sincerity reliability, openness, and tactful candor.
10. *One's character:*
    care, respect, responsibility, compassion, empathy, tolerance, generosity reverence for life and human dignity;
    reasonableness, rationality, objectivity, prudence, self control, cooperativeness
    knowledge and the optimal development of one's own intellect, emotions, anc competence;
    initiative, industry, diligence, vitality, courage, fortitude, resilience, the pursui of excellence.

Figure 5.8

For instance, firing a subordinate can involve the ethical issue of *fairness* in ways that might have challenged Solomon. A good illustration of what a manager may have to deal with was given in a recent book, *Tough Choices—Managers Talk Ethics*, by B. L. Toffler,[41] that presents many excellent examples of dilemmas, 21 from 21 manager interviews, a book that would greatly interest even the jaded.

Mac in one example was transferred from another location in the company to Johnson's department as a service engineer manager after careful review of his record, good interviews, and good references from previous superiors who, it turned out, were purposely misleading in their eagerness to get rid of him (or not get him back). A man over 60 with some value but out of date on technical knowledge, he had the aggravating traits of being insensitive, tactless, explosive, unable to listen, and unable to get cooperation. He soon had alienated everyone in the department.

Nevertheless, a tenet of the organization's culture was that superiors are responsible for their subordinate's success, and Johnson did his best. Over a 1 1/2 year period he met with him regularly to set goals mutually and to review progress, the goals were lowered each time, and he produced nothing but excuses. Plainly, Johnson had gone the limit with him, but still he felt there was an ethical problem of *fairness* in a decision to fire him.

Although he was not unaware of the organization's (and prior superiors') causal responsibility, perhaps in the back of his mind was an insecurity about the adequacy of his own teaching and guidance. But he asked himself would it be fair to a man over 60 who had been with the company a number of years, was in fact sick, and had a wife in bad health and an unemployed son? He undoubtedly would be unable to find another engineering job at his age (and Johnson vowed that his own references would be honest), and he might very well commit suicide as a result of all this. Yet too was it fair to others in the department to keep him longer, when none was able to work with him, and all were more competent and being paid less (several had left because of him)? And was it fair to the company because of the poor performance and ROI?

Naturally Johnson is entitled to ask how much can he be held responsible for this situation, including the possibility of a suicide. But he had the conscience to be concerned about these matters, and a decision had to be made, one that minimized harm to all involved. What would you do?

An organization that sincerely wants its managers to be ethical can provide a lot of help by what it does to prepare them for such problems, and choose from them based on your values hopefully improved by ethics education, priorities, and conscience.

A more comprehensive procedure for it was recently presented in a new book aimed at O.D. professionals for their own and their management development work, the procedure by W. Gellermann et al. that was labelled "A Five-Step Model for Ethical Thought and Action."[42] Consider adding the following (an abridgement of it) to the above:

Step 1: Problem analysis
a. Given that it's an ethical problem, are any ethics rules, ideals principles, or guidelines being violated? Which, if any.
b. Is there a conflict of values? If so, clarify.

Step 2: Ethics analysis
a. Analyze the situation—facts, causes, variables, responsibilities of those involved.
b. Clarify your assumptions and your vision of the desired results.
c. Determine the decision options and their consequences; draw on the alternative applicable philosophies (page 172).
d. Rank the options based on your values, education, priorities reasoning and conscience.
e. If any violation is involved or considered (#1a above), what is or would be the basis of justification?" What are your own responsibilities? Can harm be avoided or prevented?

Step 3: Decision
Choose the "best" option with the consequences (costs and benefits) fully in mind based on a combination of your values, education, priorities, reasoning, conscience and intuition.

Step 4: Action (or inaction).

Step 5: Reflection

Needless to say, it would be grossly unrealistic to expect busy executives to go through all this on any but very major ethical decisions; moreover, it's open to plenty of criticism, like the difficulty, and often impossibility, of identifying the relevant facts, factors, assumptions, options and their consequences. But, as Gellermann pointed out, the main purpose was to supply a systematic way of *thinking*, to enhance ethical sensitivity, to clarify the problem, and to encourage a review of one's own applicable values, priorities and responsibilities. Just knowing what is involved can improve decisions if only by triggering in the mind the key factors to question, whether for oneself or for a deciding group."[43]

Of course an organization committed to ethical management behavior, in addition to the education and training, will also review and upgrade all, starting with requiring ethics education and training in a mandatory management development program. As Toffler recommended, ethics analysis and education should have two parts:

- Educating to think about ethics, sensitizing, developing awareness, and becoming familiar with problems where they most often arise: performance evaluation, hiring, firing, promotions, demotions, relationships, and systems design.
- Training to incorporate ethics in one's decisions and activities, to use ethics language with ease (fairness, rights, justice), and to express ethical concerns skillfully without raising emotional barriers—people need practice on such new behavior.

The example does show a person (Johnson) duly sensitized. She also supplied a useful set of guidelines for dealing with dilemmas. When faced with one:

1. Accept the fact that problem is a dilemma without a right-or-wrong solution; the conflict of values or competing claims cannot be eliminated.
2. Define the elements of the conflict, examining the values and both the positive and negative sides of each claim or right.
3. Assess honestly the responsibilities, yours, and others', degrees.
4. Determine if there's a "key factor" to guide the decision, for example, using time to solve the problem incrementally in order not to "rock the boat" (where that's an organization value) with a quick total solution.
5. If no key factor is discernible, simply try to balance in a decision the claims of all the stakeholders according to your own values and conscience; use your imagination, be creative, and improvise to be fair as best you can.

Two cautions were added: (1) Let your conscience and the potential harm tell you when to and when not to make an open issue of an ethics situation; gauge the reception in the given climate. (2) Beware of rationalizing, avoiding, or doctoring a decision. But note also that a key skill that has to be developed, especially for dilemmas, is *ethics analysis*: apply to the problem the various principles that appear most appropriate—since science has offered none, we must turn to the philosophers (the list on page 172)— rank, and choose from them based on your values hopefully improved by ethics education, priorities, and conscience.[w]

Of course an organization committed to ethical management behavior, in addition to the education and training, will also review and upgrade all its structures and processes to ensure that they don't invite conflict (the way reward systems commonly do), prevent unintended consequences, and are ethically responsive. Also, job descriptions should allow enough autonomy and flexibility for imaginative solutions to dilemmas. The chapters ahead will cover such planning and action according to their titled subjects (and note the behavior change program in Chapter 19).

But naturally individuals can still do a great deal more on their own through:

- Courses, seminars or workshops at universities and professional training organizations on such subjects as organization psychology, human behavior, life planning, career planning, management development, leadership development (still rarely available), transactional analysis, self-management, business ethics, and interpersonal skills.
- Workshops of the NTL Institute (take especially the Stranger T-grouping) whose capabilities and calendar every personnel (HR) department should be familiar with.
- Books and articles on values, ethics in business, individual and organization change, leadership.

Unfortunately, few business schools *require* the ethics courses, but they're all available; the human resources departments of major enlightened firms pick up on a lot of it, commonly using outside suppliers like NTL.

Certainly, some readers will laugh and scoff at the idea of the self-management course in the list, especially those who figure they are in management because they're good at managing themselves. But one trait necessary just to get started on developing the competence, we know, is *introspection,* and it's one that many upward-mobiles don't have, a learned capability that in fact no manager should feel embarrassed about not having on finding out.

Generally, those who possess this trait acquired it as a result of introspective models who fostered it during their pre-job years, but its development can easily be delayed for lack of a good model and/or under the pressures of ambition, the organization's "rules of success" (pages 5-7), and the rat-race interpersonal competition in Figure A.1 (page 4), along with heavy family responsibilities and no career planning. Then one day, progress, like the trip up the Maslow ladder, may say the time has come for a higher plateau, or it may be frustration over subordinate performance, or one may have read Socrates' comment that "the unexamined life is not worth living."

So one is motivated toward greater self-knowledge, and a good course on self-management (and sometimes career planning) will provide it, beginning with helping you uncover your *frame of reference.* To explain, for an individual o process data psychologically, the information must have some form or structure. Of the information that comes in from the outside, some is already structured in the sense that it has clear meaning, but much is not, is ambiguous or amorphous, and has to be interpreted. We add the missing structure by means of a combination of our personal values, beliefs, goals, norms, fears, and so on, and it comes out as a systematic approach to perceiving.

To make objective, effective decisions, it's necessary to understand the components of one's own system in order to know the subjective slants they mpose on judgments about events and others, to separate facts from opinions and feelings, and to counter associations of events with prior experiences that seem to be but are not related.

The procedure of these courses, after they give this explanation, is to get the student to answer general personal questions like the following and dig for the reason *why*:

- On what subjects am I especially sensitive?
- On which have I been accused of being insensitive?
- What technical and social limitations do I have that worry me, and how do I compensate?
- What strengths do I have and how do I use them or fail to?
- Listing them on paper, what are my principal fears, prejudices, distrusts, hates, personality dislikes (in others), and the assumptions I make about those I dislike?
- What relationships have made me most happy?
- Which ones have made me most unhappy?
- What events have made me most and least happy?
- What are my true goals for 10 years ahead on job, position, income, family and social relationships, personal character?
- Can I discern from my past actions, thoughts, and decisions where on the good-evil continuum I honestly place people in general?

Transparently, one can work on them without taking a course, but a good instructor and the class itself can inspire one to come up with the truth and/ or show how to do it, which is much less likely when done alone. The Stranger T-group is perhaps the best introduction to discerning the truth about a lot of the questions.[x]

Then in regard to reading books, a practice of top salesmen comes to mind: they keep themselves on top and avoid going stale by reading at least one or two new books on selling every year. Ethical awareness similarly has to t be kept fresh and continuously updated. A good one each year like Toffler's will do it. A short list of favorites, several of which should be in the basic education course described above:

Ethics in Business, R Baumhart (Holt, Rinehart & Winston, 1968)

Moral Issues in Business, V. Barry (Wadsworth, 1982, 2nd ed.). Many good, brief cogent cases.

Ropes to Skip and Ropes to Know, R. Ritti and R. Funkhauser (Wiley, 1982). The realities of conventional large corporation norms, rituals, ethics. How to cope. Excellent.

Ethical Theory and Business, T. L. Beauchamp and N. E. Bowie (eds.) (Prentice-Hall 1983). Very good on theory and its applications to business.

Ethical Issues in Business, T. Donaldson and P. H. Werhane (eds.) (Prentice-Hall, 1983). A superior basic text.

Morality in the Making, H. Weinreich-Haste and D. Locke (eds) (New York: John Wiley, 1983)

Right Conduct, M.D. Bayles and K. Henley (eds) (New York: Random House, 1983)

Immorality, R.D. Milo (Princeton Univ. Press, 1984) See ahead.

The Hard Problems of Management, M. Pastin (San Francisco: Jossey-Bass, 1986)

Executive Integrity, Srivastva and Assoc. (eds) (San Francisco: Jossey-Bass, 1988)

Values and Ethics in Organization and Human Systems Development, W. Gellermann, M.S. Frankey and R.E. Ladenson (San Francisco: Jossey-Bass, 1990)

The first of them, incidentally, was principally a discourse on a survey of the state of ethics in management in 1968[y] that all evidence indicates is much the same today, and the responses to two questions in particular are worthy of note. For "What influences you most to make ethical decisions?" the ranked answers were:

1st		One's personal code of behavior
2nd ⎫	⎧ a	The behavior of one's superior
3rd ⎭ tie	⎩ b	The company's policies
4th		The ethical climate of the industry
5th		The behavior of one's peers.

And when asked "What influences you most to make unethical decisions?" the ranked answers were:

1st		The behavior of one's superior
2nd ⎫	⎧ a	The behavior of one's peers
3rd ⎭ tie	⎩ b	The ethical climate of the industry
4th		Lack of a company policy
5th		Personal financial needs.

In the minds of respondents, the answers to the first questions seemed to be saying, "I am good," to the second, "Others and especially the boss are bad." Translated by the author: *"If you want to be moral, get a moral boss."* It undeniably helps, but isn't that an evasion of one's own moral responsibility?

The book in the reference list by Milo may be particularly significant to the more conscientious. A philosopher has for the first time classified comprehensively the types of immorality, giving a clear picture of causes and remedies. A brief, oversimplified outline: he has concluded with convincing explanations that there are six (the examples supplied by the author of this work on leadership)[46]:

Perverse wickedness—
The agent does a morally wrong act not realizing it's immoral, and would feel remorse if or when found out.
Cause: bad principles or bad priorities or value misconceptions.
Examples. harsh Theory X treatment of subordinates learned from superiors and incongruous with the self. A Christian Scientist's refusal to take his/her seriously sick child to a doctor.

Preferential wickedness—
The agent does wrong knowing it's wrong (therefore has some moral concern), but has low motivation to do right. Feels no remorse.
Example: the corporate thief.

Moral indifference—
The agent believes or knows its wrong, doesn't care. No remorse.
Examples: sexual harassment; most cases of adultery.

Moral negligence—
The agent fails to realize, when he/she could or should, that it violates one of his/her own principles. Didn't take precautions expected of a reasonably informed person.
Types: impulsiveness (including thoughtlessness), self-deception, carelessness, recklessness, any resulting in wrongdoing.
Example: inadvertently humiliating someone for lack of considering the consequences of the act.

Amorality—
No moral principles pro or con. Don't care. No remorse.
Example: bosses who are authoritarian bullies.

Moral weakness—
The agent wants to do right but for lack of will acts contrary to own principles. Inadequate self-control.
Types: intemperance, irresolution, indecision, and yielding to immoral temptation.
Example: harmful lust; injury to co-worker due to procrastinating on a duty, political pandering.

And consider that both greed and injurious interpersonal competition can be any of the six.

All six are "blameworthy" except when due to duress, to mental illness, to an honest mistake, or to ignorance that could have been avoided by education (not ignorance due to carelessness, negligence, or laziness). Also, Milo pointed out that on the subject of morality *will power* is a matter of acquired skills, abilities, and habits for applying self-control, taking precautions, or taking countermeasures, many we hold people responsible for acquiring and exercising. Advanced planning like setting deadlines to counter procrastination is one; the "arousal reduction" techniques on page 204 are some others.

An analysis of these immoralities will show that there are in fact two fundamental forms and three fundamental causes, the five related as shown in Milo's matrix below. Note that four of the six types have at least some moral concern (for the interests and welfare of others) the lack of which, we are reminded, is the most reprehensible cause of immorality.

		The agents' belief-state	
		does not believe wrong	*does believe wrong*
The agent's moral defect	bad preferences	perverse wickedness	preferential wickedness
	lack of self-control	moral negligence	moral weakness
	lack of moral concern	amorality	moral indifference

Additional information for understanding the value changes that may be necessary and to aid value judgments follows in the next chapter (and more in Chapter 18).

NOTES

a.   The "relative" nature of a social value should not be confused with moral "duties" that have universality because they're based on basic human needs (table on page 143), the universality tending to give them "absolute" character; e.g., be just, respect human rights (both discoursed on pages 160-161).

b.   One might note the relationship of stages 4, 5, and 6 to the college and non-college votes in Figure 1.2 (page 10) on obeying laws you do not agree with.

c.   Another crucial point from the governor of New York in a speech at a 1987 forum on education; by not teaching values, public schools are sending a message that they are not important, indeed "that the choice between good and evil is not important" (*The New York Times*, March 8, 1987.)

d.   The econo-political use of the word "liberal" below seems only distantly related to the philosophers' definition: a set of consistent positive convictions that include ideals on justice, liberty, equality of opportunity, and individual dignity.

e.   Fascism is not included because, like Nazism and the U.S.S.R.'s pseudo-communism, it is not more than the simple primitive idea of total central dictatorial political, social, and economic power.

f.   653 businessmen attending Advanced Management Programs between 1960 and 1964, 178 research managers attending Harvard Industrial Research seminars from 1961 to 1963, and 157 scientists with at least 7 years of industry experience but no supervision over others than their own assistants.

g.   Journal of Moral Education (East Windsor, Berks, England: NFER Publishing Co.).

h.   This phrase, adopted long before Women's Lib, will be retained in comments on the subject both for simplification and in deference to the history of psychology and the related titles that have been used.

i.   Some of his recommendations:

A prudent ruler ought not to keep the faith when by doing so it would be against his interest.

I believe it to be most true that it seldom happens that men rise from low condition to high rank without employing either force or fraud, unless that rank should be attained either by gift or inheritance. Nor do I believe that force alone will ever be found to suffice, whilst it will often be the case that cunning alone serves the purpose.

Men must either be caressed or annihilated.

j.   Starting around the 1930s. The beginning of behavior research is held to have begun when Wilhelm Wundt set up his Leipsig laboratory in 1879.

k.   Instinct definition: an enduring tendency or disposition to act in an organized and biologically adaptive way that is characteristic of a given species...in *A Comprehensive Dictionary of Psychological and Psychiatric Terms* by H.G. English and A.C. English (New York: Longmans, Green & Co., 1958).

l.   A confusing thing encountered in nonscientific literature is calling physiological processes instincts. Instincts refer to behavior. Digesting and defecating are not considered behavioral any more than the secretion in the mother when baby cries of the hormone oxytocin that hardens the nipples for nursing, which has been incorrectly called a maternal instinct.

m.   The sales manager Prentice on page 274 an example.

n.   Read *Aristotle for Everybody* by Mortimer Adler (New York: Macmillan, 1978) for an excellent and easy to understand explanation of all his major thinking.

o.   Aristotle was not referring to an average or median but to an intermediate point relative to the individual's own character. The concept is complex as one of his own examples can illustrate: For instance, fear and confidence and appetite and anger and pity and in general pleasure and pain may be felt too much and too little and in both cases not well; but to feel them at the right times, with reference to the right objects, toward the right people, with the right motive, and in the right way, is what is both intermediate and best."[27]

p.   The three principles are elaborated by Mortimer Adler in his *Six Great Ideas* (op. cit.), Chapter 22.[28]

q.   Sometimes one encounters another use of "reality" in philosophy in a non-absolute sense: as applied to objective truth (that is not self-evident), truth that has been agreed to by the experts accepted as qualified to judge.

r.   At times Fromm used "God" interchangeable with "good," defining God as a symbol (the "nameless One") representing the unity of all phenomena of the universe (vs. the anthropomorphic belief in the loving protective father), and at the same time the symbol of the highest human principles and endeavors. Some critics who have chosen not to translate the symbolism have pejoratively called Fromm's philosophy a humanistic religion; yet religious philosophers rail against his psychological interpretations of religion. The dates of his writings explain the use of "man" for both genders.

s.   For those who may want a more explicit definition of ethical behavior than the explanation on page 000, it is doing good and avoiding evil in one's decisions, actions, judgements, ideas and intentions with respect to truth, justice, rights, liberty, and basic needs towards (a) other individuals, (b) institutions of society, and (c) the formation of one's own character. The decision outcomes would be the consequence of two essentials of ethical behavior: *good character and good judgement*, the former heavily dependent on the values and philosophy summarized on p. 000, the good judgement regarding leadership on the knowledge of this 3-part work.

t.   Two others not particularly relevant to managing were added by Mortimer Adler:[38]
  1(c).   Excessive skepticism—the relativists.
  2(c).   Objective value judgments—those that are universalizable, like any tied to the reality of basic needs, e.g. the statement "humans need knowledge."

u.   This, the area of greatest controversy and the most important in the true/false debate, was first clarified by Charles Pierce, who concluded at about the turn of the century that such a truth is a result of "the universal assent of those who understand," the experts of the topic's discipline applying the best "scientific" method. It is therefore a social product and a value subject to new information as knowledge about it increases.

v.   A helpful rule of thumb: What makes a moral concept both correct and a duty is its applicability to everyone, its universality.

w.   The Gellermann et al. book on Ethics and Values listed 8 factors to consider for justification of a decision to violate; briefly: 1. The moral rules violated. 2. the evils avoided, prevented or caused, 3. the relevant desires of the people affected, 4. their rational beliefs, 5. one's authority to violate (hierarchy), 6. the good it would promote, 7. would it prevent an unjustified violation of a basic moral rule by the other person? 8. would it result in punishment for the violation?"[43]

x.   It also pays to study "attribution" tendencies with regard to superiors, oneself, and subordinates and the influence these tendencies have on decision-making. For example, what is one's own tendency in evaluating a subordinate's failures? Is it to attribute them to personality and skill or to the situation? And how do you judge the successes? You might ask too if your basic philosophy about "the nature of man" is involved? And what are your subordinate managers' tendencies in judging their subordinates.[44]

y.   The sample of 1,800 executives had 47 percent in top management, 28 percent in middle management, and 12 percent at lower levels; 37 percent had graduate degrees, 38 percent bachelor's degrees, 20 percent some college, and 5 percent only high school. The study was repeated six times from 1961 to 1976, and after 4 the last, done by Brenner and Molander.[45] Baumhart commented, "Each time the results have been remarkably similar," and "Business behavior is more ethical, but public expectations have risen more rapidly." Of course business behavior in the 80s would seem to have bellied the claim for it.

REFERENCES

1.   Kluckholm, C., "Values and value orientation in the theory of action," *Toward a general theory of action*, (eds.) T. Parsons and E.A. Shils (Cambridge, Mass: Harvard University Press, 1954).

2. Rogers, C.R., "Toward a Modern Approach in Values: The Valuing Process in the Mature Person," *Journal of Abnormal and Social Psychology*, 1964, pp. 160-167. Reprinted in Readings in Psychology: *Understanding Human Behavior*, ed. J.A. Dyal (New York: McGraw-Hill Book Co., 1967) p. 444.

3. Kohlberg, L., "Education for Justice: A Modern Statement of the Platonic Viewpoint," *Moral Education: Five Lectures* (Cambridge: Harvard University Press, 1970), p. 73.

4. Ibid., p. 68.

5. Sizer, N.F. and T.R. Sizer. "Introduction," *Moral Education: Five Lectures*, op. cit., p. 4.

6. Kohlberg, L., op. cit., p. 61.

7. Hartshorne, H., and M.A. May, *Studies in Deceit* (New York: MacMillan, 1928)

8. Stein, S., and C. Smith, "Return to Mom," *Saturday Review of Education*. April 1973.

9. Steiner, G.A. *Business and Society* (N.Y.: Random House, 1971), p. 93.

10. England, G.W., "Personal Value Systems of American Managers," *Academy of Management Journal*, 1966.

11. Lusk, E.J., and B.L. Oliver, "American Managers' Personal Value Systems Revisited." *Academy of Management Journal*, September 1974.

12. England, op. cit.

13. Steiner, op. cit., pp. 109-118.

14. Martin, W.F. and G.C. Lodge, "Our society in 1985—business may not like it," *Harvard Business Review*, November-December 1975. (The 1985 date clearly the wrong guess.)

15. McCoy, R.H., "The parable of the Sadhu," *Harvard Business Review*, Sept.-Oct., 1983.

16. Guth, W.D. and R. Taguiri, "Personal values and corporate strategy," *Harvard Business Review*, Sept.-Oct., 1975.

17. Allport, G.W., P.E. Vernon, and G. Lindzey, *Study of Values: A Scale For Measuring Dominant Interests in Personality*. (Boston: Houghton Mifflin, 3rd Ed.)

18. Spranger, E., *Lebensformen*. Halle: Niemeyer. Translated as Types of Men by P. Pigors. New York: Steckert. 1928.

19. Kohlberg, L. "Stage and sequence; the cognitive-developmental approach to socialization: *Handbook of Socialization Theory and Research*, (ed.) D.A. Goslin (Chicago: Rand McNally, 1969).

20. *Morality, Moral Behavior, and Moral Development*, (eds.) W.M. Kurtines and J.L. Gewirtz (New York: John Wiley, 1984).

21. Weinreich-Haste, H., "Social and Moral Cognition," *Morality in the Making*, (eds.) H. Weinreich-Haste and D. Locke (Chichester, England: John Wiley & Sons, Ltd. 1983), pp. 88-92. (Paraphrased).

22. Toulmin, S.E., *An Examination of the Place of Reason in Ethics*. (Cambridge: Mass.: Cambridge University Press, 1950), Chapter 10.

23. Gerth, H.H. and C.W. Mills (trans.), *Max Weber: Essays in Sociology* (New York: Oxford University Press, 1946); "Bureaucracy," p. 214, an essay written in 1904.

24. Moyer, K.E. "The Physiology of Aggression and the Implications for Aggression Control" *The Control of Aggression and Violence*, edited by J.L. Singer (New York: Academic Press, 1971), p. 83.

25. Skinner, B.F., *Beyond Freedom and Dignity* (New York: Alfred A. Knopf, 1971), p. 206.

26. Plato, *The Republic* (New York: Oxford University Press, 1945), trans. by F.M. Cornford. The episode reprinted in *Ethical Theories* (ed.) A.I. Melden (New York: Prentice-Hall, 1967), p.46.

27. Aristotle, *The Nicomachean Ethics*, translated by W.D. Ross (London: Clarendon Press, 1925, Book II. Also in *Problems in Ethic*, edited by R.E. Dewey et al. (New York: Macmillan, 1961), p. 235.

28. Adler, M. *Six Great Ideas* (New York: Macmillan, 1981).

29. Fromm, E. *The Art of Loving* (New York: Harper & Row, 1956).

30. Melden, A.I. "On the Nature and Problem of Ethics." his editorial introduction to *Ethical Theories*, op. cit., p. 14.

31. Skinner, B.F. op. cit, 1971, p. 101.

32. Ibid pp. 110 and 113.

33. Ibid., p. 175.

34. Ibid., p. 173. (Italics added).

35. Ibid., pp. 136-137.

36. Fromm, E. *Man for Himself* (New York: Holt, Rinehart and Winston, 1947). The Fromm quotes in this section are from pp. 9-20.

37. Ibid, p. 20.

38. Adler, M. op. cit., 1981, Chapter 8.

39. Gellermann, W., Frankel, M.S., Ladenson, R.E., *Values and Ethics in Organization and Human Systems Development* (San Francisco: Jossey-Bass, 1990).

40. Greene, T.M., *Kant Selections* (N.Y.C.: Charles Scribners Sons, 1957).

41. Toffler, B.L., *Tough Choices—Managers Talk Ethics* (New York: John Wiley, 1986) p. 189.

42. Gellermann, et al op. cit., pp. 65-89.

43. Gellermann, et al., ibid., p. 44.

44. For a summary discourse of the subject see "Why did you do that? Attribution Theory in Organizations" by J.M. Bartunek, *Business Horizons*, Sept.-Oct., 1981.

45. Brenner, S.N. and E.A. Molander, "Is the ethics of business changing?" *Harvard Business Review*, January-February 1977. (The comments were in the same issue), p. 189.

46. Milo, R.D., *Immorality* (Princeton, N.J.: Princeton University Press, 1984), p. 187.

Chapter 6

Changing Values—An Introduction

It's apparent that, before we can hope for any improvement in the social management causing the I-0 gap that we're locked into by bad values and their systems, a lot of values are going to have to be changed. But we're faced with the problem of inadequate tools to take the very first step: that of separating the good values—which most values of mature people are— from the bad beyond those clearly discernible (like the ones on page 118).[a]

Then when we try to judge the behavior of individuals on the basis of specific good or bad values they hold (for either improvement or their own self-knowledge), we must rely either on surveys of co-workers and subordinates colored by personal relations or on self-reports by the managers themselves, reports limited by the dichotomy Chris Argyris and Donald Schon called "espoused theory" vs. "theory-in-use":[1]

> When a man is asked how he would behave under certain circumstances, the answer he usually gives is his espoused theory of action for that situation... However, the theory that governs his actions is his theory-in-use, which may or may not be compatible with his espoused theory... And we cannot learn what someone's theory-in-use is simply by asking him. We must construct his theory-in-use from observations of his behavior.

And the unobtained theory-in-use is where the relevant values are, being an integration of the person's values, assumptions, beliefs, and perception of the situation.

However, with the knowledge we have from personal experience and the research that *has* been done on the bad values (on the sources of the page 118 list) a lot of improvement on certain types of them is possible.

We know how people change their values on their own (without applied behavioral techniques), a process that they perform internally constantly through life. One research philosopher classified the ways as follows:[2]

Value acquisition—accepting a value not previously adhered to.
Value redistribution—a change in the extent or the pattern of a value's distribution in society.
Value emphasis or deemphasis—changes due to improved or worsened conditions that arouse dormant or minor values or reduce important ones.

189

Value redeployment—redefinition of the area of a value's applicability, which may result in an extension (e.g., civil rights now include equal rights to employment) or a -contraction.

Value abandonment—for example, giving up one religious faith for another. Acquisition and abandonment are the most radical forms of value change.

Value rescaling—a reranking of importance that can be done to acquisition, emphasis change, redeployment, or abandonment.

All are changes that can either be caused directly or be the indirect result of changes in other values. Examples of the direct causes:

- *New information*, e.g., direct or self-instruction or chance acquisition as from reading, TV, interpersonal relations, lectures.
- *Achievement of values*, e.g., attaining an economic status goal.
- *Disillusionment*, e.g., discovery that a held value is a poor one, such as excessive reverence of high position.
- *Political or economic events*, e.g., revolution, new-found affluence, new-found poverty.
- *Demographics*, e.g., the nation's change from a rural to an urban society.
- *Technology*, as described in the Introduction to Part II.
- *The culture*, e.g., the rising levels of education, standards, and aspirations.

And it's obvious that adults, who enter organizations with a considerable repertory of values, have acquired (and continue to acquire) bad values or value misconceptions in two fundamental ways:

(a) As a result of *ignorance* (itself resulting in assumptions):
Social ignorance about psychology, behavior, and interaction; Technical ignorance about structures and processes and their behavioral consequences.

(b) As a result of *learning*:
Obsolete values from the culture, models, organizational learning, hearsay (e.g., interpersonal aggression);
Wrong values not in the obsolete category *derived* from wrong models, literature, hearsay, misinterpretations (e.g., values on winning, losing, success).

Certainly, on the external (to the person) methods, the supply of new information, the first of the "direct" causes above should take care of the ignorance, and it is transparently the only cause in the list over which an organization itself can have any direct influence. We know too that behaviorists have developed techniques that can change many of the misconceptions acquired through learning, techniques through which organizations can apply some indirect influence; they will be described in Chapters 18 and 19. But they've largely failed on the deep-seated ones strongly imbued by society, that is, parents, education, religions, society's many organizations, the community, and the government, the deep-seated values being the heart of the culture of that society. These deeply embedded ones are widely held views that people are seldom willing to change unless all others in the community do or some cataclysmic event motivates apostacy. Also, its difficult to present convincing evidence that they're wrong, ruling out change by new information alone or by the behavioral techniques, new information being the first step in all cases. So their change must be sponsored by society, and it is a slow process over which individual organizations other than educational ones have little influence.

In sum, values can be classified as follows according to the way they may be changed, number 1 being the answer to much of the ignorance just referred to, and number 2 the solution to learned misconceptions that are not deep-seated:[b]

Value Classification by Rate of Change	Principle Mode of Inducing Change
1. Fast to change	by New information
2. Medium	by Behavioral techniques
3. Slow	by Cultural conditioning over a long period

Possible Programs. What organization managements can do to change or upgrade values is plainly limited to numbers 1 and 2, and certainly not all of that is within their power. Much of number 1 and all of number 3 is up to the institutions of society, that is, education, government, and institutions of the private sector like industry associations. It might simplify matters to think of planning two programs: an *internal program*: numbers 1 and 2 within organizations, a principal purpose of the balance of the book; and an *external program*: numbers 1 and 3 by society and its institutions.

The internal program. With these elementary facts, skeletal outlines for the two programs can be put together. The minimal requirements of the internal program would be (corresponding to a and b on page 190):

A. *Information*
   1. Social knowledge—the behavioral sciences on the individual, values, motivation, group dynamics, people leadership.

    2. Technical knowledge—structures and processes, includin
    planning, control, authority, organization design, etc., and thei
    impact on people.

B. *Learning, unlearning, and relearning* (Values and behavior)[c]
    1. Organization development techniques and technical-socia
    integration, direct and indirect.
    2. Organization development applications—T-grouping an
    integration implementation, which should include neede
    changes of organizational structures and processes; among them
    policy upgrading and the scheduling of reinforcements fo
    desired performance and behavior.

Some may question why organizations should get involved in social an
technical informational education. Naturally, small ones can't afford muc
of it, must buy adequately developed managers, but the present practice
of larger firms, including the paying for managers' outside courses (par
of "internal" programming), ought to be sufficient evidence that they're sur
of the investment return and the practical need to help on the move up th
promising, less-educated prospects. A few even operate degree-confirmin
colleges.[d]

Nevertheless, virtually all the courses that are social education or that hav
a social component have to undergo substantial improvement to adequatel
achieve their goals, which they rarely do, and the improvements require
span both the "information" and "learning" aspects of the problem.

To date, the best overall approach to these needs has clearly been in-hous
organization development, but OD too—that should be preceded b
preparatory education—has been found wanting. On its coverage of value
themselves, it is not that OD behaviorists have been unaware of the exten
of the bad ones, rather it seems that they've underrated them, partly for lac
of values analysis to clarify in their own minds their power, what can b
done about which ones, how, and the time requirements. The other failure
it appears, has been their failure to make an adequate effort to change th
more visible dysfunctional behavior they've seen, eliminating crucia
processes to speed up their OD effort in order to please the managemen
clients involved.

Consequently the successes of OD have been limited to situations wher
there was a crying need to *do something*; then after recovery, or anywher
else it was being tried out for general performance improvement, th
techniques have been dropped within 6 to 12 months, and reliance generall
shifted to participation that we now know has limited potential (see pag
390).

Of course, until the advent of OD in one's own outfit—the entry itself requiring many considerations and careful planning—there are still plenty of elementary principles of management dedicated to the consideration of subordinates' held values and needs that managers should learn and follow.

Basic principles of contests, for example, are regularly violated. A study by Rensis Likert illustrates how it happens to apply to sales management. Other principles will be described and illustrated in chapters ahead.) An abridged quotation from Likert:[4]

> Contests and similar competitive procedures are (commonly) used in an attempt to capitalize on each salesman's drive for a sense of personal worth... There are serious "side effects" from this use of one of man's most powerful drives which are costly to the organization. The motivation is one of helping only themselves and avoiding helping those with whom they are competing, of not sharing new information, better appeals, answers, strategies, new markets, etc., nor helping on tough sales problems or asking for help.
>
> The findings (in the 40 sales offices studied and reported in Part II) show that the most successful sales managers are discovering that using the competitive drive this way yields productivity but appreciably short of the best, that the best performance, lowest costs and highest levels of earnings and satisfaction occur when it is used to motivate cooperation rather than competition with one's peers and colleagues. For example, the individual can compete with his own past record or with "par for the course;" even better, the entire sales office can compete with its own past record and with a current goal.[c]
>
> All that has been said is of course equally applicable to sales managers. Pitting office against office or region against region are all less sophisticated ways to apply the drive, yielding poorer results.[5]

The External Program. Section iii of the hypothesis on page 34 took account of the fact that the internal managements of organizations cannot alone eliminate the I-O gap; society has an important part to play.

Simple logic, even without the foregoing, tells us that it must start with the upgrading of values and philosophies, the formal education establishment being in the keystone position by virtue of its teaching those who will be future employees, managers, parents, and teachers; and to it we can now add academe's growing adult education and contract development programs for the managers of industry.

Implied in the hypothesis is the assumption that the education, along with improved behavior, will lead to the external institutional structure and process improvements needed to foster the desired attitudes and conduct and to discourage the undesirable.

The minimal program for achieving all this would cover the following:

A. *Education*
1. Research on what values the nation wants to hold and should hold, and how to teach them to:
   a. children and adolescents
   b. college students and adults.
2. Educational programs
   a. Type 1 values and the relevant ethics (p. 191)
   b. Type 2 values and associated ethics by behavioral techniques
   c. A long-range plan for type 3 values and associated ethic
   d. Value systems education (within a, b, and c): orientations philosophies, and ideologies
   e. the education necessary for B and C below.

B. *Industry and professional organizations*
1. Education on and promotion of leadership development with it values upgrading and ethics as described in Chapters 20 and 21
2. The definition of and promotion of social responsibility.
3. Leading the reform of corporate governance.
4. Codes of ethics for both internal and external relations.
5. Professionalizing organizational leadership.

C. *Government*
1. Industry regulation, to the extent that industry makes i necessary, through agencies such as SEC and FDA.
2. Federal laws, to the extent that self-management by industry i inadequate, on governance, employee rights, and behavior.

The First Step—New Information

Whether value change is attempted by internal or external methods, jus a careful reading alone of basic information can start the neurons firing in the right direction for both the categories of ignorance and learning on pages 190. The list of misconceptions on page 118 itself suggests a way to organize it:

(a) Power, authority, and control
(b) Emotions
(c) Inappropriate interpersonal competition and its principal underlying causes:
   Aggression
   Winning
   Masculinity
(d) Success

The information needed to change or improve values on the first three losely related subjects in (a) is so important to managing that in addition o the philosophy of authority just presented (pages 166-170), a whole hapter will be devoted to it ahead (Chapter 11), and because emotions (b) re often confused with motivations, they'll be discussed under that subject n the next chapter.

Interpersonal competition (c). By the time we graduate from high school ve've of course come to realize fully that competition is the driving force, he key factor in the spectacular superiority of free enterprise in America nd worldwide in comparison to the performance of communist economies. As a result, the average citizen is most reluctant to criticize this sacred cow or fear of inadvertently crippling his or her whole future within the system. Even the education establishment tends to steer clear of it.

In general, the *intercompany* competition modus operandi, we know, has matured, at least on the surface, to a reasonably gentlemanly functioning n which each firm doesn't try to literally destroy others and, at the most, ngages in "limited warfare" for greater market share, largely abiding by accepted norms; formal law provides some deterrence to the less restrained.

Similarly, *interpersonal* competition seems to be innocuous enough, and ve go to considerable lengths to "toughen" ourselves to thinking it is. A part of the lore and spirit, for example, is to be up to the fray; in Harry Truman's famous words, "If you can't stand the heat, get out of the kitchen."

But the more thoughtful, accepting the competitive system's superiority, have important reservations about the universal blessing we've accorded it and, furthermore, realize that you can question the rules of the game without hreatening the whole game. The reluctance to do so is often what created he sacred cows in the first place, and, in almost every instance, such taboos ventually brought on serious malfunctioning or ruptures of one kind or another.

The sociological origin and development of this particular cow give a clear explanation of why it is still pervasive. Stated simply, in the early animal stages of human evolution when the visible resources of sustenance vere not abundant, competitive battle was obviously the mode of distribution. But eventually the species became herd creatures because of an intuitive realization that cooperative effort was essential to both defense and obtaining larger prey, resulting in a need for the resources to be *shared*.

Then with advancing socialization we evidently learned somewhere along he line that cooperation could also lead to the resources being *increased*, providing more for all.

Indeed, today Western and advanced Eastern civilizations clearly have a surfeit of resources. Selected shortages, including the energy one, will come and go, science eventually curing them all, so there are few instances outsid of deep poverty where personal competitive aggression as a public polic is really needed for resource distribution.

Particularly important now, growing organizational size and complexit in all sectors of society are requiring the highest degree and quality c cooperation and coordination to make the layer on layer of interactin systems, groups, and individuals function. But interpersonal competitio by its very nature demands *non-cooperation.*

On the other hand, competition, we know, has literally been from th beginning the way in which the species has progressively selected the bette members for species improvement through the propagation process, an it seems still to do so in a very general way today. The sciences may in th distant future develop analytical techniques to rate and rank us, but it presently inconceivable that it will ever happen. Further, competition no only does a fair job of identifying and ranking talent, competence, an quality, but it is also clearly associated with the human creative an achievement drives.

The benefits are definitely overwhelming and accrue to the point of bein somewhat blinding; we've been so well conditioned from early childhoo with the combination of an appreciation for them and their importance t "success" that virtually no one noted the liabilities until the behaviorist came along. Even today few people are listening, and few will until the understand at least the principal ones.

Liabilities. For an introduction, it's been shown by research that ther are numerous serious negative consequences in organizational life that we'v been inclined to ignore, especially that:[6]

1. Competition (in organizations) can often set individuals agains others and group against group in dysfunctional behavior.
2. It often results in a shifting of objectives from obtaining a resourc or winning, to blocking or destroying the competitor.
3. Competition inevitably results in winners and losers, and at least som of the hidden costs of losing can be rather high in systemic term

Interpersonal illustrations (individuals) of the first are so commonplac as to make examples superfluous. An interesting *intergroup* example in th business world demonstrates well the general ignorance of the subject. Whe Crane Co., the largest industrial valve manufacturer purchased th Chapman Value Co. in the late 1950s (with expected anti-trust flak), the continued it as a division in competition with the company's Crane Valv Division. The murderous inter-division price-cutting for big contracts, back

iting, and appeals to the president for mediation went on for some 5 years
efore it became apparent that some types of intergroup competition can
e seriously destructive.

Figure A.1 on page 4 illustrates quite well both items 2 and 3, hitting
n what is undoubtedly a leading cause of disgust, fear, and often alienation
mong the higher-type managers, showing too that the one-win-to-several-
ose process is continuous, all the time, all the way up.

Chris Argyris gave a telling illustration of what some hidden costs are
ven for a fairly cohesive top management team, all of whom in his example
ad in fact undergone at least some form of laboratory (sensitivity) training.[7]
The CEO of a very large company was genuinely interested in advanced
rganization development and participative management, had been
working on them with his top group for 5 years, and had made considerable
progress on problem-solving and climate. But as a group, they generally
elt that they had reached a plateau below their goal, so they invited Argyris
o diagnose their interpersonal and group dynamics.

His method was to tape three of their executive meetings, analyze them,
nd explain the meaning verbally in a procedure known as "process
onsultation." Within the presentation, he described to the executives the
ollowing condition and the domino sequence that was responsible for the
ata and their dissatisfaction (quotation abridged):

1. The group climate is strongly influenced by competitive behavior.
    When important points are made, they tend to be made in a "selling"
    manner.
    Examples of (your) selling are:
    "The real problem facing us is ..."
    "What you are really saying is ..."
    "The nub of the problem is ..."
    "You can't fail if we ..."
    "The very basic issue is ..."
    "You've got to ..."
    "Let's face it, if we would only ..."
2. "Selling" and "persuading" tends to:
    a. Make the "seller" feel he is being articulate and powerful.
    b. Reduce the probability that a "customer" will buy because the
        customer senses that the emotional component is stronger than
        the rational, may distrust the "sales pitch." He tends to immunize
        himself from the enthusiasm, turning himself off, not listening
        but preparing his own sales pitch; and if he does listen, it may
        be to find the weaknesses in the other's position. The original

        seller feels less effective and increases his selling with cyclicall
        increasing competitiveness.

3. Under these conditions:
   a. Individuals will not tend to feel they are heard and understood
   b. The time available to be "on the air" will tend to be scarce.
4. There will be very little helping one another to own up to, be open
   to, and experiment with new ideas. The predominant stance will b
   one of competing with each other to be heard.
5. All this could tend to feelings that group meetings are a waste of time
   and what is needed is a good strong leader.

        Three members did state these views toward the end of the meeting
One asked, "What the hell did we accomplish today?" Another
followed (a softer, but perhaps equally disappointing voice), "No
a damn thing."

In the text of his book, Argyris explained that the underlying cause o
this state of affairs, even with these fairly enlightened men, was the
competitive win-lose environment created by the long-held business belie
that the most effective behavior is a competitive, selling, persuading one
and, as is common, all the institutional rewards were geared to inspire it
The president himself was quoted as saying at one time, "You know, I find
myself competing at a cocktail party with people I don't really care about
and that I will never see again."

Argyris was not trying to denigrate or knock the importance of the ar
of persuasion. The objection implied is its use as a competitive strategy for
winning or dominating rather than applying cooperative communicative
reasoning toward a best decision or a solution to a problem.

Particularly distressing is that the some 650 business schools across the
country that offer MBAs instill the attitude and sometimes intentionally
In a book about the Harvard Business School that many use as a model
the author, a journalist before and after going there himself, described it
teaching and his reaction to it; an excerpt from a Time (magazine) review:[8]

> The Harvard Business School, he seems to be saying, is loosing upon an already dog-
> eat-dog world a flock of overly aggressive competitive spirits it needs like it needs another
> war. Cohen isn't opposed to competition, he just thinks it has gone slightly berserk
> in the U.S.—"individualism gone mad," he calls it—and that it has completely taken
> over at the Harvard Business School. There, not only the professors and the students
> but even the secretaries seem content "to accept that maximization of long-range profit
> is why God hath created the earth." Any semblance of a balance between competition
> and cooperation, between individualism and the community, has been lost.

Another graduate, interviewed by the author of a new (1986) book, "The Big Time," was quoted as saying (overextending his hyperbole a bit!) about the school's graduates at the time:[9]

> These kids are smart. But I'd as soon take a python to bed as hire one. He'd suck my brains, memorize my Rolodex, and use my telephone to find some other guy who'd pay him twice the money.

The school (HBS) does require a 3-week ethics course in the first semester and offers several ethics electives, one of them called "Moral and social inquiry through fiction," but how much behavior change could courses like those possibly bring about? However it was good to read recently[10] that under the pressures of such criticisms from alumni, employers and the press its whole curriculum is being redesigned.

Looking therefore at the assets and liabilities of competition together, we must ask, can we eat our cake and have it? The true nature of aggression can shed some light.

The structure of aggression. There's no getting around it, if you want results, aggression has an almost irresistible appeal:

- it demands and gets attention (the squeaky wheel);
- it commonly removes barriers;
- assertive, dominating, or forceful behavior most often works;
- in applicable situations, non-aggressive verbal effort may get some attention but is usually ignored, especially in deference to aggression;
- money, status, prestige, and recognition are repeatedly rendered for successful aggression;
- national myths and heroes model it, and we honor and motivate it through our books, songs, and statues, whether it be wars, sports, or crime, confusing the good and bad so thoroughly we honor gangsters and exhibitionists as highly genuine heroes.

But aggression, as everyone knows, is a problem, and the last point above suggests the crux of it. Until very recently we knew almost nothing about it, so schools could teach nothing, leaving average people to draw their own conclusions from the tales of history, the folklore, the incentives, and the assumption that it is an instinct rather than a learned impulse.

It is surprising in fact that, in spite of the incentives, many in the younger college generation hold that all aggression is basically evil, a view that seems partly due to the pacifist movement and partly to the church's doctrine of original sin, from which one would deduce that the human has an instinct for evil aggression. Indeed, the very definition of aggression looks evil:

Aggression is a movement, physical or psychological, calculated (controlled) or irrational (uncontrolled), into another's territory for a power purpose: either (a) to restructure the status quo, or (b) to reassert the existing power structure for its maintenance, or (c) to defend the structure against another's aggression.

But a closer look at the full meaning will show that, although much of it is evil, there's plenty of room for some good over and above self-defense buried in the statement, and a full comprehension of it has to start with why people aggress.

First, as shown earlier, research has demonstrated in many ways that the human is far too complex for instincts. An encyclopedia's summary of the research on them with respect to aggression is impressive:[11,g]

The argument that the aggressive impulse is innate and instinctive because it is so prevalent is not accepted today. In the first place, the universality of the drive is open to question. There are men, animals and entire societies that display little or no aggression... No specific physiological patterns of aggression, comparable for example, to the nest-building instinct, have been found either in men or animals. The fact that the organism is equipped for either constructive or destructive behavior argues not only against the instinct hypothesis, but indicates that learning and other environmental factors have material effect on the way we meet situations. Dogs and even lions can be trained to fight or to play; children can be reared to be aggressive or nonaggressive; if cats and rats are brought up together the rats will not fear the cats, and the cats will not kill the rats even when they are hungry (though they may sometimes kill them by playing too roughly). On the other hand, if cats are allowed to watch their mothers kill a rodent regularly, most of them will kill when they grow up—but interestingly they will only kill the (rodent) species they have seen the mother kill.

Clearly, it's a very complicated behavior, and our past failure to carefully define aggression (and therefore its adjective also) is a reason why we still commonly use it to distinguish enthusiasm from apathy, vigor from inertia, and the creative from the dull.

Science itself, however, has not found explaining it easy. Freud's effort was his self-destruction Thanatos Theory: we have an innate drive to discharge back to a tolerable level a continually rising pressure to aggress; we have to aggress against others to avoid destroying ourselves![12] It was quickly discredited as was the Frustration-Aggression Theory (1939) of Dollard, Doob, et al.[13] But the latter did point to a major issue, that of *frustration*, with their conclusions that:

• all aggression is preceded by frustration, and
• all frustration increases the probability of aggression.

Often but not always. Not only are there plenty of instances in which aggression is created without prior frustration (e.g., sports and military training), but also there are many in which frustration does not necessarily lead to aggression. For instance, it sometimes causes only righteous indignation. However, behaviorists began to look more closely at all the causes of frustration, especially:

a. A felt need to attain a goal
b. Failure to attain a goal in the desired manner
c. A sense of inadequacy or loss of self-esteem
d. A feeling of impotence
e. Another's attempt to deprive oneself of needs or desires
f. Insults and annoyers
g. Threat of attack
h. Attack
i. Another's injustice toward oneself
j. Another's injustice toward others.

... and study the possible human reactions to them, that they can be any or a combination of:

1. Anxiety, fear, or panic
2. Flight (due to the # 1 above)
3. Self-control, including delayed response to decide best response
4. Increased vigor: acquisitive, competitive, or noncompetitive
5. Persistence, which can include greater care
6. Angry aggression: psychological and/or physical.

Although only item 6 of the reactions is labeled an aggression, we know that often item 4 has an aggression consequence, which sets one to thinking about all the possible types of aggression. Our experience itself tells us that it can be constructive, destructive, non-violent, violent, psychological, or physical, and it happens that a definition of direct violence can provide a separation of them into the two basic types.

A direct application of violence is, broadly, an angry exertion of force for the purpose of injuring, harming, punishing or destroying; it can be either physical or psychological and be controlled (that is, calculated) or uncontrolled (irrational).

One can see that only item 6 has the violence, so being a consequence of anger, the behaviorists have logically labeled it angry aggression, and because item 4 can include a form of aggression without anger or violence, they called it *instrumental aggression*. Thus the underlying difference is the presence or absence of anger or violence.

An analytical person might now suspect the possibilities of further subdivisions—there are—and try to find examples to verify each category. The conceptual structure of aggression and a suitable set would be as follows:

A. *Angry Aggression*
   1. Destructive
      a. physically violent, e.g., punching
      b. psychologically violent, e.g., insulting
   2. Constructive
      a. physically violent, e.g., overthrow of an oppressive dictator, replacing it with democracy
      b. psychologically violent, e.g., throwing something against a wall, releasing the peak of frustration
B. *Instrumental Aggression*
   1. Destructive
      a. physical, e.g., fraud, embezzlement, theft of personal property, physical annoyers
      b. psychological, e.g., the aggression behind much of Figure A.1 behavior (page 4); malicious gossip or lies about another; competitive refusal of a boss to give an earned raise or promotion; and competitive efforts where cooperation is more beneficial
   2. Constructive
      a. Physical, e.g., physical games; justified nonviolent sit-ins; mutual-consent love
      b. psychological, e.g., parlor thinking games; business strategy planning; selling; advertising; collaborative teamwork; justified indignation reducing internal tension; also see quote of Rollo May on page 207.

And then there's the overlap, as for example when frustration within the "cool" instrumental increases beyond the cool to angry.

Angry Aggression. Whether from hatred, hostility, frustration, greed, or for power, revenge, or retribution, in otherwise normal people its implementation is more likely:

1. When the person has found it rewarding in past similar circumstances;
2. When the person has seen social models (parents, teachers, admired ones, local and national heroes) rewarded for it in past similar circumstances;

3. When the person can do it anonymously;
4. When the person is far enough from the effects of the aggression that they cannot be seen;
5. As the desire for the goal increases;
6. Frequently, as the goal attainability decreases;
7. When the person is a male, an only-child, or a younger child;
8. When family attitudes have fostered it;
9. The lower the family is on the socioeconomic scale;
10. Sometimes as a result of cathartic release.

Number 1 involves the basic principle of operant conditioning touched on in Chapter 4, and the inverse is true also: cease rewarding it and instead discourage it by rewarding non-aggressive responses.

The power of modeling, number 2, was also described in Chapter 4; a glaring illustration of number 3 is the Ku Klux Klan; and bomber crews in war time evidence number 4: when World War II crews were queried on their feelings about bombing cities full of people, they shrugged it off as a job that had to be done.

Number 5 needs no explanation, and we all know from personal experience that the desire for the goal as well as the degree of aggressiveness frequently increases with decreasing attainability (number 6): it has also been demonstrated by research.

On number 7, study has shown that males, only-children, and younger children in families tend to be more impulsive in their readiness to express aggression, and the tendencies have logically been attributed to bringing them up differently, but the aggressiveness of only-children and the younger ones are inconsequential compared to that of males in general. The problem of macho will be discoursed ahead.

The fostering of aggression by family attitudes, number 8 in the list, is clearly part of the same topic, and it is magnified down the socioeconomic ladder as stated in number 9, apparently in proportion to the felt need to acquire and free themselves of their various types of bondage. Additionally, fathers, peers, and, indeed, social rules of self-respect always encourage sons also to fight back in defense when insulted, and the psychological prodding is too much for a youngster to buck.

Obviously too, however, they're taught at the same time to inhibit their aggression against females. As observed by one behaviorist, "One fights with other boys, not with girls. Beating a boy in a fight or in a competition is worthy; beating a girl is worthless. It is shameful and cowardly to attack girls ... (all of which) suggests a possibility of controlling the aggression: teach boys that it's just as worthless and cowardly to attack a boy as it is to attack a girl."[14,h]

The feasibility is resoundingly manifested by some of our American Indian tribes; for example, the Northern Blackfoot Indians (population about 800) were found by Abraham Maslow to have a record of only five fist fights in 15 years and no other signs of hostile aggression. "These are not a weak people by any means," he pointed out. "The Northern Blackfoot Indians are a prideful, strong, understanding, self-valuing group. They are simply apt to regard aggression as wrong or pitiful or crazy."[15]

Catharsis, the 10th, is defined as the relief of the emotions through viewing the experience of others in a drama. The effect varies substantially with age (children vs. adults), demographics, family, personality, and other factors. In general, for children the viewing results in aggression only in very aggressive, less imaginative ones who've watched *realistic* movies or TV programs that are *susceptible to imitation* (two essential ingredients). Other children are not pushed over the edge, usually forget quickly what they saw.[16]

Adults on the other hand tend in observing angry aggression to undergo an intellectual change, a change of focus, mood, and perception, and a movement of thought away from angry aggression to alternative means of expressing their feelings. The experience in fact qualifies as an arousal reduction, the principal solution to undesirable angry aggression short of value change, and everyone, especially managers, should have at least some of the options in mind for handling those instances whether for the self or others. The easiest to implement:

a. *Distraction to another subject of interest.* Time is on the side of reduction, except when one dwells on the frustration, which can increase it.

b. *Distraction to another pain*, for example, pinching one's leg hard until the boss's diatribe is over.[i]

c. *Reinterpretation* of the aversive event to make it less aversive.

d. *Removing the sources of reinforcement* to the attacker to modify the person's future behavior in like situations.

e. *Removing the models* of aggression for the same reason; for a youngster, it may be a matter of changing the peer group.

f. *Increasing the attacker's inhibitions,* a principle that applies mainly to problem cases; "aversive conditioning" to remove undesirable impulses is one technique, "emotional role playing" to build empathy is another.

g. *Increasing the self-confidence of the attacker:* education or job training may be the answer to high frustrations that lead to defensive attacks due to feelings of inadequacy.

h. *Increasing the self-confidence of those who are habitually attacked,* such as police, in their ability to respond effectively to others' frustration without using counteraggression; a technique called "cognitive clarification," for example, was used on police to break the chain of aggression-counter aggression often observed in their handling of aggressive people. "Stranger" T-group training was part of the process (T-group, Ch. 18).

i. *Developing "frustration tolerance;"* when self-imposed, we call it self-control; two short-range techniques: (1) reinforcing waiting behavior (waiting for a long-range larger reward vs. a short-range smaller gratification such as venting); (2) converting aversive waiting into a more pleasant non-waiting period (playing a game, thinking about or planning a pleasant event ahead).

But then, too, we now know unequivocally that because angry aggression is learned, it can be unlearned (by value change).[17] The problem for adults is that for this trait the unlearning has to be a one-on-one project, which of course can hardly be done for a whole society, only for abnormal cases. So the sensible plan would be to go at it before negative aggressive tendencies have to be unlearned: teach children how to handle or avoid anger and frustration, which can be accomplished in groups through the key device of game playing (as described ahead).

Summary. Obviously, destructive angry aggression results in a violation of someone's rights or in an injustice, and it's a behavior we can do without. Unfortunately, we encourage, support, and reinforce it in our culture and do it in so many ways even though the argument behind virtually all of it is obsolete and is based on survival needs that no longer exist in social relations. The proof of its superfluity is in many cultural groups around the world that have more benevolent norms and simply don't act the way we do.

In the minds of many, unfortunately, the elimination of such aggression from our behavioral repertoire (by conditioning plus education to always be moral) will lead to dire consequences: spinelessness, loss of individuality, and annihilation by our enemies. With the knowledge we now have, it should be apparent, except to the most obtuse, that this is not at all so. Particularly, they need only examine more closely the behavior of the Indian tribes cited, the Quakers, or other peaceful sects to find they abide by such standards without diminishing their guts or character or being less able to defend themselves.

Conversely, those who are intractable pacifists should face up to the idea that some angry aggression can be beneficial—the *constructive* kind. Most organizational people are now aware of the technique for one application in interpersonal behavior, the corrective technique known as "assertiveness training."

When an individual habitually suppresses open expressions of anger, resentment, or indignation that are justified, as it so frequently is, it is generally due to strong internalized norms that result in anxiety or guilt when such reactions are contemplated or to fear of losing self-control (which may be manifested in overcontrol), and the inhibition carries over to all aspects of interpersonal relations. Difficult-to-explain violent crimes by people with admirable records of stability and compatibility are often attributable to such inhibitions—the suppressed lid, without a safety valve, blew off.

The training technique attempts to change the values underlying the inhibition to permit prosocial, moderate, appropriate aggressive expression, developing at the same time a desire for the well-being of others, a refusal to inflict suffering on others, and the ability to reduce arousal.

A key part of the process is the development of control by *discrimination learning*, which is in fact a well-developed talent in everyone that is used in many ways, both obvious and subtle, but is occasionally blocked on some issues (as in the example above). One behaviorist gave the following summary of what's involved:[18]

> Learning strong internalized norms which prohibit aggression may reduce aggression; however, good discrimination learning is necessary so that appropriate self-assertion and expression of (non-aggressive) anger or resentment remain possible. In order to effectively inhibit aggression, it is desirable also to teach prosocial values, to esteem others' well-being, because it leads to behavior antithetical to aggression, incompatible with inflicting suffering on others. Unfortunately, teaching to esteem other people's well-being is not widely practiced.

The average citizen in advanced societies does develop from infancy on through parents, schools, etc. extensive and intricate discriminations of yes-no, degree, direction, and type of behavior, but on angry aggression we certainly still only scratch the surface with it.

Instrumental Aggression. It can be deduced from the general definition of aggression on page 200 and from section B on page 202 that:

> *Instrumental aggression* is a controlled non-angry effort for the purpose of acquisition, competition, self-advancement, or self-protective action, and it may be either destructive or constructive depending on the motive behind it:

- *a destructive* one has the goal of making a person suffer, is often called "cold-blooded" aggression;
- *a constructive* one has the goal of achieving one of the foregoing without harm to others.

Item a on page 201, "a felt need to attain a goal," is most often what is behind instrumental aggression, though it may involve or be in the form of any of b to j. As such, it is both a frustration and a motivation to act, one that therefore always anticipates a payoff or reward, which may be either tangible or intangible—money, food, property, victory, status, or prestige, retribution, "cool" revenge—that may be intended for oneself, another, or a group.

Clearly, the principal concerns for organizations are the two psychological types, the B1(b) and B2(b) on pages 202—the destructive physical is either illegal or abnormal, the constructive irrelevant—and the two psychological can be broadly labeled, respectively, destructive and constructive *competition.*

To sort out behaviors accordingly and deal with them, a practical approach is to start with the good and bad consequence of competition and work back to the thinking, decisions, or actions that produce them in order not to cut down inadvertently on the wealth of good that interpersonal competition can bring us.

To list the principal positive results, the ones we want, constructive competition generally:

- Upgrades the species in the propagation selection
- Identifies and ranks talent and competence
- Motivates creativity, achievement, and excellence
- Optimizes the pace of performance
- Raises standards
- Builds strength by making us draw on reserves
- Helps one discover and gauge one's resources, peak performance, and limits and is correspondingly a means of testing oneself
- Can make boring jobs more interesting, unpleasant ones more acceptable.

And there are the more subtle beneficial consequences of some types of instrumental aggression, such as those described by Rollo May:[19]

> ... cutting through barriers to initiate a relationship; confronting another without intent to hurt but with intent to penetrate into his consciousness; warding off powers that threaten one's integrity; actualizing one's self and one's own ideas in a hostile environment; overcoming the barriers to healing.

In contrast, expanding on the points made earlier (page 196), destructive competition can do any or several of the following at one time:

1. Pervert the effort to win to one of obstructing or dominating and th effort to acquire to one of stealing or destroying;
2. Be destructively dysfunctional by setting individuals and group against each other.
3. Make our competitive "road to success" in fact a "road to failure, because for every one person who wins there must be severa sometimes many, who lose, producing numerous hidden harmfu costs;
4. Choke off communication in situations where cooperation i desirable;
5. Distort an individual's sense of value in ways that preclude soun judgment;
6. Seriously threaten self-esteem causing undesirable effects on behavio and cripple motivation and performance when the self-esteem i undermined.

It turns out that the key motivations behind the damage in any instanc can be the urge either *to win or to acquire*, between which there's frequentl a relationship including a sequence. When there is a sequence, the urge t *acquire* tends to come first, as implied by Maslow's hierarchy, sinc possessing is founded in basic unlearned needs, whereas the urge to wi in competition has been shown to be learned. Relevant too is the usua decline in the urge to amass wealth with higher amounts of accumulation along with the contrasting attitudes of lower materialism in the offspring of the affluent versus a high amount in poor families.

There's nothing complicated about the drive to acquire; property law and norms keep it fairly well in line. But there is about winning. It's on of our difficult-to-change deep-seated values inculcated by the culture, it' a sensitive spot in the ego, and it's entangled in a web of other very importan values; so it and its relationship to the others should be well understoo before meddling.[j]

Winning. We know it is presently a leading measure of *personal worth* We're brought up to see it that way by parents, playmates, and later, coaches so that winning becomes a deeply ingrained hypermotivation. Indeed, i early years, for lack of the maturity to think about it, youngsters judge thei worth largely by the visible physical aspects that their animal sid understands, by:

- Their demonstration of physical power and control over othe youngsters,
- Their ability to inflict cringing and pain,

- Having opponents admit to being losers, therefore inferior,
- Having observers see who is superior,
- The feeling of importance and prestige gained by doing these.

...the exact same criteria and goals of any male animal when taking on the pack or herd leader in order to become the new leader. In a human, the end result cannot help but produce the same arrogance plus egocentricity, a badly distorted picture of worth, and a determination in the opponent to soon return the treatment.

There are those who have romanticized the innocence and joy of children at play, calling it only the euphoria and laughter of non-competitive frolicking, ignoring the conduct and emotions during competitive play and the feelings of humiliation and disgrace felt by losers. Some learn to lose and smolder quietly; others do not and vent their reactions. Listen to two uninhibited boys playing marbles or girls playing hop scotch.

One of the most damaging consequences of the excessive stress on winning is little known. An exercise used to illustrate it in graduate school behavioral science classes is quite educational to many of the students.

Six to eight of the students are engaged by the professor in bidding against each other for an imaginary nickel, under the assumption that each has a limitless supply of pennies to pay for their own wins. Five games are each played to the win point, the professor is the auctioneer, the score (record) of winners is kept by name on the board, and the participants take turns bidding in each game. The rest of the class observes and notes the individual and group behavior. Characteristic observations:

- The first game generally runs up to a willingness to pay between 20¢ and 50¢ for the nickel; subsequent games then go as high as $2 even though they are repeatedly reminded they are bidding only for a nickel.
- Those who run the bid up high tend to get visibly excited and aggressive.
- Depending on the group, specific categories of students are often identifiable by the time several games are played: those who set a rational limit they will not go beyond, those who are satisfied to win once, those who have difficulty not being a winner at least once (seeing their name on the board), those who feel they must win always.
- Winning in each instance is the result of being allowed to win by the others and ultimately by the final opponent.

The shocker is the realization that almost all of them lose sight of the true value of the nickel in spite of numerous reminders and no material gain. Just as the complexities of group dynamics, power, and personality are involved here, so are they all in competitive interpersonal busines situations.

A careful look at this behavior tells us two things: (1) An important sourc of the winning urge is clearly *the personal worth* mentioned, with th blackboard record a stark reminder of status and prestige, which differen participants rate differently in this and any situation. (2) The valu distortion appears to be greatly amplified if there are no limits to the wa in which one is permitted to pursue winning, demonstrating item 5 on pag 208.

Number 1 is a clue to correction of the bad judgment: for children, develo in the beginning a sound base of values that will lead to a mature sens of self-esteem; for adults, upgrade the values by any or all of (as feasible the three change techniques on page 191. And number 2 reminds us of th importance of laws, rules, and reward/penalty structures.

The evolution of our sense of self-esteem itself adduces two of the mos relevant related values (along with basic concepts about winning and losing on the subject. As social creatures, all of us, including the innerdirected have for eons made the primary measure of self-esteem the opinions o others. In tribal days, the key value others conveyed was naturally th importance of angry aggression and strength needed to defeat enemie physically. With the decline in the need for the physical, their expectation evolved to a mix of angry and cool aggression to gain superiority in al competition, leading eventually to the less hostile ideas of *masculinity* an *success.*

Today, society promotes a masculine paradigm through virtually ever medium—literature, movies, TV, advertising, sports, rewards, penalties, th adoration of women—and does so totally ignoring the costs; for example

Maleness		*Cost*
Aggression	—	Hate, distance, jealousy, guilt
Power	—	Distrust
Authority role	—	Loss of equality relationship
Strength	—	Fear of losing
Decisiveness	—	Can't ask for help
Competitiveness	—	Distrust
Success	—	Threat of failure
Winning	—	Value distortion, emotional denial, reduced self-control
Sexual aggression	—	Relationship limitation
Provider	—	Ego threat (fear of failure)
Active tension	—	Passive relaxation
Rational	—	Emotional
Independence	—	Loneliness

Masculinity moreover leads us to look upon humanism as sissy rather than the major advance of human development that it is, and we carry it over into management as "hard" authoritarian leadership and a disdain for emotions.

The larger more complex issue of "success" needs to be singled out for special thought on its own (ahead), but on this subject of masculinity one might note the relationship of the two for men, that success can make up for uncertainties about masculinity, so the pursuit of status, prestige, wealth, and power over people and the system is all the more inflamed and anxiety-loaded.

Society then selects its *heroes* based on their masculinity and success to provide models for its citizenry, examples for everyone to emulate. And because insufficient discrimination has been taught, we find the populace making heroes of successful crooks (Jesse James, Dillinger, and Mafia characters) as well as law men, IRA anarchists as well as Schweitzers, the bloodiest hockey players as well as true sportsmen; and *winning* is the dominant idea, even for the president chatting at the cocktail party described on page 198, with the destructive potential of any of the six possible undesirable consequences listed on page 208.

The fact we now know is that it is well within human capability to avoid all the undesirable and still retain a readiness for the desirable in the list above them (on page 207), doing it by simple "discrimination learning" and reinforcements that can transcend the idea of winning.

Goals and solutions

These two chapters on values, 5 and 6, have attempted to highlight the principal wrong ones and value misconceptions that are at the core of the I-O gap and organization behavior problems. Plainly, the two levels of value change stated for the external program, A1a and b on page 194, are necessary for a complete job: (1) the development for children, and (2) the upgrading for adults, both having as goals the elevation of the quality of values in each of the eight areas commented on throughout the chapters:

a. "The nature of man"
b. Morality
c. Power, authority, and control
d. Individualism and conformity
e. Interpersonal competition
   i. Collaboration when needed or appropriate
   ii. Moral competition when competition is needed or appropriate
f. Winning and losing

g. Masculinity, heroes, and emotions
h. Success.

As stated, the "new information" change technique #1 on page 191 may be enough in cases of ignorance not complicated by related values, and the behavioral technique #2 can change a lot of our misconceptions. But for many people all eight (a to h) contain deep-seated value misconceptions that will require a concerted effort over time by society to change via method #3.

Managers certainly do not have the time to burden themselves with the details of the needed educational processes for method 3, but if all possessed an overview of what is already known and can be done—thus some #1 information for #3, #2 given in Chapters 18 to 20—it would complete the awareness (of goals, solutions, and urgency) that might motivate them to speed up the processes for their own organizations, themselves, and their children in schools and homes. Briefly, some of the main elements for the two levels:

(1) The educational solutions for children (#1 in the first paragraph above) naturally have to be scheduled to educability, scholastic level, and stage of maturity (e.g., Kohlberg's stages) and quite obviously, different parts of each of the eight in the list (a to h) will have different starting points, so planning and implementation for large groups and the whole nation are going to be complex.

But the Education establishment has already demonstrated in programs and in journals its ability on a number of them. For instance, a few grammar schools are teaching discrimination on when to collaborate and when to compete (e) by positive and negative reinforcement, and to it we might add the Chinese policy and method of beginning with toddlers, which we found out about through the efforts of 12 American women who were invited to visit China in 1972 as a goodwill gesture.[20,k]

For a responding American display of goodwill by the women, it was a fiasco from the first sightseeing trip, when they were shown a Canton nursery school. Two teams of children who seemed to be playing tug-of-war with a rope quickly caught their eye because neither side was getting anywhere, only cheerfully swinging back and forth while chanting. As one book reviewer colorfully described the picture, Little League motherhood awakened in the travelers; they leapt in on both sides to add their weight to the game, pulling with all their might until all the children tumbled in a heap, to the total confusion of the children and annoyance of the attending teacher and the guide.

The guide then translated the chant: "Friendship first! Competition second! Friendship first! Competition second! We learn from you! You learn from us! We learn from each other!" The game was not to win or lose but to teach cooperation and mutual support. The women noted on each subsequent tour to other schools, moreover, that all games were taught according to a related set of principles: there is a place for cooperation and a place for winning, and the winning is just a measure of achievement, principally against one's own past performance.

Apparently, they also found that the attitude and behavior carried over successfully into adult interpersonal relations, for the contrast with their own proved traumatic, building up as a sort of cultural shock in which one by one they fell ill or turned to frivolous amusements to avoid probing the nature of China further. There were two camerawomen along to record the trip, and one attempted to explain the impact of it all on herself:

> I guess I'm seeing things here that make me analyze myself, how awfully competitive I am. I try not to be because I know how destructive it can be, but I can t help it. Sometimes I worry more about what Joan (the other camerawoman) is shooting than I do my own work, and I know I shouldn't. We're both good. Why shouldn't there be room for both of us? I even have trouble communicating with her because I'm so suspicious of my own feelings... These people remind me of my own defects, and it's tough to face.

The book's author summed up the sicknesses: They simply concluded that Chinese people are nicer than Americans.[1]

(2) The educational solutions for adults (the #2) in the eight areas (a to h on page 211) would of course be no less complex, probably more so, requiring all three values change techniques, education on catharsis, and arousal reduction (page 204), plus a widespread use of structures and processes for items (b), (c), and (e) that will be recommended in chapters to come.

But in line with the "new information" presented in this chapter, there are two fundamental subjects that, were we to correctly inform both children and adults about them, would momentously speed up the pace at which society would rectify these bad values and misconceptions: *games*, which can be the principal technique for teaching sound values and attitudes about competition, winning, and losing, and *success*, the last of the eight, that plays the leading role in virtually all human endeavor.

Games. An interesting commentary on past cultures is that none had ever attempted to manage competitive attitudes in games by cultural conditioning until the seventeenth century when the British invented sportsmanship. The attitudes apparently remained at the physical survival level until then, and when sportsmanship was added, it functioned as a bridge from that level to our culture's recent concern for the psychological level. Before sportsmanship, rules were adhered to only because of severe penalties and were breached whenever penalty could be avoided (still common today of course but more surreptitiously); the winning competitor walked away with the feeling of contempt and loot, the loser was disgraced and possibly dead.

It's believed that sportsmanship actually evolved less through any English benevolence than as a practical way of filling a critical need for an unusually large number of aggressive superior leaders per capita to rule the empire. Complex sports provided an ideal way to build the aggressiveness to fight, the ability to contrive strategies, group cohesion, and the desire to win. Rules did keep the maiming down, but conditioning to sportsmanship motivated abiding by the rules, self-control, plus coolheadedness in crises; and the total package of games, rules, and sportsmanship made it possible to train leadership, followership, and aggression wholesale, and at the same time bank the fire of angry destructive aggression until it was needed.

Combine this with the empire's heavy dose in the classroom of nationalistic "rule Britannia," and you have Englishmen to this day spending their whole lives in other countries refusing to give up their citizenship!

The physical and psychological benefits to be derived from games per se plainly extend well beyond these purposes.[m] There are, we know, three types, each of which can be either a one-to-one or team game:

> Sedentary and parlor mental games
> Physical no-contact games
> Physical contact games.

All of course require the intellect, and adding the physical in the second and third develops the desired coordination between mind and muscle and among muscles. Further, doer and spectator alike gain the esthetic pleasure of observing well-developed coordination, both solo and group, when the game displays grace.

The psychological benefits to an individual of playing games are obvious to us all, but when a game is made a team affair, the additional potential psychological gains deserve special note: (a) an affiliative satisfaction and cohesion from belonging, (b) a psychic and emotional pleasure from the cooperative effort (perhaps the greatest from pair and group music and dancing), (c) an increased willingness and readiness to subordinate personal interests to group interests, (d) an ability and inclination to be supportive of others, and (e) a developed sense of fair play.

On the other hand, it is conspicuously clear that any game has the potential also for our well-developed vices of greed, hate, intolerance, injustice, dishonesty, etc., and physical contact adds all our lowest animal capabilities of cruelty, violence, and crippling to the death. Yet formal education does little more than propose a few old-fashioned normatives. We should not be surprised to still see today so much negative behavior in sports, considering the ignorance of people in general on what they're up to and why.

For a few particulars of what can be done, schools might for children at least do so elementary a thing as subdivide each of the three game types into its four parts and explain them, scheduled to educability and stage of maturity:

1. The purpose of games
2. The instructions—what to do
3. The behavioral rules
4. The consequences—winning, losing, gains, losses, side-effects

Then as their development advances, they have to be led to upgrade their conception of *the purposes* (#1) of the games they and others play beyond the superficial "have fun" they first perceive, until they're able to tag them correctly with any of the following (or more) that may apply:

Recreation, fun	Physical development
Burning energy	Intellectual development
Reducing tension	Spiritual development
Building confidence	Punishing
Building courage	Releasing hostility
Learning leadership	Exhibitionism
Selecting a leader	Enjoying sadism
Learning limits	Enjoying masochism
Rewarding	Demonstrating dominance
Comparative testing	Vainglory
Settling disputes	

There should be no difficulty in learning *the instructions* (#2), including when within the game to cooperate and when to compete, but it may be at this very point that the less controlled egos of youngsters take off competitively. The answer is in techniques of discrimination training, conformity learning, and reinforcement techniques.

The same techniques are of course the means of teaching sportsmanship on how to abide by *the behavioral rules,* and sportsmanship itself must be reinforced by the concurrently administered values education to keep the rules-following from degenerating to a simple trade-off of gains from breaking them against losses from the penalties. It takes one back to the question "why be moral?"

Then learning about *the consequences* (#4), especially those hidden by the emphasis on winning, can be largely a matter of encouraged introspection of personal experience plus case studies and role playing, examining all the effects of both winning and losing so that the purpose can be linked to the consequence in order to promote a preference for socially-beneficial higher-type games, while providing a better understanding of the appeals of (and those who relish) lower-type games.

A major target to be accomplished somewhere within the total process would naturally be to impart a clear appreciation of the difference between instrumental and angry aggression, the close link between the two, the problems of slipover from the first to second, and the fact that genuine lasting excellence is possible only with the constructive instrumental.

Certainly, wanting to win where competition is appropriate (including winning against one's own past performance), is crucial to the species' progress, and teaching must indoctrinate the power of positive thinking toward that end. Nevertheless academe has failed to impress the young that:

- all of life is not winning;
- winning is only one aspect of a game or of life, and not necessarily the most important one;
- losing can be as important or more important.

Apparently the environment prevents the first from being as obvious as it is when read, and on the second, besides the winning, there are the many positive and negative things that happen in games given on the last page. And the winning itself is often made a mockery by the frequent unearned causes of it; e.g., the winner's conspicuous good luck, the loser's bad luck, the loser's mistakes, differences in equipment, the character of the audience, the heat, the cold, sun, last night, and so forth.

In organizations, it's as often cronyism, brown-nosing, who you know, being in the right place at the right time, or a vacancy with an unqualified decision-maker filling it with the nearest body.

The third, that losing can be as important or more important than winning, refers mainly to the loser's intangible gains of faster development against a better performer, motivation to expand one's limits, learning what the limits are and how to be confident within them, developing frustration tolerance, and having fun and building friendships when the competitive attitude is mutually benevolent. Also, the psychological gains to winners of occasionally losing can be invaluable.

Losing, however, has been so denegrated that it is often devastating long after, and winning has been made so important to self-esteem that a little (or a lot of) lying, stealing, and cheating is often sneaked in. In organizational management we simply add camouflage and sophistication to "selling," "persuading," and authority in dealing with subordinates and engage in the methods of Figure A.1. in the Introduction for both peer and strong subordinate competition; the consequences: a climate of mistrust, antagonism, no-risk conformity, and over-weening ambition. Karen Horney summarized it perceptively back in 1936:[23]

> The influence on human relations of this competitiveness lies in the fact that it creates easily aroused envy towards the strong ones, contempt for the weaker, distrust toward everyone. In consequence of all these potentially hostile tensions, the satisfaction and reassurance which one can get out of human relations are limited, and the individual becomes more or less emotionally isolated. It seems that here too, mutually reinforcing interactions take place, so far as insecurity and dissatisfaction in human relations in turn compel people to seek gratification and security in ambitious strivings and vice versa.

Mistrust, incidentally, has been shown by a number of studies to increase aggression significantly.[24,n]

Of course our society and its culture cannot be accused of planning it that way. Like leaving out the behavioral side of management, it's been a matter of first things first in progress, the slowness of the learning process, institutional priorities, and resistance to change. Losing has been *allowed* to be humiliating and dishonorable, and naturally such miseries have occurred in far greater abundance than the pleasures of winning just by the fact that there are so often several losers to each winner; indeed in organizations there are so many opportunities to lose in comparison to the few to win that trying to climb the management ladder is, as mentioned earlier, more a road to defeat, according to our present values, than a road to success.

Success. This, we know, entails the larger "ball game of life," and the system in which the smaller successes of winning particular events are but parts. It's easy to imagine therefore that one's concept of success will have an important influence on the parts as well as guide the whole, functioning as a basic philosophy of one's total endeavor.

All advanced societies hope that "achievement" will be the underlying motivation of its members, so making each new generation achievement-oriented is a most important mission of their educational institutions, teaching concurrently *how* to achieve, and the incentives are clear to any youngster: along with instruction come exhortation, encouragement, praise, prestige and sanctions (+/-) from all directions—school, home, organizations, community—for high rank in the grading system and winning in games.

However, all this pressure to achieve has largely resulted in a pitting of the individual against others, so that *superiority* has become the paramount and controlling measure. Instruction is given also on the importance of growth, progress, personal character, cooperation, contribution, and standards of quality, but the reward emphasis on superiority and dominance is so great the other six important components are largely buried out of motivational sight.

No one of course would propose bucking the basic realities of the human and society. As long as we are social beings we'll forever have to cope with rank, and we must always be goal directed or perish, so we'll always have to struggle with the frustrations of subordination, non-attainment, and losing.

But patently, success does not always require superiority, and to teach otherwise should involve little more than applying the same incentives in a balanced manner to all the factors that are important.

The salient elements can be diagrammed as in Figure 6.1, a model of what is generally believed will lead to success. The germane dominant motivational force is the "self-ideal" at the top. To it has to be applied a sense of purpose, and for most people it's the tangible reward of money, notoriety, or getting to the top of the power or prestige heap. Thoughtful youth today, however, seem more inclined to look for a place and activity where they feel they're making a contribution, be it ever so small, and it's undoubtedly the soundest most enduring aspiration. Certainly, after obtaining money or notoriety, what then? An important reason why so many American families have gone from shirtsleeves to shirtsleeves.

But frequently overlooked is the essential second half of "purpose," that part of it that has to be commitment to excellence for one to gain the true satisfaction of success, assuming the "what" is worthwhile.° Moreover, making a poor contribution when one *could* make a good one would probably invite a mess of psychological problems as well as rebuke.

There seems little doubt, therefore, that the *pursuit of excellence* is a necessary component, an ever-advancing part of the purpose that can fit any endeavor, degree of competence or capacity, or rate of progress, even upgrade the "what" as one develops or circumstances change. Being a process, it can be transferred on completion of activities to new ones, giving constant challenge and, as a part of the purpose, constant satisfaction. Furthermore, a requisite of morality would seem to be to always work at one's purpose to the best of one's ability.

One naturally has to define excellence for oneself, and it emerges from the process of deciding one's philosophy of ethics and defining success. Toward the philosophy, although the text may seem to have implied that selecting humanism over authoritarianism is simple logic, it is important

The Processing of Purpose

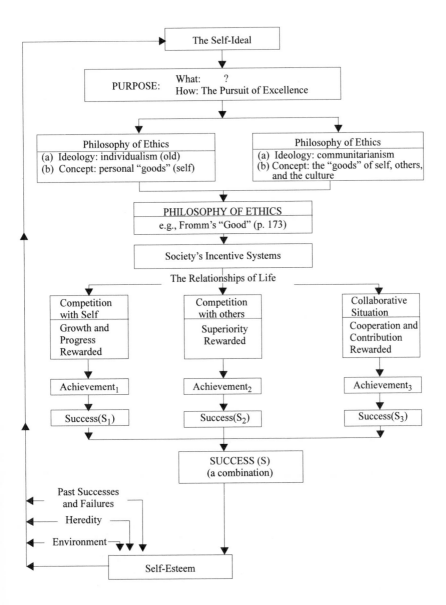

Figure 6.1

to be sure the humanism (if chosen) isn't undermined by a retained traditional view of "individualism;" one has to clarify the personal ideological concept (pages 134-138) in such a way that it will support, not undermine, the philosophy.

In doing so, two practical considerations: choosing the old individualism alone has not only the drawbacks of loneliness and high cost to society, but it is capable of satisfying too few types of excellence. Furthermore, the measure of it, superiority, is too undemanding for able persons, who can achieve it with ease by sticking to what they're very good at or selecting weak opponents. Also, in any organization or community the gauge is always average people; we have a lot of smart but complacent self-satisfied CEOs because of it.

The thinking through should result in a philosophic integration balanced by each person to his or her own individuality, something along the lines of Fromm's "Good" on page 167 that, in its concern for the *good* of each of the three—self, others and the culture—leads to the essential three parts of a complete definition of excellence: one's best efforts in the three areas of achievement for each of their specific situations.

Personal Goals of Excellence

Competition with self	Competition with others	Collaborative situations
Growth/progress	Superiority	Cooperation
Personal character	Personal character	Contribution
Standards	Standards	Personal character
		Standards

(The very fact that "personal character" and "standards" are posited in all three could be a reminder of the insufficient weight now given to the development of an admirable humanist personality alone, an achievement we see in people of very modest status and means, people who nevertheless greatly enrich society by their presence.)

Any society then motivates its desired balance of effort through incentives, positioning its incentive systems, as on the 6.1 chart, between the philosophy it has culturally adopted and the conception of success it feels is necessary to implement it, its own definition of success being the ultimate carrot.

True success here cannot be earned in but one category; it requires achievement in all three, and a society can assign the balance by ranking the rewards as, say, the least for S_2, more for S_1, more still for S_3, and the most for an optimum success mix (S) of all three achievements. When discrimination learning occurs, the society gets the best of both ideological worlds—the self-actualizing unique individual and a responsible collaborator.

As for a definition of success, the foregoing discussion indicates that one would be duly exacting and concise with:

> *Success is performing one's duty*
> *to the best of one's capability,*

assuming a comprehensive definition of duty like Fromm's on page 167 which requires all three types of achievement.

Needless to say, overt reward should not always be necessary. Aside from the fact that society's institutions can't possibly get around to honoring all important successes, they can't see many, they're not up to judging many others, and each individual has his or her own personal perception of what's important at a given time that fits personal needs and wants.

Though we actually answer partially these limitations on our own by many methods of *self-rewarding*, in organizations the same misconceptions of managers that have caused the individual-organization gap and the other behavior problems all too frequently block our doing so. Aware of this, behaviorists have shown us how to encourage it in spite of the misconceptions by motivating *goal internalization* and by structuring for *intrinsic reward*, two techniques to be described.

And of course the dominant organizational question is how do you inspire the pursuit of excellence in subordinates? Principally by *leadership behavior*, a major subject of the rest of the book.

Addendum

One can see that Education can do much toward developing effectively the key values (page 176) in the young by information alone, and for adults in organizations, humanism and the pros and cons of Theory X and Theory Y have been disseminated widely enough that any top executive who sees the light can, with due planning, tact, and timing, implement internal education and development toward the practice of Theory Y and the behavioral pragmatism on page 174—that if it works behaviorally it's right and good and vice versa.

One might observe that in many respects, this pragmatism is no more or less than a tit-for-tat of what is known as "social exchange" (described in Part II), which is also built into the chant of the Chinese children—we learn from you, you learn from us, and so forth. And we do not have to go beyond our own borders to find such children or people and such a regard for others. In addition to encountering it in small religious sects here and there, we've found it among a number of the American Indian tribes. For example, along with the Northern Blackfoot mentioned on page 204, Hopi Indian children have exhibited the same attitude. When a group of them was asked to do a task as fast as possible to evaluate the comparative capabilities of each child, none would signal completion until all the others had finished.[27,p] In another tribe when the young men were taught basketball in a new educational program, they took it up with vigor and enjoyment but refused to keep score.

In each case, what we would call winning was a measure of competence, but they had the care, respect, and responsibility that made them not want to give the others the feeling of dishonor, humiliation, or self-reproach that can come from losing. It adds up to Fromm's three inseparable concepts that form the essence of humanism (from *The Art of Loving*):

Love:	Knowledge + care + respect + responsibility
Duty:	Love + advancing the full potential of the self, others and society's institutions
The good life:	Love + duty + work

... in which duty here is a synonym for *morality* as described on pages 119-120.

A final note. Many managers (and even professors), especially those who judge themselves as successful, will be convinced that this coverage of values has overstated the extent to which present ones are dragging down performance and behavior and therefore must be made the primary target. They might consider the following. As for their effect on a society as a whole, one noted sociologist summed it up in the statement that, "In the last resort, it's always a system of values that's decisive."[28] Nationally, it is the system that permits hunger and abject poverty along-side of opulent wealth, which varies around the world only in degree.

For organizations, Chris Argyris illustrated it with the simple matter of truth: intelligent managers know, he said, that, if you can't tell the truth in an organization, it's worthless to put up with the organization; but they know too that telling the truth even tactfully gets you in trouble and can get you fired.[29] Thus the alienation and defection within organizations and the reluctance of many youths to enter them. Ominously, the "truth" problem is increasingly getting back to those best management prospects at universities.

A hopeful sign: the increasing news reports of unethical conduct of businessmen is finally goading many companies and business schools into some action. The Business Roundtable of some 200 major corporation CEOs has itself just issued a study recommending ethics programs and the minimum requisites for some results: top management commitments, written codes that clearly communicate management expectations, programs to implement the guidelines, and surveys to monitor compliance. This was reported in *Business Week* issue (February 15, 1988) along with the examples in the box below and some important comments by two ethics professors; one: "Making speeches and sending letters just doesn't do it. You need a culture and peer pressure that spells out what is acceptable and isn't and why." Another: only one in ten of the majors doing anything on it is doing it right: via a continuous program to all corporate levels.

And, there's that reservation: what the larger culture, society itself, must do.

HOW SOME COMPANIES ATTACK THE ETHICS ISSUE

BOEING   CEO involvement; line managers lead training sessions; ethics committee reports to board; toll-free number for employees to report violations

GENERAL MILLS   Guidelines for dealing with vendors, competitors, customers; seeks recruits who share company's values; emphasizes open decision-making

JOHNSON & JOHNSON   A 'Credo' of corporate values integral to J&J culture, companywide meetings to challenge the Credo's tenets, and surveys to ascertain compliance

XEROX   Handbooks, policy statements emphasize integrity, concern for people; orientation on values and policies; ombudsman reports to CEO

Data: *Business Week*

NOTES

a.   The two most popular techniques are the Allport-Vernon-Lindsay Study of Values referred to on page 138 but designed only for value orientation and the Gordon Survey of Interpersonal Values (SIV) that is principally a questionnaire on four needs plus conformity and benevolence. Other attempts have been comparisons of interests and values of managers and non-managers, evaluations of successful executives in biographies, and "content analysis" of publicly espoused values in speeches, sermons and editorials (e.g., Rescher's register in Exhibit 1) - none looking for the bad.

b.   There is no doubt that it would be difficult to separate all values accordingly, but those to be targeted initially are the unequivocal ones like the misconceptions on page 118.

c.   The answer to b on page 191, corresponding to the famous "unfreeze-change-refreeze" phrase of Kurt Lewin (explained in Chapter 18).

d.   The American Council on Education has recognized over 2,000 courses at 138 corporations as worthy of regular academic credit. AT&T, GE, GM, Motorola, and Xerox each offer several dozen of these courses, and undoubtedly there are more today. Additionally, a number of corporate schools have been accredited to give undergraduate and graduate degrees.[3]

e.   An incentive technique of pooling points toward a group goal that some firms use is on the other hand, of dubious morality, since it has the insidious effect of inciting intragrou conflict, encouraging the better performers to harass or shame the poorer ones toward resul beyond their abilities, ignoring both the punishment factor and the fact that there will alwa· be poorer performers in any group.

f.   *Time*, Nov. 17, 1973.

g.   It is generally held that humans have certain unlearned, physiologically based motives-survival factors, such as hunger, thirst, sex, avoidance of pain—that are complex unconsciou interactions of the mind, physiological needs and the situation; there are even grave doub about "survival" per se as an instinct, for there's plenty of evidence against it. The wo· aggression is sometimes incorrectly substituted for this survival drive and is often confuse with the motives of power and achievement.

h.   Research has also revealed the extent to which girls are taught to be feminine: the· are no consistent feminine traits in female children, such as dependency, affection-seekin; reassurance seeking, nonaggressiveness, etc., and manifestations that occur are not repeate from one situation to another; the universal conclusion of all research: both masculinity an femininity traits are learned, not inherited. One difference found in some studies: females we· not willing to go to as high a level of pain or violence as males, possibly due to hormon: differences, but it too may have been a result of learning, a remote learning.

i.   One reaction to this the author encountered "Baloney! If he's that much of a jerk, g ahead and hit him!"

j.   For an example, in organizations: the tendency of sales personnel to reduce effort afte reaching their personal income goals before the end of a quota period.

k.   China has the rare combination of cultural characteristics that makes such a nationwid change of values feasible: limited resources that must be shared + overpopulation requirin much other-directed collaboration[21] + institutionalized rebellion against bourgeois standarc + dictatorial authority from the top down. Clearly, a lot of long-range preparation woul be necessary to account for the differences in a democracy.

l.   Another incident: when the Chinese national basketball team played the Rutge· University team in 1978 in New Jersey the game ended in a tie, and the Chinese team heade for the locker room. Told by the American referees that the custom was to continue after th end until the first team scored, the Chinese coach said, "Why? Does someone have to win? Recent spectator riots at their own soccer games might however suggest the opposit· but those are believed to be cathartic release, letting off steam, against the disciplined li demanded by their authoritarian government (in Time magazine, June 3, 1985, p. 34).

m.   "Playing (games) and the processes of play have far-reaching consequences fc maturation, development, and socialization (of the young)." Main areas of socialization they'v been applied to: conformity to rules, controlling aggression, adaptation to social norms, sel discipline, cooperation, "socialized" competition, leadership-followership, emotional contro and tolerance.[22]

n.   In the real world of hard knocks, adults might also consider a policy for interpersona competition (e on page 211) as described in a recent book,25 one based on the "Prisoner· Dilemma:" the choice whether to compete or cooperate, knowing that when both compet· the results for both and the total are poor, when both cooperate the reverse; the dilemma: whe· one cooperates and the other competes, the competitor does very well, the cooperator poorl· so each concludes the only recourse is to compete, producing poorer results all around-precisely the situation of international arms races as well as much interpersonal executiv competition.   Also see the 1992 book entitled "Prisoner's Dilemma" that shows how it is basi to the rational side of the conflict of individual self-interest and collective good, omitting th judgmental ethics side.[26]

Values-change and trust building are clearly the answer, though feasible only over the long range. What can be done sooner, at least on the interpersonal level, to minimize the damage while working on them? The author of the 1992 book concluded from a survey of game theorists that education on the dilemma and a tit-for-tat response are about the best we can do. The policy: cooperate as long as the other does, retaliate against deviations, but respond again with cooperation as soon as the other returns to cooperation.

The importance of maturity for this in manager selection is evident, after which in-house development can teach the facts and suggest the policy as a defense until the desirable behavior has evolved and become dependable.

o.   Note the obfuscation possible in "commitment" vs. displays of energy: plenty of employees put on a consistent good show of vigor without being committed, and superiors often can't tell the difference, a point the ambitious keep in mind.

p.   A subsequent study of the same group showed that, given the opportunity to cheat, 40 percent of the children did, indicating that they felt a competitive urge even though they had been taught interpersonal consideration.

REFERENCES

1.   Argyris, C. and D. Schon, *Theory in Practice: Increasing Professional Effectiveness* (San Francisco: Jossey-Bass, 1974), pp. 6-7.

2.   Rescher, N., "What is Value Change? A Framework for Research." *Values and the Future*, edited by Baier, K. and N. Rescher (New York: Macmillan, 1969), pp. 68-71.

3.   "Survey of Continuing Education," *New York Times*, Aug. 30, 1981.

4.   Likert, R. *The Human Organization* (New York: McGraw Hill, 1967), pp. 74-75.

5.   Sales contests are far more tricky than most managers realize See J. M. Brion, *Corporate Marketing Planning* (New York: John Wiley, 1967), pp. 416-417.

6.   Tannenbaum, R. and S. A. Davis, "Values, Man and Organizations" *Industrial Management Review* (MIT), Winter, 1969, p. 79.

7.   Argyris, C. *Management and Organizational Development* (New York: McGraw-Hill, Inc., 1971), pp. 98-107.

8.   Cohen, P., *The Gospel According to the Harvard Business School* (New York: Doubleday, 1973).

9.   Shames, L., *The Big Time* (New York: Harper & Row, 1986).

10.   *Business Week*, Nov. 15, 1993.

11.   Goldenson, R. M., *The Encyclopedia of Human Behavior* (Garden City, N.Y.: Doubleday & Company, Inc., 1970), pp. 44-45, Abridged.

12.   Freud, S. *Beyond the Pleasure Principle* (New York: Liverright, 1970) (translated by James Stracken).

13.   Dollard, J., L. Doob, N. Miller, O. Mowrer, and R. Sears, *Frustration and Aggression* (New Haven: Yale University Press, 1939).

14.   Buss, A. H. "Aggression Pays," *The Control of Aggression and Violence*, edited by J. L. Singer (New York: Academic Press, 1971), p. 17.

15.   Maslow, A. H. *Motivation and Personality* (New York: Harper, 1954), p. 175.

16.   Singer, J. L. "The Influence of Violence Portrayed in Television or Motion Pictures Upon Overt Aggressive Behavior," *The Control of Aggression and Violence*, op. cit.

17.   Hokanson, J. E. et al, "Modification of automatic responses during aggressive interchange," *Journal of Personality*, 1968, 36, 386.

18. Staub, E. "The Learning and Unlearning of Aggression." *The Control of Aggression and Violence,* op. cit., p. 119.

19. May, R. *Power and Innocence* (New York: W. W. Norton, 1972), p. 151.

20. MacLaine, S. *You Can Get There From Here* (New York: W. W. Norton, 1973).

21. Riesman, D., *The Lonely Crowd: A Study of the Changing American Character* (New Haven: Yale University Press, 1950), pp. 11-26.

22. Serok, S. "Therapeutic Implications of Games with Juvenile Delinquents," *Game Play* (eds.) C. E. Schaefer and S. E. Reid (New York: Wiley, 1986), pp. 311-328.

23. Horney, K., "Culture and Neurosis," *American Sociological Review,* 1:221-235.

24. E.g., Loew, C. A., "Acquisition of a Hostile Attitude and Its Relationship to Aggressive Behavior," *Journal of Personality and Social Psychology,* 5, 1967, pp. 335-341.

25. Axelrod, R., *The Evolution of Cooperation* (New York: Basic Books, 1984).

26. Roundstone, W., *Prisoner's Dilemma* (New York: Doubleday, 1992).

27. Klineberg, O. *Social Psychology* (New York: Holt, 1940).

28. Bertalanfy, L. Von, "The world of science and the World of Values," *Teachers College Record,* Vol. 65, 1964.

29. C. Argyris, *Argyris on Organization* (New York: Amacon, 1976, four audio-cassettes).

Chapter 7

The Nature of Motivation

'he complexity of motivating people is of course now well appreciated by ost managers as well as students. It is neither a matter of a few anipulative tricks as was once thought, nor is it achieved by just engaging e participation in decisions of those affected. It demands an intricate ombination of knowledge, intelligence, values, and skills applied to the ehavioral pragmatism on page 174. To maximize the effectiveness of your otivational effort, your decisions through this combination have to have ree characteristics: be technically competent, be moral, and be behaviorally und.

Part II will cover the management technology needed, so having attended morality in the last two chapters, the way to make them behaviorally und follows. The postponed system model provides the blueprint.

ystem Model

On page 28 the statement was made that more information on the dividual was needed before the technical model and social model (Lewin's) iven there could be meaningfully integrated to form a sociotechnical one, device needed for both problem diagnosis and the testing of alternative lutions in Step 6 of the problem-solving procedure (page xxii). It is now ossible to construct one by substituting the essence of what's been presented r the elements of Figure 2.2 (page 27) producing Figure 7.1, which shows e "social system" as recommended there, though aspects of it overlap other ctors in the two columns it's in.[a]

It's easy to see from it how an employee arrives at perceptions of the rganization in column 3: the factors of his or her personality in column are applied to the components of the organization in column 2: and lainly, a leader's motivational effort has to be with respect to all the lements in column 3 in ways that will produce the best results in columns and 5.

It's evident that the Figure 7.1 model is a total organization model, not st a motivation model, that to be successful one must, for example, also elect personnel well for column 1 and design well for column 2. But sticking

The Individual-Organization Interaction Cycle
(A Management System Model)

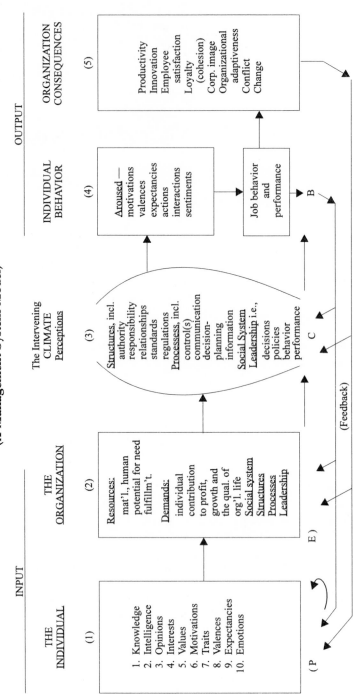

Figure 7.1

228

) the subject of this chapter, to achieve the motivation goal (above), one as to do the learning in two steps: acquire the basic information on motivation processes and content that follows, and learn the skills of how) use it toward closing the 1-O gap, the latter started in the next chapter nd carried through the book as is relevant to the chapters' subjects.

Processes

The reference is to the motivation processes of management, not to be onfused with the operating processes of the organization in column 2, and hey subdivide into those within the individual and those to be considered or the organization as a whole.

The Individual. We know that a subordinate's motivation in regard to performance is a drive based on personal needs (the page 143 definition), nd some managers (usually strongly affiliative) have known intuitively now to arouse it positively and consistently, but most who make the effort lave to learn over time by trial and error. It's an ordeal that can be largely liminated when you know what you're dealing with from the start, know he thinking process used by the individual, and know what the person puts nto it, the content. This would greatly help answer how The Individual column 1) in Figure 7.1 judges The Organization (column 2) to produce he Climate perceptions (column 3).

The fundamental forces in the human are drives, direction, and activation. The *drives* subdivide into biological maintenance, psychological maintenance, and self-actualization as shown in Figure 5.7 on page 143; the direction is the decision-making mechanism of approach and bavoidance o specific stimuli; and the activation is the arousal system:

Biological Maintenance Drives are operated principally by an internal mechanism called "homeostasis" that, in the event of tissue, safety, or substantial sex deficiencies or imbalance, arouses the needed chemistry for rebalance within an equilibrium range. The psychodynamic theorists considered these primary, the bases of all motives, a view subsequently rejected.

Psychological Maintenance Motives (the word "motive" substituted for "drive" when psychology is involved) also have equilibrium needs, the learned ones in column 3 of Figure 5.7 and the unlearned ones in column 2 that may be genetically endowed; the equilibrium is necessary to be able to integrate thinking, feeling, and action into consistent organized behavior.

The Self-actualization Motive is unique to the human, a major feature that puts us above all other creatures. More ahead.

Direction is the part of the response decision that decides the approach or avoidance on certain stimuli, a genetically endowed automatic reaction, but one can consciously override it.

Activation is the arousal system that commands the response and its energy in a range of very low or slow to panic, the amount crucial to efficient performance, too little being inadequate, a moderate amount the best on attention and coordination, and too much obstructing mental processes.

Motivation from the process point of view alone is naturally a matter of how to influence these three successfully by satisfying the needs-motives values triad through the first factor, the needs; the means: the extrinsic and intrinsic reinforcers on page 86 that translate into the corresponding two types of motivation:

The Two Types of Motivation

Extrinsic motivations: satisfactions of either material or psychological needs that are applied by others or the organization through pre-action incentive or post-action reward.

Intrinsic motivations: qualities of the work itself or of relationships, events, or situations that satisfy basic psychological needs (such as achievement, power, affiliation autonomy, responsibility, creativity, and self-actualization) in a self-rewarding process.

In the early period of trying to explain this process, however, the behaviorists simplified their approach by considering only the effect of the extrinsic, perhaps with the thought that the same principles might apply to the intrinsic, which or course they don't. But even at that, it was still necessary to account for the complexity of the individual's personality and the major variables of the situation.

Around 1964 two men, J. W. Atkinson and V. H. Vroom, succeeded separately developing similar landmark theories of motivation. They were called *expectancy theories*, based on the writings of Tolman, Lewin, and Rotter and the phenomenology personality theory, which, recall (pages 53-54), stressed the whole person, perception, purposiveness, and the immediate experience. Vroom's theory was the one that became more popular because it targeted the needs of management.[1]

In brief, a person's motivation to do something, he said, is a function of the perceived value of the outcome of the effort and the expectation that the effort will produce the outcome. His model: $F = \Sigma (V \times E)$, with F the force of motivation, V (for valence) the subjective value given the outcome, and E the expectancy.

The key concept is that different individuals have different degrees of motivation for the same outcomes and different outcomes, everyone with a unique combination of valences and expectancies, the outcome (V) in organizations having two levels. The first is the performance goal set by the organization, the outcome planned for the individual; the second is the reward for performance (incentive, promotion, praise, security) and other possible consequences. Second level outcomes desired by the person are labeled positive (+), objectionable ones negative (−) those receiving indifference zero, and all are totaled for a net figure.

The E is the degree of expectation, the believed probability ranging from zero to 1, that success on the first level will result in the desired outcome(s) on the second.

As for the model's utility, the intent was not to show how to motivate subordinates with specific devices (as attempted by Herzberg), only to help managers analyze their performances for improvement by understanding the process and major variables in the subordinates' minds.[b]

The Organization. But of course any planning for improvement must be in terms of the organization's needs, which brings into play one of the most basic social principles, the one known as the cognitive *theory of social exchange* that dates back to antiquity and was revitalized in 1958 by Homans:[2]

> Social behavior is an exchange of goods, material and nonmaterial; ... persons that give much to others try to get much from them, and persons that get much from others are under pressure to give much to them. The process of influence tends to work out at equilibrium to a balance in the exchange.

Each party, say a and b, attempts to reach a balance to his or her own satisfaction of the equation (Reward − Cost)$_a$ = (Reward − Cost)$_b$, which governs also the trade between the individual and organization shown below.[3]

The organization offers resources the individual wants in return for applied skills and energy, but the built-in conflicts of interest preclude either party from being 100 percent satisfied, so the solution has to be a reconciliation of some sort.

Two are possible. The parties can each compromise, the consequence of which is usually that each agrees to give only as much as is perceived to be forthcoming from the other. Or, management can·attempt to design and operate the individual and organization collaboratively to the degree possible, "so that both the individual and organization can maximize the degree to which their respective demands are met" without having to compromise important personal outcomes, like the feelings of achievement, competence, and intrinsic satisfaction—clearly the technical social integration defined on page 32.[4]

Examples of the first, the compromise, are factory piece-rate pay systems, the tit-for-tat attitude at all levels of bureaucracies of doing only what one feels matches the pay, and every situation where one does as one is told on the what and the how and only that for a periodic paycheck. The approach is logical to an organization with low expectations of its people, which a Theory X view would cause. The results are mediocrity with a cost that is passed on to consumers in price.

On the second. conceding that everyone still accepts some measure of compromise, the job design and management are such that they achieve the organization's goals while providing the individual with the intrinsic rewards that are possible as well as the extrinsic. The approach is optimistic; the results, optimal.

Porter and Lawler quoted above also elaborated the Vroom model with salient perceptions, equity, and two major feedbacks showing the exchange implied in it, giving one a more meaningful picture (Figure 7.2) of the motivation task.[5] Their definitions (abridged):

Value of reward refers to how attractive is the potential outcome of the individual's behavior (similar to valence).

Perceived effort-reward probability refers to the individual's perception of the reward return probability ff satisfaction from differential amounts of effort (similar to expectancy).

Effort is the energy expended to perform the task.

Abilities and traits are the characteristics of the individual.

Role perceptions deal with the way in which the individual defines the job, what needs to be done for effective performance.

Performance is the person's accomplishment on tasks that comprise the job.

Satisfaction is the degree of contentedness from the extent to which the reward actually meets or exceeds what is perceived to be equitable.

Although the logic of it is quite evident, it's important to understand the performance/satisfaction relationship. It's explained in the next chapter and the model's practical limitations caused by simplification, an unavoidable characteristic of all models, are:

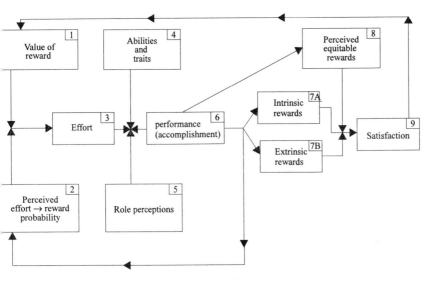

Figure 7.2

1. It is based on the assumption of situational stability and "normalcy," whereas any of frequent and significant changes of structure, technology, economics, and processes can substantially alter the key "effort" and therefore stability, normalcy and performance;
2. Effort is also importantly influenced by nonrational elements like anxiety and a variety of emotions, factors that are ever-present and need to be accounted for (but how?) and are not;
3. It assumes a direct relationship between reward and performance, which is rarely found in offices and managerial work (though it often could be);
4. Given a direct reward-performance relationship and normalcy, it is still very difficult to ascertain an individual's perceptions, effort, effort-reward probability, and reward value;
5. Although some of the major internal motives can be accounted for indirectly, there is no accounting for others that may have a major influence (e.g., autonomy, power, affiliation. security, prestige).

Yet we have to take such a model for what it is—a conceptual guide not intended to be all-encompassing, as Porter and Lawler said themselves. Any manager who studies it carefully can gain a far better awareness of the full scope of his or her own responsibility for motivation and the size of the job, that it is multivariate as to both one's own input and the others' responses, and that the manager is the initiator (as superior), whether in the matching of the person to the job (in box 4), clarifying the requirements (in box 5), providing a complete package of rewards in their full meaning (in box 7A and 7B), or ensuring that the rewards of the group are accepted by the majority as fair to get favorable responses (in box 8).

Given these details of the individual-organization exchange, it would still be an important additional help for unit planning and decision-making to have an overall conception of organizational motivation, and top executives sorely need it for policymaking. One behaviorist did a superior job consolidating it as follow:[6]

A. **Performance and Behavior Requirements**:
1. *People must be induced to enter and remain* within the system at a sufficiently rapid rate to counter defections. People of course may be within the system physically but be psychologically absent; it is not enough just to hold them.
2. *The assigned roles must be carried out dependably* and must meet a minimum level of quantity and quality of performance.
3. *Innovative and spontaneous behavior beyond role specification* is necessary to achieve organizational objectives. These include voluntary cooperation, voluntary protection of life and property in the organization, offering constructive ideas, self-training, and helping to create a favorable attitude and climate.

B. **Motivational Patterns**:
1. *Rule compliance or conformity to system norms.* Compliance is to some extent a function of sanctions, to a greater extent of generalized habits and attitudes toward authority, but they only operate to insure minimum performance. Control design and management are the means, and they have three conditions for best motivational effectiveness: appropriateness (relevance), clarity, and reinforcement.
2. *Instrumental system rewards.* Incentives for entering and remaining in the system (fringe benefits, working conditions, etc.) accrue to all members and do not lead to higher than minimum performance. Three conditions conducive to effectiveness: (a) make the system rewards as attractive as competing ones; (b) honor the rights-accumulation principles of seniority; (c) apply uniformly for all members regardless or rank.
3. *Instrumental individual rewards.* Rewards directed at individuals for higher quantity and quality of work may also help hold them but not necessarily gain innovative or nonspecific (or untargeted) performance. Three primary conditions for effectiveness: (a) the rewards must be perceived as large enough

to justify the added effort; (b) they must be perceived as directly related to the performance and follow directly after; (c) they must be perceived as equitable by the majority, many of whom will not receive them.

C. **Arousal Conditions:**

1. *Intrinsic job satisfaction.* The man who finds the job he delights in will not think in terms of minimum volume and quality; he gains gratification from accomplishment, expression of his abilities, responsibility, making his own decisions and craftsmanship. (Such job satisfaction also arises from #2 below and its conducive conditions.) Conducive conditions for this: job design providing sufficient challenge, variety, and complexity, and demanding the employees' skills and judgment; some individuals do not want them, but most do.

2. *Internalization of organizational goals and values.* Motivations associated with self-identification and value expression are, with intrinsic satisfaction, the leading ways to activate the individual's best performance in the mutual best interest of both the organization and himself or herself. Benefits can also accrue from two types of *partial* identification: professionalism and its standards of performance, which are not necessarily tied to the institution, and the internalization of a sub-system's goals and values. Conditions conducive in the overall organization: development of an attractive organizational mission, especially one with emotional significance (e.g., service to the community or humanity, adventure), imaginative leadership, perceived opportunity to grow, and high self-image from the association. Subgroup conditions (which apply also to the larger organization): decision participation, opportunity to contribute in a significant way, and sharing the rewards of the group's accomplishment.

3. *Social satisfaction from primary group relationships.* The stimulation, approval, and support from group interaction comprise one of the most potent forms of motivation. Conditions conducive for desired organizational behavior: modeling of and guidance by both the formal and informal group leadership, and desirable group values and norms. (Also see **Group Dynamics** section in Chapter 12).

Content

The theories of both Maslow and Herzberg are general content theories, each providing important insights about the major human drives and motives, those classified and listed in Figure 5.7 (page 143). But the human is too complex for generalities to be much help when it comes to "managing" the psychological in columns 2 and 3 of the Figure with consistent success; one needs to know them in detail.

For those in column I, the physiological maintenance drives, the human requirements are obvious enough, and only the research findings on "ranking" might be a useful addition. Indeed, the only thing we really need to add is that all attempts to rank these drives and motives in order of importance, power, or sequencing have failed. There does seem to be a hierarchy of strength among the basic needs of rats in the order of a maternal care drive, thirst, hunger, and sex (last), and some empirical observation 'studies have suggested (not convincingly) the same may be true for humans.

For examples of contradictions, we've all heard of many Maslow hierarchy reverses such as people starving for religions, principles, self-esteem, or self actualization. Conversely, some rankings, we know, are *learned* as the individual grows to adulthood.

A paramount point to appreciate about the psychological maintenance and self-actualization motives is that they're all products of the species interaction with its environment in one way or another. Further, those in column 2 on page 143 are considered unlearned because (a) we now know there are no instincts, (b) research has no evidence they are learned, and (c) they're not the result of social interaction.[c]

Those in column #3 however, *are* the result of social interaction, and they're plainly the dominant forces behind organizational performance. This is not to say that those in #2 are motivationally unimportant; any can either play a direct part or strongly influence ones in #3, so coverage should begin with the relevant #2 motives and the overlap.

Activity/exploration/manipulation. Activity is so glaringly necessary for a living creature to survive—it is even a force in the amoeba—it seems pedantic to list it as a motive, but because it is so important, it must of course be mentioned. Exploration and manipulation, however, are specific drives that spell personality characteristics, ones that have particular significance to organizations, and the laboratory has given us some clues to understanding them.

A hungry rat placed in an unfamiliar place like a new cage and near food will not eat until it has explored the area, a behavior we can imagine is related to its natural problem of surviving in an environment of hostile predators. This drive does not appear to have been checked out for higher type animals like monkeys, but we know that monkeys do have the exploring variation we call curiosity and, in addition, a manipulative drive. They will play with objects and manipulate levers placed in their cells for some time even though nothing is gained from doing so, then after a while they get bored and ignore them if there is no return on the effort.

The comparison with infants, crawling around examining and getting into everything, is inescapable. We explain it partly as developing the senses and muscles, but also partly as seeking familiarity with, and repetitious patterns of the environment, in order to find consistency and predictability. Babies need such consistency and predictability to be able to develop their responses and predispositions.

Also, over a period of time, different children obtain different types and degrees of reinforcement associated with these experiences, so we observe a wide range of reactions and motivation strengths, some carrying on through adulthood. For instance, some children and adults may show virtually no exploratory drive because it's been discouraged or punished out of them; others, given encouragement, become creative geniuses.

There are two particularly important organizational points about the exploration/manipulation inclination: the problem of *uncertainty* tolerance concerning external forces and that of *innovation* concerning internal motivation. It's evident that in our ongoing exploring we like a moderate amount of surprise, suspense, and change in the information we gather, and like monkeys, when it wears off we get bored with it. Many of our recreational pastimes and much humor manifest this uncertainty factor. But for both monkeys and ourselves, at a certain point of intensity, where threat is felt or harm anticipated, anxiety, fear, and possibly panic set in even though the situation may be harmless. Chimpanzees shown a fake chimp head without a body become terrified; children laugh at odd noises but they can also be made to cry with them.

The carryover of the uncertainty tolerance problem to organizational life is at both ends of the "change continuum." Any experienced manager knows that no variety, change, or uncertainty in a person's work produces boredom, and the bright ones leave. Yet, significantly, any major organizational change applied to subordinates can be disastrous if not done with adequate advance explanation in digestible stages and preferably with planning participation.

On the matter of the motivation of innovation, enough is said ahead in this text about the stifling effect of bureaucratic control, but it's well to recognize that failure to foster creativity (column 3, page 143) goes to the core of the individual through this fundamental psychological need and drive to explore and manipulate. We also see the heart of the "intrinsic" reward one can get from interesting or challenging work.

Affection/Affiliation.   Evidence was given in Chapter 3 (pages 55-57) that we are truly social organisms, and B. F. Skinner certainly underscored it with his statement (on page 21) that "without a social environment, a person remains essentially feral, will not be aware of himself as a person, to be for oneself is almost to be nothing."

Moreover, we know from genetic research that we've evolved a set of "constitutional tendencies" of feeling that emerge as identifiable traits at set times in the early maturation process (page 46). The "age-appropriate" time for the first signs of *affection* toward mom and dad is around the 10th to 11th month, and by the 15th infant begins to show affection for others. Our need to love from then on can be tied to an inseparable joint development of emotion, intellect, and personality, leading to full maturity. And naturally the need *to be* loved is an essential exchange reciprocal.

The link to sex and reproduction is probably the main reason, as mentioned, for classifying it as unlearned, but affection's importance not only may be for the individual's psychological maintenance; it may also include a "constitutional tendency" toward a general affection for all mankind, of brotherhood, as a necessary maintenance-of-the-species element through the species section of the brain referred to in Chapter 3.

A behavioral science dictionary definition of *affiliation* is "an individual's need to draw near and enjoyably cooperate with another, to form friendships, and to please and win affection of important others."[7] It is the natural relative of the more one-to-one "affection" motive but is essentially platonic in character.

On the assumption that its nature and origin might best be examined under extreme emotional conditions, such as fright, one researcher enlisted a group of college women in a study in which they were first shown, by a diabolical looking white-coated man, a supposedly powerful, complex shock machine and told in a frightening way that it would be tested on them.[8] Then during a faked delay to hook up the machine, the scared women, none of whom knew each other, were interrogated on their desire or not to wait alone, with others in the group, with others not of the group (who hadn't been made fearful), and with or without the right to converse.

It turned out that they each adamantly wanted to be with others in the same misery and didn't care whether they were allowed to talk or not. Not only did misery prefer company, but it preferred just being together with others in the same condition. The physiological need to avoid pain had engaged a measure of the deep-seated drive, affiliation.

The significance of affiliation to organizations is the range and quality of behaviors it induces. For example, persons with too little, generally due to an early feeling of rejection or from mistreatment, are unable to "communicate" normally with subordinates, resulting, among other liabilities, in not obtaining all the information needed for the best decisions. They are unable to motivate, therefore unable to get better than minimal performance, and commonly they are unusually high in the power or achievement drive, well beyond the asset value and into the liabilities the two drives can generate. These three, incidentally—power, achievement, and affiliation—will be shown in the next chapter to be the key performance drives that largely encompass the other relevant ones.

A moderate amount of the affiliation drive appears necessary to understand, relate to and manage subordinates effectively and to get along with superiors. People very high in affiliation can also manage well, but their unique priorities restrict the type of work in which they can do so. Their happiness and success are in being liked, so friendship, harmony, pleasing others, and good relationships often take precedence over job and group performance. As a result, their criterion for selecting and supervising subordinate managers is more often friendship than competence. Fortunately, they tend to seek social or helping roles, as in personnel management, counseling, teaching, the clergy, or social services, vocations in which it can be a plus.

Most people, however, have a fair balance of the three key performance drives so that even when there is a high level of affiliation, there may also be an ample amount of the others necessary for sound and effective managing.

The Competence Motive. One of the early behaviorists who objected to the psychodynamic idea that all motives were based on the primary drives was R. W. White, who pointed out that activity, exploration, and manipulation are, for both human and animal, no more than coping with the environment.[9] He therefore proposed that the three really add up to an overall "competence motive" and are simply specific components of it.

However, it is a consequence of social interaction and therefore is in the learned categories. The crucial period of its development, he said, is 6 to 9 years of age, when a youngster first goes beyond the protective family to contact peers and others, friendly and not too friendly. The contacts produce perceived successes and failures (one's own), and the net result of them is the developing level of the "sense of competence" that oscillates up and down as the two outcomes alternate. On moving into adulthood and maturity, the "smoothed" growth curve of the motive's strength flattens out at a level that averages the experiences, and from there on the level tends to predetermine the degree of the individual's future success. We see the origin of the truism that one's success in life depends a great deal on how high or low one sets goals. The consequence is that success truly breeds success, successful experiences spurring boldness and building the power of positive thinking. Conversely, the pains of failures psychologically amplify the negative and discourage a person toward withdrawal.

Clearly, luck is important, and the successes can have a multiplier effec but parents can have an even greater impact, first, through teaching c schooling on the basic abilities essential to being competent and, secon in their modes of criticism and encouragement.

On the latter, we know that a major end result of the criticism an encouragement is the child's self-assessment. If, because of harsh criticism the self-assessment is also harsh, the child will see failures where they're nc justified, reducing the sense of competence and readiness to explore. On th other hand, if spoiled with compliments, its ego can get out of touch wit reality, a condition usually followed on waking up by serious regressio or depression complications.

It's a sensitive development, one that depends of course also o intellectual, emotional, and language development, an important reason fc its common failure to grow in poverty areas. However, it can be made t flower belatedly in adulthood because of either later successes or speci efforts to make it develop, such as achievement training plus hard work o self-education.

The sense of competence undoubtedly plays a leading role in wheth a person is successful or not in any kind of work, but especially where th demands are high for initiative or creative contribution. But is it a motiv The foregoing description suggests it's a learned attribute.

The Achievement Motive. Western societies have apparently been least intuitively aware of achievement's society-wide importance fc centuries, because developing the motivation has been a fundament purpose of the competition built into their school systems, a feature passe down from Ancient Greece. In fact, studies of many societies as far bac as that time have uncovered a consistent correlation between economi development rates and achievement drive, the degree of which wa manifested through their literatures, a main achievement stimulan Surprisingly, it held true regardless of the society's level of advancement c the type of economic system.[10]

The impact is equally important at the organizational level. In industr where it is most visible, research has verified that company growth rate closely correlate with the percentage of high achievers in the managemen

And the achievement-oriented individuals that organizations get fror their societies developed the drive, as with competence, mainly because thei families nurtured it. Middle-class parents normally and almos unconsciously arouse it by the guidance they give their children to set an attain improvement goals, solve many of their own problems and b independent, doing it in a supportive and encouraging manner—a important reason why the bulk of the country's achievers and leaders come from the group.

By the same token, the family indifference, feeling of powerlessness, and environmental oppression in poverty ghettos literally block any inclination for it to emerge among the poor, and if they are black, the drive is often frustrated again in the labor market when they're confronted with prejudices and barriers to advancement. Indeed, it has been found that children of employees in both the labor class and bureaucracies generally tend to be low in it; they're apparently given a negative unhopeful attitude about trying from apathetic and alienated parents. Like competence, it can however be awakened and be stimulated where underdeveloped, starting to do so well into adulthood.

Conveniently for management, the drive can be measured with good reliability by Thematic Apperception Testing (TAT),[d] substantiated by the research of psychologist D. C. McClelland who has supplied us with much of what we know about achievement. The salient characteristics of a person with a high degree of it, he found, were:[11]

1. "He likes situations in which he takes personal responsibility for finding solutions to problems" for a number of reasons: (a) his upbringing has imbued him with an intrinsic personal satisfaction in solving problems, accomplishment has often become an end in itself, and commitment evidences the drive; (b) he habitually gives a lot of thought to the problems he takes on, thereby increasing the odds of succeeding and of snowballing his self-confidence through a good record of successes—the power of positive thinking is on his side; (c) the desire for responsibility is the natural derivative of (a) plus (b) and the resultant belief that he can do the job best without interference from others, the reason for its listing in column 3, page 143.

2. "He tends to set moderate achievement goals and to take 'calculated risks'." Thus he selects the situations and the odds that will give him a reasonable chance of success and therefore the intrinsic satisfaction he wants. He avoids the too easy and routine, which bore him, and avoids extremely difficult, where the probability is high that he will fail. If he has a choice between solving a problem and throwing dice to win, both with the same odds of success, he will take the problem, since its solution depends on his ability, not luck, and it satisfies the drive.

3. "He wants concrete feedback as to how well he is doing ... otherwise how could he get any satisfaction out of what he is doing?" Three elements of the feedback are significant: (a) that it be concrete; the

vagueness of praise for attitude, feeling, or cooperation that please: the high affiliation person is inadequate; (b) that it be fairly fas feedback; research scientists and professionals are high achievers toc but must often wait a long time, even years, for a knowledge o results—he usually avoids such careers; (c) since a fundamenta interest is improvement, he wants the negative facts as well as th positive; it is essential to the reliability of his self-confidence as h approaches problem-solving excellence.

In oversimplified summation, such a person is a confident, responsibl person who likes to solve problems, take reasonable risks, and measure anc evaluate progress with honest feedback—a most desirable set o characteristics to have in any manager. Note too that the satisfaction desirec is intrinsic. One will find with this type that the desire for higl compensation is no less than in anyone else, but that it serves principall as *evidence* of achievement.

One study by McClelland and his researchers provided an additiona insight on the last point (3). High school students from both the middl class and working class were put to work on a project, given feedback or how well they were doing against a standard, and paid for their work. Afte a while the pay was stopped but feedback continued; the middle class students kept working at the same efficiency; the others lost interest anc their efficiency declined.

The profit motive operated far more effectively for the working class students. "If anything, it is the person with little achievement motive whc expects a tangible reward for greater effort," and appeals of money alon without challenge to the person with a lot of the achievement drive is no only unmotivating, "he is likely to turn in a very ordinary, uninspirec performance."[12]

This is not to say that a dominant high achievement motive is necessaril desirable in all management and professional people; the need for higl affiliation in some situations has been pointed out, and the badly malignec power motive has as important a function in managing as they both do if not more.

The Power Motive. Of all the motive variations on the survival theme the drive to possess controlling influence over others does seem to be th most obvious survival means as either the leading manifestation of learnec aggression or the cause of it. In organizational life we see both its availability and its use in all three of its legal types (omitting the illegal "force"). Som representative methods and devices:

Types of Power Behind Formal Authority

(1)	*(2)*	*(3)*
Domination	Resource Control	Symbols
Fear	Money	Position
Command	Information	Status
Coercion	Competence[e]	Prestige
Manipulation	Promotion	Emblems
Punishment	Perquisites	

And the symbolic position is the only base of direct power that can take dvantage of all three categories though the "information" (including nowledge) does at times seem to be even more potent.

To want some power as a protective device is natural enough, but the eason for its strong dominance in some of the populace and not in others ill hasn't been answered conclusively by the scientists. There appears to e a number of causes, and the first theory on it still remains an important xplanation, the one Alfred Adler incorporated in his "Individual 'sychology" Theory that he developed in 1914.[13]

Combining his clinical experience with a little philosophy he ypothesized that, although the "individual psychology is not a highly ystematic structure, the power motive is based on about seven concepts":

1. *The striving for superiority.* The normal individual has an innate drive for superiority in the form of completion, self-actualization, and perfection rather than social superiority or domination over others. All other drives are subordinate parts of this sovereign urge that is the essence of life.

2. *The feeling of inferiority.* It arises in the infant from his helplessness and can be amplified by physical defects, developmental problems, feelings of social inferiority, or any sense of "incompleteness."

3. *Compensation.* The individual develops competence and skills to overcome the inferiority feelings and compensates in those areas that have blocks to completeness (e.g., physical limitations may be compensated for by developing mental superiorities); thus, perceived compensation needs can influence growth goals and aspirations throughout life.

4. *Overcompensation.* In some areas that fall short of perceived success, normal inferiority turns into an inferiority complex leading to over compensation, an unhealthy neurosis that manifests itself in an eccentric drive for power and self-advancement at the expense of others.

5. *Social interest.* Normal people are not simplistically self-centered but have an innate desire to cooperate and aid the common good, though, like other natural tendencies, the motive has to be allowed to develop.

6. *Style of life.* Each person strives for superiority according to the particular feelings of inferiority that most deeply affected him in his childhood (especially up to 5 years of age), and this striving evolves into a "style of life" that forms his personality. One's style therefore begins at this early stage and influences goals, perceptions, learning motivations, and methods for the rest of one's life.

7. *The creative self.* While self-realization and completion might be related to "mind," this, the creative self, was related to the idea of "soul," guiding each individual toward experiences that might best lead to fulfillment.

It is amply evident that with this brilliant pioneer thinking, Adler not only supplied many in the following decades with the foundation for their fame but gave us a number of today's most important behavioral terms. Also, not entirely apparent from these seven, there is his overriding thesis that each human is a unique organized whole that evolves as much from his or her creativity and coping with the environment as from heredity, and further, that each has a healthy measure of autonomy. Allport, Maslow, and Rogers, we know, later came to these same conclusions.

His view of *the power motive* per se, however, is frequently equated wrongly with his fourth concept on overcompensation, a view supposedly verified by the misunderstood "will to power" of Nietzsche whom Adler admired. As one professor of psychology succinctly clarified:[14]

Just as will to power meant for Nietzsche not domination over others but the dynamics toward self-mastery, self-conquest, self-perfection, so for Adler power meant overcoming difficulties, with personal power over others representing only one of a thousand types, the one likely to be found among patients.

Adler, in other words, saw the power motive as a modified achievement motive in which, according to concept #1, the achievement was the ultimate event of "completion" or "self-actualization" which was brought about by demonstrated superiority.[f] This would be the benign end of the range of power motive types one can encounter in organizations, the exploitive authoritarian being at the other end, the neurotic of Adler's concept #4.

After the Hitler holocaust, a group of psychologists decided to probe as deeply as possible the authoritarian end of the German character toward predicting future political dictators, if not prevent their emergence. Of course the organizational authoritarian is a much milder version, but there are important personality correlations.

Studying the German family life in particular because of the authoritarian national tendency, the psychologists found that there had been a generally universal incessant, excessive parental demand for obedience through adolescence that carried over to adulthood as overly obedient identification with authoritative figures.[15] The characteristics that emerged, they concluded, were a dependence on those authorities, of conformity, conventionality, overcontrol of emotions, and an exaggerated concern about power and status. An added unfortunate adult side effect in acute cases is a venting of buried childhood resentments by directing them toward the weak, minorities, foreigners, and other safe targets that can be attacked without risk, all being traits common to Fascists, antisemitists, and ethnocentrists.

Erich Fromm, it may be recalled, summarized the attitude of authoritarians who enter organizations in the form of the *authoritarian ethics* (page 169), saying that it is a conviction of one's own superior judgment in all matters over subordinates, exploitation by dominance, intimidation, and fear, obedience to authority the main virtue, and rebellion the unforgivable sin that must be punished.

Neither of these two extremes—Adler's view (the benign) and the autocratic authoritarian—present the power motive as it is usually encountered. Most managers of people are about halfway between the two; some of the authoritarian stance seems to them to be important to their success, if not to get a job done then to inspire respect they're not sure they have earned.

Adler was undoubtedly right about the origin, that the motive comes naturally in our association with people; we learn it as a means of achieving "completion." The problem is the exaggerated condition it can reach when warped by abnormal or hostile upbringing. Given good socializing forces, the kind that develops a mature personality and sense of responsibility, a motive evolves that is a crucial asset in organizational management. One of the better descriptions of a normal manager with a strong one:[16]

If a man spends a considerable amount of time thinking about the influences and control he has over others and how he can use the influence, say, to win an argument, to change other people's behavior, or to gain a position of authority and status, then the psychologists say he has a high *need for power* and derives satisfaction from controlling the means of influence over others.

Such men will usually attempt to influence others *directly*—by making suggestions, by giving their opinions and evaluations and by trying to talk others into things. They're usually verbally fluent, often talkative, sometimes argumentative and are seen by others as forceful and outspoken, but also as hard-headed and demanding.

They seek positions of leadership, and whether they succeed or are only seen as "dominating individuals" depends on other attributes such as ability, sociability, sensitivity to others' feelings, and the quality of their values.

Lastly, a most important set of facts about the power motive has recently been uncovered, and it will be presented in the next chapter (on how to manage motivation)—the part it plays in "the motivation to manage"[8]

The Status Motive. The desire for status is plainly linked to the power and achievement motives and has an association with recognition, appreciation, and prestige (right column, page 143).

Status is nothing more than relative ranking, which an organizational group or society conveys by the prestige it accords through symbols and/ or deference. Whenever a group comes together, even just two, it's for some type of activity, interaction, or sentiment (three key words in group dynamics), and status arises almost automatically. It would be a function of "natural" inequalities of intellect or ability if it weren't that society's values, prejudices, and caste systems distort the picture. It all starts with the status conferred by society and its culture at birth due to its values, and five other measures, we know, are added during movement up to and into adulthood: possessions, personality, achievement, power (socially sanctioned power), and authority.

It is the individual's disagreement with these judgments of the immediate social group that gives status its motivational force, disagreement caused partly by each of personal values, ego, and a social lag.

On the last, other than at birth society generally conveys status as a reward *after* it is earned, causing a lag that virtually always exceeds human patience, and to this has to be added the inflation of entitlement the ego creates. The sum of these believed "injustices" builds the individual's motivation to rectify it to his or her own view.

It is quite apparent, however, that free societies try to let "natural" inequalities override prejudices, caste, and many of their values. Indeed, democracy provides us through status with a patent verification that equality only means equality of opportunity: by allowing talent to freely seek its level, status differences permit optimum identification and utilization of resources. Any contrived effort to alter what comes naturally can only slow progress and promote mediocrity. A true democracy therefore will facilitate and sustain natural status differences. The values of a free society and its culture take it from there, and it is at this point in our own that the differences of opinion create our status motivations for individuals and that the wrong cultural values give us so many of our social and organizational headaches.

The benefits of status as an organizational as well as a societal tool, though, cannot be understated. Society itself uses it, in addition to its resource utilization function, as a fundamental system of order in conjunction with the role system. The specific goals and tasks of each organizational unit tend to dictate roles, to which status is assigned for recognition of the responsibility and authority differentials. While the roles allot the performance and behavior expectations between status positions, the status structures the relationships to coordinate effort toward the goals. In everyday life we see the traditional social role differentials evolve from the process—parent-child, teacher-student, policeman-auto driver—and in organizational life those such as president-vice-president, manager-clerk, fire chief-fireman, etc.

Work organizations use status and its prestige in two additional ways. It serves as an achievement feedback and reinforcement, stimulating further achievement, and it serves as the basis for signs and symbols of office that tell people internally how much, relatively, to defer to the possessor.

Large public corporations then compound its use through the CEO's pay alone. In setting it very high, most of it may be lost to taxes, but the CEO enjoys enormous prestige, it gives more room for giving good status ranking to many levels below, and the board indulges itself via the six to eight figures in establishing its own status in the industry and nation.

Self-actualization. Repeated mention of self-actualization to this point has been unavoidable because of its importance as a leading learned motive. In fact the details, it will be seen, are essential knowledge for all managers. It is not a new idea or new discovery. Aristotle himself seems to have been aware of it when he said, "We must strain every nerve to live in accordance with the best thing in us; for even if it be small in bulk, much more does it in power and worth surpass everything."[17]

But little was said or inferred about it again until Nietzsche's exhortation[18] in "Thus Spoke Zarathustra" written in 1883-1885 (that one should live a life of continual self-development toward it) and when in 1890 William James[19] declared in his personality theory of the "self" that it is a natural need. Then 24 years passed before we got Alfred Adler's explanation (on pages 243-244), his concepts #1 and #7, which were insights he drew from his clinical analyses.

From that point on the behavioral sciences began to look at it more closely and in the 1930s and 1940s the real psychology of it as a natural need began to be developed:

- Karen Horney made an issue of it in her 1937 "The Neurotic Personality;"
- Kurt Goldstein proposed it as a key concept in understanding personality in 1939;
- In 1943 Abraham Maslow not only introduces his hierarchy of needs theory with self-actualization at the top (page 9) but also showed that, while most needs and desires cease to be motivating after they're satisfied, self-actualization is an exception;

- Eric Fromm used his behavioral knowledge of it in 1947 (in "Man for Himself") to support his "humanistic ethics;"
- Sartre presented his powerful argument for Existentialism based on it in his 1947 and 1949 works;
- And most recently (1951), Carl Rogers gave self-actualization perhaps its greatest educational boost when he elaborated on his statement that "the organization has a basic tendency of striving to actualize, maintain and enhance the experiencing organism."[20] (One might note too how it dove-tails with his description of the origin of values on page 122).

It then behooved the scientists to test the validity of the theories expressed or implied, and not just of self-actualization but the whole rang of needs to which it appeared to be related; the potential utility for management alone was impressive. For example, if Maslow's ideas of a hierarchy and changing motivations on page 9 were true, one could predict the motivational consequences of successively providing ample measure of each need starting from the bottom. Research found it didn't work out that way, but it did find that:

- As needs are satisfied, others do emerge
- As lower-order needs are satisfied, they become less important, therefore less motivating; this is less so with higher-order needs (in the right column on page 143), and not so with the self-actualization one that tends to retain its strength once momentum gets going.
- Higher-order needs are not aroused unless lower-order ones are reasonably satisfied.
- Higher-order ones at times function as a cluster, e.g., achievement, recognition, responsibility, and self-actualization together.
- In light of the conclusions of Adler, Maslow, and Rogers, the achievement motive is in fact most likely a consequence of the self-actualization drive rather than being independent.
- These characteristics apply to most normal people but not necessarily everyone, usually depending on upbringing, and are influenced by acquired fears and neuroses.
- Adler linked a healthy power drive with self-actualization, but an excessive power drive may be largely aimed at coercive control over others instead of being related to self-actualization.
- The number of steps in the Maslow hierarchy ladder has been difficult to verify for lack of research know-how; the researchers have only been able to validate that two levels have reliable predictability. The limitations of their research tools are one problem.

Research, however, has developed data of major significance to management on managers' opinions about self-actualization. Figure 7.3 pictures the results of a survey of 1,900 managers in three large firms who were asked to weigh their needs in importance and rate the extent to which each had been satisfied by their organizations.[21]

One can see in 7.3a that the value attached to autonomy (and ego needs), which tends to subsume the desire for responsibility, certainly recommends the practice of delegation, and the dominant position of self-actualization does suggest that it's the most important motive of all to target for arousal to get the best out of managers.

The feelings of importance in 7.3a are naturally tied to the feelings of dissatisfaction in 7.3b. Looking at the two charts with due allowance for the relationship, it is interesting that the most important needs are the least satisfied, which brings to mind the AMA survey findings in Chapter 1 on page 11.

In another survey using a random sample of 332 salaried managers, independent businessmen, and hourly paid workers, it was found that the less self-actualization achieved, the more likely were people to: (1) daydream, (2) have aggressive feelings toward superiors, (3) have aggressive feelings toward co-workers, (4) restrict output, (5) make mistakes in their work, (6) postpone difficult tasks and decisions, (7) be more concerned with the material rewards, (8) show less interest in their work, (9) not indicate job satisfaction, and (10) think about changing jobs.[22]

What does the terms really mean? Even a high school education gives us all a general idea of what self-actualization means, but an individual could fall considerably short on achieving it or giving the opportunity for years knowing no more than that. Understanding its meaning specifically can make a big difference to those who get the opportunity and will naturally aid any planning to give the opportunity to others.

The very beginning of the desire in the individual is surprisingly the most revealing, its emergence as a "coping style" in infancy as a result of the interaction of heredity, the self, and the environment (pages 45-47). As was explained, the self develops in the early years into three parts: *self-identity* (which includes self-knowledge), *self-esteem* (through self-evaluation), and *self-ideal* (growth aspirations). The initial coping advances the identity, the self-esteem is formed mainly by the familial environment, and models are the major forces in developing the self-ideal. Given a conducive environment and normal adult models, the process of psychological growth parallels the automatic physiological growth, and the urge for self-enhancement becomes strong as part of it, continuing virtually throughout life, *as an effort to move the self-ideal to reality*, the self-ideal rising at increments of improvement.

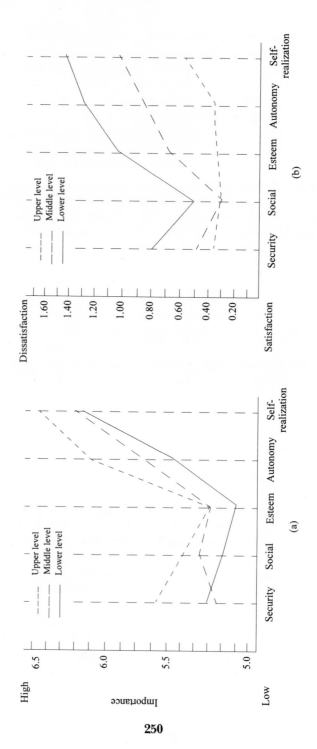

Figure 7.3

The terms coping, self-ideal, and growth are therefore the essence of it. It has nothing to do with self-indulgence, an accusation sometimes made. It describes a process toward an ideal, such that there is always room for improvement.

Those who feel they've reached it have simply become complacent, and the best defense against the feeling has to be developed early in the life game: learn from someone or somehow "the pursuit of excellence" (page 218), which not only will keep full achievement above reach but greatly heightens the motivation, the performance, and the satisfaction.

Maslow gave us some helpful insights for working toward it, thinking that is transparently basic to "the pursuit of excellence":[23]

1. Self-actualization means *experiencing fully*, vividly and selflessly— with full concentration and total absorption, free of self- consciousness, poses, defenses, shyness—throwing oneself fully into continually changing problems.

2. At each point in life there is a progression of choices ... to *make the growth choices* instead of the fear choices is to move toward self- actualization.

3. Listen to the impulse voices, that is, let the self emerge. Most of us most of the time (especially children and young people) listen not to ourselves but to Mommy's introjected voice, to Daddy's or the Establishment's—*look to the "Supreme Court" inside.*

4. When in doubt, *be honest and take responsibility.* Looking within oneself for answers implies taking responsibility.

5. Being honest also involves *daring to be different*, unpopular, nonconformist, courageous.

6. Self-actualization means both *using one's intelligence and going through the arduous and demanding periods of preparation* in order to realize one's potential.

7. Peak experiences are transient moments of self-actualization that cannot be anticipated or sought, but one can *set up the conditions so that peak experiences are more likely to occur.*

8. Self-actualization means *finding out who one is*, what one likes and dislikes, what is good and bad for one, where one is going, what is one's mission, and what are one's defenses.

One can see that #4 is essential to the "socialized power" of leadership (page 272), and a caveat should be added: be sure the emphasis on self- actualization doesn't undermine the importance of team collaboration.

It is significant that Adler, Horney, Goldstein, and Maslow all saw neurosis as the major internal interference to the natural genesis of the self-actualization drive. Neurotics are so preoccupied with their problems and defenses they leave no room for it. As Adler commented, natural tendencies have to be *allowed* to develop, in the case of this motive, given room for truth, reason, and creativity to prevail.

EMOTIONS

How do such mercurial forces like emotions fit into the organizational picture? Most managers believe not at all. Besides seeming to be difficult to predict, they all too often are counter-productive, costly, and time wasting. Yet the same managers have to admit some emotions, e.g., the simple feeling of enthusiasm, do motivate high performance. But are such forces in fact motives? Failure to understand the difference can preclude effective handling of this extremely important human capability. Learning how to differentiate might best start with a brief description of its psychophysical nature.

The genetic "age-appropriate" time for different types of emotion to emerge is a fascinating commentary on the completeness and complexity of built-in development and defense mechanisms that play such a large role in all interpersonal relations. In addition to the emergence in an infant of affection between the 10th and 15th month, jealousy appears in the second year; humor between the second and third; shame, guilt, grief, and anxiety form between the fourth and fifth; and by the end of the fifth a complete set of all the basic emotions are in operation.

Around this period, the socialization process described by Carl Rogers in Chapter 5 begins, including discrimination learning and the development of complex patterns of sentiments, those involving love, fears, moods, worry. And the cultures of the individual's society and sub-groups naturally play a major part in causing the great differences of arousal we observe. Graphic examples: a Masai warrior compliments a youth who shows great fighting promise by spitting in his face; when the men in some of our American Indian tribes become angry, they lower the voice instead of raising it; and of course there are all the diverse forms of decorum ambassadors to foreign lands are supposed to learn that arouse emotions when not honored.

Yet the seeming inconsistencies of emotional *arousal*, the event that makes us take note and get an emotional feeling, can confuse analysis. For example, not all emotions are arousing—dejection is the reverse—and of those that do arouse, the cause is not always a situational event, for example, anticipation, or getting an internal urge for some excitement or sensation. But the main emotions of concern to management are arousing and are situational, and they have five stages of development from:

1. the arousing situational cue, to
2. the perceptual appraisal, to
3. the awareness and feeling of emotion in the central nervous system, to
4. physiological changes (increased heart beat, raised blood pressure, muscle tension, glands secreting sweat), to
5. action: direction of approach (including attack) or avoidance (including escape) and activation.

Theories vary as to the order of items 2 and 4 or whether they operate simultaneously, but what is important is the existence of an integration of the psychological and physical into a spectacular psychophysical defense or attack reaction to the environment. The psychological enters at step 2 where all of learning, cognition, and motivation are combined, setting off the subsequent chain of events from items 3 to 5. Thus we see that all these emotions can have a motivational component, and research has shown us that all motives have an emotional ingredient, for example, the emotional thread tying:

Achievement and status to self-esteem
Affiliation to love
Power to aggression
Self-actualization to approval.

The overlap can plainly blur the distinction, and confusion could be added by the fact that both emotions and motives are conditions of tension or stress due to an imbalance of the homeostasis function. But there are two guidelines to help differentiation.

First, in an emotion, when the homeostatic imbalance (step 4 above) occurs, it is subjectively experienced as feelings, during which time the motivational component, if any, is quite subdued. But for a motive, the feelings are of minor importance, and the goal is the dominant feature. In sum:

Motives stress goals.
Emotions stress feelings.

Second, emotions, we know, range from quiescent to explosive and, as implied, from just feeling to feeling plus strongly goal-directed emotions. For instance, affection can be passive or impel one to embrace depending on the situation, and anger can be just indignation or motivate to destroy. Thus the intensity of an emotion (which is usually, but not necessarily, due to the situation) has a lot to do with where it lands on the scale of feelings-only to goal-directed feelings.

Of course, because each emotional feeling along the intensity continuum, having significantly unique characteristics, has been given a different label, the labels themselves often help one tell the difference.

The chart below attempts to illustrate the stress of the two words and the overlap.

Emotions		Motives	
← ———————	Goal-directing	——————— →	
With Feeling Only	With Feeling and Goal Direction	Physiological Maintenance	Psychological Maintenance
Confusion	Desire	Food	Achievement
Dejection	Anger	Safety	Power
Anxiety	Fear	Sex	Affiliation

Knowing the difference plainly does not explain why any emotions might be desirable in organizational management, and if one believes the Theory X contention that decision-makers must be wholly rational, they all become automatically forbidden. However, this is equivalent to demanding that a person remove all feelings of friendship, hostility, desire, guilt, fear, anxiety, etc. in organizational affairs. As Douglas McGregor so aptly put it, "The emotional and rational aspects of humans are inextricably interwoven; it is an illusion to believe they can be separated." Moreover, he added, loyalty, enthusiasm, drive, commitment, acceptance of responsibility, self-confidence, and creativity each contain a gross emotional component; to the extent management reduces the effects of such emotions on behavior it reduces its ability to survive and prevail.[24]

To illustrate two undesirable results of assuming they're unimportant, managers as a consequence (a) either are insensitive to them when they occur in one-to-one relationships or fail to understand those they do spot, and (b) lose important benefits of participation when trying to engage it in groups.

Performance reviews are excellent examples of the first. Every bona fide personnel manager, for instance, knows that those that are unsuccessful are invariably so because of negative emotions, often invisible, aroused by the superior's lack of tact or clumsy criticisms. And almost invariably the superior blames the subordinate for the disagreements and demotivation that follow.

Learning about the actual effect of the treatment on the person might in itself bring about a self-appraisal by the superior for a modification of the approach: knowing that when the subordinate is put on the defensive that way, he or she either rejects what is heard as incorrect, misinterprets it or fails to hear it clearly, and generally refuses to accept even facts suspected of being true. Research has produced four reasons that cumulatively compound to such an outcome:

- The level of an emotional reaction correlates with the importance of the issue to the individual;
- Therefore, an individual's objectivity on an issue decreases inversely to the importance of the issue to his or her interests, feelings, or goals;
- Emotional reactions are amplified by power and status differentials;
- The physiological consequences of emotion (increased heart beat, tension, etc.) reduce the reception of the environment by the sense organs in proportion to the increases in emotional level.

Quoting McGregor[25] again for an example of emotions' productive potential in participation:

> We say that an important reason for group consideration of important decisions is to get the benefit of different points of view. Yet by denying or suppressing the emotional factors *which are among the major cases of different points of view*, we defeat our stated purpose.

And the productive potential in both individuals and groups of enthusiasm commitment, etc. naturally goes without saying.

Research findings on the effects of the opposition to emotions have been unanimous. For an example of typical results especially well detailed, Argyris in a study of 265 upper management decision-making meetings involving 165 executives found that one of the major values common to them all was the belief that feelings and emotions must be played down; yet to the extent they were suppressed:[26]

a. the development of competence in dealing with feelings was blocked,
b. individual defenses went up inhibiting others too,
c. openness to new ideas, values, innovation decreased,
d. the probability of idea experimentation was reduced

and the general net result was lost group vitality. Some of the appalling particulars, moreover, were:[27]

- Restricted commitment—for example, less-than-open discussion often leads to labelling a less-than-fully-accepted proposal by the superior as "his baby, not mine."
- Subordinate gamesmanship—for example, the techniques used by group to present negative information to a president in order that not upset him, commonly practiced in a preparatory dry-run presentation.
- Lack of awareness—for example, failure of executives to understand both their own behavior patterns and their impact on others. Typical interview contradictions:
  "I have an open relationship with my superior;" later: "I have no idea how my superior evaluates my work or feels about me."
  "We say pretty much what we think;" later: "We are careful not to say anything that will upset one another."
- Blind spots—for example, in all the organizations studied, upper executives were unaware of their subordinates' negative feelings about them, and in middle management looking upward:
  71% did not know where they stood with their superiors,
  65% did not know what qualities led to success,
  87% felt conflicts were seldom coped with,
  65% thought the most unsolved problem of the organization was top management's inability to help them overcome intergroup rivalries, lack of cooperation, and poor communication.
  59% evaluated top management effectiveness as "not too good" to about average.
- Distrust and antagonism—the organization norms that coerce individuals into hiding emotions inevitably create an information vacuum between superiors and subordinates that the subordinates fill in with their own offended imaginations.
- Processes damaged—when the above defensive activities are set in motion the decision-making effectiveness decreases in direct relation to the importance of the decision to the decision-makers; that is, the defenses are most pronounced when they can do the most harm.
- And it is the better, most committed executives that are most upset by the performance; the others simply lament, "I told you so."

These executives were in six firms (one medium technology and five high technology) progressive enough to want to work on team development, so one can suspect substantially higher doses of the same for average companies. Argyris added that this kind of climate is not by any means restricted to business organizations; it can be found just as frequently among managements of education, research, trade unions, governments, and the ministry.

What we really want of course is to accentuate the desirable types of emotion and minimize the undesirable,[h] which can get started only after the superior learns these facts about the subject, makes eminently clear his or her acceptance of emotional expression (within common sense), and is ready to discuss those expressions with understanding and charity. The significant milestone of progress then will be the point at which there's a mutual interest in unselfconsciously probing the impact of feelings on important decisions at hand.

Chapters 17 to 21 will provide a variety of techniques and policies dedicated to building the trust and openness that are essential prerequisites to such a climate. For the present, the salient facts can be summarized as follows:

● Motives stress goals; emotions stress feelings.
● If the behavior you've observed is a motive, what to do about it is discoursed in the next chapter; if it's an emotion, first evaluate whether it is a desirable or dysfunctional one, then before acting consider that:
● Emotions are wired into and influence all behavior, from a little (that usually appears rational) to a lot (that may appear irrational).
● They are an inseparable part of all thinking and doing and cannot be turned off by internal will-power or external persuasion.
● When a defense mechanism, the degree of arousal is logically proportional to the importance of the issue to the individual.
● The desirable emotions are essential to optimum productivity and creativity, individually and organizationally.
● A dysfunctional emotion in an otherwise rational person calls for a reassessment of what happened, a cooling-off period, and/or other recourses taught in a good interpersonal skills course, which all managers should have had or should take.

It is appropriate, however, to comment at this point on the recent rash of new books promoting the emotion factor as the key to leadership success, pushing the idea that tenderness, vulnerability, and affectionate demonstrativeness are what counts, one going so far as to suggest a corporate goal of "having fun" should be on a par with making a profit.

The two most popular books, "In Search of Excellence"[28] and "A Passion for Excellence,"[29] do in fact have much of value on desirable leadership behavior, but they also go overboard. A dominant pitch: "You gotta love, you gotta care ..." (perhaps intended to jar the hardened into at least trying) All of them raise serious concern about what they're really up to, that in fact they're suggesting that "by conjoining 'love' and manipulativeness 'vulnerability' and trickery, managers can seize a competitive edge."[30]

Aside from the immorality involved when these are the intent, three majo flaws of such books as guides for organizational leadership should be kep in mind: (1) their failure to give any attention at all to values change firs reinforcing the suspicion of manipulation (or ignorance of the subject); (2 the general neglect of the requisites of leadership variability for effectivenes across different conditions and circumstances (see pages 348-349); (3) the barely refer to, let alone incorporate, the management technology half an the necessary integration of the social and technical in organizationa leadership. Result: They only deal with *behavior*, and superficially at that and are gross misrepresentations of the organizational leadership function

NOTES

a. *Explanatory Notes*: (I) The model clearly excludes the external forces; the individual organization interaction is of course not a closed loop the way it may seem here, an organization and its people being a relatively open system interacting with the outsid environment as well. (2) Column 3 illustrates how charts oversimplify reality, e.g., processe are commonly structures and structures often contain processes; leadership is a process, policie are also structures, and one can see major parts of the social system in both.

b. For example, if a goal set for a subordinate manager was higher volume output fo the manager's unit than produced in the previous period, and the output the unit subsequentl produced was less than that goal, one should ask, along with the standard ones, what wer the person's own goals vs. the one agreed to with the superior, and what did the subordinat believe were the odds of being awarded them for achievement? For example, were the persona goals a pay raise right after achievement and/or quicker promotion, and were the expectation high, low, or zero? Further, the subordinate may not believe there's a connection between th two levels, or may not believe the organization's goal is attainable. Note that because of th multiplication sign (x), if either V or E is zero, so is the motivation, and the summation sig (Σ) requires the incorporation of *all* outcomes considered by the subordinate, including suc negative ones as cost to health or hostile group attitudes for exceeding the group's norms Clearly, management can influence the motivation (F) through V, E, or both together.

c. The development of affection and nurturance is believed to precede social interaction probably because of their close relationship to the physiological sex drive.

d. Found by McClelland and others to be reliable for all three drives of achievement, powe and affiliation. Also see the modified test on pages 355-356.

e. Competence would include all the technical and social skills. It does not refer to th so-called "motive" on pages 239-240.

f. Rollo May similarly said, "Far from treating power only as a term of abuse... I us it as a description of a fundamental aspect of the life process." In *Power and Innocence.* op cit., p.20.

g. As said, the Thematic Apperception Test (TAT) is a good one for evaluating power well as achievement. The Minor Sentence Completion Scale (by J. B. Minor) is another ne used.

h. A short list of the undesirable emotions: hostility, uncooperativeness, defiance, nmaturity, aggression, greed, prejudice, hypocrisy, dishonesty, surliness.

REFERENCES

1. Vroom, V. H., *Work and Motivation* (New York: John Wiley, 1964).
2. Homans, G. C. "Social Behavior and Exchange," *Academy Journal of Sociology*, Vol. 2, May 1958.
3. Porter, L W., E. E. Lawler, III, and J. R. Hackman, *Behavior in Organizations* (New ork: McGraw-Hill, 1975), p. 109.
4. Ibid., p. 114.
5. Porter, L W. and E. E. Lawler, III, *Managerial Attitudes and Performance* (Homewood, l.: Irwin-Dorsey, 1968), p. 165.
6. Katz, D. "Motivational Basis of Organizational Behavior," *Behavioral Science*, 1964, p. 131-146 (abridged).
7. *Dictionary of Behavioral Sciences*, compiled by B. B. Wolman (New York: Van Iostrand Reinhold Co., 1973).
8. Schachter, S., *The Psychology of Affiliation* (Stanford: Stanford University Press, 1959).
9. White, R. W., "Motivation Reconsidered: The Concept of Competence." *Psychological review*, 1959, 66, pp. 297-333.
10. McClelland, D. C., *The Achieving Society* (Princeton: D. Van Nostrand, 1961).
11. MaClelland, D. C., "Business Drive and National Achievement," *Harvard Business review*, July-August 1962, p. 99. (Abridgements in which the quotations are his.)
12. Gellerman, S., *Motivation and Productivity* (New York: The American Management .ssociation, 1963), pp. 129 and 133.
13. Adler, A., *Practice and Theory of Individual Psychology* (London: Lund-Humphries, 923, first English publication).
14. Ansbacher, H. L., "Individual Psychology," *American Handbook of Psychiatry*, edited y Silvano Arieti (New York: Basic Books, 1974), p. 793.
15. Adorno, T. W. et al, *The Authoritative Personality* (New York: Harper and Row, 1950).
16. Litwin and Stringer, op. cit., pp. 18-19 (Condensed) (Ref. #4, p. 42).
17. Aristotle, op. cit., the Ross translation (Ref. #27, p. 190).
18. Nietzsche, F., *Thus Spoke Zarathustra in The Complete Works of Nietzsche* (New York: Macmillan, 1924).
19. James. W., *The Principles of Psychology* (New York: Dover, 1950, first publication, 890).
20. Rogers, G, op. cit., 1951, p. 487.
21. Porter, L. W., *Organizational Patterns of Managerial Job Attitudes* (New York: American Foundation for Management Research, 1964).
22. Bonjean, C. M. and G. G. Vance, "A Short-Form Measure Self-Actualization," *Journal of Applied Behavioral Science*, 4, 1968, pp. 297-312.
23. Maslow, A. H., "Self-Actualization and Beyond," *Challenge of Humanistic Psychology*, dited by J.F.I. Bugental (New York: McGraw-Hill. 1967). (Abridged, italics added.)
24. McGregor, op. cit., 1967, pp. 17-24.
25. Ibid., p. 21.

26. Argyris, C., "Interpersonal Barriers to Decision Making," Harvard *Business Review* March-April 1966, p. 84.

27. Ibid., p. 88 (condensed).

28. T. L. Peters & R. H. Waterman, Jr., *In Search of Excellence* (NY: Harper & Row, 198

29. T. L. Peters & N. K. Austin, *A Passion For Excellence* (NY: Random House 1985

30. De Mott, B., "Threats & Whimpers: The New Business Heroes," *NY Times,* 10/26 86.

Chapter 8

Motivating the Individual

A notable statement by Douglas McGregor makes an ideal introduction: "You don't motivate people; man is by nature motivated; when he is not he is dead." So it's apparent that a supervisor's motivation objective has to be the activation and utilization of the appropriate motives at the right time in such a way that they function in the desired manner.

What *does* a leader want most to motivate in subordinate individuals and groups? Obviously, that they perform at their very best on intelligence, judgement, creativity, skill and responsibility toward organizational objectives, and the intent here is to discourage the old traditionalists' technique (the picture below from a BW ad for one of its seminars on motivation![1]) and show how to succeed by just being nice with a little interpersonal skill—which *is* a bit complicated and must start with planning mutual behavioral objectives. The book "A Passion for Excellence"[2] stated that the most important ones for oneself and subordinates are:

- Care of customers—their needs, service, product quality, courtesy, and keeping in touch;
- Constant motivation—in the broad sense of constant helpfulness;
- Day-to-day leadership at all levels that inspires employee commitment.

.. to which should be added: increase long-term shareholder value and return (see page 325).

You and your subordinates might have learned about them from the organization's management development courses, in "coaching," or from a book like this, but though you yourself may be fully motivated to work hard to achieve them, or whatever goals have been adopted, you know most subordinates will without reminding forget them for one reason or another (like being too busy or being indifferent). And along with the reminding, you have to motivate them.

How do you do it? A great deal is of course involved, indeed much of the rest of the book, all applying to any set of goals. You have to start with the relevant broad categories and proceed from there. The basic ones:

261

1. *Leadership*—decisions, policies, behavior—that elicit trust, confidence, respect, openness, commitment, collaboration, followership.
2. Structures and process, including standards, norms, rewards, procedures, job design.
3. *Climate*-the employees' perceptions of #1 and #2 and the social system.

One can see that in essence the full function of leadership is involved, and the "how" is commonly summed up in the word *style*.

In this regard however, "style" does need a little clarification because of the loose use and misuse of it by many management writers. Three elements are involved: personality, interpersonal skills, and managerial skills (managing the management technology), and four terms show how to combine them:

| Personality style
Leadership behavior | } | : | they are synonymous, refer to the leadership of the
social (people) only through personality and interper-
sonal skills |
| Leadership style[a]
Managerial behavior | } | : | they are synonymous, refer to the leadership of both
the social and the technical aspects of the organization |

Thus the first two, erroneously the most popular concepts of organizational leadership, refer to only half the job, the second two the whole job, the internal part being the subject of the book, and the preferred phrasing is leadership style with "organizational" in front of it— *organizational leadership style*—the term desirably putting greater stress on people leadership than technical managing because, in most instances, the technical itself requires a people leadership perception.

Plainly, the leadership in the #1 is what directly activates (or not) the desired motives, with #2 and #3 functioning indirectly, and for a superior to consciously behave in a motivating way naturally requires a little more than the basics on process and content within the individual given in Chapter 7, beginning with a knowledge of the place of motivation in the leadership function and the variety of ways of doing it, followed by how-to.

As for place, it is one of seven role responsibilities of leadership:

Motivating, directing, coordinating, controlling, teaching, changing, representing.

And it is a dominant one because, besides standing alone, it has to be applied at least to some degree in each of the other six for them to be fully successful.

Then complicating matters further, there are eight basic ways, *skills*, in which one can motivate others:

integrating directly and indirectly (technical-social integration), inspiring, supporting, rewarding, reinforcing, delegating, giving participation, power sharing.

And similarly, the first, integration—the vital relating of personal needs and aspirations to organizational goals and methods—must play a part, if only by implication, in the efforts of each of the others for them to be effective.[b]

So there's a pervasive amount of overlap across and within both role responsibilities and motivational forms such that integration is a crucial activity that carries over from the skills of motivation to the responsibilities of organizational leadership, its complicated dynamic operating in a closed loop as follows:

➤ **Organizational leadership** with seven role responsibilities.

↓

The most significant role is motivation, which has eight forms.

↓

The most significant form is **technical-social integration.**

↓

In sum, both motivation and integration must be dominant concerns of all leaders; indeed, they will be found ahead to conjoin with virtually every leadership subject covered by the book. However, as described in Chapter 2 (on pages 31-32) the latter, integration, has two major parts. and the detailed coverage of them will be as follows:

Direct integration—in all interpersonal superior-subordinate negotiations, but the particular skill delayed to Chapter 20.

Indirect integration—in two stages:

- The first stage is the coverage of the general social considerations managers should know about behavior, about the needs and aspirations of subordinates, and about group dynamics for the planning of structures and processes (knowledge that is also needed to be successful on direct integration). This Part I is the start of it, and it continues through to the end of Part III as relevant to each chapter's topic.
- The second stage is on how to find out the *specific* social considerations necessary to achieve the indirect integration, that is, what subordinates specifically would like for each structure and process that affects them, the best way being the participative techniques of OD (Chapters 18 and 19), and most of them incorporate implementation planning.

For the first stage, the patterns and arousal conditions of organizational motivation, B and C on pages 234-235, outline precisely what must be learned to motivate successfully the individual and the organization (or group) of individuals:

B1,	Control	- the organization
2 and 3,	Compensation	
C1,	The job	- the individual
2 and 3,	Climate	

The "Control" referred principally to the structures and processes of #2 on page 263 and will be left to Part II on The Organization. The sections here will be devoted to the others in the order of the general to the specific, that is to climate (development), to the job (design), and to compensation.

Before proceeding accordingly however, two subjects should be clarified in introduction: the organizational culture, the major force underlying climate and norms, and the motivation to lead and manage, that is, does the manager you wish to motivate to do well at it want to lead and manage in the first place? How can you tell?

Organizational Culture

There are certain facts about an organization's culture that any CEO or board of directors wanting to lead an organization should know: its characteristics, how it develops, the three basic types and their impact, how can they be changed for the better, and the kind of leadership needed to bring about change.

To expand on the definition on page 21: an organization's (or group's) culture is its pattern of basic assumptions, mostly subconscious, that employees develop over time as they learn to cope with their and the organization's problems of external adaptation and internal integration. Note that the list of value misconceptions on page 118 is one of common basic incorrect assumptions, both conscious and subconscious, of many managements.

These cultural assumptions in fact comprise the underlying foundation of an organization's climate and norms and should be kept in mind when judging any of them, particularly in differentiating an organization's culture from its climate. Indeed, culture and climate have often been confused in managers' minds because they share features of complexity and multidimensionality, and they seem to have a similar impact on employees' thoughts and on the organization. But an aid to distinguishing them: while a culture is a cluster of amorphous assumptions that are not easy to identify, climate is an outcome of more discernible shared perceptions of employees subjected to the same leadership, policies and practices (more specifically, the page 27 definition and the discourse on climate ahead). Thus the culture might be over-simplistically described as a "cause" (itself brought about by a number of fundamental forces) and climate as an "effect" (one of them), the two still reciprocally influencing each other.

Note that "behaviors" are not included in the culture definition, because they are an indirect outcome of culture, determined essentially by the combination of the climate perceptions and the external and internal environmental conditions and contingencies.

Supplementing the page 118 list of misconceptions, Edgar Schein supplied a good understanding of cultural assumptions and their depth by describing basic ones of two very different organizations (in his Chapter 1).[3] The first, a dynamic high-tech firm with open office landscape, extreme informality of dress and manner, an absence of status symbols, high levels of enthusiasm, energy, and interpersonal confrontation and conflict glorifying "arguing back," yet intense loyalty to the organization. To understand this incongruity one need but appreciate a shared deep assumption held, that "We are one family who will take care of each other."

The second was a European high-tech company (he called it Multi Company), most of the managers European, that had offices with closed doors, many status symbols, obvious deference rituals, formality of behavior, concern for protocol, a tendency to avoid conflict, and little direct lateral communication. A consultant brought in to increase innovativeness (Schein) needed to understand the underlying forces causing such a closed arrangement because his communications to one level of managers were never transmitted or shared up, down or horizontally.

A core assumption he found was on the nature of "truth" in their minds. Truth to them came largely from the wisdom of its scientists, from experts. Though there was a high regard for the individual, a manager was to develop ideas for his or her arena only; for other arenas the person was expected just to be a good soldier. Thus Schein found it necessary to give information directly to them on each level, one-on-one, when it was accepted because it was from an expert. As such it was not considered an insult indicating the manager was not on top of the job, a possible implication of advice given by a non-expert coworker.

Cultural assumptions are in general developed over time through the socialization process as leadership, employees and events change. Without using the word "culture," Homans was the first to describe the dynamics that produce it, illustrated by the chart on page 527, the process now, with a little thought, easy to tick off in the two categories of the external (to the individual)-what he or she brings in from society or is imposed by the organization, and the internal-the factors having psychological impact on each person and on internal integration:

The external - (a) the values, beliefs and predispositions brought in from pre-membership education, groups and relations, family, nationality and race; (b) the organization's methods of adaptation to survive and prevail: its mission, strategies, goals, means, technology, and performance evaluation techniques; (c) physical surroundings.

The internal - (a) the consequences of leadership, climate, norms, group dynamics, and the organization's values (including what's to be rewarded and punished); (b) resolving the problems of internal integration with regard to power, status, interdependence, intimacy; (c) the organization's internal philosophy, idealogy, and durable felt theories of managing the unpredictable and unexplainable.

And a difficult complication in trying to analyze the culture of any organization above small is their multiple culture nature, that each enduring unit can have unique cultural aspect and assumptions of its own, for instance the different ones of the departments of engineering, marketing, finance, and R&D, described in IB on page 30 as "differentiation," a characteristic that can be viewed as an intercultural problem.

Add to that the multidimensionality shown in Figure 8.1 that pictures the total sociotechnical system context of an organization, where the culture fits in, the two way influence with climate and norms, and the influence of each technical and social factor on the performance and behavior of individuals. It also reminds us of the indirect impact on the culture (through climate) of human assumptions about the technical (structures, processes, products, markets, etc.), and correspondingly their impact on organizational effectiveness.

The main objective of all the organizational culture research and writing undertaken in the last decade or so[c] has not been just to identify and define it but, more important, to find out what kind of culture enhances long term successful performance toward the mission and goals and how to create it.

Business literature has in the past praised the power of a *strong* culture to enhance performance, and it's usually true, but only if it's the right kind of strength. Unhealthy bureaucracies (p. 448) are negatively strong—in their resistance to change, support of the status quo, and civil service mentality that cripples effort and performance, all of which can be the result of a top management that's authoritarian (producing the "we-they" syndrome) or asocial (e.g., operates only by the financial numbers).

Also the culture of plenty of firms that have had a long period of impressive success have been judged strong, but many have developed a complacency of success and arrogance of superiority, even believed invulnerability, that have impaired their view of market needs and environmental changes (see the IBM story on pages 1169-1171). Or the success can somehow effect an inability to judge correctly the causes of a declining performance, as at the former Peoples Express where the CEO became so enamored with his participative management system—thus an inward myopia—that he failed to see the threat of the quickly rising price competition—an *outward* blindness—the way Hewlett-Packard did also (a new CEO being necessary in each instance).

So it's advantageous to have a strong culture only as long as it's adaptive to change. Kotter and Heskett in their book "Corporate Culture and

The Basic Internal Determinants of Group Performance

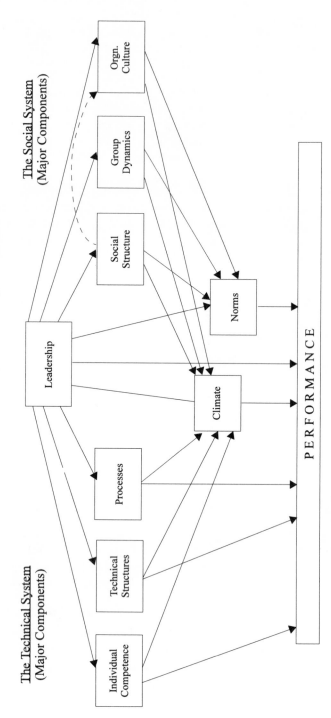

Figure 8.1

* Orgn. culture: The basic assumptions that underlie its climate, norms, and general ethos.
  Social structure: relationships, interdependencies, status and role systems.
  Group dynamics: the group behavior effects of grouping leadership, structures, and processes (e.g., goals, norms, cohesion, roles, size, arrangement).

Performance" gave an excellent description of what this involves. Their research of 207 firms in 22 different industries revealed three basic types they labelled Theories I, II and III.[4]

The analysis of the 22 showed in general a correlation between good long-term performance and strong cultures—Theory I—but a study of specific strong ones like Coors, Sears, Goodyear and Citicorp at that time showed a negative correlation due to dysfunctional elements (the performance measures: annual net income growth over 11 years, average ann. ROI from 1977-88, aver. yearly incr. in stock prices 1977-88).

However some firms with weak cultures have had consistently good performance records, e.g., McGraw-Hill, Smith-Kline, and Pitney-Bowes, some of which type may be explained as due to diversification purchases of strong cultures or divisional monopolistic market positions that allow weak cultures.

A strong culture thus is not necessarily a requisite in itself for top performance. One essential seemed to be the "fit" of the firm with the conditions of the industry it's in or being targeted. They called this Theory II. But there could be found plenty of firms that initially fit, grew and prospered rapidly, then stumbled when the environment changed, for example, IBM and Peoples Express referred to above and Citicorp that thrived from the 1950s to 1970s then took a steep dive around the end of the 1980s. Theory II therefore had some validity when judging only for the short and medium range, but, over the long-term a strong culture can blind one to the facts that don't match the assumptions.

Dynamic cultural adaptability over time as the organization's competitive and economic environment changes appears to be the key missing element, their Theory III, and to develop that character requires dynamic insightful leadership throughout the hierarchy that encourages corresponding needed changes, initiative, a willingness to take prudent risks, open communication in all directions, and dedicated attention to all four constituencies that support the business—customers, suppliers, employees and stockholders—all of them.

Such an organization will not only be best able to adapt to environmental changes over the long term but be able to anticipate them through the attention to the market and customers. Kotter and Heskett provided the helpful table below (their p. 51). Basic thinking and techniques on how managements can make it happen when needed are given herein in Chapters 19 and 20.

ADAPTIVE VS. UNADAPTIVE CORPORATE CULTURES

	Adaptive Corporate Cultures	*Unadaptive Corporate Cultures*
Core Values	Most managers care deeply about customers, stockholders, and employees. They also strongly value people and processes that can create useful change (e.g., leadership up and down the management hierarchy)	Most managers care mainly about themselves, their immediate work group, or some product (or technology) associated with that work group. They value the orderly and risk-reducing management process much more highly than leadership initiatives
Common Behavior	Managers pay close attention to all their constituencies, especially customers, and initiate change when needed to serve their legitimate interests, even if that entails taking some risks	Managers tend to behave somewhat insularly, politically, and bureaucratically. As a result, they do not change their strategies quickly to adjust to or take advantage of changes in their business environments

It's important, at the same time, to note here a finding by Schein: that considerable change can take place in a firm's operation *without the cultural paradigm changing* at all,[5] that is, the basic cultural assumptions. His "Multi Company" was a good example: through a major Redirection Project the trend toward nonprofitability was reversed; two unprofitable divisions were restructured; lines of responsibility were delegated out of headquarters; competitiveness programs were started; and senior managers learned how their culture can help and hinder them.

Indeed, most of the managers "undoubtedly would say" their assumptions had undergone great changes; but, there remained the same bias about scientific authority, the hierarchy functioned as strongly as ever, and lateral communications were still considered mostly irrelevant. Schein's comments: one can conclude that many elements of a culture may be essentially unimportant to effectiveness; in fact it seems that much restructuring and turning around can occur with only superficial aspect of it being changed; indeed, most of the time executives do not need to keep aware of the organization's culture except when it's in trouble; moreover it is not at all clear that a culture can be changed, whereas climate, values and philosophy can be (his p. 314).

Nevertheless, many organizations are, or will be, faced with the need for significant cultural modification to accommodate the new process/team "horizontal organization" structure described ahead that they are implementing, thus a major test of Kotter and Hesbett's Theory III on an organization's need for adaptability.

The motivation to manage and lead

Two recent discoveries about motivation have made it possible to find out if this is present. First, it was discovered that three of the learned psychological maintenance motives in Figure 5.7 (p. 143)—power, achievement, and affiliation—were sufficient to evaluate motivation for the position, because by and large they tend to account for most of the other major ones, if not directly at least indirectly. For example, power (Adler's interpretation) tends to cover autonomy, responsibility and recognition, and achievement to cover creativity and self-actualization, though affiliation stands alone.

Until recently it was assumed that the key motive for good management was achievement, which is most visible in the sale volume of salesmen, so those in selling stand out as logical for management, especially sales management. Furthermore, good sales people are commonly very high in *affiliation* and superior at human relations, which should contribute to their management of others. Yet in a large percentage of the time, the promotion of salespeople to sales management has been disastrous.

For the second discovery, David McClelland, who taught us much of what we know about the achievement motive (pages 240-242) found through research with another behaviorist, David Burnham, that what counts most is not one motivational drive but a hierarchy of especially two plus some qualitative ingredients.[6]

The earlier studies made evident enough that managers should be high on achievement, and we also had learned that achievement should not be higher than the power motive, otherwise they would try to achieve all important tasks themselves. The new find was that the power motive should be higher than affiliation, because all managers must have a strong desire to perform the most basic of management functions: influence others to do assigned jobs in the desired manner—*power*. But when affiliation, the need to be liked that all good managers have some degree of, is higher than the power drive (as found in many sales people), urges that are antithetical to good management exist.

For example, the typical affiliation-dominated manager is one wh readily concedes without any deliberation to a subordinate's request to sta home and care for the kids while his wife is in bed with a cold. There ar true empathetic feelings for the man and his wife; no thought is given t the fact that others in the group, who may have to do his work for him might consider the exception to the norm unfair to them. Concern fo individuals by the manager tends to take precedence over responsibility fo the group. Sociologists have long known that those with very high affiliativ needs rarely make good managers on that one point alone.

Nevertheless, the higher need for power does not rule out socia sensibilities. What counts is the hierarchy of power and affiliation in tha order. Additionally, the quality of the power motive and the possession o personal maturity were found to be crucial.

Over the last three decades behavioral scientists themselves have bee misleading by always speaking of high power drive people as authoritarian when, as described on pages 242-246, authoritarians are only th "unsocialized" end of the category's range. The McClelland/Burnham research found that the socialized type does not see power as a tool of self aggrandizement but as a means of advancing the effectiveness and welfar of the organization or group. They are in effect "institutional" managers individuals whose high power need is self-controlled and strongly inhibited people who are willing to sacrifice some of their own self-interest for th firm, thus socialized power (relate to "emotional intelligence" on page 72)

Personal maturity was found to be essential. It was defined as not behavin egotistically and having a positive self-image that is not at stake i relationships. Such people as a result are less defensive, are more willing to seek advice from experts, have a longer range view than the immature and "seemed older and wiser." The best and most durable leader-manager by and large have been found to behave this way and as a consequence tend to do the right things. They have a strong sense of responsibility about thei organization or group, clearly communicate goals, organize the work well coach and counsel supportively, are impartial, develop good team esprit and encourage loyalty to the group rather than themselves if only by example.

In contrast, authoritarians, we know, are exploitive for their own benefit manage by making subordinates dependent, powerless, and fearful, and the favored few become loyal to the personality, not to the group, which fall apart when the boss leaves for lack of cohesion and a trained replacement

The two behaviorists derived their motivation mix formula from extensive research on practicing managers who attended workshops to learn about an improve their leadership behavior. It was standard procedure for the workshops to determine at the start the internal motivational ranking of each and in the cases quoted they had access to the managers' organizations, where they interviewed subordinates and studied the performance levels and trends of the managers' departments before and after workshop participation.

Significantly, through the interviews a direct correlation was found between "good" management (defined by the foregoing criteria) and morale, then between morale and group performance. Therefore, an indirect correlation between good management and performance was deduced, a relationship normally taken for granted, and the results of the various analyses made uncovered the following:

- 73 percent of the better managers (rated on their groups' morale and performance) had higher power than affiliation motivation; only 22 percent of the poorer managers had a similar combination.
- 62 percent of the better managers scored high on democratic coaching styles; only 22 percent of the poorer ones did.
- Subordinates of the better managers classified and scored (%) their superiors as follows:

	Affiliative	*Personal Power and Low Inhibition*	*Institutional— High Inhibition*
Sense of group responsibility	11	38	49
Organizational clarity	31	41	50
Team spirit	31	52	52

The statistics are a reminder that neither the right nor wrong combination of motives guarantees a specific type of behavior or result, the reason why "tend to-" four paragraphs back was italicized. Nor does the wrong mix preclude learning adequate behavior functioning through skills training. The following are brief sketches of what happened to three sales managers who attended the workshops:

1. Briggs was high on affiliation and achievement and low on power and had for years been miserable as a manager by his own admission. His department's performance was always poor to which his response was: set very high standards and criticize for failures to attain them, and, as a result, he ended up doing everything himself. His subordinates complained that his office was poorly organized and chaotic, he delegated little responsibility, he never rewarded, and he only criticized. On discovering all of this at the workshop, he decided to go back to the selling that he enjoyed, and a follow-up check 6 months later showed that he was both happy and successful at it.

2. Prentice had the right combination with socialized power but an authoritarian style that he had adopted from his superiors: give orders and threaten consequences if not followed. The workshop apprised him of (a) his motivation mix, (b) his behavior, (c) the impact on his department, and (d) what could be done about it. Six months later his subordinates' morale and trust had changed from low to high and some of his personal values had improved (no comment on performance changes).

3. Blake had the same unfavorable motivational mix and managerial behavior as Briggs but liked and wanted to keep his sales manager job. On learning the same four points given to Prentice above (2a to 2d), he countered his motivational inclinations, planned his department's organization and work jointly with the salesmen coached to help performance, developed special rewards for outstanding performance, built cohesion and morale, and raised the department's rank over the next 3 years to third place among 16 (original rank not stated).

Thus Briggs, one of the poor fits, changed his job; Blake, the other poor fit, compensated by "learning," changing his natural misfit inclinations to doing what was right; and Prentice, the good fit with an adopted aversive behavior, changed the behavior to follow his natural correct inclinations. What is particularly fascinating about Prentice's change is how the education evolved greater maturity; the authors quoted him as saying that whereas he used to brag about his new Porsche and Honda, he volunteered the comment "I don't buy things any more."

Management behavior workshops of this sort are of course not successful on all managers, in fact do not work at all on those who've been managing people for a long time with authoritarian attitudes and methods that they're convinced are the reason for any success they believe they've achieved. But for young ones eager to advance, surprisingly good results are possible when the basic elements of (a) to (d) in sketch number 2 about Prentice are followed. (Behavior change is discoursed in Chapters 18 and 19).

Note that the participants were not *told* what is wrong, which could threaten their self-image; they were given the objective facts and allowed to draw their own conclusions. Free of defenses, their minds *learned* what was wrong, and though the pain of it may have slowed the process, they accepted the need for change. The subordinates' before-and-after vote on climate given in the write-up was impressive evidence that it can work.

In sum, it's now clear that the personality of those chosen to manage people in organizations should include the following characteristics"[d]

a. A power drive higher than those of affiliation or achievement but with sensitivity to others, and high on achievement
b. The power drive "socialized" as described
c. Maturity

Developing the Climate

Picking up at C1, 2 and 3 on page 265, as implied there an orderly approach to a comprehensive program of building and directing employee motivation would be to start on climate, that is, their perceptions of all the elements of and forces in the organization (column 3, page 228) that have a motivational effect on them - with the assumptions of the culture a powerful influence on the perceptions.

Still, one has to keep in mind *all* the gross factors that contribute to performance, Figure 8.1 picturing them, the factors and diagram but a different perspective of the column 3 that highlighted how climate operates as an intervening force between the basic determinants and performance.

It's not easy to show clearly in a diagram that climate has the most direct effect on performance-climate being a product of all the boxes in 8.1 above it and of the norms that not only have a powerful impact on climate but are in turn affected by it—and to say also that it is primarily an outcome of leadership policies, practices and behavior, without implying the other boxes are less important. They are not; they're just less directly controllable. Climate is therefore a good starting point in any analysis of how to improve performance, additionally because each of its dimensions (see Figure 8.2) lead directly back to leadership. When leadership upgrades the dimensions the climate is upgraded, the norms are, even structures and processes are, all of which result in better performance.

A logical analytical procedure therefore would be (1) to review the general knowledge about climate and the requisite skills, then (2) the organization's norms, to which should be added (3) requirements for "service climate," the importance of which has only recently become generally appreciated.

(1) **The General Knowledge.** Interestingly and logically therefore, leadership was the first focus in the studies of climate. A most famous one was that of Lewin, Lippitt and White in 1939 of the effect on performance of three modes of leadership, each of which produced a different climate without calling it such. Probably the first to clearly conceptualize and define it was Argyris in 1958. Then McGregor in 1960 wrote a chapter on it in his *The Human Side of Enterprise*, pointing out that managers create the climate by their policies, practices and behavior in the form of his Theory X and Y or a mix.

It was another 8 years however before we got a truly explicit picture of it—by the authors of the definition on page 27. Their research for their book *Motivation and Organizational Climate* (1968)[8] identified nine dimensions, those in Figure 8.2, that had a major impact on individuals' power, achievement and affiliation motives, the key human forces producing different types of performance (see pages 138-142). Knowing that individuals with different dominant motives react differently to each dimension, they surveyed and studied the motive consequences of a large sample of managers, salespersons and staff professionals applying a three step procedure. Sketches of the dominant forces for a refresher:

High power motive: Influence and control over others, high on use of structure, status stressed (with strong competition for it), tendency to resolve conflicts by using authority.

High achievement motive: Responsibility, problem solving, calculated risks, reward commensurate with performance, minimal constraints, feedback.

High affiliation motive: Warmth, support, helping, people-association, interdependence, social acceptance, and minimal constraints.

In the first step, thematic apperception tests were given to them to determine their level and ranking of the three motives; second, interviews ascertained their perceptions as to the dimensions' motivational impact and their own personal preferences; and third, the first and second steps were combined to produce the "effects" chart in Figure 8.2[e] giving also the definitions as used in the survey *in terms of behavioral reactions*.[f] They then delineated from the interviews the behavioral effects of each dimension and how each affected the three motives as perceived by the interviewees. For example, those of structure, responsibility, and support were as follows, the illustrations showing how the others also can be tabulated from the Figure 8.2 definitions (they're given in the book):

Dimensional Effects	Motive results
Effects of structure	
Reduced challenge	
Reduced worth of succeeding	.... Negative on Achievement
Constraints are placed on task	
Interpersonal constraints:	
Directive leadership	
Assignment of power and responsibility	.... Positive on Power
Status and authority hierarchy	
Competition for recognition and status	.... Negative on Affiliation
Formality and social distance	
Increased organizational defenses	

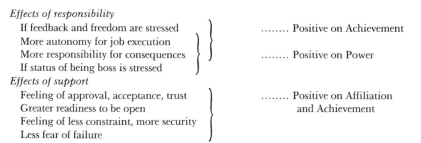

Effects of responsibility
   If feedback and freedom are stressed   .... Positive on Achievement
   More autonomy for job execution
   More responsibility for consequences   .... Positive on Power
   If status of being boss is stressed
Effects of support
   Feeling of approval, acceptance, trust   .... Positive on Affiliation
   Greater readiness to be open   and Achievement
   Feeling of less constraint, more security
   Less fear of failure

It was an impressive verification of the bond between the perceptions of climate and personal needs, here in the form of the three motives. As the researchers expressed it in their concluding statement, "In every-day language we can say that people prefer climates which seem most likely to satisfy their needs."

A laboratory simulation given in the book provided an excellent example. Conceding the short-comings of laboratory projects, it was nevertheless so well supported as "the way it is" empirically, it's worth examining. Three companies (A, B, and C) of 15 people each were formed: a president (an experienced research staff man trained to induce an assigned leadership style), three functional managers (production, product development, and controller), and eleven subordinates reporting to the managers, all but the president being outsiders hired at an hourly rate.

Organization A president was instructed to place strong emphasis on formal structure, seriousness, order, and relative status (the style he had been trained in), that is, make it power-oriented.[g] Organization B's president stressed friendly cooperative behavior, teamwork, and group loyalty (affiliation-oriented). Organization C's president emphasized high productivity, innovation, feedback, recognition and rewards for excellent performance, and teamwork against external competition (achievement oriented). Thus, each was managed to produce a climate that would arouse one motive in particular.

The three companies were put to work constructing and marketing models of radar towers and gun controls using Erector Sets, and were given two weeks to operate with all the problems of market competition, costs, and profit-making. The whole experiment was nicely displayed in the four charts of Figure 8.3. Chart (a) was the starting hypotheses about the effects of the three styles on the motives in the left column (one exception: the 'reduction" effects were only weakly supported by the research, so were labeled inconclusive). Chart (b) shows the norms that developed; (c) describes the quantitative performance after the end of 2 weeks; and (d) gives a summary of the major effects the three climates created. The *personality*

The Motivational Effects of the Key Climate Dimensions

Climate Dimension	Effect on Achievement Motivation	Effect on Affiliation Motivation	Effect on Power Motivation
Structure	Reduction[a]	Reduction	Arousal
Responsibility	Arousal[b]	No effect	Arousal
Warmth	No effect[c]	Arousal	No effect
Support	Arousal	Arousal	No effect
Reward	Arousal	Arousal	No effect
Conflict	Arousal	Reduction	Arousal
Standards	Arousal	Reduction	No effect
Identity	Arousal	Arousal	No effect
Risk	Arousal	Reduction	Reduction

[a] "Reduction" effects are related to the current level of aroused motivation. If a motive is already aroused, the level of aroused motivation will be reduced or decreased. If a motive is *not* aroused, it will remain so.

[b] An "arousal" effect refers to an enhancement or increase in the level of aroused motivation, as measured through thematic apperceptive methods.

[c] A "no effect" hypothesis means that there is no reason to expect that aroused motivation will be affected in either direction.

Structure—the feeling that employees have about authority, controls, and constraints in the group, and how many rules, regulations, procedures there are; is there an emphasis on "red tape" and going through channels, or is there a free and informal atmosphere?

Responsibility—the feeling of being your own boss; not having to double check all your decisions: when you have a job to do, knowing that it is your job.

Warmth—the feeling of general good fellowship that prevails in the work group atmosphere; the emphasis on being well liked; the prevalence of friendly and informal social groups.

Support—the perceived helpfulness of the managers and other employees in the group; emphasis on mutual support from above, around, and below.

Reward—the feeling of being rewarded for a job well done; emphasizing positive rewards rather than punishments; the perceived fairness of the pay and promotion policies.

Conflict—the feeling that managers and other workers want to hear different opinions; the emphasis placed on getting problems out in the open rather than smoothing them over or ignoring them.

Standards—the perceived importance of implicit and explicit goals and performance standards; the emphasis on doing a good job; the challenge represented in personal and group goals.

Identity—the feeling that you belong to a company and you are a valuable member of a working team; the importance placed on this kind of spirit.

Risk—the sense of riskiness and challenge in a job and in the organization; is there an emphasis on taking calculated risks or is playing it safe the best way to operate.

Figure 8.2

(a) Summary of Hypotheses Concerning the Motivational Effects of Climate

Motive	Organization A	Organization B	Organization C
n Achievement	reduction effect	no effect	arousal effect
n Affiliation	reduction effect	arousal effect	no effect
n Power	arousal effect	reduction effect	no effect

a *"Effects" are statements of change relative to other business groups, as measured by thematic apperceptive measures of motivation.*

(b) Salient Norms in the Three Simulated Organizations

Organization A	Organization B	Organization C
(1) aloofness and management formality	(1) friendliness	(1) keep busy and active
(2) procedure is law	(2) equality	(2) teamwork
(3) conflict avoidance	(3) democratic decision making	(3) individualism and responsibility
(4) isolation of workers		(4) make the job fun
(5) mind your own business and keep your nose clean		(5) beat the competition

(c) The Effects of Climate on Performance

	A	B	C
Contracts Completed	6	6	8
Contracts in Process	4	5	3
No. of Contracts Worked on	10	9	11
No. of New Products[a]	4	6	8
Total Revenue	$948.20	$661.50	$619.80
Total Costs Charged to Completed Contracts	$940.50	$666.80	$547.50
Profit; ( ) = Loss	$7.70	$(5.50)	$72.30
% Profit; ( ) = Loss	.81%	(.80%)	11.7%
Materials-Saving Innovation	$0.00	$25.10	$45.80
Units Rejected (requiring work)	0	1	4

[a] A new product contract includes all contracts except "re-order contracts" or original products.

Figure 8.3

(continued on next page)

Figure 8.3 (continued)

(d) Summary of the Major Effects of Climate

	Organization A	Organization B	Organization C
Motivation and Personality			
Aroused Motivation	high *n* Power	high *n* Affiliation	high *n* Achievement
Changes in Personality Style	decline in self-acceptance and responsibility	slight decline in responsibility	decline in self-acceptance, increase in responsibility
Job satisfaction			
General Satisfaction	low	high	high
Attitude Toward Group	closed to others, independent, rebellious	very open to others, mutually dependent	open to others, mutually dependent
Performance			
Innovation	low	moderate	high
Productivity	low	low	high

style in the summary was measured in terms of self-acceptance (outspoken, persuasive, self-assured vs. conservative, conventional, somewhat passive), communality (tact, patience, sincerity vs. impatience and deceit), and responsibility (resourceful, independent vs. lazy, immature).

It's quite evident that superior job performance is a consequence of a threeway fit of:

I.   Job
II.   Individual,
III.   Climate.

The fit idea is discernibly but another perspective of technical-social integration expressing a combining of the definition of climate on page 27 and Vroom's axiom about individual motivation on page 230—that an individual's motivation is the summation of his or her valences times the expectancies derived from the person's subjective perceptions of the configural environment.

For I, we know that jobs are composed of structure, processes and tasks, and ample research has demonstrated that jobs themselves have motivational needs. Helpfully, the authors supplied Exhibit 2 in The Appendix (of this book) for determining what the needs are and there's more ahead in the next subsection.

The individual in II, we learned in Chapter 3, is principally a composite of the 10 components on page 39 (thus all of Chapter 3 through 7), and the authors were here stressing the seventh component (an individual's motivations), the TAT being an analysis technique. Another technique was supplied by them (Exhibit 3) for quickie testing of subordinates by managers themselves.

One may remember that the McClelland-Burnham report (pages 271-275) also showed how I and II fit together for specifically management jobs, the personality, motivational, and behavioral requirements on page 273. Outside selling similarly has clear motivational needs: high achievement, risk-taking, and individual responsibility (to get the job done with little direct supervision).

And for the climate (III), to develop and maintain it so that individual motivation occurs requires not only a knowledge of I and II but also of how the individual(s) presently perceives III in order to know which of the nine climate dimensions fits now and what should be changed. The authors again supplied a do-it-yourself survey for it, Exhibit 4 in the Appendix, and numerous professional climate surveys are also offered by consultants, one of the best known being that of Rensis Likert described in System 4, Chapter 14.[h]

(2) **Norms** (the second requisite on pages 275-276 we know, are informal unspoken rules of behavior of a group or organization that most or all the members have accepted and follow; and the impact of norms on climate and performance is so significant that many behaviorists consider them the main factors to work on in order to improve the climate, even to change the organization culture itself.

Indeed, one very good way to broach the subject of climate or performance improvements with an executive is to ask, "What kinds of norms do you want?," analyze what is present (by one of the surveys described), compare, recommend improvements, and proceed to change as described ahead to what is agreed on.

On the question, the most successful organizations from the standpoint of performance through commitment (vs. luck) seem to be endowed with all of these:

1. A universal respect for the individual.
2. Informality.
3. Open communications in all directions.
4. Cooperative relationships and interdependencies.
5. A penchant for action, for participation, and for solving problems quickly, not postpone.

6. The encouragement of new ideas, experiment, innovation, constructive change, and risk taking.
7. Intolerance of bureaucratic behavior, power struggles, and politics.
8. Commitment to excellence—performance, ethical behavior, product, service.

And the ideal climate goal would be these 8 norms plus the abstracts: trust, integrity, benevolence, pride in job and organization, challenge, quiet excitement, and a sense of organizational goal "ownership"—all of which would be correctly characterized as an *integrative climate*, one in which technical-social integration has been and will continue to be achieved both consciously and intuitively as standard managerial practice.[i]

The characteristics of norms per se are a key element of group dynamics that are described in Chapter 12, and the skills of changing undesirable ones will be covered there. For here, in a section entitled "Developing the climate" the interest should be what leaders ought to do in the first place, the skills needed to develop the norms and abstracts.

The requisite skills. Figure 8.1 makes wholly evident that to achieve maximum motivation and performance success the leader's skills at any level must cover both the technical and social systems, which is to say all the knowledge and skills of a 3-volume book on organizational leadership. Naturally, the technical skills fit well under Part II's "The Organization," and this would be a good place to start on the social system skills.

An introductory explanation as to approach will help explain why it can only be a start. One can greatly simplify it by targeting the feature that all three social boxes in Figure 8.1 have in common: the *interrelationships* (thus interdependencies too) within the organization are of major importance to all, and the leadership with its policies, behavior, decisions, actions, etc. plainly impact those relationships directly through its arrows to the boxes. So the primary interest of the leader has to be his/her relationship development with everyone that has an influence on results—subordinates, peers, superiors, and all the others outside of one's conferred authority including external interdependencies (though minimally if at all relevant to internal climate)—so big an order the discourse on them will be divided this way:

- The skills in general here for leadership concerning motivation for *subordinate relations* (motivating subordinates being the Chapter 8 subject);
- In Chapter 11 on Control, given that control is in fact the fundamental intent of leadership, the specific skills of doing it acceptably in *all*

relations—with subordinates, peers, superiors, and all interdependencies inside and outside of the organization—will be covered under the rubric of "Complications of control, power and authority";
- And in Chapter 20 there will more applicable to all with a summation.

A description of the requisite skills in general must understandably be based on a philosophical presumption of a humanist view of the individual and Theory Y, the modeling and promotion of which will produce norm #1 on page 282, respect for the individual, neither the modeling or promotion of the philosophy intimating flower power nonsense or the lack of firmness where necessary.

Also required is a realistic understanding of the organizational world, especially its complexity as to the profusion of interdependencies throughout that complicate all activities and relationships, the interdependencies further complicated enormously by individual diversity of opinions, attitudes, values, interests, needs, stakes, drives, organizational politics, you name it. And all guarantee conflict, conflict that will, often if not well managed, block information needed for decisions, obstruct or distort decisions, and/or handicap the implementation of those that are made.

There are structural ways, along with the following skills, of helping to reduce the purely technical conflicts (page 31) that will be described in Chapter 16, planning them itself being an important skill. But the social conflicts, the concern here, are as much or more of a problem. Yet conflict of any type is plainly only one of the nine key climate dimensions to be dealt with, and note from the definitions of the nine (Figure 8.2) that what constitutes a good climate is favorable opinions for each including conflict, signifying an appreciation of the constructive type. The most effective skills for developing the favorable opinions (except for conflict; see index for it) generally are:

- *Structures* (including processes)—while applying the technical principles in Chapters 11 and 16 toward the functional process, team and unit goals, be aware of potential role and motivation conflicts and unintended undesirable consequences you may set up that can create ethical dilemmas for managers; thus, make the systems "ethically responsive" (motivating only ethical behavior and not unethical behavior); design the relationships in ways that encourage informality (norm 2); open communications (norm 3) and cooperation (norm 4); Chapter 16 will also show how to use structures to encourage new ideas, innovations, and a penchant for action (norms 5 and 6).

- *Responsibility and Risk*—delegate and give participation (in Chapters 13 and 19) in ways that develop the feelings—described, also promoting norms 5, 6, and 8.
- *Identity*—design subordinates' work so it's challenging to their talents, exciting, and with enough autonomy and flexibility for norms 5 and 6 and a feeling of some say over their destiny.
- *Rewards*-give appropriate recognition, appreciation and incentive for achievements, the intrinsic as important as the extrinsic and tangible (details in the next major section).
- *Standards* (and goals)—the leader's modeling, decisions, policies, behavior, and teaching, must be done in ways that promote norms 5, 7 and 8.
- *Warmth and support*—warmth a prime stimulus of good relationships, and support so crucial it's a leadership principle (page 571), thus both very important to norms 4 and 6.

The risk in the second dot has two sides to it, one of which warrants special note. Recall that it was described in Figure 8.2 (p. 278) as a sense of the riskiness and challenge in the job, which refers to the chances of technical or performance success, the risk that a high achievement person was found to have a need for in a moderate amount, called "calculated risk" on page 241.

But then there's also the feeling of risk involved in the degree of job security to severe insecurity induced by one's superior, a continuum that produces an emotional range of from complacency to motivation to deep anxiety. Experienced leaders appreciate the overlap with the above aspect and that they should try to keep the emotional feeling around the motivational middle, that too great a feeling of insecurity can seriously reduce performance, too much security generally results in apathy, and a balance yields a beneficial amount of tension that adds to the technical challenge.

So a leader's goal in this regard is to *manage the tension level* as a sub-task of managing motivation, doing one's best to gain and maintain this balance, and keeping these climate dimensions in mind can be helpful. For obvious examples, the extremes, we know, are the intimidation and coercion that induce a climate of destructive fear, and the laissez-faire non-leader attitude that guarantees complacency.

Thus a fairly high feeling of anxiety and insecurity is inevitable under a directive authoritarian personality style, and the nonleader deserves the poor performance received. But for that preponderance of traditional managers who are reasonably considerate, a perceived high level of anxiety can be reduced substantially by giving timely appropriate recognition, appreciation, rewards and support, while the desired level of tension can be gained by establishing participatively challenging achievable goals, high standards, and powerful incentives, followed then by fair periodic appraisals.

All nine dimensions should of course be important concerns to leaders of all levels, but CEOs in particular need to be fully aware of the extent to which their own personal behavior can arouse and sustain sizable increments of favorable opinion on them whether on seemingly insignificant or very significant matters (per "standards" above). For instance, again in behalf of the eight norms: for #1, eating in the employee cafeteria and parking their cars wherever there's a space in the lot, private dining rooms and parking spaces seen as an affront to the dignity of those lower down.

For norms 2 and 3, their personal unassuming and friendly demeanor is a principal way of promoting both the informality and open communications; e.g., besides carefully learning and using first names everywhere themselves, they insist on its being a universal practice, some requiring first-name name-tags (without last name), which clearly encourages the open communications too. On the latter, one firm even has a well-publicized (internally) program of "Talk back to the boss!"[j]

Then for norms 4 to 6 the most progressive CEOs have built OD into their management systems, becoming personally involved in its activities wherever feasible. If innovation is crucial they've incorporated structures like those described in Chapter 16's "The parallel organization" and promoted the needed norms down the hierarchy by repeatedly talking up the importance of innovation, championing entrepreneurial effort, giving support in the face of errors and failures, and getting together ad hoc teams right away themselves to solve problems on the spot—always modeling for all levels down the management team.

Peters and Waterman, incidentally, stressed appropriately the value of such behaviors and norms 2 to 6 by giving them collectively a memorable label, saying that organizations with them possess "fluidity." They found that orientation was a principal response to the complexity of the successful large firms they studied, organizations that made a point of attending to the ideas, problems and issues "that either fall between bureaucratic cracks or span so many levels that it's not clear who should do what; consequently nobody does anything."[10]

On the norm 7, there's no doubt that for an intolerance of bureaucracy and politics to exist there has to be a minimum of bureaucratic management to begin with; thus if bureaucracy and politics are problems, developing the norm must start with a major effort to institute effective organization design and the needed behavior change (Chapters 18 and 19) accompanied by appropriate top management modeling with all eight norms for goals plus strong signs of disapproval for violations of the #7 norm.

Recall that the commitment to excellence in #8 was given special attention from a personal performance standpoint at the end of Chapter 6, and what the most progressive CEOs do for specifically organizational *ethical* excellence should be added here. They usually know from personal experience the inseparable connection between motivation and ethical treatment; allow even a little immorality in supervision and you get minimal to no motivation, indeed over time the reverse: low morale, indifference, alienation, contempt. So ethical behavior across the organization at all levels is a top priority, and they go about promoting it by attempting to make it a strong norm, the most committed doing it as described on pages 177-178 and making ethics a legitimate, acceptable, and easy topic of discussion through:[11]

- Policies—clear statements on the subject in the basic HR policy (see the subsection on it in Chapter 21), and a blunt statement and strong system for the protection of whistleblowers.
- The mechanisms, processes and education needed to make the policies work (also in Chapter 21) plus management's readiness to listen and to support the processes.
- Modeling (requiring it of all top executives)—statements on the ethics of decisions and action wherever appropriate, open comments about a and discussion of some of one's own and their dilemmas, and clear messages to answer to the expectation that employees voice and concerns they have.

These "requisite skills," as this subsection is entitled, plainly are only generalities; no more could be given at this time because of the complexity of the subject, but it might be helpful for a gestalt while reading ahead to add a preliminary list of the specific interpersonal skills to be treated and give a sample of the kind of interpersonal leadership that competent trainers want to develop.

As said earlier, first there has to be the crucial foundation one that warrants repetition lest any of its parts be overlooked: the philosophical presumption of humanism in the leader and Theory Y, and the application of the 8 leadership principles and seven role responsibilities, all delineated in Chapter 20. In fact, it would not be over-doing it to emphasize again the importance of the personal values and philosophy that must underpin every interpersonal skill, especially (though it may sound maudlin to some):

- believing that people are basically good,
- being honest, forthright, sincere, empathetic,
- being considerate of others' dignity and self-regard,
- respecting individual differences of personality and temperament
- being dedicated to open two-way-influence (transactional) communication.

Feeling this way is fundamental to the direct integration described in Chapter 20, inevitably shows that one cares (Fromm's "love"), and somehow leads managers to share feelings and opinions, be sensitive to others' needs, and produce appropriate responses. Moreover, it goes a long way toward developing others' tolerance and forgiveness for unintended offenses and otherwise unacceptable constructive-intended suggestions.

For the skills list, much of it would be "old hat" to the experienced, but they might give special attention ahead to those they may be overlooking among the motivation skills (p. 264), or on coaching, counseling, performance review, MBO, joint job planning, goal-setting and budgeting, participative career and development planning, conflict leadership and management, gaining compliance against resistance, interdependency relations, political skills, team development—all of them requiring direct integration in some regard.

And of course much of the motivation skills are strictly leadership behavior, which was well illustrated in a study a while back by Texas Instrument's HRD, the results in the chart below that they gave to their managers as recommendations on how to handle day-to-day interpersonal relations. It was produced by a survey of 1,344 of their managers at all levels to determine their degree of motivation, the leadership behavior of their managers, and the amount of correlation between the two.[12]

J.P. Kotter in his book on interpersonal skills, *Power and Influence,*[13] made a strong pitch on the importance of appreciating, learning and practicing all such skills as early as possible in one's career—relationships down, up and laterally—because of the time it takes to solidly develop them in order to produce the network of goodwill and of collaborative associates needed for success, consistent success itself yielding a reputation that compounds the cooperativeness. And, early impressions, good and bad, do tend to endure.

But make this endeavor as easy as possible, he recommended, by being smart in your choice of job: its fit to your talents and temperament, the kind of person you'll report to (whose several interviews before hiring usually make the appraisal possible), the person's competence, apparent authority (to get resources) and criteria of judging performance (yours), the situation's visibility and growth opportunity, and why there's a vacancy. Naturally, growth, advancement and a good track record will come much more easily in a good fit than in a mediocre one, and for sure, they'll be substantially helped by a highly regarded mentor up the ladder if you can get one interested in you (but students and HRD planners should be aware of both sides of the mentor subject. See "The Down Side of Mentoring" by R.L. Keele et al. in *Trainer's Workshop*, May 1987, pp. 61-64).

Several examples of actual cases were given by Kotter that effectively demonstrated many of the interpersonal skills, and one that well illustrated a particularly trying subordinate relationship situation was that of an MBA on graduation, researching for a fit and starting as a department head in the one chosen. Outlined briefly:[14]

- Preliminary self-analysis strengths, weaknesses, likes and dislikes as to people, types of work, industry technology.
- Interviewed (at college) for 12 jobs in 10 firms of 3 industries and selected the best fit by the above criteria.
- In the recruiting process interviews of the one most interested in before the job offer, he viewed them as the start of relationship building; found out what he could about the department he might manage—chief complaint not enough office space, main weakness poor planning and work scheduling—and demonstrated this acuteness in the brief interview he had with the president.
- On hiring, in the welcoming meeting with the president he succeeded in getting a commitment of 30 percent more office space, and during his first week the president stopped by for a short chat, something he'd never done before, duly impressing the subordinates; the subsequent announcement of the added office space raised his stature even further.
- The first 4 months: Concentration on developing relationships with subordinates, boss, and interdependent peers. Re the subordinates, met with each to discuss their jobs and reach agreements as to responsibilities, authority, and priorities, made progress on planning and scheduling to their liking, and created a sense of commitment.
- From the 5th through 12th month, due attention to relationship building continued plus important management changes: in the 5th and 6th month new information and control systems installed, in the 7th and 8th the department reorganized, and in the 9th confronted two personnel problems aware of from the start (one fired, another transferred).
- By the 12th month he began to be recognized up the hierarchy as a successful organizational (technical and social) leader with promotion potential.

This was contrasted with the story of an MBA classmate of equal technical talent who was convinced that "good (technical) performance speaks for itself" and gave no attention to the subtleties of the social up, laterally, or down. After a good start, things began to go wrong, obstacles increasingly appeared, his boss saw it as a lack of knowledge of the "basics," other department managers complained, and two subordinates sent anonymous letters to the boss. By the 8th month, he began looking for another job.

Put simply, the unsuccessful MBA worked at only half his job, the successful one at the whole job. And note that one of the latter's first concerns for effectiveness on the technical was upgrading the *job design* (re C1 on page 265) of each subordinate, who was motivated by participation in the process. But before going on to that, some important points on that crucial part of performance, *Service.*

Service. B. Schneider provided an excellent summary of the recent literature and research, including his own, on the subject in the book *Organizational Climate and Culture* that he edited.[15] The following includes the principal points among others.

Service policy naturally has to be based on the nature of service, that it is intangible and most often produced and consumed simultaneously, for example, the attention of a retail clerk, or a seat on an airplane flight. Thus the quality of service is difficult to control by management during the process. The only control can be indirectly through the design and management of motivation and the supporting factors—leadership, staffing, training, facilities, equipment, information systems, communication (especially of what is valued), and the motivation of the collaboration across the organization of all the activities necessary to achieve the desired service quality. In short, the creation of an organization-wide *service climate* that inspires commitment and substitutes for the close and immediate supervision that's anathema to employees.

So the subject is *service management* at all levels of the organization, particularly HR management—HR policies and processes, openness, decision involvement, participative career planning, hiring standards, appraisal system, feedback, and rewards—directed by enlightened leadership.

Plainly now, it's not only applicable to all types of service organizations, that constitute some two thirds of all employees in the U.S., but it has become widely apparent that superior service is competitively imperative wherever customers (including the internal ones) must be contacted.

First, to design the service function and manage it effectively, one must of course know in detail what customers want and expect. Figure 8.4, assembled from extensive interviewing by three researchers,[16] provides in essence 10 subdimensions under "standards" in Figure 8.2. Equally

Dimensions and Examples of Service Quality:
Customers' Views

Reliability:
Consistency of performance and dependability

- Accuracy of billing
- Keeping records
- Performing the service at the designated time

Responsiveness:
The willingness or readiness of employees to provide service

- Calling the customer back quickly
- Giving prompt service

Competence:
Possession of the required skills and knowledge to perform the service

- Knowledge and skill of the contact personnel
- Knowledge and skill of operational support personnel

Accessibility:
Approachability and ease of contact

- Waiting time to receive service is not extensive
- Convenient hours of operation

Courtesy:
Politeness, respect, consideration, and friendliness of contact personnel

- Consideration for the customer's property
- Clean and neat appearance of the contact personnel

Communication:
Keeping customers informed in language they can understand, and listening to them

- Explaining the service itself
- Assuring the customer that a problem will be handled

Credibility:
Trustworthiness, believability, honesty

Credibility is achieved by
- Company reputation
- Personal characteristics of the contact personnel

Security:
The freedom from danger, risk, or doubt

- Physical safety
- Financial security

Understanding/ Knowing the Customer
Making the effort to understand

- Learning the customer's specific requirements
- Providing individualized attention

Tangibles:
The physical evidence

- Physical facilities
- Appearance of personnel
- Tools or equipment used to provide the service
- Physical representations of the service

Source: Adapted from Parasuraman, Zeithaml, and Berry (1985).

Figure 8.4

Dimensions and Examples of Service Quality: Employees' Views

Bureaucratic Orientation to Service	• Following all rules and procedures • Doing job in routine fashion
Enthusiast Orientation to Service	• Keeping a sense of "family" in the branch • Designing new ways to serve customers
Managerial Behavior	• Planning and goal setting for service delivery
Service Rewards	• Incentives and other rewards for service excellence
Customer Retention	• Active attempts to retain customers • Not giving special treatment to big accounts
Personnel Support	• Staffing levels and training permit good service
Operations Support	• Easy access to customer records • Error free records
Marketing Support	• Understanding of customers • Care in introducing new products/services
Equipment/Supply Support	• Equipment is available and up and running • Necessary supplies are available

Source: Adapted from Schneider, Parkington, and Buxton (1980).

Figure 8.5

important, one needs to complement the 8.4 with the employees' concept of the requisites, knowledge of the two sets essential for training and the design of rewards. Schneider and two others assembled 8.5, also from extensive interviews.[17]

The crucial importance of this subject was made wholly evident by a number of surveys. In one, for instance, interviews of 2,374 customers found a clear correlation between employee welfare and the customers' perception of overall service quality; where their welfare (through HR planning and management) was facilitated customers reported superior service experiences; correspondingly, it was found that companies with high turnover offered poor service quality to customers.

What all this says: in order to develop a motivationally effective organizational climate, not only must the details of each of the 9 dimensions in Figure 8.2 be attended to but in today' s highly competitive world special effort must also be applied to the ten 8.4 subdimensions of 8.2's standards. Schneider's succinct summation: "When management provides for the employees, the employees will provide for the customers." And as the managing director of quality consulting at The Hay Group recently pu it: "If you don't establish an internal climate that's open and encourage employee involvement, then your quality program is unlikely to benefi anyone."...quality in all regards—R&D, manufacturing, marketing and finance as well as service.

Job Design

Indeed for job designing itself to maximize manager motivation at any level, a series of issues extending right up to top management must be taken into account, but they will be explained ahead. On the interest here, one need initially to visualize the scope of the 3 factors involved introduced on page 280, its parts, and how the fundamental leadership techniques are applied

One can get it from the following chart, the term "individual-job fit" used to stress the objective, and compensation is displayed separately because of its relative independence of the other elements of job design due to the psychology and market forces involved. It will be covered in the next major section.

Job Design Structure

Individual-Climate Match

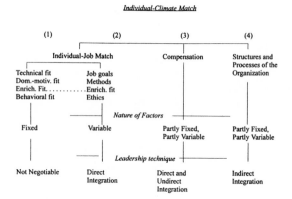

	(1)	(2)	(3)	(4)
		Individual-Job Match	Compensation	Structures and Processes of the Organization
	Technical fit Dom.-motiv. fit Enrich. Fit.......... Behavioral fit	Job goals Methods .Enrich. fit Ethics		
Nature of Factors	Fixed	Variable	Partly Fixed, Partly Variable	Partly Fixed, Partly Variable
Leadership technique	Not Negotiable	Direct Integration	Direct and Undirect Integration	Indirect Integration

The "fixed" nature of column 1 and the unnegotiable nature of fixed elements certainly need little explanation. The technical fit (that includes the necessary knowledge, intelligence, and skills within the technological requirements) is of course the first test a prospect has to pass. The dominant-motivation fit has been described. The enrichment fit is partly a matter of the fixed structural requisites of column 1 and partly the negotiable variables of column 2. And the behavioral fit is a crucial factor that is new to most managers, the lack of which explains many inadequate performances that ould otherwise be good. But also, special caution has to be taken that the b's design motivates ethical and not unethical behavior (column 2). For xample, ask what values conflicts may the person encounter with others r the organization and what dilemmas in decision-making are possible, nd give some job design help in how to resolve them ethically.

The two in column 1 yet to be described, therefore, are the enrichment nd behavioral. And after that's done an "individual-job fit" section will ombine all four for the job-planning procedure that's been delayed and hows what else has to be done for a motivating climate. But first, there's measure of how well the fit is being achieved that every manager should learly understand: *job satisfaction.*

Job satisfaction. Naturally, a person satisfied with a job is apt to stay in and do it well, a fact documented by C1 of the motivational patterns on age 235. However, management planning for it has commonly been obbled by a misunderstanding of what it means, beginning with the ssumption that given job characteristics and managerial actions are niversally satisfying to everyone, others universally dissatisfying, when in ct job satisfaction is a highly subjective opinion for each individual, and here are different kinds of satisfaction that have significantly different onsequences on work effort.

In the Chapter 5 England survey on manager values, managers—who are he principal determinants of job satisfaction for their subordinates—ranked as of major importance (page 132), yet job dissatisfactions is commonly at he heart of negative attitudes in most situations. And, parenthetically, there s no hope that dissatisfaction that occur will disappear through habituation ver time. In a study of nonmanagement personnel over a 14-year period, not nly did dissatisfaction not decrease, but alienation and aggression towards he bosses and companies increased.[18] It would undoubtedly happen to nanagers too if they remained in the same positions for long.

The early scientists were regrettably as confusing about this subject as hey were about learning. In the 1950s, based on their intuitions, the human elations theorists sold the idea that job satisfaction would lead to better erformance, simplistically:

a. assuming with insufficient evidence that the satisfaction caused performance (in this immediate discussion each use of the word "satisfaction" will refer to job satisfaction),

b. assuming with only one type of satisfaction, the extrinsic, to the neglect of the other involved (aside from complacent contentment).

It takes no more than an elementary postulate on job satisfaction to get he correct answer for (a). In general:

Job satisfaction occurs when the value received is equal to or more than the expected return.

And performance may be irrelevant in any given case. Certainly, the reasoning in (a) should be reversed if there is a satisfaction-performance connection at all, with satisfaction the result of performance and what i yields.

On the (b) one has to start by asking what is the core factor causing satisfaction? Reward. Which, as shown in Figure 7.2 on page 233, come in two forms derived, like the two of motivation, from the two of reinforcement on page 85:

- *Extrinsic* rewards administered by the organization: they are comprised of factors external to the work done, e.g., pay, working conditions, social relationships, security, etc.
- *Intrinsic rewards* self-administered by the employee: they are educed from the work itself such as the list on page 85, the design of the job (e.g., its utilization of talents and the opportunity it gives to grow), and the character and supportiveness of the leadership

And, the consequence is two types of satisfaction, extrinsic and intrinsic

The error of the first assumption (a), moreover, was compounded by another assumption within it: that pay, the chief extrinsic satisfier, is always linked to performance, when unfortunately (although most organization say and like to believe they tie their managers' pay to performance) almost every study of what they do shows its connection is minimal at best, and many managements, either indifferent or recognizing the difficulties, don' even try. As a result, pay universally tends to be seen by employees as merely for doing the specified tasks of the job (role specification) and showing up on time each morning. (An excellent charting of pay satisfaction alone is given on page 318.)

So the human relations theorists were wrong on both (a) and (b) in two regards: ignoring intrinsic satisfaction and assuming that pay-performance linkage is always present, leading to their inadequate "be nice" theorem that brought grief to the organizations that tried it. They should have said extrinsic and intrinsic satisfaction together would lead to better performance, because their joint consequence produces the key requisite *commitment*.

A research study by Porter and Lawler[19] that contributed to the construction of their motivation model on page 233 is an interesting illustration of this reciprocal interdependence. In a survey on job satisfaction in five companies they found that managers who were ranked high by their superiors reported significantly greater job satisfaction than did low ranked ones, and yet the highest ranked did not see themselves as receiving much greater pay and security (extrinsic rewards) than did the lower ranked. Nevertheless, they reported significantly more opportunity to participate in decisions, to express autonomy, and to obtain self-realization (intrinsic). The researchers concluded that the five organizations seemed to be:[20]

allowing their best performers to gain more self-fulfillment than low performers but not providing perceptibly different extrinsic rewards. Pay did not show an appreciable relationship to rated performance.

But the intrinsic satisfaction they got from the nature of their jobs and how the leadership allowed or assisted them to fill their basic psychological needs (column 3, page 143) translated into *commitment* that produced better performance and higher ranking by their superiors.

Thus, if you believe, or your research has shown, that your managers feel job satisfaction, it's important to determine what kind of satisfaction you've got. If it's extrinsic only, say, from high pay, you may get better motivation and performance for a while after a change from low rates, but soon the high pay is taken for granted, and without intrinsic satisfaction, performance slips back to being perfunctory ... *unless* you've succeeded in truly tying pay to performance.

The measurement of job satisfaction added to that of quantitative organizational performance is a particularly important combination in that it can give top management a valid and insightful judgment of its team's leadership competence. Quantitative results are certainly basic, but with all the uncontrollable variables that influence it, it's not alone a reliable measure of leadership. However, if climate surveys report intrinsic job satisfactions as among those ranked high in the example above, and quantitative results are consistently commendable (allowing for the uncontrollables), top management will know its superiors are intrinsically motivating their subordinates through job design and leadership.[k]

It might help one's grasp of these complications to examine now how well the page 233 motivation model explains them. In constructing it, Porter and Lawler, it can be seen, put the horse before the cart, performance ahead of satisfaction, as contrasted with the human relations theorists in (a) on page 294. It is true that in tying them together, which is in theory the way it should be, they did not acknowledge the real world where actually there is rarely an extrinsic reward linkage to performance, but the model does provide the right managerial guidance for producing better performance. Moreover, Porter and Lawler in their research on the two types of reward did verify that "intrinsic rewards are more likely to produce attitudes about satisfaction that are significantly related to performance than are needs that can be satisfied primarily by extrinsic rewards." And from their study of the five companies just referred to it's clear that the intrinsic alone can produce the desired results—commitment—if the extrinsic is at least average.

So from the page 233 model one has to conclude that for managers the chain of events for better results, given average pay, starts *principally* with box 7A:

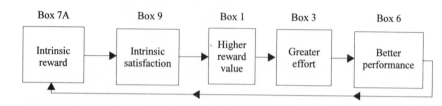

In a start-up situation box 6 (performance) of course may begin the process, performance justifying or producing the reward, but for a going situation it should be apparent to superiors that if performance is unsatisfactory and the competence is there, the problem lies in a lack of sufficient intrinsic satisfaction through either job design and/or their own leadership style.

Models being simplifications by definition, one doesn't attempt to incorporate all the elements that influence satisfaction or motivation, only the key ones. An additional element the operating manager might keep in mind is that satisfaction is both present and future oriented. Individuals can be and will report they are satisfied if they believe they're on the way toward getting it even though well short of it. Good leadership and supportiveness can do much in this regard if trust has been established.

Also, there are a variety of factors, many beyond a superior's control, that are very important influences and should be considered in the equation when judging specific individuals. Here's a short checklist of some that research has substantiated, including obvious ones that might be overlooked:

- Managers typically report higher general job satisfaction than do non-managers.
- Higher level managers report higher satisfaction.
- Line managers are a little more satisfied than staff.
- Independent professionals are the most consistently satisfied.
- A manager's overall satisfaction generally appears to be related to perceived influence on the superior.

- Satisfaction is much more likely to arise as a result of intrinsic rewards than extrinsic ones (as explained).

- The satisfaction of intrinsic needs at lower organizational levels has the interesting effect of generating a desire for more satisfaction when needs are only partially satisfied until the needs are adequately filled. For example, allowing some participation in a department's decision-making will lead to demands for more, up to the point where the subordinates feel they're being allowed a reasonable amount of influence over their destiny.

Incidentally, it is important to mention Herzberg's two-factor theory in this connection, because it has been so widely publicized and it seems to make sense. With a somewhat unique interviewing technique, he and his associates concluded that job satisfaction is essentially divided into two parts:[21]

- The primary determinants of *job satisfaction* are higher-order need factors intrinsic to the work itself (achievement, recognition, "the work itself," responsibility, advancement, growth);
- The primary determinants of *job dissatisfaction* are lower-order need factors associated with the job environment, therefore extrinsic to the work itself (company policy and administration, supervision, interpersonal relations, working conditions, salary, status, security).

Their relationships to the intrinsic and extrinsic rewards on page 294 are easy to see. Herzberg's explanation of how the determinants function: employees, he said, are strongly motivated to obtain more of the former, so they were labeled "motivators," but they are motivated little or not at all by the latter factors only satisfied or dissatisfied, so they were called "hygiene"—thus the two-factor theory title. Furthermore, the two factors, he said, are relatively independent, a characteristic he explains this way:[22]

The opposite of job satisfaction is not job dissatisfaction, but rather no job satisfaction; and similarly, the opposite of job dissatisfaction is not job satisfaction, but no job dissatisfaction.

All of this was equivalent to saying that pay and interpersonal relations have little capacity to motivate, and it seemed to overlook the complex interrelationships possible among psychological needs and the great variety of differences possible among individuals.

The comparison with Maslow's hierarchy in Figure 8.6[23] brings out other points that warrant questioning. A listing of Herzberg's ranking alongside

MASLOW   HERZBERG

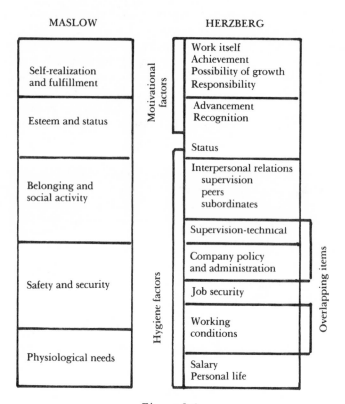

Figure 8.6

the hierarchy suggests some similarity in their theories, but one may recall that Maslow believed that (1) any unsatisfied need in his hierarchy can motivate, and (2) as the needs, except for the top one, are increasingly satisfied, they decline steeply in their motivating power. In contrast, Herzberg said that none of the hygiene factors in the chart can motivate to any appreciable degree, only the factors integral to the work itself.

Perhaps, in fact, some additional explanation about both theories is due. Although neither has adequately been validated by the research of other behaviorists, each has made valuable contributions in different ways. Maslow only intended generalities for guidance and a point of departure for further study, and the frequency of reference to the hierarchy confirms the help it has given.

On the other hand, Herzberg made specific claims that could be verified or disproved, and to date little has been verified. For example, the way the factors were segregated has raised many questions, the methodology supporting the theory has often been challenged, and there's plenty of evidence that some extrinsic (hygiene) rewards can be very motivating. Moreover, in a subsequent writing he revealed that he believes (a) there is for all employees a "normal" profile of similar motivations, and (b) all jobs have demands and goals that can best be attained by persons with a dominant motive of achievement.[24] The evidence in this and Chapter 7 should make it unnecessary to say more.

Yet Herzberg does deserve a great deal of commendation for the general education on motivation he brought to practicing managers across the country, and he made a particularly admirable contribution to management by instilling the awareness in academe as well as managers of the importance of job enrichment, which ties in importantly with Maslow's own conclusion about his hierarchy of needs: in view of the advanced development of the American economy, trying to motivate by means of the three lower levels— more pay, more security, or enhanced social satisfaction—will seldom be enough, especially for managers. Managements must simply learn to design jobs and manage employees in ways that will increase self-esteem and self-actualization, enrichment being the key to that design.[1]

The Enrichment Fit. Any jobholder knows that certain aspects of the job structure must remain unchanged if the job's goals are to be attained. But after holding one for a while, they soon come to realize that not all the structural elements need be designed as they are. Further, there's often much to be criticized about the processes involved, the information needed but not provided, the inadequate feedback, insufficient responsibility, the lack of authority commensurate with the responsibility delegated, the lack of challenge.

Design factors such as these are what enrichment is about. Some are predetermined by the nature of the work and its goals, some, like the demands for judgment, creativity, decision-making, directing, teaching, and the above are variables that can be altered to motivate better performance. In fact, negotiating such changes will be shown in the full chapter on leadership (#20) to be a principal part of direct integration, and it's important for superiors to learn the fundamentals of making a fit in preparation for doing so.

The process of planning a fit understandably implies changing only the job, not the person, so one looks first at the givens of the person per column 3 of Figure 5.7 on page 143 and attempts to discern what design characteristics best satisfy the job-pertinent ones. In light of the Chapter 7 motivation descriptions and the a-b-c to manage on page 275, they would be:

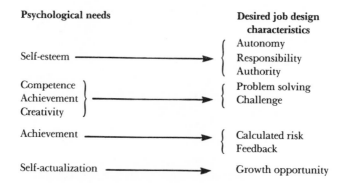

Porter, Lawler, and Hackman added two other characteristics they derived indirectly through the general concept *meaningful work* that the whole group of design characteristics implies. To be truly meaningful to the employee, the job would have to (a) be a "sufficiently whole" job that the person and others could see as having value, and (b) utilize enough *present* skills to demonstrate one's competence, again to both the self and others, and (c) offer growth opportunity through the development of *new* skills. The job should therefore be made high on *job identity* for the first and have for the second and third significant *variety* as to challenge and use of the incumbent's skills and abilities.[25] The eight design characteristics plus these two comprise a complete picture of enrichment.

Parenthetically, a reservation that many experts have enjoyed stressing is that not everyone is interested in autonomy, responsibility, growth, or self-actualization, which of course is true. Some individuals have not risen up the needs hierarchy sufficiently, some have neurotic complications, and others have been under the heels of authoritarians for so long they may never rise above being "indifferent." But what company or superior would want a subordinate manager without a need for responsibility, let alone the other psychological needs? Any discovered are usually removed immediately.

Readers of business news have undoubtedly noticed recent case write-ups in which these enrichment factors have been applied, Volvo and Texas Instruments being two outstanding examples, but the extent of job enrichment throughout the industry is still surprisingly sparse when the performance benefits are considered. From a random sample of 125 companies among the *Fortune* top 1000—presumably the more progressive of the country's corporations—the data in Figure 8.7 covering both management and non-management were assembled, and though it may seem dated, there's no evidence of greater or more meaningful application today.[26]

a. **Extent of Job Enrichment**

Response Category	Responding Firms	
	No.	*Percent*
Formal job enrichment program	5	4
Informal job enrichment program	32	25
Plan to use job enrichment	29	23
Do not plan to use job enrichment	59	48
Total	*125*	*100*

b. **Functional Areas in Which Job Enrichment is Being Applied***

Functional Areas	Formal Programs (4)	Informal Programs (18)	Total (22)†
Production and operations	4	11	15
Marketing	1	7	8
Engineering and R&D	1	8	9
Finance and accounting	1	9	10
Personnel and labor relations	2	11	13
Data processing	1	8	9
Other	0	1	1

*The question provided for multiple responses.
†The number in parentheses represents the number of firms answering the question.

Figure 8.7

The survey does assume that the respondents were careful to distinguish between horizontal enlargement and true vertical enrichment. Enlargement comes in three types: increase the load by adding more of the same, chop up dull specialized jobs and combine the parts differently for reassignment, or rotate jobs that need to be enriched. No motivation is added.

Herzberg published two of his consulting cases with associates, which supply interesting exercises for job planners and students to critique (both condensed here):[27]

Case #1. A company with a 38-man sales force had lost share in its market to competition, and though the share had stabilized in 1966, the stability was unreliable. The salesmen received straight salaries (no commissions) and enjoyed considerable job satisfaction (from a special survey).

An experimental group of 15 salesmen was quietly set up, the other 23 considered the control group; the experimental design effectively kept the external variables similar for both groups:

Objective: regain marketing initiative and hopefully some share.
Criteria: sales volume and profit; a job satisfaction survey at end.
Changes Made for the experimental group:
  a. No more sales reports were required on calls; the men were only to pass on information they thought appropriate, request actions desired.
  b. The call frequency schedule was made their own responsibility, records to be kept by themselves for reviewing.
  c. The technical service department provided them first priority service on demand, paper work to be made out later.
  d. Authority was given to settle complaints immediately on their own up to $250.
  e. If faulty material was delivered, they had complete authorization to handle it in any way they saw with no value limit.
  f. They were given a discretionary pricing range for negotiating of 10 percent.

Results: Sales volume of the special group went up 19 percent over the 9-month period applied, only 5 percent for the control group (both had a decline of 3 percent the previous year); the spread between the two had a constant rate of increase.

Gross margin of the specials was "as high if not higher" than the control, so the sales increase was not due to use of their new pricing authority; in fact the authority was used less often than previous requests for concessions; given the authority, they discovered that price was not the obstacle they had imagined.

Job satisfaction increased among the specials by 11 percent even in this short time and remained unchanged for the control. (The period was apparently too short for other meaningful quantified differences, such as turnover.)

Case #2. The management of a factory was concerned about the erosion, due to the increasing complexity of the business, of the traditional role of the engineering foremen providing maintenance, resulting in decisions on planning, technical control, and discipline being pushed up the line or turned over to staff specialists. The consequence had been the isolation of the foremen, the overloading of the managers, and a weakening of the foreman-worker relationships. The sizes of the special group and control group were not stated, but efforts were made to balance ability and experience between the two. A summation:

Objective: integrate the foremen more fully into the management and capitalize on their potential; motivate by responsibility and opportunity for achievement.

Criteria: the budgets; disciplinary records and work stoppages; written assignments by staff managers; a job satisfaction survey at end.

Changes made for the experimental group:

Planning and technical: increased involvement in organization developments and design; complete control of certain "on cost" budgets; more recognition for achievement of plans; writing of monthly reports.

Management: more responsibility for "on the spot" situations and for preventive maintenance; maintenance of records; conduct of employment interviews; formal responsibility for assessment, training, and development of subordinates; greater involvement in job design; special project management; complete disciplinary authority except for dismissal; direct consulting and negotiating with union officials; more recognition of plan achievement.

Results: **Budgets**: costs as planned or reduced with no sacrifice of effectiveness, done as well as higher up managers previously.

Discipline: effective with reduction in "repeat offenses" by problem-men, substantial reduction in short-term stoppages.

Hiring: in 6 months 100 men of better caliber at better rates; interpersonal skill noticeably improved by interview experience.

Training: much better quantitative results over the control group.

Projects: estimated annual savings of $125,000.

Staff Assessments: markedly better than the control group, effective handling of increased responsibility, better overall performance; within the experimental group management could better identify "the wheat from the chaff."

Satisfaction survey: some modest increase.

In both cases there were increases in autonomy, responsibility, task identity (the "whole" increased), problem-solving, and variety; and each offered better opportunity for growth in managerial judgment, though case #1 is limited to self-management by salesmen.

No comments were made about feedback; maybe it was adequate. It is impossible to tell how much of a Hawthorne effect there was on both the employees and superiors—doubtlessly some—but both sets of change did importantly enrich the jobs, and the satisfaction appeared to be intrinsic. However, there was a fortunate coincidence with a Herzberg assumption here. His apparent belief that the motivational demands of all jobs are primarily achievement related nicely fits selling, the first case, and it's also a high requirement of a foreman's job. But the latter's people-management, we know, also has the need of higher power over affiliation. If one were enriching for a particular foreman who was higher in affiliation, possibly chosen because he was so well liked, the changes would probably have had little effect or other effects.

Additionally, the stated goals of each project undoubtedly limited the scope of each effort, and enrichment seemed in these cases to be the solution to the problems. But there could have been causes other than the job's lack of intrinsic motivation, such as shortcomings on the other three requirements of "fit," not the least is the behavioral fit.

The Behavioral Fit. The scientists are still having considerable difficulty developing validatable procedures for determining the behavioral requirements of a position. Campbell et al. commented on it and the entire subject of managerial job description in this way:[28]

Describing requirements of managerial jobs is usually difficult because such jobs are subject to so many changes. Any given job or position at the managerial level changes from time to time, from person to person, and from situation to situation. This means that a managerial job title tells us very little about actual job demands or about how any given manager may meet those demands. Since managerial job titles provide such limited information, other means must be developed for discovering the behavioral requirements of managerial jobs. What is needed is a set of fundamental dimensions to describe or measure the job behaviors desired at a particular time and for a given situation.

In recognition of this, the experts have painstakingly assemble exhaustive task lists (up to 3,500!), compiled critical incidents of jobs (e.g. 1,847 for a grocery store manager position), experimented with cluste analysis, and applied factor analysis wherever possible. Most of the effor have produced no more than descriptive tabulations of technica expectations or abstractions of personal styles. However, one study has stoo out as a promising beginning because it provides the set of fundament dimensions referred to—10 dimensions for 5 basic management functions– to which behavioral requirements universal to the dimensions might b applied.[29]

Five-hundred-and-seventy-five tasks listed by 93 managers in five larg companies in a structured survey (three levels, five functions) wer condensed by factor analysis into 10 task clusters, A to J in Figure 8.8a, 1 dimensional elements that the study concluded were a general base fo almost all management positions. Figure 8.8b is a brief summary of th report's description of the elements (observe that each element is but on important requirement of the typical titles given, the index showing th measure of importance), which one can see, are essentially technica performance requirements of the job, not behavioral ones; but the table ca be used as a route to the behavioral in three steps:

(a) Determine the behavioral requirements for each dimension of the jo being evaluated by a survey of managers for whom the function i the past was a major responsibility (suggestions on how are ahead

(b) Staff work: (i) summarize the results of (a) for a description of th behavioral requirements of each dimension; (ii) construct "theoretical behavioral requirements" description for each importan management position using Figure 8.8a to provide weights for th requirements.

(c) Modify and tailor the theoretical description to the actual position by a discussion between a staff person and the most qualifie managers who have held the job, and perhaps the incumbent, in joint meeting.

Proportion of positions (as originally classified by level and by function) which measure relatively *high* on each of the ten dimensions

Category of positions	A Staff service	B Supervision of work	C Business control	D Technical products & markets	E Human affairs	F Planning	G Broad power	H Business reputation	I Personal demands	J Preservation of assets
LEVEL										
Upper Management (24 positions)	.46	.21	.71	.29	.55	.63	.55	.46	.46	.42
Middle Management (48 positions)	.54	.54	.60	.54	.41	.47	.35	.39	.23	.31
Beginning Management (21 positions)	.90	.62	.62	.71	.19	.43	.14	.52	.19	.19
FUNCTION										
Research & Development (11 positions)	.91	.54	.55	.91	.27	.82	.00	.54	.27	.18
Sales (24 positions)	.42	.16	.79	.62	.54	.29	.50	.21	.17	.21
General Administration (22 positions)	.68	.54	.67	.55	.18	.49	.36	.27	.27	.32
Manufacturing (26 positions)	.43	.54	.81	.31	.39	.46	.42	.62	.27	.39
Industrial Relations (10 positions)	1.00	.70	.00	.30	.70	.70	.20	.80	.60	.50

Figure 8.8a

305

A. *Providing a staff service in non-operational areas.*
Staff service to line superiors such as gathering information, interviewing, selecting employee briefing, checking statements of facts, making recommendations; typical titles high on th dimension: secretary, plant engineer, assistant treasurer or P.A., director of personnel, manage of industrial relations and R&D.

B. *Supervision of work.*
The incumbent plans, organizes and controls the work of others, has a direct contact wit workers, concerned with efficiency and motivation; typical titles high on this dimension: work manager, manager of manufacturing, accounting, section supervisor, district traffic manage line manager in general.

C. *Internal business control.*
The emphasis on the technical and routine applications of various controls, concerned wit determining and achieving goals and budgets, enforcing regulations; typical titles high o this dimension: division manager, budget administrator, plant manager, general sales manage division auditor.

D. *Technical aspects of products and markets.*
The main concerns are market demand, developing new business, competitors, assistin salesmen, analyzing, contacting customers; typical titles high on this dimension: division sal manager, director of research, v.p. of sales, engineering section manager.

E. *Human, community and social affairs.*
Requires effectiveness in working with others; involved in nominating key personnel fo promotion, appraising performance and selecting managers; also involved in communit affairs, public speaking; typical titles high on this dimension: district, regional and genera managers, plan managers, manager of industrial relations.

F. *Long-range planning.*
Systematic, future oriented long-range thinking and planning covering objectives, strategie management development, solvency, the business mix, new ideas; a tendency not to get involve in routines or detail; typical titles high on this dimension: upper level positions, R&I managers, engineering executives.

G. *Exercise of broad power and authority.*
Broad power, final authority in many areas, interprets policy, makes use of staff, has very hig status and unusual personal freedom; typical titles high on this dimension; any to management line position plus divisional general managers, general sales managers and to staff executives.

H. *Business reputation.*
A general responsibility for the intrinsic aspects of the organization's products or service decisions broadly to enhance quality and public relations and dealing with desigr improvement, delivery and associated corporate image; typical titles high on this dimensior managers of manufacturing, engineering, R&D, purchasing, traffic, industrial relation

Figure 8.8b

(continued on next page

Figure 8.8b (continued)

. *Personal demands.*
Stringent demands on the personal behavior of the incumbent, especially in interaction with superiors and felt obligation to portray the conservative industrious businessman; typical titles high on this dimension: v.p. of manufacturing, director of purchases, controller, high staff executives.

. *Preservation of assets.*
Representative concerns are the preservation of physical and other assets, large capital expenditures, taxes, losses, but not technical operations; typical titles high on this dimension: Timberland manager, v.p. of manufacturing, ad and promotion manager, v.p. of purchasing, assistant treasurer.

It's a pragmatic solution and logical. There are no research techniques in sight that can surpass an adequate sample of good, experienced management brains for an understanding of and integration of the complex variables and demands of jobs they themselves have held.

One problem: although it would be desirable to know the behavioral requirements of all the management jobs in the organization, in medium and large scale firms where meaningful job descriptions are most needed, the cost and time to prepare them would be prohibitive. But doing it for the key positions is critical, not only to avoid misfits where the most important decisions are made, but also to better spot behavioral weaknesses in either incumbents (by performance) or prospects (by prior evaluation). These positions are the principal means of forecasting top management potential, and top executives should have a high percentage of the behavioral strengths in the list below.

Some considerations on the three steps: for step (a) staff personnel of the human resources department can compile a laundry list of typical traits and behaviors needed in management, including ones such as:[m]

Common Behavioral Requirements In Management[n]

Achievement orientation	Self-confidence	Low anxiety
Affiliation orientation	Emotional maturity	Introversion
Power orientation	Insightful	Extroversion
Ambiguity tolerance	Responsibility-loading	Energy
Frustration tolerance	Interpers. skills & ethics	Initiative
Pressure tolerance	Verbal skills	Systematic
Ability to evaluate,	Organizing skills	Intuitive
and willingness to	Autonomous	Receptive
take, good risks	Dominance	Perceptive

Select a substantial sample of managers (20 to 30) for each dimension in Figure 8.8a for whom the dimension was in the *recent* past (to account for memory) a major responsibility, give them orientation on the behaviors, and ask them to assign the needed behaviors in rank order to their dimension, applying a weight of their own.

For step (b), the summarizing (i) of the results of (a) and preparation of the theoretical behavioral requirements (ii) for each position would be routine for the staff people. Descriptions for five of the dimensions might look like the following ("educated" guesses without a survey):

> *Providing a staff service in nonoperational areas:* high achievement oriented (for high competence), high frustration tolerance, good interpersonal, verbal, and organizing skills, systematic for technical staff work, both systematic and intuitive for managerial staff work.

> *Supervision of work:* high socialized power motive higher than affiliation, high pressure and frustration tolerance, systematic for the planning, self-confidence, maturity, responsibility, dominance, good interpersonal, verbal and organizing skills.

> *Internal business control:* power-affiliation ranking, maturity, self-confidence, responsibility, autonomous, intuitive, low anxiety.

> *Human, community, and social affairs:* strong affiliation need, maturity, insightful, extroversion, interpersonal and verbal skills.

> *Long-range planning:* ambiguity tolerance, ability to evaluate, and willingness to take good risks, organizing skills, low anxiety, a combination of systematic and intuitive.

On (c), the modifying and tailoring of the theoretical behavioral requirements to an actual *position* are then done by bringing together the most qualified authorities on the position, such as the superior, position holders of the recent past (recent here to account for evolutionary changes of the position's characteristics), and possibly the incumbent, in a joint discussion led by the staff person. The procedure somewhat as follows:

i. Have the managers do the same for the position that the survey managers did for their dimensions: assign and rank behaviors from the laundry list to the job. Also, have them fill out the Appendix Exhibit 3 questionnaire (the Task Analysis) for the achievement, affiliation, and power orientation to aid judgments on the first three in the behavior list.

ii. Summarize the foregoing data and set it up for the position similar to the "theoretical behavioral requirement" of the position prepared in (b) ii, making the format similar for easy comparison.

iii. Guide the managers through the comparison to a reconciliation.

iv. Do it about every 5 years to account for the dynamic changes over time in demands on the position.

Though not scientific, just going through the procedure forces consideration of, therefore better odds of filling, previously neglected behavioral job demands that are as important, often more important, as functional skills.

Too much work and expense? How many subordinate positions does a superior have on the key-position ladder? And what are the many costs of a bad fit in these positions?

Individual-job fit. All the "individual-job fit" elements for manager jobs in the chart on page 292 can now be assembled into an effective procedure, and starting the description with what is the present standard practice in matching will help by contrast to show the importance of upgrading the procedure.

The traditional job description, we know, spells out the functional requirements as to responsibilities, authority, accountability, relationships, and standards, all of which:

- make it possible to ensure there are no gaps in the total of all the tasks to be done by the job and unit,
- clarify for the incumbent the fundamental expectations of management and the minimum performance standards of the job,
- provide a point of reference in cases of conflict among employees or disagreement with the manager.

So executives who ban them as forcing rigidity, the way a few who consider themselves progressive have, lose these advantages. Since descriptions are only as rigid as the superiors who administer them, it would be well to examine the supervision if it appears to be a problem.

While making these contributions, however, traditional job descriptions at the same time cause serious misconceptions by being limited to the tasks of the job. As a consequence, a search for someone to fill a position is considered mainly a matter of evaluating for the technical requirements of the job and compatibility with the superior. That success on these could still lead to a mismatch doesn't occur to most managers, nor to many personnel staff who've not learned that, as the prior sections have demonstrated, *jobs are not motivationally or behaviorally neutral*, points that are fairly recent discoveries.

Consider the risks of mismatching on the dominant-motivation fit, for example, putting a high achievement individual in a routine job that the person would soon leave in boredom, or putting a high affiliation employee where there's little interpersonal contact. Mismatches on behavioral fit would be putting an essentially intuitive person in a job with high demand for systematic analysis and little for intuition or a mainly systematic person where there's considerable ambiguity or frustration. And the two Herzberg cases illustrate poor enrichment fit.

Furthermore, there is seldom any thought given to subsequent adjustments where feasible on near-matches to make the jobs more motivating. This incidentally, does not contradict the common sense general rule that all job and systems analysts are aware of, that one should not design a job to fit a person. It should be clear that no recommendation made herein violates it. The proposals for adjustment are intended to improve the fit within the limits of flexibility the jobs may possess, in a trade-off of the theoretical ideal in exchange for better performance without sacrificing essential "fixed" job requirements.

These critical comments are no condemnation of the managers involved. Present unsatisfactory fittings simply reflect the slow pace of putting the pieces of the state of the art together and communicating them. A job matching procedure for either new manager prospects or incumbents should in general approximate the following with the chart on page 292 in mind (the "compensation" of column 3 ahead, and the planning of column 4 under "Strategy" and "Structure" in Chapters 15 and 16):

1. Prepare the functional description as in the past on the technical requirements of the position, the responsibilities, standards, and accountability, plus guidance of subordinate teams if any (explained ahead).
2. Determine the other climate parts of the job in column 1 page 292, and include them all with #1 above in the description:
    a. the functional with the elements that have been missing: interpersonal skills needed (see subject index), role responsibilities (Chapter 20), and organizational relationships (better than in the past);
    b. the job's dominant motivation need;
    c. the job behavior requirements.
3. Evaluate the candidate or incumbent for all the "Individual Job Match" parts of the job (columns 1 and 2), using appropriate appraisal techniques where applicable (in the next Chapter):
    a. the adequacy as to required intelligence, technical knowledge and skills—*the technical fit;*
    b. motivational strengths vs. the job's needs, and for managing jobs the power-affiliation ranking and maturity—*the dominant-motivation fit;*

   c. the person's higher-order needs and the extent to which the job can (or can be made to) satisfy them for intrinsic motivation— *the enrichment fit;*

   d. the suitability of the person's traits, behavioral characteristics, interpersonal skills, and ethics—*the behavioral fit.*

4. Evaluate all job goals and performance measures for potential conflicts or the creation of ethical dilemmas; eliminate those identified if possible, minimize the negative, reconcile in the description, or change the measure used, and give some guidance.

5. Evaluate the person on values and philosophy relevant to managing people (as G.K. Chesterton said, "For a landlady considering a lodger it's important to know his income, but still more important to know his philosophy.").

6. If, as a result of the appraisals in #3 to #5, he or she appears to be a good match for the position and accepts it, start the process of "direct integration" for the variable parts of the job (column 2, page 292) along the lines of McGregor's example in the Integration section of Chapter 20. Also consider leadership development (in Chapters 17 and 20).

In numbers 1 and 2, however, an overriding issue is the part the job plays in the total process to which it contributes. The common job design approach is to concentrate only on task specialization without thought given to the intended outcome of *the process* of which it's a part; the result is myopic job cells with minimal process interrelationships when maximizing them is essential to process effectiveness.

Job description planning according to process and its outcome, a team concept being one, forces a complete rethinking and redesign of what each job in the process should be toward that effectiveness, and the best way to inspire the rethinking is to bring together the managers of the functions involved in the process for a cross-functional perspective, questioning all the assumptions underlying the present design and redesigning for the best process outcome, motivational results, and customer satisfaction which means integrating the needs of column 4 on page 292 with those of columns 1 and 2. The result is usually a process team.

Process/team. This process/team planning and set up is not applicable to all situations, for example, a number of management and specialist positions, and there will always be some hierarchy above them, but it is applicable in most organizations to a substantial degree. Doing it is in fact a basic reengineering procedure and method of flattening the organization toward what is now being called the post-hierarchical "horizontal organization" (more on it in chapters ahead).

Three approaches have evolved, the selection made to fit the situation:

1. an individual is made responsible for the whole process leading it as a team;
2. an informal team of the functional managers collaborating on call as needed (per the team leader) to manage the process;
3. a formal relatively autonomous team of the functional managers, fully responsible and accountable for the process.

The first is particularly applicable in Marketing/Sales. In almost every industry today companies have as competition plenty of quality products at competitive prices, so one key to *competitive advantage* for a seller generally boils down to developing a *selling advantage*, and most have found the solution to be process design, following certain basic rules for *all* process/team applications:

a. focus all activities of the organization on their processes, not tasks, and on customer needs, wants and satisfaction;
b. a senior executive must be involved and consistently attentive to each team;
c. each team should receive the training and development according to its level and program as described in Chapter 13's "Team philosophy" section, and below middle management each member should develop in time several to all of the team's needed competencies for effective cross-functional performance.
d. build close long-term relationships of team members with customers and suppliers;
e. use the sales organization in team with other relevant departments to fill customer needs and solve their problems;
f. Reward the team and team members both as a group and individually, the group according to achievement of team goals, and individuals for pay increases and/or bonus sharing according to the team's evaluation of the individual's sharing attitude, teamwork and collaboration conveyed to management for its annual review, at which time management also evaluates the person's achievement of goal responsibility and applies either its skill-based plan, gain-sharing plan, or other method it may have.

Wal-Mart is an excellent illustration of all of (a) to (d), the way they link tightly suppliers, warehousing, trucking, 24-hour shelf-replenishment, billing, selling attention, and so forth; and from principally a service standpoint they are also especially applicable to industry-to-industry selling where a "customer sales representative" may be made responsible to see that all functions from the sale contact to delivery are kept on schedule, for example, order entry, credit checking, product spec. maintenance, delivery, and installation where applicable—all separate relatively disconnected sequential functions commonly given the indifference to individual customers typical of any assembly-line worker. With the "customer sales rep" the customer need only contact one person for added information input or order status (delivery time). Most every executive is also familiar with the limited internal version in the form of product and market managers (in Chapter 16).

For (b), the CEO of Home Depot has gone so far as to make himself "salesman-in-chief;" and on (c), GE assigns staff full time to customers' factories as virtually in-house consultants. Examples of (d) are DuPont using teams of sales reps, technicians and its own factory managers on request to help solve customers' problems; and Kraft sales people helping supermarkets improve their profit (trained for it). And a technique for (e) is to build customer satisfaction incentives into pay plans using customer surveys for the rating on both team and individual effort.

On the second of the three process approaches listed above, it is essentially the standard project management technique applied to whole processes, and an example of the third at the management level can be found at General Mills where relatively autonomous twenty-person work teams run complete plants. They're given the marketing plans for the product, production costs, and performance data and do everything—scheduling, quality control, supervision, etc.—and get bonuses as a group on results, the executive superior acting only as a monitor and facilitator.[30] See pages 584-599 for a detailing of team philosophy and development, Chapter 14 for the use of work flow software in groupware for process analysis and design, and Chapter 16 for "horizontal organization' planning detail.

Of course, in each instance of (a) to (e) in (1) and in (2) and (3), the job descriptions have to cover the assigned responsibilities, utilizing the potential of up-to-date information technology (e.g. electronic support to suppliers and customers, and the customer sales rep above having access to all sales quoting and order status data on his/her portable PC).

Underlying the process thinking, it should be added, is the realization by all progressive firms doing it that the former inward-looking management concentration on costs, control and growth is no longer enough just to stay even with competition let alone be a leader. While they are still very important, the dynamic changes in the competitive environment have, as they know, made the crucial outward-looking *quality*, *service* and *innovation* the prime factors to target, and process thinking and operating is fundamental to success; motivation toward those ends must be built into job descriptions as much as possible.

A few final comments. An important issue is the degree of detail that should be written into job descriptions for non-team positions, which can have a range of from too much discretion, risking a neglect of essential tasks, to functioning like a straight-jacket. The designer must hit a balance that gives both sufficient autonomy and flexibility to allow creative planning, problem-solving, and action and to allow room for ethical responses to dilemmas (pages 175-184).

Also, the #4 on page 311 on ethics is an essential precaution. At times there may be unavoidable conflicting responsibilities within a given job (or deliberate ones to force collaboration as will be shown in bThe Parallel Organization, Ch. 16), but quite commonly there are serious problems of conflict particularly due to goals and their performance measures that encourage undesirable decisions and actions; and the measures themselves are often not directly relevant to the person's performance or are beyond his/her control. When on the other hand conflicts or dilemmas are unavoidable, the designer should be aware of them and give some warning and guidance either in the description, the performance review, or the collaborative planning in column 2 on page 292 (the reason for "ethics" there a along with goals and methods).

And lest #5 be underrated, incompatibility of a subordinate manager's values and philosophy with those of his or her superior or with members of the group is unquestionably a major reason—and one that's little appreciated as such—for friction, dissatisfaction with a person, and eventual removal. One common mistake regarding the values of the unit that was mentioned earlier: putting an authoritarian person in a manager's position after the departure of a progressive one who had conditioned the subordinates to participate.

In sum, job planning is admittedly complex, and to the extent that steps are omitted one can be sure of proportionally less job satisfaction, poorer performance, higher costs, and higher turnover.

Even in small organizations that can't afford staff help, superiors can considerably upgrade the traditional method by simply applying intuition to the required steps and working intimately with the subordinates. But the full procedure is particularly important to top managements of medium and large firms that desire high performance, in that effective procedures must make up for the remoteness of the top from most of the individual position-filling. At least good and comprehensive minimum job-filling standards have to be set and positions planned accordingly.

Compensation

To complete the process of making the "individual-climate match" one will recall in the chart on page 292 that after the job designing of column 1, columns 2, 3, and 4 have to be undertaken. As said there, the direct integration of columns 2 and 3 will be in Chapter 20 and the indirect of columns 3 and 4 extends from here through Chapter 19 (in its two stages; page 000). Success on the match throughout the organization would produce the integrative climate defined on pages 264-265, one in which technical-social integration has been and will continue to be achieved, both consciously and intuitively, as standard managerial practice.°

(It may be helpful to keep in mind here that at the top management level the first structural concern is a technical one, the *industry-organization-job* match applicable to the whole organization, a subject that will be discoursed in Chapter 16).

Compensation in column 3, displayed separately because of its independence of the other subjects, refers, we all know, to the extrinsic rewards, those administered by the organization (vs. the self-administered intrinsic), therefore all pay, incentives, and administered intangibles. Good decisions on it in any substantial organization have been growing more difficult for some time. It always required an integration of the facts on organizational resources (especially its limits), system structure, cost effectiveness, and market rates,[p] plus managerial philosophy; but now with rising standards and expectation, psychology has to be added and given major consideration.

One can see in this mix that part of compensation is virtually predetermined ("fixed"), the rest is variable, and that the philosophy strongly influences how to handle the variables (e.g., exploitation and manipulation as opposed to equity via participation). Which takes one back to the values chapters, so this major section will add no more on it, deal only with the other factors and the incorporation of the psychology.

As for the total compensation design theme (the subject referring to the management level), it's a good idea before starting to plan it to review in one's mind what each type can and cannot do. Foremost, while base pay tends to be the primary inducement to the individual to fill the first two of the organization's needs listed on page 234—A1 to enter and remain, A2 to carry out the assigned roles—it cannot on its own gain innovative or nonspecific (untargeted) performance (A3), intrinsic satisfaction with the work itself, or internalization of the organization's, unit's, or job's goals.

Adding incentives is one improvement in those regards, a limited one in that they motivate performance on only the factors they're tied to. And the intangible extrinsics are generally not tied to any specifics of performance at all, but still must be managed well in order to hold onto the most desirable personnel.

Thus the role of pay alone is essentially that of membership, attendance, and minimum performance; the role of incentives is targeting specific performance; and the role of the intangibles is to provide the conditions needed to sustain the membership, attendance, and minimum performance, having some overlap with intrinsic reward and its benefits.

That's the organization's side of the coin, the easy one to comprehend. It's the individual's side, how they view their compensation, that has presented most of the problems, complicated by the fact that employees' views result in behavior as well as performance. So if their interpretations do not match what the organization wants, the behavior is apt to be poor to dysfunctional, dragging down the performance.

Unsatisfactory consequences should therefore be expected for any plan that is not based on both the compensation roles and potential interpretations. The organization gets what it pays for, so it had better know what each type of compensation elicits if it is to motivate what it wants. Inversely, much of the behavior in an organization can be understood by examining the compensation system, which is a major reflection of the leadership style at the top as well as its managerial competence. what follows is the principal knowledge the organization needs in order to get what it wants. The subdivisions will be:

> Base pay
> Incentives
> The intangible extrinsic rewards
> The overall policy

Base Pay. The subject needs to be introduced by some comments on money in general, regardless of the form in which it is received.

In the terminology of behaviorists, money is a generalized conditioned reinforcer, which means it's a multiple incentive for the attainment of many potential outcomes, and it can be either an incentive before the fact or a reward and reinforcer after the fact.

Plainly, it's what can be done with it, its instrumentality, that gives it its motivational power. However, managements have universally assumed incorrectly that it has much the same instrumentality to everyone, especially that money is the most important want, so paying more will solve any attitude, effort, or productivity problem. When it doesn't work, the fault is all placed on employee inadequacies, and Theory X remedies are invoked.

The correct explanation of course is that money is valued in proportion to its perceived ability to fulfill the individual's needs—the reason why the saying, "everyone has a price," doesn't always hold up. So with all the possible psychological needs in Figure 5.7 on page 143 plus personality, economics, and environment, in addition to the problems of expectancy, equity, satisfaction, etc. in the Figure 7.2 motivation model on page 233, with all these, both the importance of money and the reasons for the importance can be widely divergent among persons, and can moreover vary over time for individuals as circumstances change.

The big questions therefore would seem to be who does money motivate, how much does it motivate, and how much does it take? But that is not enough. We must further ask, when and why does money fail to motivate? What in those cases are the corrective actions or alternatives? As complex as it all is, the sciences have given us some helpful guidance. For a summary of the main discovered generalities and verified intuitions:

- Money has the greatest reinforcing power on upward mobiles and hardcore workers, a strong effect on working class people (McClelland's study on page 241), and the least on true professionals; for managers in general it's a safe assumption that the range is at least from important to very important.
- But the importance of money does decrease the higher the position and the higher the compensation (an important overriding factor on a number of these points is *greed* (page 120) when it can be "pulled off;" for example, during the 1980s and 1990s the egregious compensation of many major firm CEOs who controlled their boards).
- It naturally motivates in terms of needs, doing so loosely according to the Maslow hierarchy and depending on the management level, being sought first for its ability to satisfy physiological needs, second for security, after which it becomes of increasingly less direct importance at the social level (#3) and ego level (#4) with little if any at self-actualization (#5).
- One thing for sure is that employees to whom security is very important assign a comparatively low valence to the value of money, so for them it is less able to motivate superior performance; other methods are needed.
- Each individual has a compensation point above which he or she become more interested in satisfying other needs, e.g., the point where a private office is more important to satisfy the need for esteem and recognition, the point where office quality factors play a part, etc.
- Highly motivated good performers in middle and lower management have high money aspirations; token increases are generally taken as insults, except in a depression, or are seen as hostile or competitive acts of superiors trying to encourage departure.

- Compensation satisfaction is basically determined by the elements of the motivation model on page 233, with the emphasis on the seven factors in the second tier from the left of Figure 8.9.[31]

The seven factors, however, are markedly complicated not only by the difficulty mentioned of getting employees to relate base pay to more than minimum performance but also by employees' own normal subjectivity and the standard organizational policy of compensation secrecy. The performance-pay linkage will be covered in the "Incentives" section ahead. On *subjectivity*, the perceptual skewings caused by it that research has reported seem prosaically evident, but they are important considerations in appraising individuals' satisfaction with their compensation. Examples: (a)

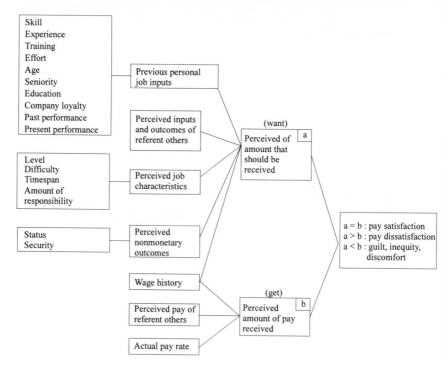

Figure 8.9

Managers commonly value their own output and compensation worth much higher than they are valued by others including those who administer the plan. (b) They usually think they're above-average performers and should get more than associates in comparable positions. (c) There are some strong biases on nonperformance factors: old timers feel seniority should have very important weight, the well-educated that education and degrees should, and so on. So one has to expect some degree of conscious dissatisfaction generally and at all times except when they're clearly overpaid.

And the opinion distortions, especially of the comparisons, are sorely amplified by a policy of pay secrecy.[q] Superiors claim that secrecy keeps managers from making the comparisons that they feel would increase their dissatisfaction. There is no doubt that many also hope it will result in less requests for raises (even talking about pay is often frowned on) as well as less disputes about the inequities that exist.

Lawler's own studies (1965, 1966, 1967) among others have conclusively shown that the reverse, greater satisfaction, occurs:[32]

- Pay comparison is a most important feedback to employees of their organization's rating on and opinion of their general performance; in its absence individuals cannot judge the ratings correctly or tie their pay to the general performance.
- Secrecy leads people to overestimate others' pay in comparison to their own.
- Secrecy leads them to feel they themselves get less than the average and get lower raises.

The evidence is that secrecy unquestionably results in less satisfaction with pay and, furthermore, in less satisfaction with the whole organization. Those organizations that have opened up have found a significant improvement in attitude as a result of not withholding the truth, a new belief that the company is doing its best to both appraise fairly and pay fairly. As a consequence, the employees are much more willing to accept, and interested in taking, the risks of a merit system, which they naturally don't like when they believe it's unfairly manipulated, a belief secrecy will almost always induce (e.g., the common opposition of teachers and their unions to instituting merit pay in the Education bureaucracy—no trust).

This translates into the fact that an organization must have an open information system on pay if it is to maximize the motivational effect of either or both of its pay and incentive system; inversely, it cannot maximize the desired results with secrecy.

The carryover to participative management should be evident. Participation is patently dependent on subordinates' openness which is directly in proportion to their degree of trust in their superiors. How could there be trust and truly open discussion between superior and subordinate or between management levels with secrecy on facts so crucial to hones communication? Yet how many with pay secrecy profess to be participative

There is of course a certain amount of logic to their inconsistent policies Although the genuinely participative organization is still rare, many mak the effort, and most of them are making some progress, are in stages o transition toward the goal with an openness proportional to the progress Subordinates do give ample credit for the effort and are commensuratel more communicative. Pay openness would produce a quantum leap ahea(in this regard.

However, it's questionable whether an open pay system itself can b(successfully introduced in stages. The key pay information to any employe(is naturally what others in the organization are getting for the same work Knowledge of only the salary ranges and/or the average of raises given (on "partial" approach some have tried unsuccessfully) can hardly relieve doubt about the fairness of distribution. Cases have been reported in which sucl partially open systems or other varieties have, on introduction, only lowere(morale, increased rumor, and reduced the perception of the pay-performanc tie if any is being attempted. Among other things, a partial approach seem to reaffirm that the authoritarian style will be around for some time to come

Two preliminary "democratization" moves do have to have been mad for a high probability of introduction success:

1. First, all pay inequities have to be removed (to the extent feasible on any level of management that openness is to be applied to, th most practical approach naturally being to apply it to the whol management team as quickly as possible, accepting that it could tak(as long as a year or two just to the inquiries.
2. Each level has to institute a performance appraisal procedure fo subordinates that is equitable, open, and respected.

Then after a genuine participative management effort is underway, th(release of the pay information would be accepted by all with a fair amoun of equanimity.

Some writers, incidentally, have contended that an open system is no feasible where groups of employees operate so interdependently as a team that their individual contributions cannot be identified for rewarding. Th(stand seems to overlook the option of giving equal pay and assigning ¿ bonus to the group, the group collaborating with the superior on how th(bonus should be divided or doing it on their own.

Another solution being tried by a number of firms (much of it stil experimental) has been labeled "skill-based pay," increases given t(individual workers or team members based on improved or acquired nev skills. Compared to bonus plans (called "gain-sharing" systems) that are or what employees do, pay-for skills is for what they know how to do.

HRD that manages the system determines the "skill units" of the individuals' or team's tasks, skills that are technical, interpersonal or "soft," and the individuals demonstrate mastery by paper-and-pencil test, satisfaction of an expert (supervisor, trainer, facilitator), or satisfaction of the team's members, pay increases tied to achieving the standard set.

There are some problems. A skill-based system requires a massive amount of planning and data, job redesign, training, and evaluations; interpersonal and soft skills are not easy to measure; the systems cost more than traditional compensation ones; and if its benefits are not going to offset the costs, the firm should probably not adopt it.[33]

On the other hand, the benefits can be considerable though also difficult to measure:

- Skill-based pay increases are (assuming equitable base pay to start with) logical for developing basic management talent, particularly for white collar and production workers where it's most applicable, and naturally production goes up; moreover, career advancement in most situations requires expertise in a range of functions (why the importance of lateral moves also are now becoming widely appreciated).
- All the "restructuring" going on has often greatly changed, stretched out, or eliminated career paths and many promotion opportunities; skill-based and gain-sharing plans tends to convey and substitute for needed expressions of interest and appreciation.
- The pay increases and bonuses change the management pay-raise decision from subjective by the superior to mainly objective, putting the criterion of learning in place of control; additionally, the technique makes the logic and fairness of transfers more apparent than traditional pay systems.
- For teams, other merit payments are generally less equitable and less feasible; sometimes they're made zero-sum situations: of the total amount available an increase to one person means less for the others. No problem on it with skill-bases pay.
- Employees or teams with multiple skills provide the organization with flexibility to reconfigure quickly to meet changing markets or work-flow emergencies.

Moreover, it would behoove organizations that are upgrading themselves to the team philosophy to carefully evaluate the extent to which their existing compensation system may be rewarding anti-team behavior; for example:

- rewarding only individual effort
- tying pay increases to seniority
- failing to encourage development of needed skills
- failing to reward commitment (discernible collaboration, involve ment, and dedication to team goals)
- linking moves up to ability to earn more money, thus stressing hierarchy and status when a flatter more organic structure is desire

Incentives. Numerous surveys have shown that 65 to 70 percent of medium and large organizations today have incentive plans (also calle bonus or merit plans) at one or more levels, but a number of analyses of them indicate they don't work and propose that the whole idea should be abandoned.

These could be the conclusions of analysts insufficiently versed in either the technical or social requisites of a good plan and its implementation Many do work adequately now, and the principle can be made very effectiv in many other situations. Certainly they're not feasible in all of them, but a 1993 study by consultants Hewitt Associates of some 2000 firms reveale that 68% of them had an incentive plan, and they expected, due to the succe rate, that virtually all large firms would have them by the year 2000.

Where they are feasible, planning good ones depend on the attention give to four factors and the way they're handled:

> Compensation principles
> Incentive objectives and structure
> Goal setting
> The measurement of performance
> Appraisal

In introduction, the purpose of an incentive, we know, is to motivate b promising a reward before the desired performance, and the paymer becomes a reinforcer for performance repetitions when the promis continues. A close cause-effect may be perceived because it is self-eviden or management has tried to make it so by the payment and explanation

However, the very nature of managerial jobs (compared with nor managerial) tends not to allow a close cause-effect relationship because o

- The multiplicity of managerial responsibilities necessary to b effective: analysis, planning, decision-making, leadership, delegation motivation, coordination, teaching, controlling, taking risk handling conflicts, etc.

- The qualitative nature and complexity of all of these, precluding precision and inviting controversy.
- The dependence of managers on:
  a. The performance of subordinates who have eccentricities and at times get sick, have accidents, make mistakes, and so forth.
  b. The cooperation, services, decisions, and effectiveness of other departments or personnel beyond control.
- The uncontrollability by managers of major items in any department's budget.

The consequence is that very few organizations have succeeded in selling o management or employees the idea of specific linkage, and the high probability of argument and bad feelings over appraisals has alone prevented many superiors from even attempting incentive plans. Campbell t al. found that some 25 of 33 companies they themselves studied on the subject did not do so for managers[35] (which contrasts with the surveys on ll employees mentioned in the first paragraph above).

Indeed, every organization should periodically examine and reexamine because of changing conditions, the potential for incentives to improve their managers' performances. Their feasibility will be manifested if it is found hat:

a. A cause-effect linkage can be seen in the chain of desired performance, the action necessary to produce it, and the reward.[r]
b. Agreement is possible on the selection and evaluation of the measurement of the action that produces the desired performances.
c. The performance-effect is not so long after the action-cause that the connection is lost, for example, tying the reward to any long-range decision or long-range result.

If it is clearly not feasible—like staff services and long-range planning obs—straight salary is normally the only recourse. Then along with the foregoing tests, determination for most positions generally depends also on he principles involved. Consideration of relevant principles as to either on-going or new plans can be covered and assured by simply answering the ight questions, such as:

1. What, first, are the effects of the base pay on performance? If there is none, the need for an incentive may be clearer. If base pay encourages specific acts or behaviors that are detrimental, or deters ones that are desired, can an incentive be designed to discourage them?

2. Is the base pay of specific individuals too low? If they know they're underpaid for work they now deliver, will they trust the incentive or believe any incentive will itself be inadequate? Can an incentive be designed to increase performance in such a situation?

3. Is the base pay too high for a plan? For instance, can more reward profitably produce *more* performance? Perhaps the whole compensation plan needs an overhaul.

4. Should the plan be tailored to organization levels, classifications or individuals? What degree of commonality is there among groups of managers for reinforcers, payment schedules, intervals, or timing?

5. On a plan in force, are performance improvements possible by making changes in any of these last five factors (in item 4)?

6. Do the incentives in any way encourage destructive competition between individuals or groups when cooperation is desired?

7. Are there any group incentives that encourage internal dissention or set the group against the less able members, remembering there will always be less able ones? (a matter of ethics).

8. Do the incentives in any way discourage desired changes or innovations of processes or products (e.g., a short-range profit goal for general managers that discourages new product development and/or introduction, risks that should perhaps be taken from the divisions and given to headquarters task forces to ensure longer-range go-no-go decisions in the interest of the whole firm, assigning those approved back to a division)?

9. Are there any job design-change opportunities for increasing *intrinsic* incentives to complement the extrinsic ones?

10. On feasibility of a new plan, has due weight been given to the organization's climate, leadership styles (especially as to mode of appraisal), industry dynamics (e.g., average product life), product/market diversity, and the organization's structure and processes (all of the subjects discoursed in coming chapters)?

Unfortunately, it takes professional analysis to obtain reliable answers to many of these questions; nevertheless, what is most important to any manager is to know what additional questions to ask when they are brought in and to know the main options. Then additionally, think through for any incentive system the principles stated by Katz on page 234 with regard to B3, that:

a. the rewards must be perceived as large enough to justify the added effort;

b. they must be perceived as directly related to the performance and follow directly after;

c. they must be perceived as equitable by the majority, many of whom will not receive them.

And keep in mind Figure 7.2 on page 233.

Next (in the p. 322 list), the planning of **Incentive objectives and structure.** It is finally becoming apparent to many managements that the fundamental goal of their management effort should be to increase *long-term shareholder value and return* as measured by increases in the combination of "total return" (dividends, cash payouts, plus earned and unearned capital gains) and market price increases (see the end of Chapter 5 for both economic and market value added—EVA and MVA, explained here). It's generally recognized now that success on this depends heavily on two skills: the planning of competitive strategies (in Chapter 15) and management incentives, especially for upper management.

The way to do the latter has to start with visualizing the linkage between the use of corporate assets to create value, the market that gives the assets value, and the intervening variable, the employees. More on the linkage in Chapters 13 and 15; for here on management incentives, the approach has to be what has to be done to motivate managers to achieve *customer satisfaction* leading to the desired increases in sales, profit, ROI, and the other measures of value and return. For upper executives with an important impact on these factors (that is, total return and stock prices), understandably an effective way to get the desired executive commitment would be through stock ownership that is a significant part of the individual's net worth.

A January-February 1990 issue of the *Harvard Business Review* gave an excellent example of how one firm did it.[36] The company's board realized that the standard stock options for upper executives added to already generous compensation packages had generally proven inadequately effective, because the added gains were not important contributions to total income, and there was no penalty for poor performance.

Agreeing with the above statement that each executive's equity stake should be a significant part of his or her net worth and put them at risk both positively and negatively—big total income for outstanding performance and punishment for poor—they persuaded the executives to buy some 5 percent of the company's total shares by providing each about 90 percent of the financing at an attractive rate. Each bought on the average over $500,000 worth, and needless to say, when the market price and dividends went up they did very well, when down it hurt.

However, an essential part not mentioned: the firm has to make sure those executives fully understand what it takes to produce and sustain customer satisfaction and the ultimate goal of long-range total return, crucial knowledge that must be taught in executive development programs and repeated in refresher ones.

An intriguing and very successful program that did was an option plan for *all* employees by PepsiCo, Inc. they installed in 1989. The first of such plans was instituted by Pfizer, Inc. in the 1950s, but the idea didn't get much attention until PepsiCo did it, after which Merck & Co., DuPont and several others followed, many more expected to do so soon.

The plans adopted differed in a number of ways. PepsiCo grants new options to all full-time employees (some 100,000) every year on July 1st giving them the right five years later to buy stock at the July 1st price equal to 10 percent of their pay. Say the option is given with the price at $20 per share. The employee pays nothing. Five years later it's up to $60/share. The employee can then buy it at $20 or not, and if buy, hold it or sell it immediately, the company obtaining the shares for the person on the open market or by issuing new stock. There's no risk to the person, but it can be expensive to a very successful firm.

Merck also had a 5 year wait (then) but limited the purchase to 100 shares. DuPont has a 1 year wait with the 100-share cap; but in each case the preparation program of education, as commented above, can be crucial to goal achievement, and PepsiCo is thorough about it, gives all two years of indoctrination on everything that affects shareholder value and return teaching them how to incorporate the learning in all planning, decisions and reporting systems.

Indeed, a definite trend is underway brought about of course mainly by the widespread criticism of the gross over-payments. One consulting organization (Hewitt Associates) found that of 100 companies responding to a survey (reported in *The New York Times*, 5/9/93), 16 of them then had formal stock ownership guidelines for executives, 4 had informal ones and 17 more were considering one or the other. The written formal ones are what's new—none before November 1992.

Some of the formal require all v.p.s earning $50,000 or more buy a percentage of their salary, others are more specific; for example, Union Carbide requires the CEO hold four times his/her annual salary, the COO three times, and 14 other executives (with salaries above $150,000) an amount equal to their annual salary—no corporate financial assistance. Most plans, like this one, only apply to executives.

This of course deals only with the stock options part of incentive compensation, the part that boards of major firms have recently abused so badly for top management (e.g., the top five CEOs receiving a total of $322 million in 1991, the large part of it from options), and a popular type, the restricted stock option, frees the gift of any linkage to performance: the executive gets shares with the restriction that he or she may not sell them for a specified period, usually 5 years, but during the period is given the dividends and the right to vote the shares. If the price goes up, fine; if down, one just doesn't buy—no loss, no pain, and the dividend cost to the firm. Grael Crystal analyzed 161 large firms that granted options, 61 of which were restricted, and all of the 61 trailed the others over a 5 year period by every measure of return from 11 percent to 32 percent. He found that it's commonly been the choice type of boards that recognized their firms weren't going anywhere yet wanted their executives to collect on their incentive plans. His advice to those invested in firms with restricted options: sell.[37]

To make matters worse, the SEC has for all options compounded the opportunity to abuse; it has ruled that executive pay should be related to *stock* performance. As one experienced board compensation committee executive said, linking pay to stock price "is just an invitation to management to manipulate figures and actions." One study of 324 firms that had adopted stock price option plans in 1978 showed that over the following five years R&D was reduced 10 percent, ROI dropped 4 percent, and profits fell 10 percent, all compared to similar companies.[38]

The manipulations have been particularly obvious for the five years before CEOs retire, during which period their retirement pay and bonuses are based on the firm's profit and stock price increase. The common pattern: R&D, advertising, and HR development are cut. From the head of the non-profit Institutional Shareholder Partners: "The real problem is the lack of accountability. CEOs today (1992) are absolute monarchs and their boards are the House of Lords." More on it with solutions in the last two sections of the last chapter (22).

And at the divisional top management level the performance linkage is all too often no better, even though the opportunity to be quite specific about responsibility is present. For example, a large compensation consulting firm (Towers Perrin) studied 163 major companies and found that only slightly more than 1% had divisional incentives tied to divisional results; the balance received regular or restricted corporate options. Needless to say, the linkage should be to what the person can control that benefits both the division and corporation, being based, for example, on service, quality, sales, costs, gross margin, productivity, market share (GE demands market leadership). Good ones for functional executives: new accounts for sales, rejects and scrap for production, innovation for engineering, development and design. And two bases growing in popularity is the pegging of bonuses and even promotions on either or both of profit and customer satisfaction. At IBM, for instance, their 300,000 sales force now has 60 percent of their compensation above base pay tied to profit, a user information system supplying them with product margins, the other 40 percent based on customer satisfaction...customers have expressed great satisfaction; and on the profit linkage an American Compensation Association study has found that, in general, companies are earning back in increased sales and productivity twice what they're paying out.

Note that so far only *asocial* factors have been considered to the neglect of the qualitative *social* that so often determines the quantitative results. Incentive payouts at all levels should be related wherever possible to a variety of qualitative matters, and especially for divisional CEOs to those of climate and morale (employee opinion surveys), the development and advancement of subordinates, loss of promising ones, the amount of participation applied (see pages 000-0), team development, and of course an appraisal of customers satisfaction as affected by their direct responsibilities, the education on all naturally covered in executive and management development.

For incentives below the top level, Lawler quoted earlier supplied some helpful plan-design guidance. In his book *Pay and Organizational Effectiveness*, he commented, complementing the 3 Katz principles, that for any plan to be truly motivating it must (1) create a belief that good performance will lead to higher pay, (2) contribute to the importance of pay, (3) minimize the negative consequences, and (4) increase the belief that good performance also leads to other positive non-pay outcomes.[39]

Interestingly, a number of social psychologists claim that the motivation value of all incentive plans is debatable. While there's truth in some of their contentions, one suspects that much of the negatives are a result of studying plans presently in force, most of which, as previously mentioned, are not particularly good. A sampling of their negatives:[40]

- Incentive compensation plans produce short-term performance improvement but not lasting-improvement and seldom change attitude or behavior;
- People who expect rewards for work done do not perform as well as those who expect nothing because the minds are on the rewards not the work;
- Rewards can be punishment and are manipulative, saying not only "do this to get that" but also, "do this or here's what will happen to you";
- The pressure to get rewards can create competition destroying needed cooperation;
- The #1 casualty of incentive rewards is creativity, because (a) they focus on the "that" away from top performance on the "this," and (b) it results in avoidance of the risks often necessary in creativity, e.g., the readiness to try something different.

What then do they say does work? Pay workers well and fairly and get their minds off money—which is best done by motivating commitment via leadership, meaningful work (p. 300) and an inspiring climate.

True, but design is just as important, a well designed plan neutralizing most of such negatives and capitalizing on the immutable desire for the "that" by accounting for the major variables effectively. Lawler supplied the table below to help out.

Climate	Authoritarian	Need objective hard criteria; pay clearly tied to performance
	Democratic	Can use participative goal setting and softer criteria
Production type	Mass and unit	Can usually develop hard criteria; rewards on individual or small group basis
	Process	Need to encourage cooperation; individual performance not highly visible or measurable
	Professional organizations (i.e., hospital, school consulting firms)	Individually based plans; soft criteria; high individual involvement in own evaluation
Size	Large	Organizationwide bonuses poor for all but a few top-level managers
	Small	Organizationwide bonuses possible in some situations
Degree of centralization	Centralized	Hard to base performance on subunit (i.e., plant) performance
	Decentralized	Pay can be based on profit center or subunit performance for members of management

Moving on to the characteristics of the plan itself, the effectiveness of any is naturally dependent on the measurement of performance, goal setting, and appraisal (the next chapter), the first based on a choice that's elementary to any thoughtful manager, whether the basis of measurement should be:

- performance against standards,
- performance against budget, or
- performance against specific goals.

Standards are inadequate, because by definition they only set the level of performance that's considered effective for routine tasks needed to "complete" the work. It is non-routine decisions and activities that, given the routine support, make the managerial performance difference.

Budgets are important for significant leadership positions; however, even for top positions, there are, we know, major uncontrollables in them all, there are no qualitative measures, and important activities are buried and unspecified in the gross figures. So budgets alone as incentives will usually produce distorted results and need to be supplemented in a number of ways.

Performance against goals is certainly the best and for obvious reasons, primarily ones for top executives still being profitability (top executives at IBM now have 75 percent of their compensation above base pay tied to earned corporate profit) with the quality of climate and human resources development added. The principal ones for divisional executives and middle managers were listed on page 327.

Then on the modus operandi for all of goal setting, measuring and appraisal, be sure to honor what every progressive executive now knows: that a unilateral handling of any of them is a sure invitation to trouble and poor results whether on the qualitative or quantitative, especially for management positions because of their high qualitative content. Indeed, since much of their extrinsic rewarding has to be based on qualitative factors, their participation in handling all three is imperative—an interesting commentary on the emphasis authoritarians, who can't stomach participation, place on the extrinsic to get results. More specificity on all three ahead in Chapters 9 and 10.

Some additional general suggestions for better chances on incentive success:

- Don't tie a manager's bonus or incentive to the performance of management above; when there is too little payout or none it could undermine the regard for the competence of those above.
- Don't base it on zero-sum ranking in a group; e.g., when dividing a group into above and below average, if the average moves up significantly, some with substantial improvement might still be labeled below-average.
- For interdependent managers, try to plan incentives that motivate the needed cooperation. A method is described in the MBO goal-setting section on pp. 408-409.
- Don't expect perfection; compromise is always necessary between some individual and organizational needs, and no system can be completely free of subjective judgments by superiors.
- Again, because of their importance, be particularly careful to (a) balance the incentive for short- and long-range goals, (b) be sure short-range ones will not be achieved at the expense of long-range ones (#8 on page 324).

And Lawler presented in his quoted book two sets of warnings that are worth repeating, some of them summarizing points that have been made. The first:

1. Do not assume that pay is necessarily the most important factor to your subordinates.
2. Do not fall prey to the frequently held cry of social scientists that pay is about sixth in importance.
3. Do assume that pay is about as important to people one level below you as it is to you and other managers at your level.
4. Do look beyond economic complaints and demands on the part of subordinates to see if there are noneconomic causes lurking in the background.
5. Do tie pay to performance (to the extent that it can be), and make it a form of recognition it you want pay to be important enough to motivate good job performance.
6. Do look at the backgrounds of people who are going to work in incentive jobs to see if you can identify those for whom pay is likely to be important.

For the second set, he listed those situations in which one should not try to tie base pay or incentives to performance, concurring with and adding to what has been said. Don't, when:

1. the trust level is low;
2. individual performance is difficult to measure;
3. performance must be measured subjectively;
4. inclusive measures of performance cannot be developed;
5. large rewards cannot be given to the best performers.

Staff positions illustrate item 2. The subjectivity in item 3 does not include the use of managerial judgement, the use of which is unavoidable in the many indispensable qualitative measures, factors that make trust crucial. An example of item 4 would be any situation where the accounting or information system only partially measures the performance to be judged. And failure on item 5 is *one* of the reasons why traditional organizations cannot hold top performers: they're mentally locked into mediocre raises, poor-to-no incentives, and slow promotions, and haven't the imagination to see what is necessary to hold them or the flexibility to act.

Finally, a few opinion patterns about the reward-performance tie have been identified that tend to be revealing of motivations and fears, a knowledge of which might be useful in judging the attitudes of the subordinates on one's own team:

- Generally, managers do prefer to be paid in proportion to performance.
- Less educated managers are less in favor of it.
- Good managers are more for it than are poor ones.
- European managers are less in favor than Americans (perhaps due to a more pervasive authoritarian style).

The Intangible Extrinsic Rewards. These in general are the rewards given for overall performance and as such are not usually tied to particular performance events, though the last event in a series of performances or behaviors may trigger the award. The principal ones:

- *Promotion*—a multiple reward and the most important for most managers.
- *Status*—by promotion, position, and perquisites.
- *Recognition*—by promotion, pay increases, compliments, one-shot intangible awards like time off for superior performance.[5]
- *Social relations* (with superiors, peers, subordinates)—principally a function of personality but heavily influenced by job design and status, therefore promotion and position.
- *Job security*—by promotion, pay increases, recognition, contract, labor union.
- *Working conditions*—the differences for managers clearly through promotions.

The intrinsic rewards (page 294) are of course intangible also, but the important distinction, as explained, is that they are derived from the work itself and are self-administered, whereas these are conferred by the organization or superior. Still, some overlap does seem to be present. What is conferred of the six factors does have an important impact on an employee's perception of the job as has the means used (the comments on the right) and the managerial behavior behind it, but none make the work itself more inspiring.

The major point that should be kept in mind about the extrinsic: they must be managed well to sustain the purposes of pay and incentives (memberships, attendance, and specified role performance), and they are particularly important to holding the most desirable personnel. Yet it is precisely the management of them that all too often defeats these purposes.

The principal problems that arise are related to the most important of them all, the *promotion*, which is both the primary intangible reward and the main means toward granting most of the others as the explanations in

the listing show; and, commonly the cause is poor leadership in one regard
or another.

When, say, three managers lose to the one winner in a promotion, the
three will always feel somewhat-to-badly cheated unless the winner's
superiority is conspicuous, which is not usual. While the one winner may
work harder in the future and be a greater asset, the three losers generally
slow up, develop negative attitudes, and think about leaving, some doing
so eventually if not abruptly, and sometimes all leave.

It need not be so costly or even costly at all. Such problems can be traced
to either dubious reasons for the promotion, misperceptions by the
contenders as to the reasons for it, or aversive behavior of the superior.

On the first, all too often promotions are given for, or strongly influenced
by, non-performance factors—friendship, prejudices, sex, appearance,
energy, verbal capabilities, favors. Superiors that do it and expect no
repercussions, needless to say, are deluding themselves.

But when it's not true yet perceived as so, the second, it's naturally equally
damaging, and on the third, one can be sure that the aversive behavior
(whether it's avoidance, silence, glares or actions) will guarantee distrust
and bad communications.

Yet, if the behavior is not too objectionable, two simple procedures can
cut the losses significantly: (1) have the selections for all but the top positions
chosen by a committee of the superior, the superior's superior, and a
personnel executive to give the selection visible objectivity; (2) explain to
each loser the reasons (assuming they're fair) for the decision right after the
promotion, giving them also an honest appraisal of the opportunities ahead
for themselves.

These proposals naturally rub the "exploitive authoritative" executive the
wrong way, and in fact are not easy for any traditional manager to accept,
but well-run organizations working hard on participation usually adopt them.

Another deplorable practice of many upper executives needs highlighting
if only as a caution not to slip inadvertently into it: using "job security,"
one of the intangibles, as a method of control. While participative superiors
consider job security a dividend derived from the good performance-pay-
promotion sequence, others tend to manage it along a continuum from
paternalism to a "go-no-go" extreme.

At the paternalism end, *security* is intended to be a dominant incentive
to stay and do the assigned job (in line with the philosophy that the
organization decides; you do what you're told); adequate performance is the
criterion; you get fired only if it's extremely bad. At the "go-no-go" end,
a qualified superior performance is the criterion, and *insecurity* is supposed
to be the incentive, superior performance being the achievement of the goals
set by management above. You're fired if either you can't make them

consistently enough or if the performance is consistently extremely good and threatens the superior's own sense of security.

However, it's been reliably established that managers in general, especially ambitious upward-mobiles, do not rate security very high in importance; as measures of achievement, high salary and status are much more important, the insecurity mainly an irritant. In other words, the CEOs only increase turnover unnecessarily when they try to capitalize on insecurity this way. Results on both turnover costs and performance would be much better if the true problem is found when goals aren't attained—goal-setting, the market, the management, and so forth—and consider the responsibilities of top management to help subordinate managers be successful.

Overall Policy

To the uninitiated, possibly the most surprising thing to realize is that, while money (base pay or bonus) can motivate in many situations, in some it doesn't; in others, different incentives work better. And it may be difficult to believe that as virtually all research has shown, neither base pay nor annual or sporadic bonuses successfully *motivate* to any significant degree in any but a few organizations, the failures caused by either the climate, the technical design, the administration, or a combination of them. On design, for example, it was found that base pay and increases themselves, instead of being tied to performance, were related to job level, seniority, or other nonperformance factors.[41] One comprehensive 25-year longitudinal study showed that the raises do not even have year-to-year consistency.[42]

There is the additional complication that what a superior or organization can achieve with money cannot be applied universally to all people. Its influence hinges not only on the value each individual places on money (as described on page 317-318) but also on the recipient's needs, and the situation can be a factor. Then even when it is valued highly, a disrespect for the *pay system* can destroy its effectiveness. Assuming a situation where money is valued highly and can motivate, the respect understandably depends on the presence of a climate conducive to trust—without which no compensation plan for managers can really be effective; and the subordinates' belief that the system is fair.

The benefits of opening up the pay system, the most important means of achieving trust on the subject, should in themselves suffice as an argument for the respect it would gain. To recount:[t]

- The payees get needed feedback on performance.
- They will not overestimate the pay or raises of others nor underestimate the comparative value of their own.

- Efforts to tie pay to performance will not be blocked by distrust as to the believed pay adequacy.
- The potential for intrinsic satisfaction and commitment by job-design and leadership will not be blocked by distrust on pay.
- The resulting improvement in trust makes the progress review more logical, productive, and motivating to the subordinate (which can be improved still more by adding also an open appraisal and selection system, both described in chapters to come).
- The urge to compare one's pay with the outside market is reduced; there is enough comparison inside with the people who count most.

It was pointed out, however, that the only way a superior is going to gain respect for the selection of performance measures, for the goals that are set, or for the fairness of performance appraisals made, all fundamental to trusting the system and necessary whether there's an incentive plan or not, is to enlist subordinate participation on those applied to them. Further, since genuine participation is not possible without the full truth, the pay system has to be opened up first.

In fact, the development of a solution to the problems caused by an authoritarian climate has to precede both. Before any upper management decides to have an open participative compensation system to get the trust, it had better assess the leadership style of its managers, working down from the top, for its fit with such concepts; authoritarians will sabotage both. The organizational answer is to undertake first the necessary behavioral education followed by appropriate change techniques described in Part III.

Thus, in all but the few behaviorally advanced organizations, three sequential steps are necessary: first, education and behavior change, second, opening up the pay system (and the others mentioned that should be opened), and third, participatively planning and managing the total compensation procedure.

A preliminary of the planning, however, has to be the establishment by top management of its own overall compensation objectives and design for the organization as a whole. The basic thinking for dynamic results...

Medium to large-scale firms commonly find it impossible to have the same compensation plan for the entire organization, major variances being necessary to accommodate different functions, different product lines, controllability of costs, profit contribution, measurability, etc. The only factor that tends to dictate uniformity, in fact, is long futurity of results where it is present, as in R&D, corporate planning, and some of the other staff services, in which cases the method has to be straight salary, and the motivation intrinsic satisfaction and leadership.

So there will be several to many plans in virtually all of them; but the return on the *total* compensation investment can be greatly improved if the plans are governed by an overall compensation policy, one that couples the total compensation to the organization's resources, that is, its ability to pay.

Obviously, through the years and through good and bad times, none can afford to pay everyone the top market pay rate in each category—which would give the poor and mediocre performers an undesirable and unwarranted sense of security, though it can usually minimize turnover (and profit). Needless to say, too high a pay scale for all is a bad idea, but is very low turnover a good one? Not by this technique.

Conveniently, the most motivating approach to compensation is one harnessed to resource limitations as follows, demonstrating again the value of being consciously aware of the three basic motivational needs of organizations on pages 234-235: motivating to join and stay, to perform the specific jobs, and to do more than the minimum.

In all three, job design, leadership, and future prospects, play a part, especially in the third, but sticking to compensation planning, the first (to join and stay), we know, is achieved (the extrinsic part) by offering an appealing starting pay and pay range, and the second and part of the third are mainly pay increases and/or promotions, the increase based on either:

1. the subjective evaluation of the superior,
2. across-the-board percentage increases, or
3. performance.

The inadequacy of #1 and desirability of #3 must now be clear, but an examination of the across-the-board technique, as illogical as it is, will provide the clue to the best corporate policy.

Indeed across-the-board pay increases would seem to be congruent with a desire to please everybody; however, while the poor performers would be very satisfied with such an increase, the best ones would be dissatisfied, and most important, the poor ones would be raised above their market value and become locked into the company, and the best would end up below the market, encouraging them to go out into it where they're sure they can do better. Companies that make a practice of doing this even partially—and most strongly authoritarian ones do—chronically hang onto the mediocre and poor and lose the best.

Patently, too low or no turnover at all due principally to compensation will ruin the organization with deadwood, and the way to achieve the desirable rate of return is to tie the payout to the "normal distribution curve" that describes the competence pattern in any substantial group: the largest percentage of employees will be average and a considerably smaller percentage will be in each of the above- and below-average groups. An analysis of the total past compensation payout and the record of profit goal attainment over several years will show clearly the amount the organization can afford. Distribute it in proportion to satisfying employees along this distribution curve. For example:

- Make the 25 percent who are the top performers *very* satisfied;
- Make the 50 percent who are average just satisfied; they are important contributors but might be urged to do better;
- Leave the bottom 25 percent unsatisfied.

The consequence: a most desirable continuing self-renewal process in which the best are highly motivated to both remain and continue the superior performance, the middle are made aware by the upper group example that higher rewards are possible with better performance (they should be told so too, at least in the performance review session), and the bottom are given notice to step up their effort, move out, or be moved out.

One can see that *satisfaction* and *dissatisfaction* are and should be the controlling forces, and the organization must periodically check them to see if the policy is being applied effectively. Note that this is the company-wide part of "managing the tension level" described on page 284-285. Two things have to be determined:

a. How well do managers perceive the relationship between their rewards and performance (thus how well are the two being tied together)?
b. What is the satisfaction level of each manager, and does it relate correctly to the performance grouping of the individual according to the three categories just mentioned?

The first can be determined by either a special opinion survey on compensation or be included in the periodic climate survey every organization should have. The second is a task to be determined in annual joint performance reviews of superiors with their subordinates.

Finally, two supportive policies are necessary if one like the above is to work, policies that are discernibly advisable in any case:

- Superiors must either be granted the authority to reward in proportion to performance or have their payment increase requisitions for subordinates rated and awarded accordingly.
- Superiors should be recognizably well rewarded for properly rewarding above average subordinates; *their* superiors should also sufficiently communicate job security and performance satisfaction to

free them from fear of subordinate competition while spurring them to encourage their best subordinates.

Addendum. A new phenomenon—a fringe aspect of turnover management—has evolved over the last decade or so, one that many managers view as a competitive strategy. Strategy planning for competitive advantage and profit maximization has become quite sophisticated, one of the features emerging being the concept of "core competencies," the specific technology and production skills of the organization that underlie the firm's product lines (detailed in Chapter 15). And it has apparently inspired many managements and boards to divide their employees into two groups, "core carriers" and "all the others," followed by a policy of shedding the company of as many of the others feasible and subcontracting out as much of non-core production and supportive services as possible.

The policy has become widespread resulting in a plethora of work forces now called "disposables;" in fact, some 20 percent of Fortune 500 employees are in the category, and some 30 percent of all employees in commerce and industry are part time most all of whom long to be full-time. Significantly, "disposables" are generally not counted as employees; quoting one executive: "They're not here long enough to matter," and they're looked upon by the permanent staff as borrowed fixtures and treated as second-class personnel (thus available for abuse?). Certainly, this employment practice alone makes reported claims of productivity improvement suspect.

Interestingly there is virtually no limit now on the type of work available from temp agencies. For "peripheral" personnel: secretaries, sales clerks, factory and retail workers, CAD/CAM designers, guards, etc.; for "professionals": managers, lawyers, engineers, doctors, bank officers, biochemists, x-ray technicians, top executives. One Chicago agency is so large it has 560,000 on lease; another in Connecticut has a stable of top executive turnaround specialists.

The profit logic is unassailable: costs are minimized on health-care, pensions, training and development, paid vacations, unfair termination suits, sex harassment suits, and the problems of complying with the many employment laws. And, it avoids the guilt felt for firing loyal permanent employees; if a temp is unsatisfactory, one only asks the agency to send another; and of course with a decline in the need, less temps or no temps.

Needless to say, the policy is a prime illustration of the traditional interest in only the technical part of management, little-to-none for social concerns or social responsibility, and a short-sighted attitude that inevitably peppers the company with people who are indifferent about the firm, motivated only for the paycheck, unforthcoming with new ideas, with zero loyalty, and with no incentive to avoid the variety of material temptations and sabotage.

On the broader perspective, the long-term consequences for both companies and the nation will be creeping decline not only from the reduced training and development but the reduced motivation, commitment and creativity adversely affecting the quality of product, service and image, and the hidden costs undoubtedly reduce the above claims for profit improvement by cost avoidance. Further, it is essentially a disinvestment in a firm's human resources and the nation's human capital, raising serious doubts about the wisdom of the policy as a wise competitive strategy for a company and for the nation's global industrial and economic leadership. To make matters worse, there's as yet no evidence that the practice will decline with very prosperous economic conditions. But the advantages of a committed, creative, quality conscious work force are so compelling, the nation must do all possible to make the "disposable" concept an unattractive option by reducing the claimed cost benefits; for example, by instituting universal health and pension insurance (not based on the number employed), and demanding the education of all executives on all the particulars, especially the long-range consequences—let alone the immorality.

NOTES

a. "Management Style" is also encountered.

b. A criterion for investors and investment counselors looking for well-managed firms offered by a knowledgeable one: "In our acquisition search we saw it wasn't well managed in terms of motivating employees, and we said, 'We don't want that company'."[2]

c. See the tally on page 15 of *Organizational Climate and Culture*, (ed) Schneider, B. (San Francisco: Jossey-Bass, 1990).

d. New research on managers who feel the need for control (vs., for example, the primarily affiliative) was recently summarized as follows: They're potentially the high achievers, tackling difficult tasks more persistently, setting higher goals and pursuing them more realistically, but they commonly find it hard to delegate, overburdening themselves and depriving subordinates of the autonomy they want and in doing so reduce their trust and motivation.[7] The (a), (b), and (c) with good leadership development should eliminate these weaknesses.

e. The authors entitled the results "preliminary evidence," pointing out that the verification would require either experimental study of the effects of controlled climates or long-range studies of people living and working in organizations with known climates, either of which would require prohibitive time and money.

f. Although a high level of mutual trust can be inferred in the combination of "warmth," "support," and "identity," shouldn't it be listed as one of the dimensions in Figure 8.2 because it's so important?

g. References to power-orientation will always mean authoritarian in the text ahead as it does here, to be distinguished from the "socialized" power described in the last section.

h. A distinction commonly made in management literature (vs. a climate survey): An employee opinion survey is the term used for a general survey of the attitudes and opinions of all employees about the larger organization, its policies, benefits, managing, image, etc.

i. "Integrative climate" should not be confused with the term "integrative environment" used by R. M. Kanter in *The Change Masters*,[9] that she said is an environment in which the structures and processes are designed to foster across unit and level boundaries the communication, collaboration, and cross-fertilization needed for innovation if those involved are so inclined; conducive managerial attitudes and behavior are recognized and seem to have been assumed by her, but nothing is given on when or why they happen or how they can be made to happen. What she is referring to is principally the technical integration within the organization in the definition on page 31, though "environment" normally includes the conditions outside the organization.

j. Dana Corporation. From "A Passion for Excellence," op. cit., p. 215.

k. Job satisfaction one can see, is differentiated from climate satisfaction in that the latter is a measure of the degree of general satisfaction with the work unit as to all the climate variables of structure, processes, and leadership, and it usually includes job satisfaction.

l. See the "Job design" section Chapter 16 for a summary of the other major variables to consider in job design for maximum motivation.

m. The strict definitions of behavior and performance in footnote c on page 113 generally are not adhered to in management literature because of the heavy overlap of the two in practice; indeed, the close link in management between behavior, performance, traits, and skills is such that references to behavior commonly include them all as is done in the table below of common behavioral requirements in management.

n. See *Cognitive Style*, Chapter 14, for descriptions for the last four in the list: though cognitive "styles," they manifest particular behaviors. Also see AT&T's list on page 362. Note sound judgment is a "relational" capability associated with intuition and development of the brain's right lobe; the need for some of it in all management positions is assumed.

o. Recall footnote i above.

p. For those unaware of it, the American Management Association issues annually updated data on domestic compensation for 16 categories (a book for each) ranging from top management to and including clerical, plus the compensation paid in major foreign countries.

q. The literature uses "pay" in this term to include incentives if any; the discussion of the subject will follow.

r. The Conference Board in a 1985 survey of senior HRD executives in 486 corporations found that their two top goals in the coming years would be controlling employee benefits costs and improving productivity, and their principal efforts to achieve them would be on (1) health insurance cost containment, (2) improving the link between merit pay and performance, and (3) performance appraisal systems for managers (covered in the next two chapters).[34]

s. Time-off is one of the more forgotten effective lower-level incentives where it is applicable. For one example, the author instituted it during World War II in the maintenance of airforce bombers (B-24's) accompanied with tight final inspection. Crews of seven in each of five hangers on 8-hour shifts, led by staff sergeants, were taking an average of 12 to 16 hours per plane for 50-hour and 100-hour inspections (standardized procedures) when they should have been done in about half the time. Told they could leave at time of completion but must do overtime if necessary until completion, the *average* time dropped to seven hours per plane and only reached 10. Satisfaction with the system was universal.

t. Note that the benefits of eliminating pay secrecy do not depend on a perceived pay-performance tie.

REFERENCES

1. "Human Resources Managers," *Business Week*, December 2, 1985.

2. Peters, T. and Austin, N., *A Passion for Excellence* (New York: Random House, 1985).
3. Schein, E.H., *Organizational Culture and Leadership* (San Francisco: Jossey-Bass. 1985).
4. Kotter, J.P. and J. L. Heskett, *Corporate Culture and Performance* (New York: The Free Press, 1992).
5. Schein, E.H., op. cit., p. 267.
6. McClelland, D.C. and D. H. Burnham, "Power is the great motivator," *Harvard Business Review*, March-April 1976.
7. *The New York Times*, October 7, 1986, Section C-1.
8. Litwin, G.H. and R.A., Stringer, Jr., *Motivation and Organizational Climate* (Boston: Graduate School of Administration, Harvard, 1968), p. 64 modified by pp. 90-91.
9. Kanter, R.M., *The Change Masters* (New York: Simon and Schuster, 1983).
10. Peters, T.J. and R.H. Waterman, Jr., *In Search of Excellence* (New York: Random House, 1982), pp. 121-134.
11. Toffler, B.L., *Tough Choices: Managers Talk Ethics* (New York: Wiley, 1986), pp. 337-339.
12. Myers, M.S., "Conditions for Manager Motivation," *Harvard Business Review*, January-February 1966.
13. Kotter, J.P., *Power and Influence* (N.Y.: The Free Press, 1985), Chapter 7.
14. Ibid., pp. 120-122.
15. Schneider, B. (ed) *Organizational Climate and Culture* (San Francisco: Jossey-Bass, 1990).
16. Parasuraman, A., V.A. Zeithaml, & L.L. Berry, "Service Quality," *Journal of Marketing*, 1988, 49.
17. Schneider, B., J.J. Parkington V.M. Buxton, "Employee and customer perceptions of service in banks," *Administrative Science Quarterly*, 1980, 25.
18. Lodahl, T.M., *Man on the Assembly-Line: Job Attitudes at Two and Fourteen Years* (Cornell University, School of Business and Public Administration, 1965).
19. Porter, L.W., and E.E. Lawler, III, "What job attitudes tell about motivation," *Harvard Business Review*, January-February 1968. (Abridged).
20. Ibid., p. 163.
21. Herzberg, F., B. Mausner, and B.B. Snyderman, *The Motivation to Work* (New York: John Wiley & Sons, 1959).
22. Herzberg, F.B., "One more time: How do you motivate employees?" *Harvard Business Review*, January-February 1968.
23. Davis, K., *Human Behavior at Work* (New York: McGraw-Hill, 1972), p. 59).
24. Herzberg, F., "Motivation-Hygiene Profiles," *Organizational Development*, Fall 1974.
25. Porter, Lawler, and Hackman, op. cit., pp. 302-303.
26. Reif, W.R. et al., "Job Enrichment: Who uses it and why," *Business Horizons*, February 1974.
27. Paul, W.J., K.B. Robertson, and F. Herzberg, "Job enrichment pays off," *Harvard Business Review*, March-April 1969, p. 61.
28. Campbell, J.P., M.V. Dunnette, E.E. Lawler, III, and K.E. Weick, Jr., *Managerial Behavior Performance and Effectiveness* (New York: McGraw-Hill, 1970), p. 99.
29. Hemphill, J.K., "Job descriptions for executives," *Harvard Business Review*, September-October, 1959. Discussed by Campbell et al., pp. 94-98.
30. Lawler, E.E. III, in "Managements' new gurus," *Business Week*, August 31, 1992, p. 47.
31. Lawler, E.E., III, *Pay and Organizational Effectiveness: A Psychological View* (New York: McGraw-Hill, 1971), p. 215.

32. Ibid., pp. 174-175, 255-257.

33. Osborn, J.D., L. Moran, E. Musselwhite, J.H. Zenger with C. Perrin, *Self-Directed Work Teams: The New American Challenge.* (Homewood, IL: Business One Erwin, 1990), p. 185-194.

34. *Issues in Human Resource Management 1985* (New York: The Conference Board).

35. Campbell et al., op. cit., p. 366.

36. Rappaport, A., "The staying power of the public corporation," *Harvard Business Review*, January-February, 1990.

37. Crystal, G., "Incentive pay that doesn't work," *Fortune*, August 28, 1989.

38. *Business Week*, July 6, 1992, p. 37.

39. Lawler, op. cit. (1971), p. 157.

40. *New York Times*, 10/17/93, 11F.

41. Lawler, E.E., III and L.W. Porter, "Predicting managers' pay and their satisfaction with their pay," *Personnel Psychology*, 1966, 19, 363-373.

42. Haire, M., E.E. Ghiselli and M.E. Gordon, "A psychological study of pay," *Journal of Applied Psychology Monogram*, 1965, 51.

Chapter 9

Appraising the Individual

At the start of Chapter 3 on Personality the question was asked, "Can an ideal leadership personality model be constructed?" This would seem to be the place to answer it for two reasons: the crucial elements of the components of personality on page 39 have now been covered, and it is at and through the appraisal process that we have to know what we're looking for when selecting for leadership.

The hypothetical problem-solving executive (page xxii) had to conclude initially that the answer is "no," but at this point he realized that a *high probability* personality model of an effective leader-manager *can* be constructed, a depiction that would be enormously helpful in selection and development, and he proceeded to do so as will be shown.

Of course, immediately following it in importance is the appraisal technique for identifying the characteristics in applicants and employees, appraisals also critical for being the *origin* of all unsatisfactory performances as well as good ones, because the resultant decisions impact down to the lowest level—for placement and promotion (Step #3, page 311); development, compensation, motivation, and planning—determining the effectiveness not only of the immediate units but also of the whole organization through those decisions. Indeed, it is often forgotten that these judgments down the line additionally determine to a large extent, through the selections and promotions, the quality of the candidates for and choices made for top management in the years ahead.

The functions of appraisal therefore are many and critical, and one will find in progressive firms that all the top executives consequently make a conscious effort to ensure education on and attention to them, even the CEOs repeatedly stressing their importance and personally reviewing many of the evaluations.

What to appraise, we know, falls into the two categories of personality and past performance, each having their own what and how.

Personality appraisal

The importance of personality appraisal to leadership as seen down through the ages will itself help separate what does and doesn't count in the search for leadership talent. The ancient Greeks and Romans seem to have started the theorizing about the subject with their "great man" idea of inherited talent, that leaders are born not made. This has been dubbed the original "trait theory" of leadership.

But nothing particularly imaginative was added right up into the 20th century, maybe because the aristocracy and wealthy had a monopoly on all top positions, even in the armies, and the great man idea simply verified their right to their advantages. There was no perceived need for another view among those in control of everything.

World War II, however, precipitously increased interest in the subject. The sudden requirement in this country for hundreds of thousands of leaders to be drawn from the population raised a massive problem of how to spot them among the draftees, so the scientists were pressed into service. The British did likewise at the same time.

Regrettably though, the same thing happened on both sides of the Atlantic. Having only the great man theory to start with, they all dusted it off and devoted the entire effort to the study of what traits to look for and questionnaire development for wholesale identification.

Then after the war it was more of the same as the scientists and academe moved into the study of bureaucracy. Taylor's "scientific management" assumed it, those in power delightedly perpetuated it (some were heard to claim divine right!), and it became so ingrained that to this day we still see many organizations using long lists of traits for appraisal rating, characteristics that society as a whole deems desirable, but most of which have only a nebulous relationship if any to the performance requirements of specific jobs. For example:

Personality	Work	Attitude	Resourcefulness
Sociability	Functional skill	Temperament	Initiative
Maturity	Volume	Job interest	Versatility
Self-control	Quality	Loyalty	Ingenuity
Self-discipline	Accuracy	Compatibility	Adaptability
Communicativeness	Neatness	Cooperativeness	Flexibility
Persuasiveness	Completeness	Responsibility	Forcefulness
Industry	Efficiency	Ambition	Effectiveness
Dependability	Methods	Courage	Energy

Judgment and Skills

Acuity	Integrity	Analytical skills	Verbal skills
Discretion	Standards	Planning ability	Timing

And generally each word is given a numerical range, say 1 to 5, representing poor to excellent, the grade to be added for totals to compare employees.

There is no question that all can contribute to effectiveness, and research has verified it;[1] however, not only are they all either qualitative, abstract, or a matter of opinion, virtually guaranteeing bias and subjective distortion, but also subordinate failure to display any may only be a reaction to what they have seen as successful in past and present bosses they liked and what they abhorred in those they didn't whether successful or not.

Personality characteristics thus became *the* measure of leadership ability, and many executives still believe it even though the organization behaviorists pointed out its limits over 30 years ago. There is no single pattern of personality traits and abilities, McGregor among them has said; the traits required differ with the situations; his conclusions: leadership is a relationship of (1) personality, (2) the followers (their needs, attitudes, traits), (3) the organization (structures, processes, goals), and (4) the environment (economic, social, political).[2]

Numbers 2, 3 and 4 add up to "the situation" the employees' perception of which is the climate, so one can see the connection of leadership to the individual-climate match, the goal set up in the last chapter (page 310), where "followers" can be substituted for the individual, the situation for the climate. When an agreeable relationship between the individual and situation has been effected that improves performance, the superior will have brought about the match—an act of leadership.

Another perspective—the definition given in a behavioral science dictionary[3]:

> *Leadership* is (1) the exercise of authority in initiating, directing or controlling—the behavior or attitudes of others with their consent, (2) incorporating those qualities of personality and training which makes the guidance and control of others successful.

What to Look For.[a] Item 1, personality, in the McGregor statement, however, tends to confirm once again our conviction that it is nonetheless of major importance to appraising for leadership, and scientists have continued to work hard trying to find out what of personality can be correlated with effective managerial performance, the factors most targeted being intelligence, traits, and interests.[b]

In the 1960s an impressive study was made summarizing the results of hundreds of them.[4] Though it lumped together and averaged a lot of the detail because of the great number, it did give evidence of their value as measures.[c] Campbell et al. commented.[t]

> We conclude from Ghiselli's course summary of all the studies of executive effectiveness that measures of intelligence and of personality and interest may be "good bets" as potential predictors of managerial effectiveness.

The guardedness of this approval probably reflected their awareness that most had in fact not linked the tests to either the job or the organizational function, primary elements of "the situation." But they did conclude that analyzing personality filled an important niche. As a result of a study of their own of test validations up to 1970, they asserted that some 30 to 50 percent of general management effectiveness can be expressed in terms of personal qualities. A sketch consolidating (by the author) their findings:

> *Cognition*: high on all of intelligence, verbal skills, interpersonal skills, organizing skills, and judgment in handling the technical and the social.
>
> *Disposition*: a liking for hard work and interpersonal relationships; active, ambitious, moderate risk taker.
>
> *Temperament*: dominant, confident, straight-forward, independent, low on anxiety.
>
> *Background*: scholastic and extracurricular leadership in high school and college, assumption of important responsibilities rather early in life, community participation, consistently good health. In sum, a "life-style" of success.

Clearly, people who are already intelligent, mature, ambitious, energetic, and responsible and have a prior record of achievement have a higher probability of managerial and leadership effectiveness in the future than those with a mediocre or poor profile, a fact that does not deny the possibilities of less attractive profiles; and plenty of excellent leaders, we know, have been "late bloomers."[d]

The description, however, falls considerably short of a personality model for lack of personality components that have been shown to be very important, such as values, motives, numerous other advisable traits, and the crucial knowledge about the requisites of leadership (especially as in Chapters 20 and 21). But it does contribute valuable particulars, as has a recent study that analyzed an effective manager in terms of *competencies*,[e] in this instance a competency defined as a composite of motives, traits, knowledge, self-image, and talents that manifests itself as a superior managerial skill.

They were determined by studying over 2,000 managers in 41 jobs of 12 large organizations taking 8 years. The 19 in Figure 9.1 were the result, those with a (TC) being what they called "threshold competencies," because they were not found to be causally related to superior performance as the others were, only necessary to do the job.[6,f]

You will notice that the outstanding feature of the competencies can, with a little study, be identified, that in:

10 it is a trait, disposition, or emotion (2, 5, 7, 8, 10, 12, 15, 16, 17, 18),
3 it is a motive (1, 14, 19),
5 it is a skill (3, 6, 11, 13, 14) the skills in greater detail at the right.

With all this and the past chapters in hand, it's now possible to assemble a fairly respectable "high-probability personality model of an effective organizational leader" as in Figure 9.2, using the 10 personality categories 39 of page 39 and selected ones from the sketch above.

Competencies of an Effective Manager

Competencies	Skills
The Goal and Action Management Cluster	
1. Efficiency orientation (= the Achievement motive)	Goal-setting, planning, organizing resources
2. Proactivity	Problem solving; information seeking; initiating
3. Diagnostic use of concepts	Pattern identification through concept application; deductive reasoning
4. Concern with impact (= the Power motive)	Symbolic influence behavior
The Leadership Cluster	
5. Self-confidence	Self-presentation skills
6. Use of oral presentation	Communication skills including psychology
7. Logical thought (TC)	Organization of thought and activities; sequential thinking
8. Conceptualization	Pattern identification through concept formation; pattern analysis
The Human Resources Management Cluster	
9. Use of socialized power	Alliance-producing skills
10. Positive regard (TC)	Verbal and nonverbal skills that result in people feeling valued
11. Managing group processes	Affiliative behaviors; group process skills
12. Accurate self-assessment (TC)	Self-assessment and reality testing skills
The Directing Subordinates Cluster	
13. Developing others (TC)	Feedback skills for their self-development
14. Use of unilateral power (TC)	Compliance-producing skills
15. Spontaneity (TC)	Self-expression skills
The Focus on Others Cluster	
16. Self-control	Self control skills
17. Perceptual objectivity	Effective distancing skills
18. Stamina and adaptability	Adaptation and coping skills
19. Concern with close relationships (—the Affiliation motive)	Friendship building skills

Figure 9.1

High-probability Personality Model
of an Effective Organizational Leader

Intelligence, knowledge and skills: High on intelligence and on judgment in handling the technical and social; high on leadership knowledge (especially the principles and role responsibilities); intimate knowledge of the organization's technical purposes and processes; skillful in the 8 leadership role responsibilities (Chapter 20), communicating, organizing, planning, problem-solving, decision-making, team development.

Interests, dispositions, emotions: a liking for hard work and interpersonal relationships, ambitious, independent, moderate risk taker, enthusiastic, confident, creative, responsible, self-controlled (pp. 63-65).

Values (including opinions and assumptions): Theory Y philosophy; inclination toward moral decision criteria (on page 176).

Motives, valences, expectancies: the motivation to manage (a, b and c on page 275); high on drive, creativity, the pursuit of excellence; high but realistic expectations for both the self and subordinates; commitment to the principles of leadership (Chapter 20).

Traits and temperament: strong personality (including dominant, social, outgoing, self-accepting, page 52); proactivity; high on both systematic and intuitive "cognitive style" (#7 and #8 in Figure 9.1 and Chapter 13); spontaneity, energy, stamina, adaptability, perceptual objectivity, efficiency orientation.

Maturity: criteria on pages 59-63.

Background: scholastic and extracurricular leadership in high school and college, assumption of important responsibilities rather early in life, community participation, consistent good health. In sum, a "life style" of success.

Figure 9.2

Note that, while both models (Figures 9.1 and 9.2) are good guides for leadership selection, placement, promotion, and succession planning, they are considerably less so for leadership development planning to the extent of what has to be brought to the organization. For instance, only about 7 of the 19 skills in 9.1 are teachable within the organization, and regardless of the model, genetic endowment can play an important part both positively and negatively, for example, recall that a special motivational mix is basic to the necessary desire to manage (page 275), a mix that is at least partly inherited, and surely a genetic tendency to depression would destroy the desire, not to mention its effect on followers.

Thus the "great man" theory is essentially wrong and leadership, especially organizational leadership, mainly developed, but inheritance can obviously help or hinder. And although Figure 9.2 is a "too good to be true" ideal (that can serve the useful purposes of any ideal), we have to admit that a serendipitous confluence of inheritance, environment and upbringing has occasionally produced what one feels is a "natural." But only a natural yet to be educated and developed, and then too there are important limitations. While the person may have much more flexibility for different situations than the average person, the requisite of variability across different conditions and circumstances is too great to be able to say that one paragon personality mix is best; for example:

- the functional and behavioral variations required of them to be effective in the role responsibilities: motivating, directing, coordinating, controlling, teaching, changing, and representing, that include the range from supporting to disciplining or discharging;
- the differences of leadership necessary for different subordinate personalities (page 39);
- the variety of behavioral changes to be elicited from subordinates;
- the differences due to different echelons, functions and external contacts a leader must work with;
- the differences of situations, including the different leadership requirements at different levels (see "Planning issues" in Chapter 17).

As McGregor said, there's no single pattern. In any evaluation one can only look to a guide like 9.2, the past record of fulfilling the "effective manager" definition, and the predictive techniques ahead. The summing up section at the end of Chapter 20 should also he helpful.

But first before the techniques, there is one characteristic in the model, "dominant," that's commonly not fully understood, and then there may be some wonder as to why "charisma" is missing. A few comments on them:

Dominant. The difference between dominant and dominating (with which it is often confused) is as great as the difference between sanguine (optimistic, hopeful) and sanguinary (bloody and bloodthirsty). Surprisingly to many, a dominating person is not strong but weak, whereas "dominant" seems to be an essential ingredient of a strong personality, probably the most important determinant of strength in the page 52 definition of one.

All subordinates expect their superiors (when male) to be strong, which certainly can be traced back to the original reason why leaderless groups eons ago selected the leaders they did: they wanted those most likely to maximize the benefits to the group by the way they led, which for a long time meant those who could kill the most animals or enemies. We still tend to pick by appearance or impression, to pick men who are tall and big, who have deep resonant voices, calm confidence and a way with words, erroneously believing those possessing them will always have superior leadership competence that will benefit us.

It comes naturally then that, whether elected or appointed by management, male managers tend to have intuitive feelings that they have to project a clear impression of being strong. If their personality and maturity have already made them dominant they generally don't give it a second thought, but others who are not sure of what strong means, or do not feel they have what they think it takes, improvise, generally guided by the misconceptions of Theory X and those on page 118, which to them add up to: be dominating, unilateral, impersonal (therefore inconsiderate), be "tough"—which also describes authoritarian women.

The strong personality of *dominant* individuals is in contrast a learned summary quality resulting most often from a lucky combination of genes, intelligence, upbringing, education, good models, and experiences that produce maturity and much of the Figure 9.2 personality model, an occurrence that plainly happens frequently in a democracy, an environment that tends to make the most of the available genes.

Interestingly, the dominating person's use of the word *tough* in managing is diametrically opposite to the dominant person's use of it. There are mainly four types of toughness (other than that of the neurotic or power corrupted toughness):

1. The dominating weak person as described who puts on an act.
2. Personal insensitivity, or callous-covered emotions from repeatedly receiving emotional abuse and humiliation either in childhood or over time in an organization.
3. Unilaterally holding subordinates to one's own high standards.
4. Leadership that successfully sets high standards and goals by participative integrative processes, motivating subordinates to hold themselves to the standards and goals.

The second invariably leads to being authoritarian if only because of superiors' modeling, and the third may be due to managerial ignorance or a neurosis, but the authoritarian attitude behind it is transparent. The fourth simply describes the consequences of competent technical-social integration; combine it with the characteristics that motivate leadership identified by McClelland and Burnham (page 275), and one will have what subordinates most admire.[g]

Charisma. Webster's defines it as "a quality of extraordinary spiritual power attributed to a person capable of eliciting popular support in the direction of human affairs." Katz and Kahn have added, "It is not the *objective* assessment by followers of ability to meet their specific needs. It is a means by which people abdicate responsibility for any consistent, tough-minded evaluation of specific policies."[7]

The psychology of social exchange is again involved but strictly on an emotional level. The spiritual message arouses a romantic faith that "a person like that is good for me and my interest." It may seem true to the person for the short-range satisfaction of emotional needs, but a clue to the long-run practical value is in the meaning of romantic—unreal, fanciful.

Drucker reminded us that, "leadership,is not a magnetic personality— *that* can just as well be demagoguery."[8] And the president of MIT, when asked about it in a recent national survey on leadership, said, "It would be nice to have charisma (in the leader), but you'd like it to be based on an understanding of what the hell is going on."[9]

Whether a leader does or does not, however, a top one can sometimes foster virtually the equivalent of charisma given certain conditions: (1) The leader is enough like the followers in a readily perceptible way that a common bond can be formed, yet is far enough above in echelons that day-to-day intimacy doesn't destroy the illusion (referent power occurs between subordinates and immediate superiors more so than charisma). (2) The followers believe the leader has global powers to get results. (3) The leader supplies in some way a wishful symbolic solution to their needs that arouses excitement.[10]

And they can foster the wishful thinking (#3) with some good internal PR. Of course it will often be seen for what it is, the truthful way being admirable performance, such as providing the organization with consistently good decisions, successful organization growth creating new job opportunities, and/or top personnel policies along the lines of those recommended in Chapter 21—or the fanciful.

How to Find It.   Regrettably for employees and job applicants in the not too distant past either the quality of formal personality appraisals or the level of importance assigned to them, if they were done at all, virtually guaranteed abuse and injustice whether on hiring, compensation, or promotion. By the 1960s knowledge and techniques had advanced enough to make fairness and substantial reliability possible, but then came the EEOC Guidelines on Employment Testing Procedures that virtually wiped them out.

However, court decisions in the 1970s, common sense, and additional technique advances restored them to respectability, and we now realize that they achieve their goals better than any other method, providing they're properly constructed and managed.

Understanding what the attainable goals of personality appraisal are is of course primary, and to best circumscribe them it helps to look at the goals of all three major techniques together, those as well of past performance and the hybrid management by objectives (MBO), which combines evaluation and planning. The matrix below gives the basic ones (checks meaning "yes"):

Appraisal Technique	Appraisal Goals		
	Predict	Evaluate	Plan
1. Personality[+] Appraisal	√		
MBO	—	—	
2. Past Performance Appraisal	√	√	
MBO	√	√	
3. Future Performance Appraisal	—	—	—
MBO	—	√[++]	√

[+] Term for appraising intelligence, traits, motivations and interests.
[++] Evaluations deduced from MBO's "past performance" component.

And their principal purposes, that is, what a manager can achieve through them, are:

> *Predict*: hire, allocate resources for best utilization (placement), develop, promote
> *Evaluate*: rate and differentiate, compensate, motivate
> *Plan*: plan for the short-range, motivate

Translating the three into specific managerial tasks, it goes without saying that hiring and placing personnel entail predication, which requires both the personality and performance appraisals preceded by resumes and interviewing.

All experienced managers realize however that even honest resumes have a fair amount of puffery in them if only due to subjectivity, they commonly have a lot, and checking past performance with former employers has been so curtailed by legal suits that comments of value from these sources are rare.[i]

Then interviewing by the superior is by its very nature useless for predicting because of the interviewer's bias, guessing, amateurishness, and here the subjectivity of both parties. Their value as a final check for compatibility and mutual regard is unquestionable but it's limited to that. As a result, a group interview in which the hiring executive retains the right f rejection is increasingly being required in large organizations, a process hat, besides inducing the superior to be more objective, shows how the person will tend to interact in group tasks, that major requirement of any managerial job.

But one can see from the chart that to predict for the purposes listed below t takes both personality and performance appraisals, but each type has imitations. To obtain a prediction to promote, past performance data can of course be extrapolated, but the difference between the old and new work and new relationships may significantly reduce their value. And while personality appraisals can importantly help the decisions with missing needed knowledge, their application for this purpose is mainly to lower evels, less and less up the ladder for obvious reasons, the interview being he sole recourse at the top.

And understandably, for management development and motivation planning, both the personality and past performance appraisals together (again the former mainly at lower levels) are desirable, while compensation planning can only be based on past performance and the market.

The inclusion of activities planning here (on the subject of appraisal) may at first seem irrelevant to appraisal, but those familiar with MBO know the relationship, past performance being the planning base. Moreover, the evaluating and predicting that take place (for the future planning via MBO's past performance appraisal) also make the technique an ideal setting for certain parts of the development planning (as will be explained ahead). Additionally, we know that MBO sessions present one of the best opportunities for direct personal motivation, the common demotivation results that occur during them being due to mismanagement.

Figure 9.3 expands the matrix in these ways, showing also at #9 and #10 he two major requisites described on pages 282-289 for developing the climate, MBO being one of the most effective techniques for the #10 building the relationship). More on it in Chapter 10.

As for "how to find it," that is, find leadership competence in an individual through personality appraisal, there are two basic approaches, mechanical and clinical, plus their combination, giving the six modes in he chart below, box #3 also often called psychological testing, #3 and #4 together psychological assessment.

Mechanical Methods. Of the three mechanical modes, boxes 3 and 5, are still in development; #1 is the one of importance to managers at present, and it has two types: "maximum performance" and "typical behavior" measures.

Maximum performance tests attempt to determine quantitatively how well a person can perform cognitively—intelligence (including verbal

Management Appraisals

Techniques	Appraisal Goals									
(Pr = Prediction) (E = Evaluation) (Pl = Planning)	Hiring and Placement	Promotion	Development Planning	Compensation	Work/Operations Planning	Managing the Subordinate	Responsibility Allocation	Motivating Performance	Understanding the Subordinate	Building the Relationship
	1	2	3	4	5	6	7	8	9	10
1. Personality Appraisal										
Appraisal Procedure	Pr	Pr	Pr				Pr			
M B O	—	—	—	—	—	—	—	—	—	—
2. Past Performance Appraisal										
Appraisal Procedure	Pr	Pr	Pr	E	E	E	Pr		✓	
M B O		E	E	E	E	E		E	✓	✓
3. Future Perform. (job plan'g)										
Appraisal Procedure	—	—	—	—			—	E	—	—
M B O			Pl		Pl	Pl	Pl	Pl	✓	✓

Figure 9.3

354

:ompetence, arithmetic ability, and reasoning), spatial relationships, nechanical comprehension—and on motor abilities. The answers are right)r wrong, and the total scores do contribute to the rating of managerial :ompetence. The most effective of them are the intelligence tests. The ones with the best validation records[j] are:

> The Miller Analogies Test (MAT)
> The Wonderlic Personnel Test
> The Wechsler Adult Intelligence Scale (WAIS)

	Mode of Combination and Analysis[11]	
Mode of Data Collection	Mechanical	Clinical
Mechanical	1. Pure statistical	2. Profile interpretation
Clinical	3. Behavior and trait rating	4. Pure clinical
Both	5. Mechanical composite (e.g., regression equation)	6. Clinical overview or composite

The MAT is the best on high-cognitive skills (most only test the elementary),[k] is short, and has exceptional validity. The Wonderlic test has the most extensive variety of factors:

Vocabulary	Proverbs	Number series
Reasoning	Analogies	Alphabet items
Syllogisms	Perceptual skills	Scrambled sentences
Arithmetic	Spatial relations	

And it and the WAIS that are commonly used for IQ scoring.

Guion has pointed out that all in this maximum performance category are less than "general" intelligence tests for management because they don't measure important intellectual powers involved in creative thought, planning, and judgment, but they nevertheless seem to be good "risks" when applied to managerial and sales occupations and also for predicting trainability.[13]

Another inadequacy of maximum performance measures, as might have been guessed, is their inability to reveal anything about behavior and motivation, motivation being the force that moves many very average people to superior performance. The typical behavior measures, on the other hand, help somewhat to fill this behavior and motivation gap. They also are of two types: "personality tests" and "interest inventories." Both are self-reporting with no right or wrong answers, and the result is a description of the respondent's main predispositions. The most prominent *personality tests* are the:[1]

> Minnesota Multiphasic Personality Inventory (MMPI)[m]
> California Psychological Inventory (CPI)
> Guilford-Zimmerman Temperament Survey (GZTS)
> Thurstone Temperament Schedule

Their goal is, broadly, to measure an individual's adjustment to interpersonal and situational demands on a variety of scales; the GZTS, for example, measures essentially ten:

General activity	Emotional stability	Friendliness
Restraint	Personal relations	Masculinity (of course
Sociability	Objectivity	for men only)

The most prominent *interest inventories* are:

> Strong Vocational Interest Blank for Men (SVIB)
> Kuder Preference Record
> Edwards Personal Preference Schedule (EPPS)
> Minnesota Vocational Interest Inventory (MVII)

Descriptions and critiques of all eight tests can be found in the two books referred to, those of Campbell et al. and Guion. For the limited intention here, the summary comment of Campbell et al. is sufficient warning against using any as a "package" (unaltered regardless of job or situation) for managerial predicting:[14]

> Only a few of the published typical behavior inventories have been developed empirically. Armchair methods, behavior "theories" and factor analysis have been the bases for most. Since the development of such scales was not behaviorally based initially, the odds are against their being related to important aspects of managerial job behavior. Thus, scales of occupational choice (e.g., SVIB) or psychological aberration (e.g., MMPI) can hardly be expected to predict managerial behaviors such as effective planning and delegation.

The fact that all were originally constructed for either clinical use on problem people or for general counseling of students should have itself disqualified them for use that way, but it was the validation attempts to correlate test outcomes with global measures of success[n] that made it apparent. Almost none was found.

When, on the other hand, some of the tests were carefully keyed into the managerial needs of the organization, the effects were quite different. Examples for those interested are the Standard Oil of New Jersey (SONJ) long-term "Early Identification of Management Potential" study and the SCORES battery applied to Lockheed engineers.[15]

Two points about the SONJ deserve special note: (1) The tests were related to the *general* management needs of the firm regardless of function and yet done sufficiently well to give impressive validations. (2) Biographical information of those tested was also keyed (mechanically) to organizational needs and they produced the best validation results of all.

In sum, to determine the 30 to 50 percent of managerial effectiveness through personal qualities that Campbell et al. said is possible, the various tests, especially the personality and interest ones, have to be related by modification to "the situation."

Nevertheless, some additional advice for testing someone from *Training* magazine is worth keeping in mind. You yourself may not have had to deal with test selection and testing in your current function, but with the growing need to retrain managers at all levels, you might unexpectedly find yourself intimately involved in it for subordinate managers or yourself:[16]

1. Retain an expert if at all possible, a veteran, not just a statistician or psychologist, and remember that you're ultimately responsible for the results and what happens.
2. Don't rely on tests alone; look for the whole person (phenomenology), not just the scores.
3. Understand the limitations of the tests. Different tests and different scoring procedures may be necessary to evaluate for different jobs or elements of jobs, and tests by themselves are simply inadequate; they supply useful information but only part of the decision-making needs.
4. Understand the strengths of the specific tests. For example, in general, intelligence tests predict especially well for the executive level, interpersonal skills assessment for middle managers, technical skills assessment for the supervisory level, but get the evidence of past experience of each test in comparable situations. Also, tests get at points that may be overlooked, and often tell us things to look for in the interview and reference check.

5. Show test results to the testees and discuss them.

Still, there's the other 50-70 percent of effectiveness to account for, most of which is with regard to behavior and motivation plus that all-important linkage to the situation, so much more than test modification is capable of achieving. The clinical and combination methods go a long way toward supplying it.

Clinical and combination methods. The "pure clinical" of box #4 on page 355 means an evaluation by a professional clinician, which may include interviewing and/or the observation of any of leaderless group discussions, in-basket exercises, role-playing, or business games.

The author has utilized with good results outside clinical psychologists applying a 2-hour Rogerian interview as a final check of lingering doubts about otherwise highly qualified prospects, but it is entirely inadequate for standard predictive personnel decisions like hiring and promotion, as will be explained below. Even Rogers supplemented his interviews with other techniques.

This comment refers to interviewing by professionals yet we know that interviewing by amateur managers is the predominant method for these decisions, each an event in which, although the manager can add specifics of "the situation," all his or her emotions, biases, stereotypes, and irrelevant impressions dominate the final decision.

The functional difference between the professional and amateur is most important. In contrast to the amateur's seeking an emotional "feel" for or against the person, the professional is restricting his or her task to *collecting information*, admittedly interpreting in the process where the information is sparse, but as a Rogerian (unless you've hired a Freudian), the psychologist judges the information as samples of behavior, not as signs from which to infer deep-seated drives and motivations. Wherever such inferences have been made, the validations of predictive value have been disparaging beyond belief.

One of the main problems with clinical interviewing alone, however, is that the clinical interview can only incorporate the responsibilities of an individual job in a very general way, so those who are trying to predict job success supplement it with exercises known as "situational measures," and the outcome has proved the combination to be one of the better techniques developed.

These exercises naturally can also be in combination with tests or stand alone, need not include the interviewing. The three principal ones are:

Leaderless group discussions: A group of examinees is assembled and asked to discuss something; they may be given a subject or left to generate it themselves; the examiners do not participate, only observe (they've been trained how to) and rate (descriptive behavior checklists tailored to the management needs may be provided).

In-basket technique: The examinee is asked to play the role of a manager administering in 2 to 3 hours the contents of an in-basket stacked with tasks carefully selected to uncover the relevant job behaviors. Typical behavior and performance patterns revealed, for example:

Analysis of the situation	Exchange of information
Organization of work	Unwarranted assumptions
Planning work distribution	Delegation
Decisiveness of action	Communication
Directing the work of others	Consideration of others

Business games: A management simulation, observed and rated by the examiners, in which a group of participants play management roles in a company that manufactures and markets a product; they buy materials, manufacture, inventory, and sell under a variety of economic and market conditions.

The value of tying appraisals to job realities in these ways certainly is clear enough, and the validations that have been made of those tests that do have given them high grades on prediction.

A distinction about the word "situation" might better be mentioned, though it may be obvious to some. A "situational measure" refers to direct requirements of a managing job, whereas a manager's situation is the circumstance the manager is in at a moment in time, McGregor's numbers 2, 3, and 4 together on page 345.

The "profile interpretations" of box #2 on page 355 is where the clinicians deduce the meaning of mechanical tests without interviewing, based on their own behavior training and experience. It is easiest and least expensive after pure mechanical, and good professionals predict with fair accuracy some of the major traits and behavioral tendencies that show up later on the job.

Some may also use "projective techniques," the main ones being the TAT described, sentence completion tests, and the Rorschach (inkblot) test, but only the TAT (for motivation) has stood up. The sentence completion ones, which purport to measure personality traits, have up to now been found moot and the Rorschach useless if not misleading on normal people; it has no organizational application, including the phony use to determine executive "types" that one occasionally sees published.

Finally, the techniques of boxes #3 and #5 are, as mentioned, still in development, are in the experimental stage, and may never be adequately refined. #3 is the translation of the clinician's mode of judging into mechanical rules so that a technician can produce comparable results by applying them to observation written by a clinician. #5 would be doing the same (rules) for a composite of the mechanical and clinical, the ultimate being computerization of the plethora of variables involved.

Box #6 is but a thumbnail description of the final stage of the assessment center as now done, and it is the most significant and effective appraisal technique developed to date.

Assessment Centers.° A quick review of the conventional methods of appraising for management hiring and promotion, expanding on the earlier comments about them (pages 351-352) can help illustrate by comparison the superiority of this off-premise combination of the techniques described. For the two sources:

External selection

College graduates—four steps:

1. Campus interviews by a personnel or line manager, open-ended with the criterion "I know what I like and don't like." Main acceptance reasons: grades, personality, expressiveness, like the person; main rejection reasons: unrealistic goals, lack of sincerity, don't like the person.
2. Visit to the company, interviews by department managers.
3. If mutual acceptance, about 90% of firms apply a battery of tests— intelligence, personality, interest.
4. The person is taken on as a "management trainee," may be retested just before moving into management.

Experienced managers:

- The major determinant is the series of interviews with executives he or she will associate with in the organization, the higher the entry level the more the interviews, the more intensive they are and the longer is the deliberation time. The criteria seems to be first compatibility and no competitive threat, second functional potential.
- Most firms test applicants for lower management, fewer do for middle management, almost none do for top levels.
- Large firms test in-house, others use consulting specialists or organizations.

Internal selection

- Internal candidates for openings are usually known by the position superior, and comprehensive personnel and performance records are available, therefore studied in advance. Then if a transfer is involved, the new superior has to obtain permission for the transfer from the current superior, who has absolute "Career authority" over subordinates (see "Candidate/Career Authority," pp. 868-869). If permission is granted an interview determines interest, compatibility and mutual regard. After, testing, if applied, has the following pattern:

— on first move into management, 70-90% of organizations test;
— on promotions up to middle management, about 40% test and it declines to 4% for moves into top management. Commonly the promotion above middle management is based entirely on the interview and a look at past test results that may be obsolete because of growth and change.

That the principal technique of selection is the subjective interview by the superior may best be explained, one psychologist said, as far more a reflection of the needs of the interviewer than those of the organization. Plainly too, a consequence is an expensive rejection of talent and competence for personal reasons. And, as mentioned earlier, that all promotions at the first 2-3 levels so often depend primarily on the immediate superior has the monumentally insidious effect of unqualified people deciding the composition of an organization's future top management, selecting and rejecting prospects at the start of their careers based on their (the selectors') own limited competence, fears, biases, and narrow organizational perspective.

The assessment center eliminates these weaknesses and supplies incomparable additional benefits. Originated by the German army of World War II, picked up by the British army and the American OSS, then developed by AT&T for industry (starting in 1956), it has now been advanced to such sophistication there is no question about its predictive effectiveness when professionally operated. AT&T itself was processing some 30,000 a year as early as 1978 through 70 centers for both the recruiting and promotion of managers[17] (policy changes after AT&T breakup unknown), and over 20,000 companies today use theirs at least partially.

Some moreover were using them for a variety of other purposes as well. G.E., for example, has added the training of managers in how to assess subordinates by assigning them to the centers as assessors, raising their ratio of examinee to assessor to 1:1 for the purpose; SOHIO attempts to determine the best type of climate and leadership the individual is able to work under (e.g., organic vs. mechanistic); and J.C. Penney tries to determine whether the person is better suited for large- or medium-size store management.[18] When managers above the first level are assessed, some management development with special exercises and critiquing is often added, and some use the centers on middle and upper levels to diagnose managerial strengths and weaknesses.

The content of a complete program (there are some "short forms") is as follows. Generally about 12 manager candidates or incumbents (a range of

6 to 12) are processed by 6 to 9 assessors for 2 to 3 days, after which the assessors take another 2 to 3 days for the evaluation and prediction process. The assessors may be full-time psychologists, but more often are executives from the same organization as the candidates, usually 2 or 3 levels above them, so they are familiar with where the examinees are headed, rarely know them personally (to favor any), or have reason to fear any competitively. Proper training of the assessors takes from 1 to 3 weeks, during which time they must learn (a) the basic principles of job behavior and the behavioral needs of jobs,[p] (b) the tests and exercises and the behaviors they evoke, (c) how to observe and what criteria to apply, and (d) how to translate the observations into the behavioral dimensions selected by the center as critical.

The number of dimensions have ranged up to 52. AT&T had the following twenty-five:

1. Organization and planning	14. Perception of social cues
2. Decision making	15. Self-objectivity
3. Creativity	16. Energy
4. Human relations skills	17. Realism of expectations
5. behavior flexibility	18. Bell system value orientation
6. Personal impact	19. Social objectivity
7. Tolerance of uncertainty	20. Need for advancement
8. Resistance to stress	21. Ability to delay gratification
9. Scholastic aptitude	22. Need for superior approval
10. Range of interests	23. Need for peer approval
11. Inner work standards	24. Goal flexibility
12. Primacy of work	25. Need for security
13. Oral communication skills	

One might note that the 25 includes intelligence, learning, traits, motives, values, and emotions, all of which can contribute to the prediction of the future performance and behavior of a manager and the extent to which the person will approach the page 348 model.

The typical battery of tests and exercises applied to examine each candidate on these dimensions normally include:

An interview of about 2 hours to determine personal goals, values, interests, interpersonal relationships, idiosyncrasies, and attitudes toward the organization (information gathering).

A leaderless group discussion of some six participants with an assigned subject.

An in-basket project as previously described.

A business game involving six participants.

Projective tests: the TAT and one to two incomplete sentence tests.

Objective tests: intelligence, personality, and interests.

And some companies add one or more of the following:

- A 5- to 10-minute oral presentation by the candidate on a selected topic.
- The Q-sort (see footnote 1 on page 385).
- The "irate customer phone call" (originated by J.C. Penney) especially of interest to retail organizations.
- A role-playing mock interview, hiring, or appraising a subordinate.
- A personal history questionnaire.[q]

One to several assessors write a report on each person for each test or exercise after the event, a clinical psychologist writing up the projectives. On completion of the battery, each candidate is studied for 1 to 2 hours by the assessors jointly somewhat along these lines: first, the reports are read aloud, then each assessor rates the person on the 25 or so dimensions, the ratings are openly reviewed, and more discussion with adjustments are permitted; finally, each assessor predicts for non-management personnel the potential for management and if reaching middle management can be expected within 10 years, followed by a discussion of the results and consensus predictions of the group. Managers are assessed for strengths, weaknesses, and further advancement.

Feedback of testing results to the examinee may be automatic, optional, oral, or written. Some 60 to 90 percent of assessees have wanted it, those who are certain they did very well or very poorly tending not to ask for it.

It must be apparent that the reasons for the centers' superiority over the conventional methods are:

The multiple-assessor approach vs. the usual subjective judgment by only one

The objectivity and training of the assessors

The close attention to dimensions (criteria) of measurement, the use of only pertinent ones, and the inclusion of all principal ones of importance

The situation exercises that measure performance and behaviors for specifically managerial jobs (but not specific management jobs), which traditional tests are seldom made to do

And the gains to the organization because of these and the way the program is structured and operated are:

- Optimum use of management potential in the organization is far more possible through early identification, faster movement, and reduced subjective control by immediate superiors.

- Upper management receives a written report on each person for (a) a promotion use to supplement on-the-job performance evaluations, and (b) better fitting of individuals to jobs.
- The reports are a major contribution to (a) the firm's long-range human resources planning, including the shaping of hiring patterns based on the relationship of present resources to future needs, and (b) the modification of jobs better to fit individual abilities and potential.
- The recognized attention and interest that the organization gives to the objective advancement of competence has an inevitably positive effect on loyalty and morale, and it may also aid recruiting.
- The training of line managers in how to assess; it:
  a. educates on criteria of effective performance, subordinate behavior, and leadership behavior;
  b. teaches them how to analyze both individuals and job behavior needs;
  c. develops greater perception (observation skills) in evaluating behaviors, performance, and potential for different jobs;
  d. adds insights into group dynamics;
  e. improves their management skills through mastery of the exercises;
  f. broadens their repertory of responses to problems;
  g. improves their sensitivity to being objective;
  h. upgrades the entire management team through greater awareness of the quality of the organization's interpersonal relations, its values, and its personnel standards.

But any process as elaborate as this only naturally has complications that can result in problems. In most cases, however, there are solutions, and managers would do well to be aware of both the criticisms and the options for the quality of their own relevant decisions. The principal complaints have been:

1. *The nomination of the candidate* (to go to the center): Selection by the superior on the belief that the subordinate has management potential tends to perpetuate the superior's biases, values, and style, can eliminate the individualist and feared competitor, and can be unfair to competent subordinates not noticed or not liked.[r] Solution options: (a) permit every person to go who wants to; (b) send everyone who reaches a given management level; (c) send by peer group vote; and (d) select by personnel department analysis of history and performance record. Solution (a) has the advantage of fitting in with

the desirable "open market" selection system described in *The Selection System*, Chapter 17.

2. *The nomination and use of managers as assessors*: They are usually nominated by their superiors on request for assessors by the center. The procedure has occasionally been a way of easing out deadwood on the belief that the person will flunk the assessor training, making dismissal easy. It can be prevented by the center's tactful check before acceptance for training.

   A bigger question: Are professional psychologists better? Generally yes, assuming competent psychologists; their knowledge of behavior and their observation skills are distinct advantages; however, managers learn quickly to do very well, and if an organization uses psychologists, it of course forfeits the important gain of management training and experience in appraising and judging subordinates on the job.

3. *The "crown prince or princess" syndrome*: Those reported back by the centers as exceptional performers can be so favored by management on treatment and promotions that their success becomes a self-fulfilling prophecy (affecting also the assessment center validity tests), and they are resented by co-workers. No research has supported the criticism, but effective periodic on-the-job performance appraisal sessions should tie everyone to reality.

4. The *"organization man" syndrome*: It has been said that the assessment center process can promote conformity in that the criteria for judging are standards established by management. Studies of the subject at both IBM and SOHIO have disproved it; however, the nomination of candidates by immediate superiors clearly can do it, the solution being in #1 above.

5. The *"kiss of death"*: Aside from the effect on an employee's morale of doing badly, the poor performer is likely to assume the bad showing, which may have been caused by a temporary problem of #6 below, will block future progress in the organization. It's a justified fear, though no data have been collected to prove it, and it is complicated by the emphasis the center's program may have, as described in #7 below.

6. *Anxiety*: Having one's future destiny determined in a few days by the standards of others can be a frightening experience to the less than extroverted; even extroverts can be panic-inclined on paper-and-pencil exams, and the original or unconventional thinker can be made to look bad by a glib conformist in the group exercises. Again, all these can occur, but if management of the tests and exercises is handled expertly and supportively, not perfunctorily, anxiety should be

minimal. Nevertheless, the types of stress that are common to management situations do warrant testing.

7. *What is truly being tested by the center?* A recent study of assessment center ratings has shown that the major influences on them are self-confidence, energy level, persuasiveness, and oral communication; others have found assessed managers generally convinced that interpersonal skills play a major role, confirming it.[20] Each center must carefully test its weighing practices to avoid the inadvertent ignoring or screening out of other highly valuable managerial competencies, some of which may compensate for introversion, communication, or group performance limitations.

8. *The cost*: AT&T in 1968 estimated that the cost/examinee ran from $800 to $1,500 depending on depth, figures that capitalized on volume, continuous operations, and professional management. Assuming even $3,000 per person today, the long-range return on investment still seems most attractive. While supporting a continuing center is obviously out of the question for a small company, any one of them could set up an in-house program every few years as needed with consulting help to gain most of the benefits. A few consulting firms now provide exercises, testing, and psychologists; the day may soon come when some of them will supply the complete assessment center service.

A few possible structural improvements. Presently the center program is designed to test really only for the first move into management, the other uses being essentially appendage. It would not be difficult to have three programs within them available for the three major needs: the move into management as now done but testing also for the specific management position that is often in mind, promotion above that level, and the formal (not just adjunct) evaluation for development, the second and third capable of being related.

Column 1 of the chart on page 292 made clear what is needed for both the first and second, evaluations for the "fixed" elements of the *individual-job match* on the intended position, which would of course entail determining in advance each job's requirements at least for key positions, adding the past performance record but tying the record to the needs of the job.

On the evaluations for development, some centers, as said, already do modify their procedure to appraise managers' strengths and weaknesses for it, and a couple add 2 days of development effort right after the assessment. The evaluation part demonstrates good planning, but tacking on the development does ignore the manager's side of the issue. It virtually admits the absence of "career planning" the way it ought to be done, the technique detailed in Chapter 17.

It explains there that to make career planning successful for both the individual and organization, their respective goals have to be reconciled by face-to-face discussion of the superior (who is not at the center) and the subordinate, one of the "direct integration" activities described on page 32. The total procedure, therefore, should be as shown in the flow chart below, the assessment center doing #1 and the training and development program tailored to the career planning outcome.

Management Development Planning

(1)   (2)   (3)

Assessment	→	Career Planning	→	Training and Development Planning

Assm't of strengths & weaknesses   Making Indiv. & Org'l goals congruent   For personal growth per mutual needs

We also can now use the "High-probability Personality Model" in Figure 9.2 to aid evaluations for the first two programs (management entry and promotion)[s] and add the new knowledge about competencies on pages 347-348 for all three, the list of skills in Figure 9.1 being particularly useful in development planning for those skills that are teachable.

Tests should be added to ascertain the presence of or potential for the competencies and skills, and one test that should be particularly helpful is the special form of TAT the researcher[t] formulated. Called by them the *Picture Story Exercise*, it covers six crucial variables: (1) Achievement, (2) Affiliation, (3) Power, (4) Activity Inhibition (disposition toward self-control), (5) Self-Definition (disposition to discover opportunities and see self as an initiator), and (6) States of Adaptation (regarding maturity and ego development).

Past performance appraisal.[u]

The job of organizational leadership can be summarized as comprised of five functions:

Analyzing + Planning + Decision making + Managing + Leading.

So to evaluate prospects for the competency or rate incumbents, techniques are naturally selected that will measure the degree of potential or ability in each of the five, a reason why the assessment center that does so to a fair degree has universally been considered the best approach.

A problem of course has been the assessment center cost, and certainly individual techniques are often adequate for limited goals. Also, a center may give little or no attention to *past performance* as shown by what is tested on page 362, and the importance of past performance in evaluation for promotion or development planning certainly goes without saying; indeed it is commonly analyzed for each and every goal and purpose described on page 354." A summary of the methods for all of them:

Methods of Appraising for Management
(The numbers ranked to some degree by popularity)

Hiring and Placement—Prediction
1. Interview
2. Past performance appraisal
3. References
4. Intelligence, personality, and interest tests
5. Clinical analysis
6. Situational exercises
7. Total assessment center—items 1, 4, 5, and 6 plus decision making and behavior tests
8. Not applied but also recommended:
   a. Evaluation for the motivation to manage (page 271-275)
   b. Analysis of behavioral fit and cognitive style (Chapter 13)
   c. Evaluation of "competencies" to the extent possible per page 347.

Promotion—Prediction
1. Past performance appraisal[v]
2. Interview
3. Intelligence, personality, and interest tests
4. Total assessment center results
5. Same as #8 in "hiring and placement"

Compensation-Evaluation
1. Past performance appraisal
2. Assessment center for potential

Development Planning—Prediction and Evaluation
1. Interviewing
2. Past performance appraisal
3. Intelligence, personality, and interest tests

4. Situational exercises in training
5. Total assessment center results for strengths, weaknesses, potential
6. Joint career planning

Counseling-Motivation-Feedback—Evaluation and Planning
1. Past performance appraisal (during progress review or MBO)
2. On-the-job assistance
3. MBO short-range planning (utilizing #1)
4. Joint career planning
5. Joint development planning (after #4)

The well-known dominant position of past performance appraisal is plainly corroborated, but novices are generally not aware that for it to contribute importantly toward any of the foregoing appraisal goals, much more than the traditional comparison of performance against goals may be required. Any or a combination of the following may be necessary (#14 being the traditional comparison):

1.	Global ratings	8.	Peer ratings
2.	Graphic ratings	9.	Scaled biography
3.	Forced-choice ratings	10.	Personnel records
4.	The essay	11.	Performance against standards
5.	Rankings	12.	Committee
6.	Critical incident appraisal	13.	A budget
7.	Self-ratings	14.	Performance against goals

Most are self-explanatory, but the thumbnail sketches that follow, besides defining those that are not, supply some pointers on application and utility, the main criteria of utility being: content (traits, knowledge, competencies, results), reliability, consistency, comparability, facilitation of feedback, and test acceptability to the superior and subordinate.

1. *Global ratings.* The footnote n on page 385 defines them. Because such judgments integrate many causes of performance and behavior they are valuable to a manager's own analysis and to research studies, but they are disliked by subordinates as feedback for lack of specifics they can do something about; if not complimentary, they sound like personal attacks; when trust and openness are low they're rejected, and even if trust is high motivation can be affected negatively.
2. Graphic ratings. These are useful when particular strengths and weaknesses may need diagnosing to evaluate job effectiveness; the

Graphic Rating Scales

(a) Quality   High └──────┴──✓──┴──────┴──────┘ Low

(b) Quality   High └──────┴──✓──┴──────┴──────┘ Low
                    5   4   3   2   1

(c) Quality └──────┴──────┴──────┴──────┘

| Exceptionally high-quality workmanship | Work usually done in a superior way | Quality is average for this job | Work contains frequent flaws | Work is seldom satisfactory |

(d) Quality └──────┴──────┴──────┘

| Too many errors | About average | Occasional errors | Almost never makes mistakes |

(e) Quality   5   (4)   3   2   1

	Performance Grade			
Performance Factors	Consistently superior	Sometimes superior	Consistently average	Consistently Unsatisfactory
Quality: Accuracy Economy Neatness	☐	☒	☐	☐

(g) Quality

1 2 3 4 5	6 7 8 9 10	11 12 13 14 15	16 17 18 19 20	21 22 23 24 25
Poor	Below Average	Average	Above Average	Excellent

(h) Quality of work

     15   13   (11)   9   7   5   3   1

| Rejects and errors consistently rare | Work usually OK; errors seldom made | Work passable; needs to be checked often | Frequent errors and scrap; coreless |

(i) Quality of work   Judge the amount of scrap; consider the general care and accuracy of his work; also consider inspection record.
Poor, 1-6; Average, 7-18; Good, 19-25.   20

(Note that b, e, g, h, and i are ways of quantifying; the others are not.)

Figure 9.4

variety (options) possible for "quality of work" alone is shown in Figure 9.4.[21]

The main weaknesses are (a) in making the judgments the frequent inclusion of irrelevant traits and behaviors with the exclusion of important ones: (b) the "halo tendency": the observer makes an initial overall judgment of the person in his or her mind as good, mediocre, or bad and rates all questions accordingly; one remedy: require the grading of all subordinates on one factor before going on to the next, and so on; (c) the "central tendency": the observer rates everyone about the same; (d) the "leniency tendency": a variation of (c) in which everyone is rated favorably.

Reliability, consistency, and comparability are further reduced by inadequacies of the rater or by the person's poor relationship with the ratee; but for many purposes the technique is adequate, raters have no objection to them, and they are the most widely used.

One of the most promising types of graphic rating is the "retranslation method," in which managers familiar with a position, like office manager or store manager, jointly build the questionnaire out of specific tasks critical to the job's success. The result is a direct rating of the manager's ability to be "effective" in that specific job, and many of the problems of observational error are overcome.

3. *Forced-choice ratings.* The rater is required to choose from a set of statements on each factor, usually two favorable and two unfavorable statements, though there are many variations. Each factor has a weight and the answers are totaled for a single score; the higher the score the "better" supposedly is the employee. It reduces bias because the rater is not told the weightings, but the halo tendency may still occur, and appraisers generally dislike the technique: (a) often none of the choices for a factor suitably fits, and (b) they feel they are prevented from giving a rating of their honest opinion of the ratee; their global judgments are precluded.

4. *The essay.* Either a superior's superior or the personnel department may ask the superior to write a paragraph or two on the subordinate's strengths, weaknesses, and potential; it is a helpful supplement to graphic scales, but (a) alone the content is too spotty tending to include only the points that impressed the writer, points often job-irrelevant; (b) essays of two or more subordinates have little to no comparability; (c) many managers write badly.

5. *Ranking.* When managers of different departments or functions have to be compared for a promotion or salary increase, essays, tests, or forms are either incomparable or insufficiently meaningful.

Subjective judgments of overall competence are necessary, so the ranking of global ratings are usually best (supplemented by predictive tools for the promotions).

There are two approaches: "alternation ranking": the most valuable person is selected then the least valuable, the next most valuable, the next least valuable, thus working toward the middle; and "paired comparison ranking": each manager is compared on a factor like value to the organization with each of the others, thus 5 managers would entail ratings for 10 pairs on each factor. The name with the most "better" ratings is the most valuable, the rest ranked by the number of "better" ratings they received—a time consuming process if there are many people involved.

Both are good for the purposes mentioned, better when two or more independent raters are used. But few techniques could be more demoralizing then the use of ranking as an appraisal tool for the members of one organizational unit with the intention of communicating the ranking to the employees in order to motivate or justify pay increases. One particularly bad method is the zero-sum ranking described on page 330, the second item in the list.

6. *Critical incident appraisal.* If the superior keeps a "little black book" of actual "critical" good and bad incidents effected by his or her subordinate managers, the progress review sessions could at least deal with clear-cut facts and about performance, not personality. But superiors are generally too busy to remember to record them, and the time from event to discussion will often be too long for remembrance of essential details. Additionally, when subordinates know their superiors do this, it can prevent their taking reasonable risks, damage trust and relationship, and demotivate.

7. *Self-ratings.* Sometimes it is very helpful, as well as diplomatic, in counseling to ask the person to self-rate either with graphic ratings or an open-end type questionnaire of strengths, weaknesses, and needs; as Carl Rogers has reminded psychology, people are an invaluable source of information about themselves, information only they may be able to provide.

8. *Peer ratings.* Considerable research has shown peer ratings on an employee to be potentially the most accurate of job behavior, but prediction value seems to depend on what is being rated; e.g., they are usually good on promotion factors (except when rated by competitors) like leadership, independence, and analytical ability, but are poor on rating cooperation, maturity, and tact.

9. *Scaled (or keyed) biography.* As commented before, the grading of a verified personal history record on factors relevant to the job and

weighted by importance to the job has produced good predictions of future job performance, so it can be especially valuable when applied to new-hires (the biography verified) and promotions to new responsibilities.

10. *Personnel records.* Reviewing the records of a candidate from another unit for a position in your own makes sense, but one has to guard against judging on the irrelevant or the obsolete (due to growth or change). It's often best to resort to them only for technical or functional experience not readily apparent.

11. *Performance against standards.*[w] Examples of the quantitative: costs, schedule maintenance, turnover, absenteeism, quality (e.g., rejects); qualitative examples (though nebulous, determinable by surveys, analysis, co-worker interviews): subordinate morale, HR development, subordinate decision participation, interdepartment cooperation, customer or supplier goodwill. Also, superiors must be sure to include the appraisal of the appraising done by subordinate managers.[x]

12. *Committee.* Campbell et al. have reported that appraisals at higher levels of 33 organizations they surveyed were most likely to be performed by a committee rather than the superior alone; the normal composition was not stated.[23] More enlightened firms do require the involvement of at least the superior's superior and the use of some objective performance data for pay increases and predictive tools for promotions.

13. *A budget.* This control device is certainly a valuable gauge of administrative abilities on quantitative controllables but not on the uncontrollables. At that, its limitation to the accounts of the responsibility accounting system, its minimum requirements nature, and the absence of qualitative measures brands it as only a minimal measure of effective management.

14. *Performance against goals.* Reaching-goals for key quantitative results and qualitative activities are naturally core elements of motivation and progress, so setting them and measuring the results are of top importance, but their value is greatly reduced when the goals are set unilaterally, affecting the subordinate negatively on all of performance, motivation, attitude, and morale, a situation MBO is supposed to prevent (note too the advanced performance measuring technique of EVA and MVA on pages 762-764).

If there are any doubts about the indispensability of performance appraisals, one need only recall the elementary fact that any assigned responsibility needs to be checked on its execution in order to plan how to go forward from there; thus the organization's goal hierarchy must be paralleled by an appraisal system for control and planning. To quote one consultant highly regarded for his appraisal experience.[24]

> When we talk about appraising the manager's performance, we are really discussing the management of the enterprise ... (and) if even one link in the chain is weak, the entire process suffers. This is particularly true where individual performance appraisal is concerned, for people and their efforts make the difference between outstanding and poor corporate performance around the world.

It has not been the purpose here to give past performance appraisal procedure in detail, only the critical essentials upon which the detail can be built.[y] And an appropriate base would be the differentiation between broad functional requirements of the three fundamental managerial levels:

1. *The department managers.* Their main concerns are achieving goals, maintaining schedules, controlling costs, and managing people, the people problems being in the greatest volume at this level— motivation, work quality, turnover, development, commitment— while at the same time the technical demands are highest. Thus interpersonal and technical skills are the dominant requirements, most of the performance problems arising from a lack of the interpersonal skills training. See page 913 for their "homeostatic" responsibilities.

2. *The functional executives.* Their main concerns are functional policies, planning, volume, profit and market share. Evaluations of this group commonly overlook their interdependencies and lack of any influence over economics, markets and competition; they should be rated as members of teams (pages 406-410) on controllables as well as standing alone. Also see 914 for their "mediative" responsibilities.

3. *The general management executives.* They should be appraised principally on their planning and long-range results for the 12 key result areas listed in "The decisions" in Chapter 14. This is the origin of the short-range profit pressure down the line that is undermining U.S. industry in international markets: the solution resides in incentives for long-range results. Also see 915 for their "proactive" responsibilities.

Except for the heads of major units, however, the *mode* of appraisal by their superiors within any of the three may be quite similar even though their requirements for success are so different, and it is in the mode and related policies that almost all the problems arise. Discussing them can be more understandable if the subject is divided into its two operating phases: the appraisal before participation, and the joint "progress review" that follows it. And the most promising approach to the latter—and most successful when done correctly—remains the hybrid appraisal/planning process we know as MBO. Doing it effectively is so important it warrants a full chapter on its own, the next one, but the following applies to the interpersonal part of performance appraising whether MBO is instituted or not.

Before participation. It would clearly be inept and irresponsible to undertake a progress review with a subordinate manager without first having given considerable thought to the subject beforehand: planning the appraisal, gathering the needed information together and spending the necessary time on each rating. Both because it can be a disturbing task for a conscientious superior and because a poor job can be very costly, progressive organizations provide a great deal of assistance, from forms, procedures, computerized performance records, and trends, to the ultimate, the periodic use of the assessment center evaluation with its extensive testing. To what extent these are done by the organizations or how much effort the managers devote to prior study must naturally be strongly influenced by cost-effectiveness (effectiveness that includes motivation results).

But the qualitative factors will of course always be difficult evaluations as to both accuracy and subordinate acceptance. For example, determining a subordinate manager's effectiveness in optimizing the use of human resources is plainly something that has to be interpreted by the superior just as it has to be for innovativeness, personnel development, public responsibility, and other qualitative requirements. What comes off the computer, the accounting system, or transactional data is naturally inadequate for these, and even frequent contact doesn't make up the difference, because the subordinate manager is understandably on best behavior in front of the boss. One important source for the superior of what is missing is a periodic anonymous attitude and opinion survey of the subordinate's subordinates, providing, additionally, information to the superior on the subordinate manager's own:

- leadership behavior and its effects,
- relationships and interpersonal skill,
- appraising and its impact,
- managerial and leadership competence (e.g., the revelations on page 274 about Briggs) and the effects on subordinate performance.

Fortune magazine asked the #1 ranked firm in the 32 industries it surveys annually for its "Most Admired" firm, and asked do they undertake such opinion surveys, and if so, why; and found that most do, among them:

Alcoa   Herman Miller
Amoco   J.P. Morgan
AT&T   Morgan Stanley Group
BellSouth   Motorola
Boein ;   Proctor and Gamble
Burlii gton Resources   Reader's Digest
Coca-Cola   Levi Strauss Associates
DuPont   3M
General Mills   United Parcel Service
Hewlett-Packard

Commonly called "upward evaluations" or "360 degree feedback," subordinates are typically asked to answer in writing 100 or so questions, usually anonymously. Some firms subject all managers to them, others like Dupont only to senior managers and those on the fast track; and the results may be used in their annual evaluations or purely for self-improvement as at AT&T.

Companies can choose from among more than a dozen standardized quizzes on the market, some consultants also providing training of staff in their use and interpretation for a fee.

Certainly, authoritarian superiors would rebel against having their subordinates surveyed, but the leaders of those organization trying to be participative should be able to recognize their feedback value to all; moreover any well-intentioned, achievement-oriented subordinate manager ought, in self-interest, to be eager to have that kind of information on his or her own performance. There are few more rewarding experiences than to learn that one is highly regarded by one's own unit, but if it isn't so, it can naturally only be made so by first knowing the opinions.

Then there's the crucial information that surveys can give on customer satisfaction, the starting point of volume and profit, that should be a concern of everyone in management; indeed, some firms have now instituted a Customer Satisfaction Department that comprehensively studies it, recommends on findings, and monitors it.

The internal quantitative performance data and calculations that reflect it are fairly obvious: volume, sales returns, customer retention rate, defect rate, response time, delivery. A good department will naturally survey also the opinions of customers, distributors, and others in the marketplace on product quality, design, price, service, competitive comparison, etc. Additionally, there's the obvious competitive strategy of buying and analyzing major competitors' products the way the big three do with Japanese cars, often an eye-opener for potential improvements.

And plainly, virtually all deficiencies are traceable and traced (by the department) back to their origins for improvement—marketing, sales force, manufacturing, engineering, R&D, information, human resources development, incentives, leadership development ... all of which may be more necessary for survival than is realized.

The progress review. Participation by subordinates in appraising their performance has been pushed by textbooks for a long time because the gains to both parties are so substantial:[z]

- For the superior: the appraisal *before* participation can only be tentative because all the needed appraisal information is not in yet: the unrecorded, unobserved (by the superior) and unreported happenings, the subordinate's opinions, explanations, and judgments influencing results, etc.
- For the subordinate: the psychological importance to the subordinate is well established; it's needed for the attention, recognition, appreciation, feedback, belonging, and the need to present one's side of, and have a chance to influence, evaluations of oneself.
- For both: although the informal on-the-job contact (with its suggestions and feedback) ordinarily has the most important influence in improving subordinate performance, a periodic formal meeting, especially early in a career, is a major managerial opportunity and technique for monitoring, teaching, summing up, getting feedback, clearing up rumors, pulling the loose ends together, complimenting good work, keeping the organizational goals targeted, and maintaining priorities.

But these gains occur only to the extent that the procedure is well designed and effectively carried out. The well-known truth of the matter is that progress reviews are almost always high anxiety points on the calendar that both parties would skip if the organization didn't require them. The principal reasons for this are fourfold:

a. appraisal system inadequacies,
b. interpersonal skill inadequacies
c. fears of the consequences,
d. a high level of appraisal-reward conflict;

and most of the solutions to the problems become quickly apparent through a simple analysis of them.

(a) When there are inadequacies in the appraisal system, usually neither party is aware of it unless they've had prior experience with or study of effective appraisal systems. Examples: the system's forms are poorly designed (e.g., irrelevant content due to unclear goals, poor rating scales, not tailored to the department needs); the information is often incomplete (no systematic collection); or the appraising is not built into operating procedure, so the appraisal is often delayed or forgotten. The solutions are evident from the criticisms. Additionally, subordinate managers being evaluated are seldom provided in advance, as they should be, with the performance information, including any surveys of their own subordinates' opinions. The meetings should be as surprise-free as possible to avoid emotional jolts, which can be aided by their filling out self evaluation sheets for joint discussion. Advanced organizations go a major step further by developing computerized performance profiles, also for joint discussion. The Corning Glass case in Chapter 17 (see Index) is an example.

(b) The failure to train superiors in the art of appraising seems to be largely a hangover from past one-way Taylorian "scientific management"; the mandate: command and control an indifferent employee, and the control entails ticking off unilaterally what was done right and what was done wrong with instructions for correction—the way one treats a child.

On the other hand, some point, and incorrectly, to Douglas McGregor's famous plaint about being put in a position of "playing God" as an excuse to eliminate appraisals altogether. The inappropriateness of the interpretation of the comment was explained on page 37. Well-trained (or well self-trained) mature managers don't feel that way, realize it's part of what they're paid to do, and do it effectively, their maturity adding the humility and responsibility necessary to make it so.

No superior should conduct any appraisal or progress review on a subordinate without successful training, and that means right up through top management. The chief HRD executive should make wholly evident to the CEO (if it isn't already) the importance of appraisal to performance improvement, gain the person's commitment to training the entire management team, the senior executives first, who should become the trainers of their subordinates in the skills on down the ladder, so that "linking-pin" (Chapter 13) family group training occurs.

The planning of the appraisal training program itself, how to train the superiors in how to teach appraising, should be a joint effort of top-line management and HRD to ensure that it's based on the realities of their management practices/needs and to gain line "ownership," taking the number of meetings necessary to produce a consensually accepted procedure of goals, measurable standards, sound practices, and maximum utility as a performance improvement tool.

Then each superior teaches to his or her family team the framework they're taught by the senior executives, and they customize it to their own specific needs by tying the content to their on-the-job activities. That has to be followed immediately by appraisal interview training with critiquing of videotaped role-playing. (Also see pages 410-414 on counseling and coaching and Chapter 17 for other interpersonal skills training.)

(c) The third cause of the anxiety, the fears of the consequences, can plainly be daunting for either party.

The *superior's* fears can be very complex, beginning with a fear of opening the door to questions and subjects they can't handle smoothly. Suppose the subordinate presses for a raise, presents a list of complaints, or asks for a transfer?

And in most current climates one can't win politically, unfavorable evaluations commonly arousing negative emotions from both subordinates and peer managers; further, the latter get competitively jealous if there are too many favorable ones, become unfriendly, and look on the department as a source of recruits. The only solution, some managers have concluded, is to appraise as neither very good nor poor and follow a rule of mediocrity; moreover, "do not collect accurate information about your subordinates, for it will very likely be held against you."[26] Naturally, everyone loses.

The *subordinate's* fears are (1) untrue evaluations; (2) unfavorable ones; and (3) the effects of evaluations on rewards. Where there's any lack of trust there's always the belief that superiors manipulate evaluations to manipulate their subordinates, and trust or not, there are commonly important distortions made and caused by the superiors' biases and idiosyncracies; additionally, superiors and subordinates will always have a different perspective on many subjects.

The fears of both parties are of course a product of the core problem, the I-O gap, and they will be minimized only when the climate is cleaned up, minimized (not removed) because the superior-subordinate relationship will always tend to have some adversary elements to it.

The particular cleaning up techniques that will help relieve these appraisal fears will be the interpersonal skills training referred to in (b) and the opening up of three more systems along with the open pay one that has been described—the four:[aa]

- The open pay system (pages 318-320),
- The open appraisal system (immediately ahead),
- The open personnel file system (immediately ahead),
- The open selection system (Chapter 17),

and the participative handling of a two-meeting appraisal arrangement as described below.

(d) A high level of appraisal-reward conflict is, perceptively, the subordinate's fear #3 above that needs highlighting. Fully appreciating the relationship, the person naturally acts accordingly in a formal performance appraisal session in which reward (pay, promotion, perquisites) is to be judged for change. In conventional climates the superior can invariably count on:

- subordinate defensiveness and manipulation or changing of the facts to look good, and
- misleading feedback about both the individual's own activities and performances and on anything volunteered about others or the department that might have a bearing on his/her own appraisal.

So some organizations have tried to eliminate the conflict by eliminating the evaluation for compensation from the appraisal process, simply let the superior hold an informal meeting at the end of the year if asked about it. The results: a little better truth in the quarterly ones on performance, but a year-end 10-second meeting on the compensation, because most superiors have already made up their minds on the pay, they don't want to discuss it, and the fears in (c) above loom large; further, it angers them to have to go over the same data twice and perhaps reopen arguments on any of them. However, the subordinate is obviously left very unsatisfied, unless a substantial increase makes up for the lack of communication, and the possibility of instilling a pay/performance linkage perception is precluded.[bb]

Again, it's a matter of minimizing, in this case the conflicts, by the same solutions described at the end of (c), that is, the open systems and a two-meeting structure. The latter conveniently also makes it possible to undertake competently two other personnel procedures of major importance that are commonly neglected: participative career and development planning, steps 2 and 3 in the diagram. The two require the same data and should be held annually for all managers up through middle management and into middle age (45?). The procedures will be described in Chapter 17.

The past performance *progress review*, therefore, should always be a two-step operation for both psychological and practical reasons (and to separate unrelated subjects; see pages 401-402):

Functional progress review—the review and evaluation of the subordinate manager's progress against operating goals, performance of special tasks, and role responsibility performance, followed by planning (or replanning); usually undertaken quarterly (or monthly or otherwise to suit the need).

A new computer software program can be very helpful: "Employee Appraiser" for Windows ($129) from the Austin-Hayne Corp. of San Mateo, Cal. Used by the superior initially "before participation," the person is optimally prepared to face a subordinate in the participative "progress review" (using the results there) with constructive, thought-out critical comment that can be recognized as objective, well-intentioned and helpful instead of being either untrue praise to be perceived as a nice supervisor (sometimes followed shortly after by dismissal and an unfair dismissal lawsuit), or having subjective harshness or language that can be misconstrued as sexist, racist or discriminatory.

It's not only an education in appraising, it's a time saver, it's far more accurate than the many conventional formats, it stimulates analysis covering a wide array of behaviors and skills, it helps on phraseology, for the discourse with the subordinate and for the final report, and it can be used by peers and subordinates of the appraisee (in lieu of the opinion surveys) as well as the superior to ensure better objectivity.

To illustrate briefly,[27] it starts with a menu of categories for evaluation: planning performance, decision making, leadership, communication, initiative, dependability, customer satisfaction, and so on—you click on (the window) one at a time as you work on each of your choice. Under each selected another menu appears, for example, for communication: writing, listening skill, openness, receptivity to feedback, clarity, keeping others informed. Then under any selected comes phrases that can accurately describe your opinion, the build-up across skill and behavior categories resulting in a detailed report that can be modified by a word-processing capability to best fit the appraisers views and style.

The result: a good probability of acceptability of the appraisal as valid and with the best intentions to help one improve performance and grow.

General evaluation review. This is a participative review of the "functional progress review," leading to and including discussion of compensation, its linkage to performance, career planning, and the prospects of or requisites of promotion (see "The Calendar" on page 402 and "the joint sessions" section in Chapter 17[cc]). Where the qualitative aspects are high, success understandably depends heavily on open, non-critical, constructive discourse.

In summary of the four appraisal problems (a) to (d) back on page 377, one has to accept the tendency of some degree of friction and conflict because of the adversarial nature of superior/subordinate relationships, but these can be virtually eliminated by developing a climate of trust and (re)designing and operating the structures and processes such that they will be conducive of trust.

When there is at least average subordinate technical competence, all the problems generally originate in the managerial philosophy and values of the leaders and organization. The appraisal system inadequacies of (a) are usually traceable to the view that how appraisals are handled, including the control of the information, is the private autocratic domain of the superior. When the problem is interpersonal inadequacies (b) for lack of training, one normally finds the belief that managers should sink or swim on their own. And (c) and (d) are fairly universal because of the amount of distrust in all but a few organizations due to Theory X attitudes.

But even given Theory Y behavior and the genuine participation that foster the needed trust, inappropriate structures and processes, we know, can block it. The two-meeting arrangement resolves some of the conflicts of the appraising, but the appraisal system has to be opened along with the other three in the list of four on page 379 for an overall climate of trust to reign.

The four problem areas thus not only are related but tend to compound each other. As a result, all the solutions for all the problems have to be instituted to remedy any one of them effectively, and leaving out one will make adequate effectiveness on all very difficult to achieve.

On the open systems still to be described, the one on "selection" calls for a major system change and will be postponed to Chapter 17, but *the open appraisal system* means no more than letting each individual know the objectives, procedures and rules of the system plus any decisions that are made relevant to the person in order to remove all the mystery and secrecy that in the past has hung over it. The opening up would include a revelation and explanation of status on the "runner-up chart" of the department's promotables, Figure 9.5 an example of one,[28,dd] and what the guidelines are for getting on it. Some firms have been doing it on principle without putting the open-system label on it.

Then at the same time the appraisal system is opened up, the personnel file system has to be. *The open personnel file system* combines open access to employees of all information on themselves anywhere in the organization with an appeal procedure for challenging and changing any data believed by an employee to be untrue or unfair, matters that should in fact be cleared up in the General Evaluation Review session before reaching the procedure.

Most progressive managements do have such a file policy, and important to it are the associated policies of privacy and file maintenance. A recommendation on the former (privacy) is given in Chapter 21; an answer to the latter is to divide appraisal data into factual and judgmental, and, whether the files are kept by the manager or centrally, retain the factual data as long as the individual is employed, but keep the judgmental conclusions only for 1-2 years, which would be an equitable way to allow for growth, improvement and the mistakes often necessary to learn. When higher management wants more, it can be obtained verbally from the superior.

Runner-Up Chart

Manager—ABC Department Present Incumbent (Age)		
Candidate 1	Age	Color Code
Candidate 2	Age	Color Code
Candidate 3	Age	Color Code

Position A Present Incumbent (Age)		
Candidate 1	Age	Color Code
Candidate 2	Age	Color Code
Candidate 3	Age	Color Code

Position C Present Incumbent (Age)		
Candidate 1	Age	Color Code
Candidate 2	Age	Color Code
Candidate 3	Age	Color Code

Position B Present Incumbent (Age)		
Candidate 1	Age	Color Code
Candidate 2	Age	Color Code
Candidate 3	Age	Color Code

Submitted by ————————————————

Date ————————————————

Color Code:
Green—ready now.
Blue—ready in 1 to 2 years.
Red—ready in 3 to 5 years.
White—not likely to be qualified, but best available.

Figure 9.5

NOTES

a.   A review of some definitions;

A *trait* is a consistent, persistent, stable predisposition of behavior that is the consequence of either an inherited characteristic (constitutional traits on page 46) or learned characteristic (motivation, habit, attitude) in interaction with the environment.

An *attitude* is a learned predisposition to consistently react positively or negatively toward a person, idea, or object, the reaction shown by either verbal or non-verbal friendliness, hostility, posture, mood, etc.

Knowledge is a learning.

A *value* is a learned normative standard that guides behavior (some undesirable ones on page 118, desirable ones on page 176).

A *motivation* is an internal state that energizes and directs a person toward a particular goal.

A *skill* is a learned aptitude.

A *role* is a position's or function's expectations as to the activities and behavior needed to perform its task effectively.

b.   Behaviorists' writings have often confusingly used "personality" for "traits" alone and vice versa, though it is a compound of the ten on page 39.

c.   Success in terms of salary levels and promotions over time had to be the principal measure of managerial effectiveness in all of those studies for lack of a better available one, on the assumption that increases and promotions are most often for effectiveness, though any one knows it is frequently not.

d.   A large proportion of those who have reached the top have had average grades in school and college, not to mention those who never went to college.

e.   Not to be confused with the attribute using the same word described on page 239-340.

f.   Definitions of those in 9.1 that may not be self evident:

Proactivity: The predisposition to take action, initiate.

The Leadership Cluster: the personal characteristic that enable some managers to be inspirational in people leadership (only).

Logical thought: the main feature of the trait "Systematic cognitive style" (Chapter 14).

Conceptualization: the main feature of "intuitive cognitive style" (Chapter 14).

Use of socialized power: as described on page 275.

Positive regard: belief in others and seeing them as good (re the "nature of man").

The Focus on Others Cluster: synonymous with psychological development, or maturity, but the research did not cover moral development.

g.   It is interesting that the dominant personality would most likely possess a high potential for all the competencies in Figure 9.1 (page 347), #19 being less than #4 in order to have the motivation to manage.

h.   While "predict" includes an evaluation component, the verbal distinction from "evaluate" is in their own subgoals given on pages 368-369.

i.   There are no laws forbidding background and reference checking, only against their use in ways that discriminate, but communication has virtually ceased for fear of suit. See "Freedom from defamation" in Chapter 21 for more.

j.   The scientific research procedure for the predictive validity of tests: the test is administered to the applicant and filed away unscored until the applicant after hiring establishes a record for the criterion (e.g., salary increases and/or promotions). When sufficient data have been collected, the test is scored and the correlation made. A major source of error as been in assuming applicability across different situations. "Every test or other predictor hould be freshly validated for every new situation to which it is applied."[12]

    k.   See Guion, ibid., p. 70 for complex meaning of cognitive skills.

    l.   The Allport-Vernon-Lindzey "Study of Values" illustrated on pages 138-143 is also in his category, but is of a more specialized nature, as is the "Q-sort." In the latter, the subject s asked to sort a stack of cards that describe attributes into two stacks, one that best describes imself or herself, the other the least; it can be used for either a self-description or for describing he ideal self.

    m.   A complete updating revision is periodically undertaken.

    n.   Global measures can be of two types: (1) ratings or rankings by superiors on the ubordinates' total managerial effectiveness; though they have the advantages of integrating n one judgment many behaviors over time and compare the person with peers in like work, hey're contaminated with biases, competitive fears, and irrelevancies (appearances, liking, or lisliking, etc.); (2) pay increases and/or promotions over time, which are not contaminated nd reflect pooled estimates of numerous superiors' judgments over the period, but clearly social ompetence alone can be the reason for them.

    o.   Some personnel specialists have made a definition distinction in their writing between he word *appraisal*, that it applies only to performance, and *assessment*, that it is for the valuation of potential.

    p.   Those who use assessment center results need to be warned that the claimed behavioral equirements of jobs have not been those of the candidates' specific or prospective jobs as lescribed in Chapter 8 (pages 304-309).

    q.   Surprisingly, no use appears to have been made scaled personal histories; this refers only to a self-report.

    r.   Example: Of 1,100 non-management employees tested at an IBM center, all nominated y their managers as potential promotees, a quarter were judged as without potential, and alf were rated in the lowest two of a possible five levels.[19]

    s.   Also see the summing up at the end of Chapter 20 for which traits and skills to give he greatest weight to.

    t.   McClelland, D. C, G. O. Klemp, Jr., R. E. Boyatzis, and staff.

    u.   The term includes behavior appraisal.

    v.   Keeping in mind that the predictive value of past performance appraisals is substantially educed for promotion to a position with different performance requirements.

    w.   A standard being a determined level of effective performance that is reasonable to expect. Also see pages 329-330.

    x.   An example of what should be taught about it in an appraisal course: highly effective nd less effective managers tend, as appraisers, to have different definitions and expectations of job behavior; the former put a high value on initiative, persistence, broad knowledge, and planning ability; the latter more often put their priorities on cooperation, company loyalty, good teamwork, and consideration.[22] This is a generality not to be used for stereotyping a ubordinate manager, but it suggests trying to discern what the emphasis of each is. What s being overrated and underrated? Also, does his or her rating pattern reflect competitive fear of selected subordinates?

    y.   A new book, *The Performance Management Sourcebook*, can be very helpful to HRD taff as well as operating managers: 393 pages, the first part contains new articles on appraising performance, planning, development and rewarding; the second gives questionnaires, role-playing techniques, other material, case studies, and how to work with consultants.[25]

    z.   A comprehensive coverage of participation is given in Chapter 13.

    aa.   These are of course "internal" open systems; one also encounters the open systems term or an organization that appropriately integrates itself with its environment—stakeholders, technology, economics—the next step forward being the "total integration" defined on pag 32.

bb. In a study by The Conference Board, surveyed human resources executives forecaste that, with the growing stress on productivity, "increasing interest in improving the linkag (therefore the perception) between pay and performance will mean greater emphasis o performance appraisal." Reported by *Behavioral Science Newsletter*, September 27, 1983. Relat to the footnote r on page 340.

cc. The final decisions are best reported later after the superior has had some time to relat the discussion to the organization's constraints and needs.

dd. Note that this chart must be approved by the superior's superior and will be an integra part of the larger chart of the total organization that would include top management's "ke position ladder." Its weaknesses as a planning tool can be seen by contrasting it with th procedures in the "Succession planning" section of Chapter 17.

REFERENCES

1. Bass, B.M. (revised and expanded version), *Stogdill's Handbook Of Leadership* (Ne York: Free Press, 1981) see Chapters 4 to 8.

2. McGregor, D. op. cit, 1960, pp. 180-182.

3. Wollman, B.B., *Dictionary of Behavioral Sciences* (New York: Van Nostrand Reinhol Co., 1975), p. 217.

4. Ghiselli, E.E., *The Validity of Occupational Aptitude Tests* (New York: John Wiley 1966).

5. Campbell, J.P., M.V. Dunnette, E.E. Lawler, III, and K.E. Weick, Jr., *Manageria Behavior*, Performance and Effectiveness (New York: McGraw-Hill, 1970), p. 29.

6. Boyatzis, R.E., *The Competent Manager* (New York: John Wiley, 1982) 9.1 adapted fron Table 12.1, p. 230.

7. Katz, D., and R.L. Kahn, The Social Psychology of Organizations, 2nd Ed. (New York John Wiley, 1978), p. 545.

8. Drucker, P.F., *The Practice of Management* (New York: Harper & Row, 1954), p. 159

9. *Time*, July 15, 1974 p. 23.

10. Ratz, D., and R.L. Kahn, Ibid., p. 546.

11. Campbell et al., op. cit. Adapted from p. 151.

12. Guion, R.M., *Personnel Testing* (New York: McGraw-Hill, 1965), pp. 20-22.

13. Ibid., pp. 237-238.

14. Campbell et al., op. cit., p. 138.

15. Ibid., pp. 165-170, 195.

16. Zemke, R., "Testing: Return of the Prodigal Process," *Training*, May, 1983 (Paraphrased.

17. "A Test to Uncover Management Skills" *The New York Times*, January 21, 1979.

18. Byham, W. C. "Assessment centers for spotting future managers," *Harvard Busines Review*, July-August, 1970.

19. Kraut, A.I., and G.J. Scott, "Validity of an Operational Management Assessmen Program," *Journal of Applied Psychology*, Vol. 56, 1972, p. 125.

20. Wilson, J.E., and W.A. Tatge, "Assessment Centers—Further Assessment Needed? *Personnel Journal*, March 1973.

21. Guion, op. cit., p. 98.

22. Kirchner, W.K. and D.J. Reisberg, "Differences between Better and Less Effective Supervisors in Appraisal of Subordinates, *Personnel Psychology*, 1962, 15, p. 295.

23. Campbell et al., op. cit., p. 66.

24. Patton, A., "Does Performance Appraisal Work?" *Business Horizons*, February 1973.

25. Schneier, C E., R. W. Beatty, and L. S. Baird, *The Performance Management Sourcebook* (Amherst, Mass.: Human Resources Development Press, 1987).

26. Pau, A.L, "Performance Appraisal: Useful But Still Resisted," *Harvard Business Review*, May-June 1975. An example, not a recommendation.

27. An example given P. H. Lewis in the *N.Y. Times* 12/19/93.

28. From *What to do about Performance Appraisal* by M. S. Kellogg (New York: Amacom, 1975 Revised), p. 206. Also see the book's pages 143-146 for some suggestions for discussing the chart with a subordinate.

Chapter 10

Management by Objectives—MBO

This hybrid form of the performance appraisal has now been developed and refined into a major management tool, such that it now incorporates all of appraisal, control, planning, coaching, counseling, and motivation.

Historically, the initial idea was only one of control by goal planning and performance review, the idea traceable as far back as ancient Egypt and Greece. But its value to a business organization was apparently not fully appreciated until the increasing size and complexity of General Motors in the late 1920s recommended a closer look.

At that time, Pierre S. DuPont concluded that decentralized divisionalization would be the best solution to the firm's problems of growth and bureaucracy, and that a goal-setting/progress review process carried out by divisional top managements was the way to make it work. The process was later called "management by objectives" by Alfred P. Sloan, but it was as yet a unilateral function of superiors—no participation.[a] The logic of it and potential benefits were easy to grasp, so many firms quickly followed, first Standard Oil of New Jersey in the early 1930s and most of the major ones in the 1940s and 1950s.

But soon the failure to attend to the subordinate's opinion through participation began to show in surveys of the procedure's effectiveness. Clear successes were few, most installations were marginal, floating on faith and hope, and too many were disasters. Yet even after the behaviorists pointed out the omission and participation was added, the results showed only small improvement.

Then Douglas McGregor (1960) introduced his concepts of self-management and integration that explained why the participation practiced was ineffective. The fundamental goal one has to have in mind for the subordinate, he said, must be self-management, and self-management doesn't happen unless the subordinate is committed (Theory Y, #2, on page 16), which in turn only occurs when differences of opinion on the goals of the organization are reconciled in the participative process so that the individual accepts the goals (and methods) as in his or her own best interest as well as that of the organization. At that time the person will self-manage toward the goals with commitment.

The process is plainly one of "integration," the type Chapter 2 classified as direct, and the consequence would of course be the individual's best performance:

Integrative participation → Internalized goals →
Commitment → Self-management →
Maximum performance

The participation that had been undertaken was actually superficial, a simplistic manipulative brand of human relations that remained authoritarian.

Of course, installation of an efficient MBO participation *process* is primary; it provides the framework for the integration. But for the integration to succeed, it must also have the psychology appropriate to it built in. When it is not, the process itself can cause the best efforts at integration to fail.

The way it should be designed and operated, therefore, has to be mastered in detail first, only after which can direct integration produce the desired self-management and high performance. MBO is the *job planning* of activities part integration; a description of how to undertake the *job design* part is used to illustrate the skill of integration in the summary of leadership principles in Chapter 20. The *career planning* and *development planning* parts are given in Chapter 17.

Introduction

Most know that MBO, as said, is an appraisal-planning procedure; the performance of the last period is appraised, goals are agreed to for the next period, and a general outline of how the goals are to be attained is planned, the details left to the subordinate's own judgment.

The principle of relating the goals-plan process to the appraisal is sound for a number or reasons, particularly:

- In order to be effective, the goals and plans obviously have to be based on a past performance appraisal;
- Good management includes coaching and/or counseling, especially for the less than experienced, and the discourse on how better to carry out the plans has to be based on the person's strengths and weaknesses as well as past performance, all revealed by the appraisal(s);
- The appraisal tends to highlight the development needs some of which can and should be incorporated in the activities planning.

And the appraisal principle applied is also sound. There are four *criteria alternatives* for appraising an individual's performance:

1. A concept of excellence,
2. Comparison with others doing the same work,
3. Against his or her own past performance,
4. Against mutually set goals, using #1 and #3.

The fourth, that MBO uses, largely shifts the burden of the evaluation from the superior to the subordinate, whereas each of the first three on their own implies unilateral judgments by the superior, the second often psychologically threatening and unfair. Thus #4 makes the procedure much easier for the superior; it fosters a good relationship; and because it is mainly self-evaluation (when well managed), it facilitates, and is the only one that does, any effort that may be made to motivate self-management.

As for gains to the organization as a whole, there can be many. Different companies can have a number of reasons for adopting MBO; some of the more prominent are:

- Introduce or improve a formal planning system—better goals, programs, schedules, controls, and results.
- Implement a total integration of the organization's planning function from top to bottom of goals and plans short and long range—which MBO is ideal for.
- Control decentralization better.
- Provide an appraisal system that
  a. greatly reduces subjective personality evaluations by the superior,
  b. gives the right signals to subordinates in an acceptable manner of what performance and behavior is and is not wanted.
- Increase the motivation to perform better at all levels.
- Introduce or improve the allocation of goal and task responsibility and accountability.
- Improve interpersonal relationships and climate.

An MBO system can be either the means toward, or contribute importantly to, achieving any of them, undoubtedly a main reason for the phenomenal spread of its use throughout the free world.

Yet, as virtually every manager involved in one knows, it always seems to have problems, sometimes enough of them to negate its value. Even when the superior's philosophy is right and the commitment is strong, things go wrong from the beginning, which is in fact where a lot of the difficulties originate: the deceptively simple procedure—the reiteration of an appraisal planning-execution cycle—makes them think it's easy. All in the chain of managers from the top down as a result push ahead with it almost oblivious of the thousand human and situational variables to be accounted for, assuming it's just a technical process, so that preliminaries are ignored, entry preparation is insufficient, execution is sloppy, and shortcuts are rife.

The most damaging specific causes of MBO failure and weakness that researchers have identified are (the numbers are for future reference, not rank):

1. *Insufficient involvement or commitment at the top*: a pattern of indifference is set for the rest of management.
2. *It was allowed to become a perfunctory chore.*
3. *Manager evasion of responsibilities*: delegating the MBO to staff personnel; ignoring cross-functional responsibilities.
4. *Manager resistance*: fear of personal inadequacy, little or no training, incompatible personality style or climate.
5. *Planning incompetence*: failure to define key result areas, poor goal setting, feedback ignored, overemphasis of techniques, and forgetting long-range needs.
6. *MBO not integral to operations*: tacked on as an appendage so fails to influence operating decisions and actions.
7. *Poor planning system*: conceptual inadequacy, goals and plans up and down the organization not integrated vertically, poor controls, badly designed procedures, excessive paperwork, inflexible procedures, forms or rules.
8. *Suboptimization*: overemphasis by subordinate's of his or her own individual goals, motivating interpersonal competition at the expense of needed collaboration.
9. *Lost opportunities*: failure to see or seize new opportunities in concentration on achieving the established goals.
10. *Interpersonal skill incompetence* of superior for lack of skill training, resulting in damaged superior-subordinate relationship.
11. *Absence of participation*: goals and plans are made unilaterally from impatience or are done that way from the start.
12. *Goal myopia*: overemphasis of selected quantitative goals to the neglect of essential processes and qualitative support activities.

On close examination, one can see that the first three are due to indifference, #4 to dysfunctional behavior, and all the rest to insufficient preparation or training or to incompetence.

None, therefore, is due to flaws in MBO principles; indeed, rarely has MBO produced a condition after trial or installation that was actually worse than before unless it was riddled with ineptness or serious sabotage. Its addition has sometimes made it *appear* worse by opening up a new awareness of these problems and others that were there all along, but abandonment because of their consequences has generally only left a bigger mess and lost the better functional planning of MBO that is almost always one sure gain.

As said earlier, the intent here is to discourse on the way MBO should be designed and operated in light of the psychology necessary to make it succeed, which adds up to combining the technical and social to eliminate the problems of #5 and #12. It will be done under the two headings of "System setup" and "Education" and be limited to highlighting the points that experience has shown to be crucial to success, leaving the routine to good how-to books.[b]

System setup

A simple classification of the setup issues would be: the need for a preliminary study of feasibility, planning the control, and the planning considerations unique to MBO.

Feasibility. A failure to understand the requisites of MBO has unfortunately led to the assumption that it will work in any organization or for any function, when it will not. As for the *organizational* fit, it's primarily a matter of the style of the top executive of the corporation, division, department or unit, and then the extent to which the subordinate managers follow suit as superiors.

The feasibility study therefore has to be done by an outside consultant to ensure the independence and objectivity of the feasibility appraiser as well as the person's MBO and behavioral expertise. And plainly, it assumes the consultant has the integrity to be candid if MBO will not fit, thereby losing an installation job.

MBO will not work if the top person:

a. is an authoritarian, likes the organization that way, and cannot accept the necessary participative goal-setting relations with his or her own immediate subordinates.[c]
b. is unwilling to make the structure and policy changes necessary for MBO to work, though perhaps willing to try a less authoritarian style;
c. is unwilling to apply it fairly quickly to the whole organization from top to bottom;
d. is unable to be committed to its successful operation, be personally involved, and give it continuous vigilant leadership through the years.

On the first (a), the very nature of an authoritarian, described on page 169, is sufficient explanation. Besides assuming the divine right to decide for subordinates, authoritarians have difficulty stomaching the participative goal-setting of MBO. And from the subordinate's point of view, the many qualitative factors that require appraisal judgments by an authoritarian superior preclude MBO: they resent being judged on them by people they don't trust.

(b) The CEO, regardless of style, must be willing to implement the organizational changes the study finds are necessary in order to make it work, some of which may be quite drastic, e.g., structural elimination of position and responsibility duplications (one firm described in the literature had to eliminate three vice presidents because of it); information system changes (give all the necessary feedback to each manager needed for MBO decisions and goal measurement, which may be much more than the CEO was previously willing to divulge); and policy changes (such as greater delegation and freedom of action, well beyond present constraints, that may be essential to achieving the goals).

(c) Because the goals of a manager at any level except the top cannot be set properly unless based on those of the larger unit and successively up to the organization's long-range plan (with the exception of relatively autonomous staff units), MBO in one unit only, or just here and there, would be a short-lived futile exercise of little lasting value. Further, the longer the installation delay at any point the more frustrated the levels below can become to the point of shelving it. Both the totality and momentum maintenance are vital.

Figure 10.1 pictures the planning hierarchy, and therefore goal hierarchy also, of a corporation; the annual and quarterly plans for the divisions, functions, or departments are the MBO plans of the respective managers.

(d) If the CEO is only superficially familiar with MBO, the person's commitment may not develop until the consultant presents a complete orientation on its potential, but the eventual commitment must be to the extent of heavy involvement for at least the first 3 to 5 years, only slightly less from then on. MBO is not just an appendage; it's a total approach to managing all individual managers and interrelating them, and the CEO's amount of attention will convey the importance ascribed to the procedure. More specifically, as someone once said, managers do what the boss *inspects* as opposed to *expects* and will slight a task if the boss seems to slight it.

An added complication of an authoritarian boss at any level is the type's manipulative attitude. Certainly the underlying reason for interest in MBO is better management of the planning system for better profits, but the authoritarian is inclined to see MBO as a good device to pressure managers rather than as the participative management system it is intended to be. One,

Corporate Planning Cycles for a Large Business

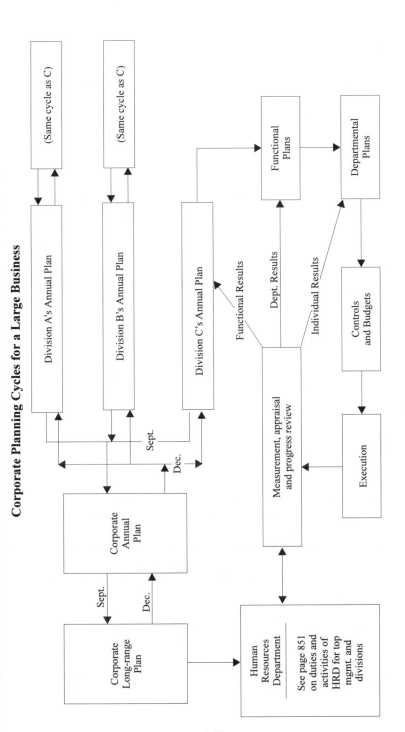

Figure 10.1

for example, made a practice of playing the units of a division off against each other, using the highest goals of the group to force all the others up (the typical labor union negotiating whipsaw) regardless of the others' operating constraints. The psychological consequences generated are easy to guess.

The consultant who discovers a, b, c, or d (page 393) and can't turn it around but recommends a go-ahead anyhow to get the installation fee may find the resultant failure and damage will make it the last assignment in the whole industry. The best solution for such an organization—wait for a more enlightened person at the top.

As for the *functional* fit (vs. the organizational, page 393) of MBO, in all cases, but the exceptions described below, in which the primary goals of subordinate managers can be directly quantified, it should work well. In fact it can also be effective when virtually all goals are qualitative if there is high mutual trust. When it isn't high, a few techniques can make it (the qualitative) sufficiently feasible anyhow, procedures like bringing a third party from Personnel into the evaluations, relying mostly on guided subordinate self-evaluation, quantifying the qualitative, or heavily systemizing the process as will be illustrated in Chapter 17 (the Corning Glass System).

Those situations in which it doesn't work, or in which the results have been poor often enough to warrant special care in the feasibility appraisal, are those with exceptional conditions of either futurity or instability. Some examples:

- Many staff functions, the achievements of which are too uncertain or too long-range so cannot be evaluated fairly in a short-range period; e.g., R&D specialists, numerous staff activities like planning, personnel, and technical advice.
- Volatile or rapid-change functions where the MBO cycle (from goal setting to performance evaluation) is too often disrupted or too short for a fair evaluation; e.g., assistant to an "intuitive" boss, a trouble shooter job, any new product stage before introduction.
- Too frequent leadership or incumbency changes for stable relationships between superior and subordinate, as in politically appointed positions in many government bureaucracies.
- The team members of most project-type matrix organizations, unless the teams remain intact with the same members for long periods of time (more ahead on team MBO, another subject).

Assuming the situation is favorable or hopeful, much of the balance of the feasibility study could be dedicated to:

- Preparing a draft of the MBO system to be installed.
- Identifying where in the organization MBO is functionally not feasible as in the four situations given above.
- Identifying organizational changes that will be necessary to make MBO work, for example, in the present information system, communication, control, staffing, and policies.
- Estimating the functional and interpersonal educational needs down through the hierarchy.
- Preparing a preliminary introduction plan for top management discussion in formulating the final one.

The first, the MBO system draft, is an aid to each of the subsequent tasks. Its preparation helps uncover the exceptions and necessary organizational changes (any of which may be roadblocks to acceptance by the CEO), it aids the survey of educational needs, and it provides a framework for the introduction planning.

Planning and control. Managing an individual or a subordinate manager (therefore the manager's unit as well) by "objectives and results" where applicable has sometimes been mistakenly held to be a self-sufficient system of controlling the person's performance, failing to realize that while self-management toward the objectives is motivated (hopefully), so can excessive self-interest and interpersonal competition at the expense of important needed cooperation, collaboration and coordination up, down and across the organization.

Moreover, (1) qualitative requisites of desired performance that are stated in the objectives and evaluated tend to be neglected, (2) *results* commonly do not reveal problem causes for the planning of improvement or correction, and (3) the very principle itself recommends waiting on everything for results, when it may be too late to avoid serious losses that might otherwise have been foreseen and prevented.

Thus the need to plan controls specifically for MBO. The larger subject of organization control itself is so important that the whole next chapter is devoted to it. However, some of its basic principles are essential knowledge for this set-up planning, so they have to be introduced here.

The core factor of course is the superior's commitment to the basic MBO management principles involved: the participation of the subordinate both in the planning (controls as well as objectives) and in the results evaluation, along with considerable freedom to decide how the objectives will be achieved, all of which helps the subordinate recognize that the controls are as much for his or her self-management use as for the superior's guidance and evaluation of performance. The overall consequence: managing through the person's *internal* control in lieu of only *external* controls.

Certainly the external controls *are* very important, and planning them requires an understanding of their basic characteristics. Three topics in particular have to be taken into account: (a) the basic types of external control, (b) the quantifiability of the activity involved, and (c) the degree of influenceability by the subordinate of each factor measured.

(a) the purposes of the three *types of external control* are almost self-evident from their titles:

Precontrols: preplanned devices to guide individuals or units toward desired goals, performance and/or behavior.

During action controls: systems and procedures to facilitate control during action or performance; they may or may not utilize precontrols.

Postcontrols: systems that facilitate the evaluation of performance or behavior against precontrol goals or standards.

However, managers have to be well aware of what they're trying to achieve with each, know what category each control being considered falls under in order to make correct choices, and understand the key issues that make for the success or failure of the choices made.

It's no small order. There's a list of 29 control devices under "Control Basics" in Chapter 11[d] and some elaboration under its "The key variables" section from which one will see that planning most of the controls is largely the province of staff specialists. But on the *precontrols*, the average manager does have to plan many of them on his or her own most of the time, and the text ahead will point out the main issues on all as they become relevant within the chapters' subjects.

One particular caution for the planning manager: the design of a precontrol can help or can seriously hinder during-action controls and postcontrols. For two fairly transparent negative examples: policies on information or communication can stultify the decision-making system, the information system, or communication system; and standards that are not clear (they should spell out what constitutes *effective performance*) can foul up any of numbers 18, 21, 24, 27 and 28 in the "Control Basics" list.

There are two points about *during-action controls* that should be stressed here in order to aid proper design or selection: why they exist, and how to plan them to foster the MBO assumption of self-management (MBO itself being partly during-action: control #23).

They exist because they fill a vacuum caused by the absence or insufficiency of precontrols for guidance, a situation that occurs when there isn't enough information or sufficient reliability of the information to preplan them. The questions in such a situation therefore: is there any information important to decisions or operations on the spot that's missing? If so, which during action control(s) in the list of 29 can best supply it to lead to it in some way.

The MBO behavioral goal of self-management is naturally the main factor that should govern the design. When possible numbers 17-19 should be tapped by the individual, so the controls have to be shaped not only to facilitate it but to encourage, not discourage, their use. Plainly, staff assistance (#20), lateral relations (#22 and as described in Chapter 16), fast feedback of performance results, and involvement in the relevant decision-making can each make important contributions.

Then for planning postcontrols, it's only a matter of deciding jointly which parts that are available of the numbers 26, 27 and 28 would be most helpful (the nature of MBO making the evaluations joint). Number 29, however, is still a future hope, an explanation in Chapter 11.

(b) Recognizing *quantifiability* of a quantitative performance requirement is easy enough, as is planning its measurements, but most managers know only one way to handle the qualitative other than to bypass them: make subjective judgments.

For a small number of them (the qualitative) it may be the only recourse, but there are in fact few instances in which some quantification cannot be applied to the qualitative. Furthermore, the separation of *general* and *specific* evaluations according to the two types of performance review on pages 380-382 (MBO meetings are functional progress reviews) can make it quite easy. Take the five qualitative leadership requirements of:

1. The development by the subordinate manager of the manager's own subordinates,
2. the development by the manager of a committed, cohesive team,
3. the morale of the manager's department,
4. the manager's cooperation with the managers of other functions,
5. the manager's contributions toward the effectiveness of teams or committees he or she is on other than his or her own.

The general performance of a subordinate manager on all of these is appropriately evaluated jointly in the annual "general evaluation review," at which time an improvement and development program of activities for the next year based on the evaluation should be planned, activities to be fitted in at quarterly (and weekly) meetings as opportunity presents. Examples: courses on coaching and team development, participating in cross-functional meetings of the superior, chairing departmental meetings, special projects, and substituting for the superior in his or her absence. At each of those quarterly "functional progress review" meetings, fit the specific events into the weekly plans ahead with detail on who is to be involved (e.g., which of the subordinate manager's subordinates), measurements, controls, follow-up; and evaluate the event performances in the following quarterly meeting. Next year the general-specific process is reiterated. Advanced managers will recognize that this is no less than the on-the-job part of a management development program to cover mainly the requirements of the current position (vs. the most likely next one).

Among the measurements possible: the time devoted to counseling subordinates can be a measure for a short-range gauge of #1 of the five, the record of pay increases and promotions a general indication for the long-range; employee opinion surveys and carefully analyzed turnover data can tell much for the second and third; and evaluations of the last two can be aided by personnel department interviews of other-function managers and team or committee members.

(c) The degree of *influenceability* is a problem on both quantitative and qualitative performance measures. The performance results on most of what one wants controlled are seldom 100 percent controllable by one person, so one had better determine collaboratively what percentage to assign to each and who is responsible for the balance. More on this in the subsection ahead on MBO "Goal-setting."

Additionally, the dynamic changes that take place in managerial jobs require a periodic review of the figures that are assigned. It is just one more reason why it's wise to have subordinates closely involved in the design of their controls and in their evaluations, even if the superior previously held the position and is well acquainted with it.

Planning considerations unique to MBO. The planning flow chart in Figure 10.1 portrays how MBO can fit as an integral part of a corporate organization's total planning system, MBO providing the goal hierarchy. A chart for a non-corporate organization would look much the same, and the basic principles of planning described in Chapter 15 hold in all cases. Here are the more important considerations unique to MBO.

MBO Advisor. In medium and large scale firms it has been prudent to have for start-up a respected high-ranking executive on temporary but full-time assignment, reporting to the president, and fully responsible for introduction, administration, counsel, and constant follow-up. Properly trained, he/she supplies often-needed assistance to individual managers (the consultant(s) who would report to him/her should be phased out of continuous service within months or as soon as possible), helps the president be continuously involved in an economical manner, and maintains the essential top management pressure to keep up the momentum.

Installation. It has been said that the plan should be introduced to the whole organization at one time; this is intended to mean, within 6 to 12 months, to fit in a pilot operation or a project-type introduction as seen advisable by the consultant. For instance, a manager unfamiliar with planning can sometimes start more easily with a simple short-range project that teaches goal setting, planning, feedback, and participation with subordinates, moving as quickly as possible after it to full planning for the whole unit.

Going It Alone. On occasion, a fairly self-contained autonomous unit can go it alone, even without help, if its top executive is already well versed in the philosophy and system. An excellent example concerning a regional sales manager is given in Chapter 13's Evidence section.

OD Techniques. When a new CEO takes over an organization or large unit that has been authoritarian or in trouble, it would be well to consider for a start up technique Richard Beckhard's "Organization confrontation" that involves the entire management team; see Figure 19.4 in Chapter 19. Other OD approaches, like Team Development, described in Chapters 19 and 20, can also make major contributions; the consultant for them should have solid references or successful experience with them.

System changes. To get MBO started successfully some of the recommended changes in the management system had better be undertaken either in advance or at the beginning. Particularly important are: giving the managers all the information they need, delegating whatever added authority they'll require, ensuring adequate performance reporting (feedback) systems, and setting up any lateral communications and relations that may be necessary.

Others that take longer because of their complexity, like the open pay system, should be commenced as soon as possible, the employees informed that they're on the way.

The scheduling of the two meetings. The additional reason for having two types of appraisal meeting (pages 380-382 has to be mentioned at this point because it is basic to the avoidance of messing up MBO, which happens when only one meeting is used, and because it concerns how best to schedule the appraisal and planning tasks.

When there is only one, two subjects are mixed together that should not be: *employee-centered* personal factors and *task-centered* functional factors, such that the emotions of the former unnecessarily distort the latter (which one recognizes would occur also in a non-MBO appraisal system that has only one meeting). This traditional mixing in one usually takes place in the fourth fiscal quarter when the preliminary functional plan for the next year is prepared, so the distortions are particularly serious because they affect the full next year's performance planning.

The problem brings to mind a recent popular article, "Management by *who's* objectives?" that applied the right idea to the wrong place.[1] It stated that the major failing of MBO is the neglect in the goal-setting of the personal goals of the subordinate, when at no time during the MBO meeting (the functional progress review) should personal goals be raised; the place for them is in the direct integration effort during the general evaluation review.

The general evaluation review, moreover, should be held in the first quarter of the following year, when all the data for the evaluation are in, and take place after the first functional progress review of the year to better relate the career planning and development to the coming year's final technical plan. A typical schedule for a January 1 to December 31 fiscal year would have a pattern like this (more on this in "The calendar" subsection of Chapter 17):

January:	First, the *functional progress review* (MBO) meetings with subordinates on their 4th quarter and total previous year, and an updating of the tentative Sept./Oct. technical plans for the new year, finalizing the goals and programs.
	Then, the *general evaluation review* meetings the next week with subordinates on general performance for compensation, promotion prospects, career and development planning.
March/April:	Functional progress reviews and updating.
June/July:	Same
Sept./Oct.:	Same, plus preparation of the tentative operating plans for the next year.

The echelon level, experience, and age of a subordinate manager plainly have a bearing on how such a schedule is applied to the person. The format would be followed for lower and middle management, but for upper management MBO (the functional progress review) is usually in the form of quarterly and annual operations or budget meetings, the personal goals and interests covered less frequently in informal meetings that, though seemingly casual or ostensibly for another reason, will be carefully preplanned by the perceptive superior and be periodic.

On older experienced managers at any level, the time between general evaluation review meetings naturally is a matter of judgment, with the consideration in mind that no one likes to be forgotten when it comes to compensation and promotion. A discussion serves as proof that they're not.

Education

The second key to making MBO successful is clearly the education prior to start-up and during set-up of those who are to use it, both superiors and subordinates, that is, on how to do it and sustain it.

The requisites are standard, the same as for planning in general: how to forecast, set goals, plan programs, schedule the activities, budget, measure, evaluate, and control. As said earlier, the routine detail will be left to how to books, and only the issues that experience has shown are the most critical causes of MBO success and failure will be covered.

Of the listed requisites the forecasting has to be by-passed because it's a special art-science beyond the concerns of this work. There will be more on budgeting along with control in Chapter 11, and managers generally do a commendable job on the programming and scheduling, but the goal-setting is often a stumbling block and unknowingly so.

Also, two other especially critical success-factors that should be commented on are the often neglected maintenance and the art of coaching/counseling by superiors, the latter an essential that so often sours the MBO process.

Goal-setting. Assuming that what the goals are set for can be handled routinely, there are three factors that are particularly important to their success, all capable of being controlled and managed well by the superior:

(a) the superior's goal-setting "style,"
(b) the characteristics of the goals set,
(c) the goal interdependence among managers.

(a) The superior's goal-setting style is of coarse only one facet of the person's leadership style, the full subject covered in Chapter 20. It may seem unduly redundant to repeat again that participation is the right approach, but there is the matter or degree of participation. Superiors have always varied it depending on the perceived competence of the subordinate, compatibility, or just what they are comfortable with.

Figure 13.3 in Chapter 13 shows seven degrees that are applicable to any type of decision-making. One can consolidate them into four for goal-setting, the four that two researchers found all in one typical large organization:[2]

1. *High mutual involvement*: The superior first held a department "information" meeting in which the unit's goals and projects for the coming operating period were discussed. The subordinates then used the information to prepare their own personal goals toward unit achievement. At the same time, the boss independently prepared sets of goals and targets for them individually, after which he met with each, and they negotiated a mutual agreement on the difference.
2. *Moderate mutual involvement*: After the information meeting, the subordinates prepared their own goals and target dates and gave them to the boss who edited and altered them, then met with each to discuss the changes.
3. *Low mutual involvement*: After the information meeting, the subordinates prepared their own goals and target dates and gave them to the boss, but no discussion followed; the subordinates never found out if they were acceptable.
4. *Boss centered*: No information meeting was held. The boss prepared the individual goals and targets, met with each, and presented them as final.

One can see that only the first is truly oriented to the psychological needs of the subordinates; #2 tries, but the boss's needs dominate in the end; #3 is a superficial stab at participation, probably for the appearance of it; #4 is pure authoritarian behavior.

Need anything be said on which can motivate subordinates to commitment and best results?

(b)   The second goal-setting factor, the characteristics of the goals set, is considerably more complex. Any good book on management planning will teach that each operating plan in each of the Figure 10.1 boxes should have up to five types of goals as they may be found needed, aside from differences of goal futurity:

- Key result areas[c]
- Capitalizing on strengths and opportunities
- Correcting major problem areas
- Improving substandard performances
- Supplying essential supporting activities and processes

The importance of on-the-job experience with goal-setting in order to know when and where to include them as needed speaks for itself. There'll be more on it in Part II. The intent here is to stress the behavioral side, that, concurrent with the same comment about plans, goals as the starting point of plans are the start of motivational arousal toward achievement, affiliation, power, rebellion, indifference, etc. through their design. The principal concerns should be:

- *Achievement*—its motivation is heavily influenced by the degree of goal difficulty:
  (a) Very difficult goals are motivating only if they are accepted by subordinates. If they are not and are believed unattainable, they will either give up, be resentful, falsify the facts to appear successful, achieve the goal by damaging or scavenging other parts of the organization, or reduce their output according to their conception of equity, or do some combination of these.
  (b) Very easy goals will not motivate, will give low or no intrinsic satisfaction and poor performance. Bright new employees will usually quit when they find their new jobs unchallenging even if the jobs seem well designed.
  (c) Moderately difficult goals (challenging and achievable), it was explained in Chapter 7, appeal to *high achievement* people, so would be ideal where the job has high achievement requirements.
- *Affiliation* and cooperation with other persons or departments will be ignored, increasing the possibility of suboptimization, if their need is not recognized and built in. The normal affiliation needs of most managers is so closely interwoven with their cooperativeness that it pays to ensure sufficient frequency of contact among those who do have to cooperate or coordinate activities; it's especially important when they have interdependent goals, as described in the next subsection.
- *High power motivation* can be stimulated, as explained in Chapter 8, if the superior backs up difficult or moderately difficult goals by designing-in a noticeably high emphasis on authority and status, but it should be apparent that it is unwise to do so unless the manager is clearly mature and with a strong sense of "socialized" power.
- *Specificity* has been found to be much more important than one would suspect. When required to set specific goals, managers can be counted on (using, say the moderate or high mutual involvement approach) to set higher functional goals for themselves and thus to produce better performance than if allowed the friendly laissez-faire of "do the best you can."[3] Therefore the combination of specific and moderately difficult goals will best motivate a high achievement individual, but they should not be so specific as to prevent creative input and flexibility on method.

Assuming due attention also to the principles of organizational motivation on pages 234-235, especially item 5 on internalizing goals, respect for these should go a long way toward getting the desired results if applied to sound basic standards. For a quick refresher of what the standards are, each goal in the MBO plan should:

1. Be clear and be specific as to expected results and deadline date for achievement
2. Be mutually agreed to by the superior and subordinate
3. Be quantified if possible, but be included if a qualitative requirement of the job
4. Contribute to a related goal of the larger organization
5. Be both challenging and attainable
6. Be known to all internal parties involved or affected
7. Be flexible to changing conditions or changed strategies
8. Aim to optimize cross-functional and collaborative performance where there is goal interdependence with others.

(c) The last (#8) brings one to the third major determinant of MBO goal-setting success on page 403, the goal interdependence among managers that calls for building into such goals the responsibility to collaborate.

The complexity of today's organizations and their environments are such that almost every manager has a multiplicity of goals, and, as just pointed out under "influenceability," few of them can be worked on or achieved by one person on his or her own. They need the cooperation of two or more people, which can be any mix of subordinates, peers, different-level managers, and/or departments. This subsection deals with what should accompany the assignment of the percentage of influenceability to a subordinate's goals: a system to insure it's carried out. A very effective one is possible for most situations; each should be evaluated for applicability.

Figure 10.2 shows three simple multiple-responsibility goals spread out among manufacturing, marketing, accounting, and engineering.[4] No one individual can achieve any alone. All the parties, as individual specialists, have their own ranked set of goals among which these may or may not be listed, and the ranking they apply is almost invariably a suboptimization to suit the specialists' or their departments' needs (on which pay and bonus are paid), not those of the larger unit.

The general manager should develop with the functional heads a goal planning-and-action system that requires each of these subordinates to spell out what the goals are for each, the percentage of influenceability, the percent due from other parties, and the specific tasks required, doing it in

The Goal Grid

		Goals							
	1	2	3	4	5	6	7	n	
General manager									
Manufacturing manager	●		●						
Maintenance foreman									
Foreman A									
Foreman B	●								
Foreman C									
Operator									
Operator	●								
Production control manager									
Inventory controller									
Scheduler									
Purchaser									
Warehouse foreman									
Warehouseman									
Marketing manager									
Sales engineer									
Sales engineer		●							
Controller									
Financial accountant		●							
Cost accountant		●	●						
Order processor									
Engineering manager									
Process engineer			●						
Estimator									
Quality control manager									
Tool engineer			●						
Personnel manager									
Clerk									

Figure 10.2

a procedure that will motivate the desired attention to both individual and group needs at one and the same time.

The author of the method referred to above for Figure 10.2 described a system for achieving this technical integration that proved effective in his own organization back in 1976. First, divide the joint goals, he said, into their two basic types, *functional performance goals* and *change goals*; then set up permanent "teams" for the former and temporary ones for the latter, using the following guidelines.

Functional goals in this instance are the regular operating ones that require the same collaborators year after year. The "teams" that work toward them rarely exist formally as such except at the top (where insufficient emphasis on teamwork is also common). To designate them as formal teams simply gives formal recognition to what should be recognized as an operant reality. A more advanced approach for most instances is the team/process structure described in Chapter 8, but this is an alternative worth considering, especially where the culture is as yet not up to the team/process design.

The change goals are those that are for significant improvements in either structures, processes, or performance, with a point of completion in a set period of time, usually short, the reason why the teams are temporary, dissolving when the goals are attained, the time is up, or the superior decides it.

A separate grid is set up for each type of goal, functional and change, and the goals themselves, one can see in Figure 10.2, choose the teams. When the grid is "published" to the parties involved, the responsibilities and accountability are glaring, the forces of group dynamics tend to stir, and the parties think of holding the respect of the others by doing their share.

When anyone, superior, subordinate, or a team, sets priorities for goals or sub-goals, the goals should be divided into two groups: (1) those most wanted and for which resources are available, and (2) those that can or have to be deferred. No time is wasted on tedious ranking; all those in #1 must be achieved, and those in #2 (usually change goals) can be activated as those of #1 are attained.

A special consideration in setting up a *change* group is that at inception, ordinarily no one person including the superior knows exactly how to reach the change goal, nor may standards or measurements be in existence, so it's best for the superior to assign all aspects of the project to the group—self-organization, rules, procedures, planning, scheduling, measuring, etc. Just designate the authority to the chairperson needed to obtain the required resources and get the job done, then provide the planning guidelines.

Experienced managers may at first question the wisdom of forming either type of team since, for the functional, current goal-setting methods appear to work, and on the change type they already have the two ways that seem satisfactory: an appendage to the structure, like a product manager, market manager, or development group, or the project team, that is in reality outside of the basic organizational structure.

The significant advantages of the teams as described are that they are composed of operating managers, all those responsible for the goals; the teams are melded into the organization's structure, not appended; accountabilities, as said, are published, glaring and unavoidable; and on "changes" of any nature clear recognition is given to the fact that all improvements and changes depend primarily on line managers.

On the last point one need only compare the concept of goal-teams for changes with the appendages and project teams which are composed of only staff personnel. The existence of either as "staff" allows the line managers vague accountability and an opportunity to pass the buck, and the absence of line authority predestines weak collaboration, coordination, and individual efforts since they depend on the staff person's persuasiveness against strong-minded line people.

All of this time and effort devoted by subordinate managers to teamwork does appear to complicate the job of appraising their individual performances. However, the Figure 10.2 grid itself should emphasize the amount of both time and effort that ought to be devoted to teamwork and should raise some questions about the adequacy and equity of past evaluations that did not include the indicated responsibilities, giving or receiving (see Subject Index for more on teams).

One can see that the appraisal of any one team member should be based on the three types of goals:

- the personal goals that are wholly within the individual's scope of influence
- the contributions due the team,
- the contributions due from other team members.

And the appraisal of a team leader if one is designated would of course involve the same, only heavier responsibility for attainment of the team's goals.

Parenthetically, it's often not realized that the MBO system of evaluation in terms of achievement of the individual's personal performance goals cannot give an evaluation of *worth to the organization*, because (a) the determination of the goals has to account for the limitations of the individual, and (b) the relationship with the superior plays a major part in the agreed-on level of the goals set, so the goals may be a lot lower, or even higher, than they should have been. One should keep in mind therefore that performances of different managers by goal achievement are clearly not comparable, nor should pay increases or promotions be based on comparisons of MBO results except in a very limited way.

Coaching and counseling.   We know that the nature of these two activities has to be fitted by judgment to the character, experience, and needs of the subordinate manager, and applying the former when the latter is called for or doing either badly can do serious damage to the relationship. Indeed, neither may be appropriate at any time for those who've become "professional," policy-imbued and skilled over the years and have moved into the upper reaches of management. Generally the counseling need itself diminishes to the point where, if at all, it is limited to the quarterly review of operating plans and budgets.

But those are the few, and to avoid the gaffs and achieve the goals on the others, all superiors would do well to have an in-depth grasp of the two and review the essentials from time to time. The detail can be learned from good how-to books like Kellogg's with its handy check lists and Peters and Austin's chapters on it in "A Passion for Excellence" on leadership behavior, but here are the key points.

Coaching   means teaching, instructing, training, informing on how to do what needs to be done as a manager of functions and people, what hasn't been done, or done well enough, the coaching undertaken by the superior or HRD trainer using any of manuals, job descriptions, college courses or seminars, or distributed educational material. The principal subjects and skills:

> *The subjects*: The organization's values, philosophy, policies, goals; team collaboration; the desired norms to be instilled; the job's goals, skills, procedures, techniques; programming; human resources leadership and the HR policy statement (Chapter 21); relevant general information about the company (see Chapter 15); your own expectations not within the above.

On the organizational values and philosophy, it should be noted, it's important to distinguish between the two categories, the operational and the ethical. Two examples of the former are "IBM means service" and Ford's "Quality is job 1," and examples of the ethical are IBM's respect for the individual,, those in Figure 21.2 in Chapter 21, and any promoting a criterion on page 176:

> *The skills*: The pre-meeting analysis and during meeting procedures ahead; listening (really), questioning diplomatically, empathizing, explaining, stories for examples, direct instruction, feedback, patience, honesty; building self-regard, confidence and enthusiasm; giving credit for good work and support for trying on tasks though failing,

and add facilitating as to any resources needed. All of this whether individual or group. (Details in chapters ahead).

A comment on story-telling: The teaching value of having a repertory of at least a few graphic, dramatic examples of what you're trying to convey is fully apparent to effective coaches. Especially when they're colorful or even jarring, you can count on them being passed around, multiplying your teaching arithmetically. An example: when the CEO of McDonald's became irritated some time ago that his shift managers weren't spending enough time out at the counters with customers, he sent an order around to be executed immediately: "Saw the back off of each manager's chair!" The importance of keeping in touch! It's still told—pointedly—today.[5]

Counseling, on the other hand, implies only consultation or what may arise in conferring, or when asked for help to solve a problem, to plan, to handle a major change or mishap. And understandably, it is the advisable face-saving approach to a low-performing experienced manager when you see the need for and would like to coach the person.

The occasions are probably obvious: other than counsel on request, there's always some, at least by implication, in all progress and evaluation reviews, and particularly important for all of values, philosophy, goals and methods are the informal opportunities you can capitalize on:

at the water cooler,	joint sales and service calls.
at a company cafeteria table,	casual chats in the elevator,
during social events such as	wandering around ("Interp. skills," Ch. 20)
bowling, softball, dinners,	speeches or memos to employees.

The skills for both formal and informal would naturally be much the same as they are for coaching but with consummate tact and subtlety, the impersonal story-telling being particularly helpful here.

The most demanding coaching and/or counseling events certainly are the periodic **progress reviews**, a mastery of which will have you prepared for any other occasion also. Here is an outline, and note that it can be inserted as the last part of the "high mutual involvement" procedure on page 404.

1. The start of course is one's evaluation of the subordinate's performance on the assigned tasks over the past period, then his or her potential for task changes expected in the next period (is the job description an adequate guide or should it be modified?).[f] To help judgments, decide, which events in the past period would be considered "critical incidents" and ask how well were they handled?

2. Review the situational factors that affected the past performances and adjust the judgments accordingly; the factors in abstract:

- Existing internal problems with regard to structure, processes, resources, products, policies, compensation, management.
- External forces or events concerning the economy, markets, competition, customers, creditors, suppliers, environment, etc.

3. Tentatively plan the training and development needs indicated by this preliminary evaluation and consider the adequacy of the development planning and action that had previously taken place.

4. Get mentally prepared on how to carry out the face-to-face meeting. For example:

(a) Remind yourself of the "skills" just listed, especially those of sincere listening, supportiveness, openness, tactful candidness, feedback, and the dangers of criticizing behavior (behavior change covered in Chapter 18).

(b) Review in your own mind the psychology basics when recommending improvements that need to be made.

- The person agrees with the recommendation and believes in it.
- It is specific and achievable in the expected period of time.
- It involves added know-how or knowledge, not personality change.
- The improvement can be related to a perceived need.
- The personal cost/return ratio is attractive.

And for the meeting itself:

1. Have past performance reports sent directly to the subordinate manager to avoid surprises and show you're not hiding anything.

2. Review with the person your list of critical incidents that you feel show outstanding performance and those that indicate needs for improvement.

3. After reviewing these, the subordinate's performance, and the events affecting them, ask for a self-critique and ideas for future progress and improvement.

4. Jointly prepare the final task list, goals, and priorities for the immediate period ahead (up to the anticipated next progress review), goals that are a fair share of the group's goals for which the person is responsible (so some negotiating may be necessary). Fit in here the coaching or counseling you believe is needed, but be sure to leave execution detail to the individual unless the person's a rank beginner.

5. Discuss and come to an agreement on the resources needed (including staff assistance) and training and development. Discuss also the progress on the schedule of development tasks that was set up in the last career planning meeting, if any (which has special appraising and counseling requirements of its own; see *Career Planning*, Chapter 17), and what can or should be added for the coming period.
6. Make notes after the meeting of the highlights for your own reference and review in the next meeting with the person, who should do the same.

Kellogg's own checklist below provides a useful simplification of the detail:

Typical Managerial Actions to Help Employee Improve Performance

With Employee:
1. Clarify work assignment.
2. Clarify results expected.
3. Clarify work standards, measurements.
4. Review likely obstacles and roadblocks and ways around them.
5. Clarify role in and contribution to employee's work.
6. Review alternate ways of getting results.
7. Review progress at suitable milestone points.
8. Contribute relevant personal knowledge.
9. Coach employee to develop needed skills.
10. Share relevant personal experience.

Independently:
1. Provide additional manpower, money, facility, and equipment resources.
2. Pave the way through personal contacts.
3. Provide added monetary and other incentives for successful performance.
4. Identify sources of help; provide, as appropriate.
5. Make desirable organization changes.
6. Make methods or systems changes.

However, there's always the chance that the performance or behavior of one of your subordinate's will be found seriously unsatisfactory, and the point is reached when you've got to put the person on notice with what you might call disciplinary counseling. One expert on personnel development and administration recently ticked off the following helpful set of steps for handling it:[6]

1. Prepare for the interview:
   a. Thoroughly analyze the problems in advance.
   b. Have all your facts ready.
   c. Know what you want to accomplish.
   d. Arrange for complete privacy.
2. State your case clearly, succinctly, and immediately.
3. Give the employee ample time and opportunity to tell his (her) side of the story.
4. Do not interrupt him/her; do not lose your temper; do not argue with him/her.
5. Stick to the facts; focus on job-related behavior that fails to meet essential performance standards.
6. Have available critical incidents of actual job behavior to help illustrate your point.
7. Indicate clearly the seriousness of the problem and state what your expectations are for the future.
8. Try to get a personal commitment for change on the part of the employee.
9. Attempt to have him/her feel positive about the organization, the department and, hopefully, about you.
10. End the interview on a positive note indicating your confidence in the employee and his/her ability to meet performance standards.
11. Maintain a close follow-up to determine if corrective steps are in fact being taken and that improvement in work performance is taking place.
12. If no improvement is forthcoming take prompt steps to discharge the employee.
13. Maintain proper documentation of the entire case.

Plainly, most of these points can be fitted into the Huberman nonpunitive system on pages 111-113 that generally should be considered first.

Maintaining vitality and momentum

An effort to achieve these two goals naturally assumes that the "setup" and "education" have been done effectively. When either aren't any vitality that may have been present at the start quickly vanishes and doubts that top management can competently manage the whole organization become a distinct probability all the way down the line.[g]

Such a state was illustrated in a previously cited study of a large organization where MBO was hastily installed; a survey several months later of 150 of its managers showed that:[8]

A. There was generally a lack of awareness of the rationale and value of the MBO approach.
B. There was insufficient mutual goal setting (only 28% with high mutual goal-setting involvement—page 404).
C. There was not enough time spent on periodically reviewing performance during the year.
D. There was a feeling that the MBO program was too rigid and formal.
E. There was inadequate knowledge about top management goals.
F. Superiors and subordinates lacked understanding of how to set goals and targets.

The criticisms might have been directed by some at the nature of MBO but the more perceptive would know that the leadership or lack of it was in fact basically responsible. Indeed MBO managers generally come to realize in time that MBO is, where feasible, no more or less than a superior structure on which to hang the whole management system of performance control, all the structures and processes that should be in force anyhow. Managers inevitably learn more about them when applicable MBO is installed properly and become more aware of how well they're functioning. It's only a short mental step to recognizing that if the components work poorly with MBO they would work more poorly without it. Thus MBO failure tends to reveal the true quality of the organization's leadership.

Certainly the fact that MBO is entirely a product of human endeavor makes it particularly susceptible to trouble especially to the human weaknesses and inclinations to short-cut, postpone, neglect, forget, and—that bane of all human-operated systems—be viewed as a perfunctory chore. So a conscious effort by top management to maintain vitality and momentum must be built into the process.

This does not mean that after it is operational the CEO should be personally involved more than one level down. It means the CEO must apply to his or her immediate subordinate executives an uncompromising program of systematic periodic review of the factors that will keep MBO alive and strong, the program requiring review by each next level down of its relevant responsibilities, all backed up with recurrent, measured reminders of accountability. Particularly important factors to examine:

- The training and refresher programs on each key capability and the transfer of the learning to the job (particularly for new managers).
- The information and communication systems and their adequacy.
- The openness of communication up down and laterally including and especially the quality of feed-up to top management.

- The "linking-pin function" operation (see "Planning" in Chapters 13.
- The control system adequacy and balance (in Chapters 11 and 15).
- The goal quality and goal record of achievement.[h]
- The goal-setting "style" and the success of direct and indirect integration down through the organization.
- System change needs for changed conditions
- The evolving opinions and attitudes of the entire management team about the system and what they can contribute to improvement (from opinion surveys).

With all the problems, risks of failure, demands for basic managerial change, and needs for constant attention, one would be wholly justified in doubting that it's worth the effort. Much of the answer is in the list of reasons why MBO is adopted given on page 391, and CEOs need to stress periodically to their managers as obvious as it is that none of those reasons targeted can be achieved simply by the system's presence. Moreover even when functioning adequately MBO cannot improve the leadership styles of superiors or superior-subordinate relationships but its presence does greatly increase the probability of success on them all.

Managers at all levels must eventually learn to manage all the MBO parts anyhow for their organization to survive in the coming decades—clear objectives, good planning, integrative participation, interpersonal competence, meaningful work design, and helping systems; so since MBO is the best structure to hang them all on when MBO is feasible, those still without it can enormously enhance their performance by installing it.

A forecast

As with any socio-technical system there will always be room for improvement and we still need to learn more on alternative ways to translate MBO's principles into practice and how to adapt all of it to individual organizations. But the competitive drive of industry and commerce virtually guarantees that improvement will be a continuous process and the dynamics and flexibility of MBO make it highly susceptible to better ideas and any characteristics the changing environment may demand.

One leading MBO consultant who has made important contributions to its development published a forecast a while back of what one can in fact look forward to in the not too distant future, one that suggests new avenues of general management thought for all executives.[10] His timing seems to have been a bit too optimistic; the date on the first line was "1980s" and has been changed to "1990s and beyond," which he would certainly agree to:

What will we (as managers) know about MBO in the 1990s and beyond that we do not know now? We will know how to describe any job in output terms through a job effectiveness description; how to measure any job; how to link an organization together by tying one's manager's output into another's input; how to separate individual and team outputs; and how to integrate social values, individual needs and organization objectives. We should have a really good link with organization development by then, and ... more will be known about how to make a second-generation start-up in an atmosphere which is anti-MBO. In addition, there will be a greater application of MBO in the service industries.

MBO will change in the same way life will change. It will be less linear, sequential, and fragmented, and be more interactive, involving and participating. MBO will be less authoritarian, disciplinarian, and paternalistic, and more stimulating and resource developing. It will be used less for accuracy or for answers and used more for understanding methods and consequences. MBO of the future will not be used to produce stability with clear goals but to produce flexibility with changing goals; it will not be closed and finite but open-ended and system oriented.

He added the following symbol to the end of his article:

NOTES

a.   Peter Drucker, who first heard the term from Sloan, is given much credit for initially spreading the news.

b.   E.g., G. L. Morrisey, *Management by Objective and Results* (Reading, Mass.: Addison-Wesley, 1970) for the elementary mechanics: P. Mali, *MBO Updated: A Handbook of Practices and Techniques for Managing by Objectives* (New York: John Wiley & Sons, 1986) for in-depth detail of the mechanics. Individual research studies seem still to be the best source of information on the behavioral aspects; many of them have been summarized here.

c.   An "authoritarian" organization should not be confused with a "mechanistic" one; although the latter tends to foster the former, it is a function of industry technology (explained in Part II's Introduction).

d.   The major control devices in Part II repeated here for reader convenience:

Precontrol	Pre-, During-, and Postcontrol Mixes
1. Purpose	16. The hierarchy (Pr, D. Po)
2. Strategy	17. Information systems (Pr, D)
3. Org. structure(s)	18. Decision-making systems (Pr D)
4. Processes	19. Communication systems (Pr, D)
5. Forecasts	20. Staff Assistance (Pr, D. Po)
6. Plans (goals, programs)	21. Compensation systems (Pr, D. Po)
7. Profit centers	22. Lateral relations (Pr, D, Po)
8. Budgets	23. Management by objectives (Pr. D. Po)
9. Policies	24. Personnel appraisals (Pr, Po)
10. Standards	25. Personal observation (D, Po)
11. Rules, procedures	Postcontrol
12. Job descriptions	26. Accounting systems
13. Training	27. Periodic checking systems
14. Mgmt. development	28. Deviation signalling systems
15. Org. development	29. Cybernetic systems

e.   Different jobs can have very subtle key result areas that are difficult to discern; it's often best therefore for each manager in the beginning to use the help of a staff person who knows the subject in order to locate and define them (it may take several hours), after which the conclusions can be reviewed with the superior. Also note in "The decisions" section of Chapter 14 the 12 on page 630 that are fundamental ones to the top managements of most organizations.

f.   Procedure on pages 310-311.

g.   One organization behaviorist underlined the point about MBO education and training with the statement that, although they won't guarantee success, ignoring them will make failure almost certain. See his article for more on behavioral problems.[7]

h.   An insidious behavioral event for all top management to guard against: the tendency of a firm's managers to treat management by objectives as a game to win, not a way to manage it more effectively.[9]

REFERENCES

1.   Levinson, H., "Management by who's objectives?", *Harvard Business Review*, July-August 1970.

2.   Tosi, H., and S. J. Carroll, Jr. "Improving Management by Objectives: A Diagnostic Change Program," *California Management Review*, Fall, 1973, p. 57. (Abridged.)

3.   Locke, E. A.. "Toward a Theory of Task Motivation and Incentives," *Organizational Behavior and Human Performance*, 1968, 3, 157.

4.   Sherwin, D. S., "Management *of* objectives," *Harvard Business Review*, May-June 1976.

5.   Peters, T. J. and N. K. Austin, *A Passion for Excellence* (New York: Random House, 1985). p. 275.

6.   Stanton, E. S., *Reality-Centered People Management* (New York: Amacom, 1982, p. 101.

7.   Jamison, B. D., "Behavioral Problems with Management by Objectives," *Academy of Management Journal*, September 1973.

8.   Tosi, H. and Carroll. op. cit., p. 58.

9.   Wikstrom, W. S., *Managing by—and With—Objectives* (New York: The Conference Board, 1968).

10.   Reddin, W. S., "Management Effectiveness in the 1980s." *Business Horizons*, August 1974.

Appendix

Exhibit 1

A tentative register of American values*

I. *Self-oriented values*

1. personal "material" welfare (the right to life and the pursuit of happiness)
   a. health (physical and mental well-being)
   b. economic security and well-being ("materialism" and the American way of life)
   c. personal security (stability of the conditions of life)
2. self-respect (the right to be treated *as a person* and *as a member in good standing of the community*; honor, honorableness)
3. self-reliance (self-sufficiency; rugged individualism and the pioneer tradition)
4. personal liberty (the right to endeavor to "shape one's own life," to work out major facets of one's own destiny and to go one's own way)
   a. freedom (from interference)
   b. privacy
   c. property rights
5. self-advancement ("success," ambition, diligence)
6. self-fulfillment (and "the pursuit of happiness")
7. skill and prowess
   a. the intellectual virtues (intelligence, education, know-how, realism, practicality, versatility, etc.)
   b. the physical virtues (strength, dexterity, endurance, good appearance, cleanliness, etc.)
   c. the virtues of the will strengths of character)
      1. readiness for hard work (industriousness)
      2. toughness (fortitude, endurance, bravery, courage)

421

      3. initiative and activism (the "go getter" approach)
      4. self-control (temperateness, sobriety)
      5. perseverance and steadfastness
    d. competence (pride of workmanship)
    e. inventiveness and innovativeness
    f. initiative (the "self-starter")
    g. well-informedness (access to information, being "in the know")
    h. faith ("believing in something" including "having a sense of values")
    i. appreciation and appreciativeness (of "the good things of life")

II. *Group-oriented values*

1. respectability (group acceptance, avoidance of reproach, good repute, conformity, the "done thing" and the "herd instinct")
2. rectitude and personal morality (honesty, fairness, probity, reliability, truthfulness, trustworthiness—the "man of honor")
3. reasonableness and rationality (objectivity)
4. the domestic virtues (love, pride in family role, providence, simplicity, thrift, prudence, etc.)
5. the civic virtues (involvement, good citizenship, law-abidance, civic pride—the "greatest little town" syndrome)
6. conscientiousness
    a. devotion to family, duty
    b. personal responsibility and accountability
    c. devotion to principle (especially of one's religion—"the godfearing man")
7. friendship and friendliness
    a. friendship proper
    b. loyalty (to friends, associates)
    c. friendliness, kindliness, helpfulness, cooperativeness, and courteousness (the good scout; "getting along with people")
    d. fellow-feeling (compassion, sympathy, and "love of one's fellows")
    e. gregariousness
    f. receptivity (openness, patience, "the good listener")
    g. personal tolerance ("live and let live," "getting along with people")
    h. patience
8. service (devotion to the well-being of others)
9. generosity (charity, openhandedness)
10. idealism (hopefulness in human solutions to human problems)
11. recognition (getting due public credit for the good points scored in the game of life; success and status)

12. forthrightness (frankness, openness, sincerity, genuineness; keeping things "above board," the fair deal)
13. fair play (the "good sport")

III. *Society-oriented values*
1. social welfare (indeed "social consciousness" as such)
2. equality
   a. tolerance
   b. "fair play," fairness
   c. civil rights
3. justice (including legality, proper procedure, recourse)
4. liberty (the "open society"; the various "freedoms")
5. order (public order, "law and order")
6. opportunity ("land of opportunity" concept; the square deal for all)
7. charity (help for the "underdog"
8. progressivism optimism (faith in the society's ability to solve its problems)
9. pride in "out culture" and "our way of life"

IV. *Nation-oriented values*
1. the patriotic virtues (love of country, devotion to country, national pride)
   a. national freedom and independence
   b. national prosperity and national achievement generally
   c. patriotism and national pride
   d. concern for the national welfare
   e. loyalty (to country)
   f. chauvinism (nationalism, pride in national power and preeminence)
2. democracy and "the American way"
3. "public service" in the sense of service for country (the nation)

V. *Mankind-oriented values*
1. the "welfare of mankind"
   a. peace
   b. material achievement and progress
   c. cultural and intellectual achievement and progress
   d. "brotherhood of man"
3. internationalism
4. pride in the achievements of "the human community"
5. reverence for life
6. human dignity and the "worth of the individual"

VI. *Environment-oriented values*
1. aesthetic values (environmental beauty)
2. novelty

Note: *Reference on page 120.

Exhibit 2*

Source: *Motivation and Organizational Climate* by G. H. Litwin and R.A. Stringer Jr., pp. 175-7.

"The following questions were designed to aid in the analysis of motivational demands of tasks."†

Task Analysis
Is it an Achievement Task?
1. How much latitude does a worker have in setting his work pace and work methods?
2. How much choice does a worker have when it comes to getting help or direction from someone else?
3. To what degree does errorless and efficient performance contribute to increased sales or company profits?
4. To what extent does the task challenge the abilities and skills of the worker?
5. Does the task provide clear, unambiguous feedback about the quality of performance?

Is it a Power Task?
6. How much opportunity does a worker have to personally direct his co-workers?
7. How much time is available for personal interactions while working?
8. To what degree does the task require the worker to deal directly with his superior?
9. How much control does the worker have over his work pace and work methods?
10. How many times can the worker leave his work area without reprimand?

Is it an Affiliation Task?
11. How many people must the worker interact with every two hours?

12. How many people can the worker interact with in his working area?
13. How dependent is successful task accomplishment on the cooperation of co-workers?
14. How much time is available for personal nontask interactions while working?
15. To what extent does the task allow for the maintenance of stable working relationships?

Rules for using these questions for task analysis are as follows:

1. Each task measured is to be ranked high, moderate, or low in response to each of the 15 questions.
2. A ranking of high = 3 points
   A ranking of moderate = 2 points
   A ranking of low = 1 point
3. For each question, standards will have to be set as to what constitutes a high, moderate, or low score. For example, high for question #11 would be 8 to 10 people, moderate would be 3 to 8, and low less than 3.
4. Total scores mean little. It is the relative scores in each of the three groups that measure the motivational demands of the task.

A Sample Task Analysis for an Assembly Worker.

	High (3)	Moderate (2)	Low (1)
Is it an achievement Task?			
1.			X
2.		X	
3.		X	
4.			X
5.			X
Total: 7			
Is it a Power Task?			
6.			X
7.		X	
8.		X	
9.			X
10.			X
Total: 7			

Is it an Affiliation Task?		
11.		*X*
12.	*X*	
13.		*X*
14.		*X*
15.	*X*	
Total: 12		

This means that, in and of itself, the task is one that seems to satisfy a person's need for affiliation." Ibid., p. 177.

Notes: * Reference on page 280.
†Parts of the following stem from the "Requisite Task Attributes" scheme developed by Arthur N. Turner and Paul R. Lawrence in *Industrial Jobs and the Worker* (1965).

Exhibit 3*

Task Motivation Questionnaire

Source: Motivation and Organizational Climate by G. H. Litwin and R. A. Stringer, Jr., pp. 173-4.

"The following list of key questions may help the manager identify different kinds of motivated behavior:"

A. *High Achievement:*
When he starts a task, does he stick with it?
Does he try to find out how he is doing, and does he try to get as much feedback as possible?
Does he respond to difficult, challenging situations? Does he work better when there is a deadline or some other challenge involved?
Is he eager to accept responsibility? When he is given responsibility, does he set (and meet) measurable standards of high performance?

B. *High Power:*
Does he seem to enjoy a good argument?
Does he seek positions of authority where he can give orders, rather than take them? Does he try to take over?
Are status symbols especially important to him, and does he use them to gain influence over others?
Is he especially eager to be his own boss, even where he needs assistance, or where joint effort is required?

C. *High Affiliation:*
Does he seem to be uncomfortable when he is forced to work alone?

Does he interact with the other workers and go out of his way to make friends with new workers?

Is he always getting involved in group projects, and is he sensitive to other people (especially when they are "mad" at him)?

Is he an apple-polisher, and does he try to get personally involved with his superiors?

"Yes" answers to these questions mean that the motivation in question is strong.

Note: * Reference on page 281.

Exhibit 4*

Climate Questionnaire Form B

Source: Motivation and Organizational Climate by G. H. Litwin and R. A. Stringer, Jr., pp. 204-7.

Items in the Revised or Improved Climate Questionnaire (Form B)
Listed by Scale

Note: The subject could respond Definitely Agree, Inclined to Agree, Inclined to Disagree, or Definitely Disagree.

---

1. *Structure*

   The jobs in this Organization are clearly defined and logically structured.

   In this Organization it is sometimes unclear who has the normal authority to make a decision.

   The policies and organization structure of the Organization have been clearly explained.

   Red-tape is kept to a minimum in this Organization.

   Excessive rules, administrative details and red-tape make it difficult for new and original ideas to receive consideration.

   Our productivity sometimes suffers from lack of organization and planning.

   In some of the projects I've been on I haven't been sure exactly who my boss was.

   Our management isn't so concerned about formal organization and authority, but concentrates instead on getting the right people together to do the job.

2. *Responsibility*

   We don't rely too heavily on individual judgment in this Organization: almost everything is double-checked.

   Around here management resents your checking everything with them; if you think you've got the right approach you just go ahead.

   Supervision in this Organization is mainly a matter of setting guidelines for your subordinates; you let them take responsibility for the job.

   You won't get ahead in this Organization unless you stick your neck out and try things on your own sometimes.

Our philosophy emphasizes that people should solve their problems by themselves.
There are an awful lot of excuses around here when somebody makes a mistake.
One of the problems in this Organization is that individuals won't take responsibility.

3. *Reward*

We have a promotion system here that helps the best man to rise to the top.
In this Organization the rewards and encouragements you get usually outweigh the threats and the criticism.
In this Organization people are rewarded in proportion to the excellence of their job performance.
There is a great deal of criticism in this Organization.
There is not enough reward and recognition given in this Organization for doing good work.
If you make a mistake in this Organization you will be punished.

4. *Risk*

The philosophy of our management is that in the long run we get ahead faster by playing it slow, safe and sure.
Our business has been built up by taking calculated risks at the right time.
Decision making in this Organization is too cautious for maximum effectiveness.
Our management is willing to take a chance on a good idea.
We have to take some pretty big risks occasionally to keep ahead of the competition in the business we're in.

5. *Warmth*

A friendly atmosphere prevails among the people in this Organization.
This Organization is characterized by a relaxed, easy-going working climate.
It's very hard to get to know people in this Organization.
People in this Organization tend to be cool and aloof toward each other.
There is a lot of warmth in the relationships between management and workers in this Organization.

6. *Support*

You don't get much sympathy from higher-ups in this Organization if you make a mistake.
Management makes an effort to talk with you about your career aspirations within the Organization.
People in this Organization don't really trust each other enough.
The philosophy of our management emphasizes the human factor, how people feel, etc.
When I am on a difficult assignment I can usually count on getting assistance from my boss and co-workers.

7. *Standards*

In this Organization we set very high standards for performance.
Our management believes that no job is so well done that it couldn't be done better.
Around here there is a feeling of pressure to continually improve our personal and group performance.
Management believes that if the people are happy, productivity will take care of itself.

To get ahead in this Organization it's more important to get along than it is to be a high producer.

In this Organization people don't seem to take much pride in their performance.

8. *Conflict*

The best way to make a good impression around here is to steer clear of open arguments and disagreements.

The attitude of our management is that conflict between competing units and individuals can be very healthy.

We are encouraged to speak our minds, even if it means disagreeing with our superiors.

In management meetings the goal is to arrive at a decision as smoothly and quickly as possible.

9. *Identity*

People are proud of belonging to this Organization.

I feel that I am a member of a well functioning team.

As far as I can see, there isn't very much personal loyalty to the company.

In this Organization people pretty much look out for their own interests.

Consistency of the Climate Scales in the Improved Climate Questionnaire (Form B) (N = 518)

	Scale	No. Items in Scale	No. Items Clustering[a]	Mean Intercorrelation
1.	Structure	8	5	.31
2.	Responsibility	7	4	.23
3.	Reward	6	4	.42
4.	Risk	5	3	.29
5.	Warmth	5	3	.33
6.	Support	5	2	.37
7.	Standards	6	2	.21
8.	Conflict	4	2	.19
9.	Identity	4	3	.49

[a] This column describes the number of items on a scale that correlate most highly with another item on the same scale (as opposed to correlating most highly with an item on another scale).

Note: Reference on page 281.